It seems we hit our seventh anniversary while I was working on the previous volume. We never would have made it this far without so many of you reading this manga. Thank you. *Haikyu!!* first began serialization in 2012, but I actually started working on it right after the end of my previous series, so 2010-ish. Funnily enough, Kenma and Kuroo haven't changed much at all since I created them as random doodles back then. Drawing them now, for the cover of volume 37, was a pretty emotional experience for me.

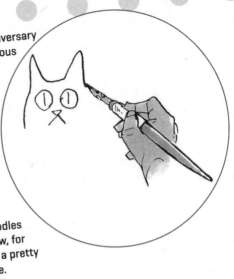

HARUICHI FURUDATE began his manga career when he was 25 years old with the one-shot *Ousama Kid* (King Kid), which won an honorable mention for the 14th Jump Treasure Newcomer Manga Prize. His first series, *Kiben Gakuha, Yotsuya Sensei no Kaidan* (Philosophy School, Yotsuya Sensei's Ghost Stories), was serialized in *Weekly Shonen Jump* in 2010. In 2012, he began serializing *Haikyu!!* in *Weekly Shonen Jump*, where it became his most popular work to date.

HAIKYU!!

VOLUME 37
SHONEN JUMP Manga Edition

Story and Art by
HARUICHI FURUDATE

Translation ■ **ADRIENNE BECK**
Touch-Up Art & Lettering ■ **ERIKA TERRIQUEZ**
Design ■ **JULIAN [JR] ROBINSON**
Editor ■ **MARLENE FIRST**

Printed in the U.S.A.

Published by VIZ Media, LLC
P.O. Box 77010
San Francisco, CA 94107

10 9 8 7 6 5 4 3 2 1
First printing, March 2020

VIZ MEDIA
viz.com

ratings.viz.com RATED T TEEN

PARENTAL ADVISORY
HAIKYU!! is rated T for Teen and
is recommended for ages 13
and up for mild language.

SHONEN JUMP
shonenjump.com

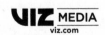

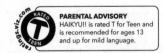

HAIKYU!!

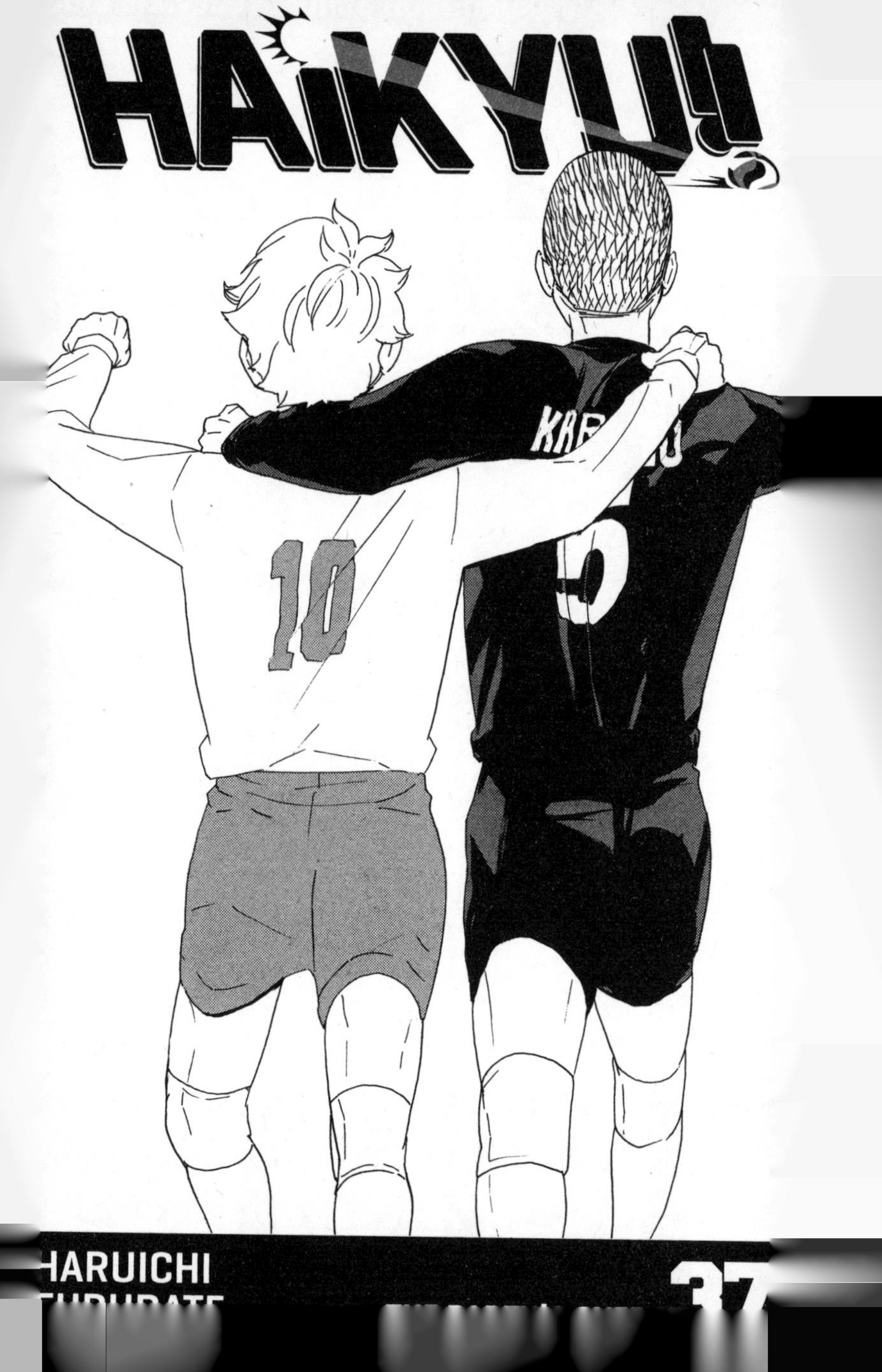

HARUICHI [redacted]

37

Karasuno High School Volleyball Club

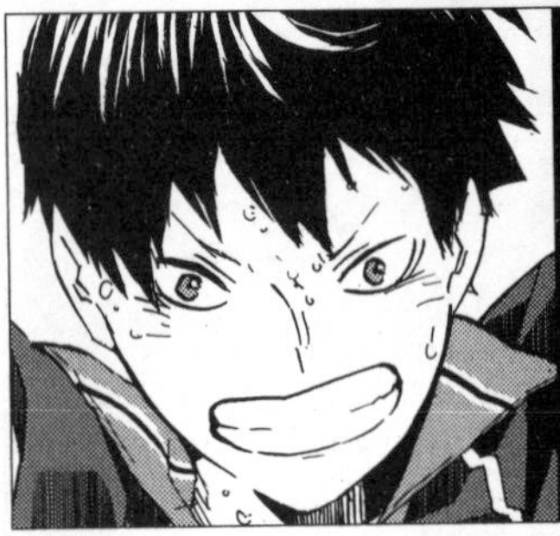

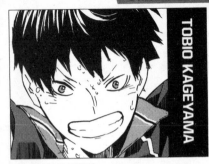

TOBIO KAGEYAMA

1ST YEAR / SETTER

His instincts and athletic talent are so good that he's like a "king" who rules the court. Demanding and egocentric.

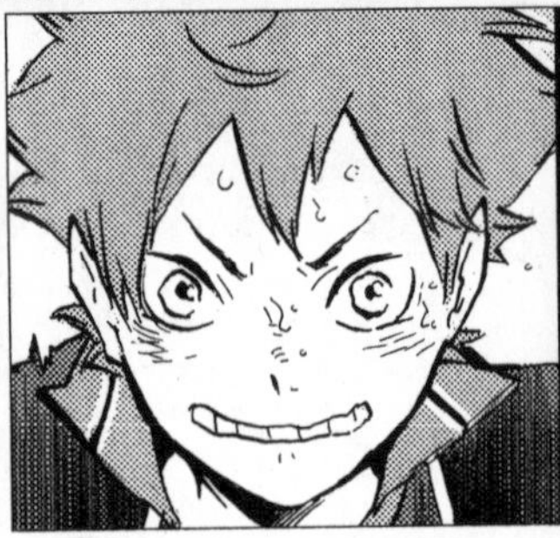

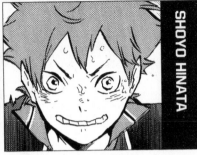

SHOYO HINATA

1ST YEAR / MIDDLE BLOCKER

Even though he doesn't have the best body type for volleyball, he is super athletic. Gets nervous easily.

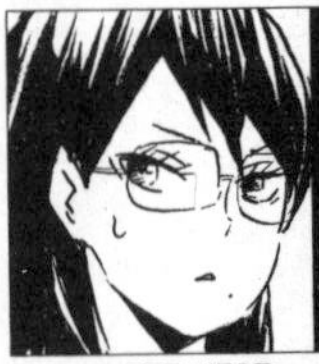

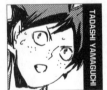

KIYOKO SHIMIZU

3RD YEAR
MANAGER

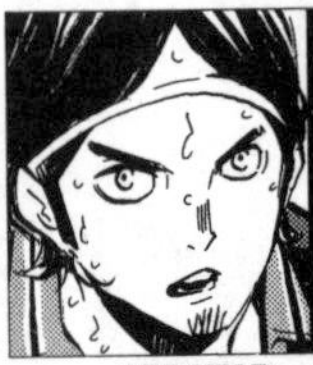

ASAHI AZUMANE

3RD YEAR
WING SPIKER

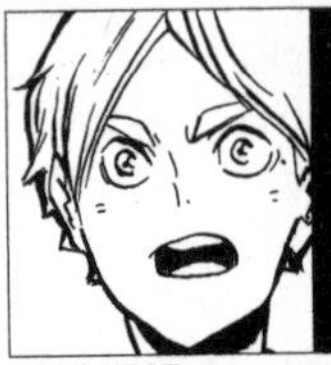

KOUSHI SUGAWARA

3RD YEAR (VICE CAPTAIN)
SETTER

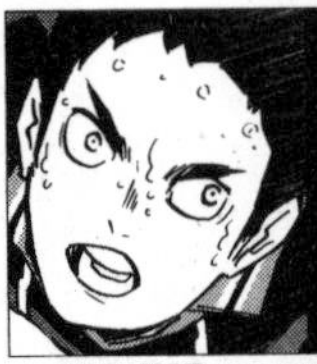

DAICHI SAWAMURA

3RD YEAR (CAPTAIN)
WING SPIKER

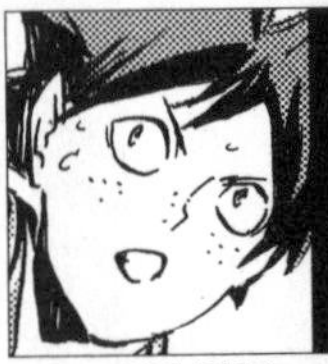

TADASHI YAMAGUCHI

1ST YEAR
MIDDLE BLOCKER

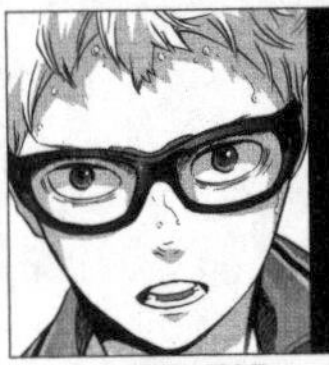

KEI TSUKISHIMA

1ST YEAR
MIDDLE BLOCKER

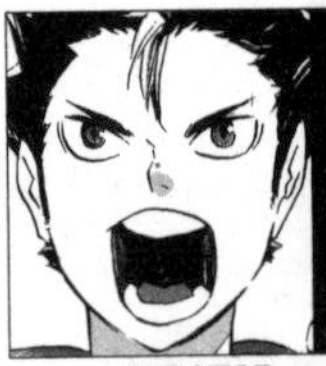

YU NISHINOYA

2ND YEAR
LIBERO

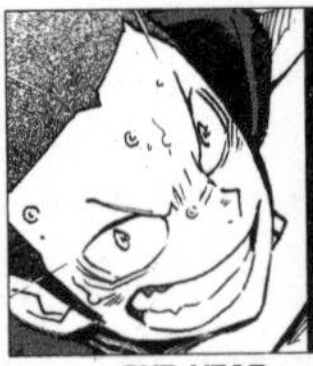

RYUNOSUKE TANAKA

2ND YEAR
WING SPIKER

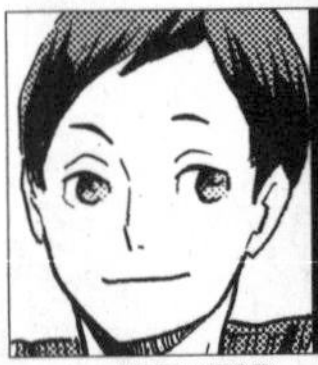

CHIKARA ENNOSHITA

2ND YEAR
WING SPIKER

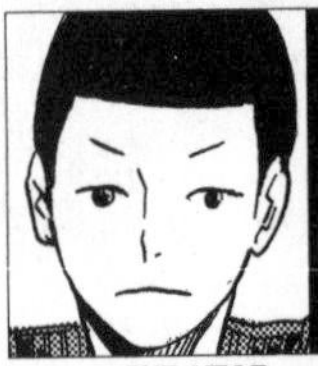

KAZUHITO NARITA

2ND YEAR
MIDDLE BLOCKER

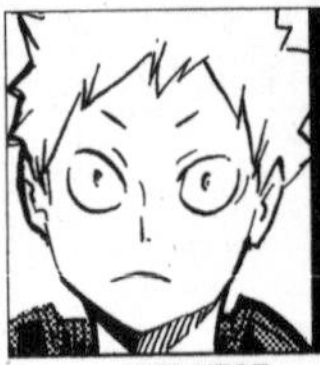

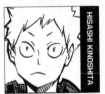

HISASHI KINOSHITA

2ND YEAR
WING SPIKER

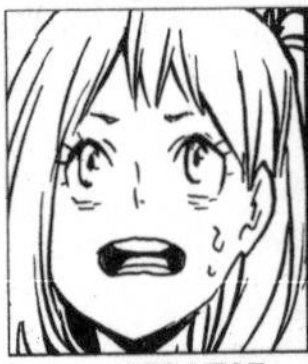

HITOKA YACHI

1ST YEAR
MANAGER

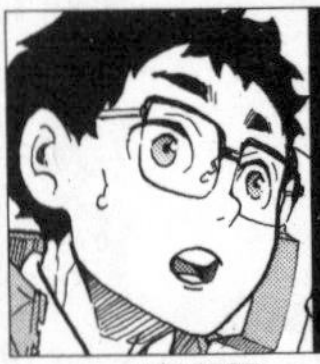

ITTETSU TAKEDA

ADVISER

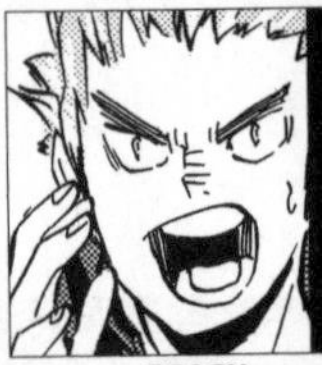

KEISHIN UKAI

COACH

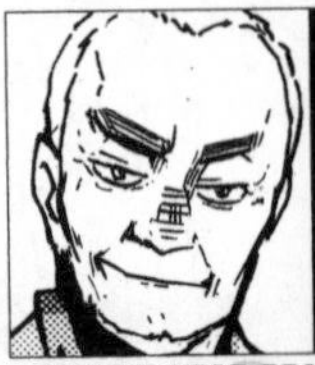

IKKEI UKAI

FORMER HEAD COACH

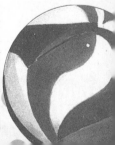

CHARACTERS

NATIONAL SPRING TOURNAMENT ARC

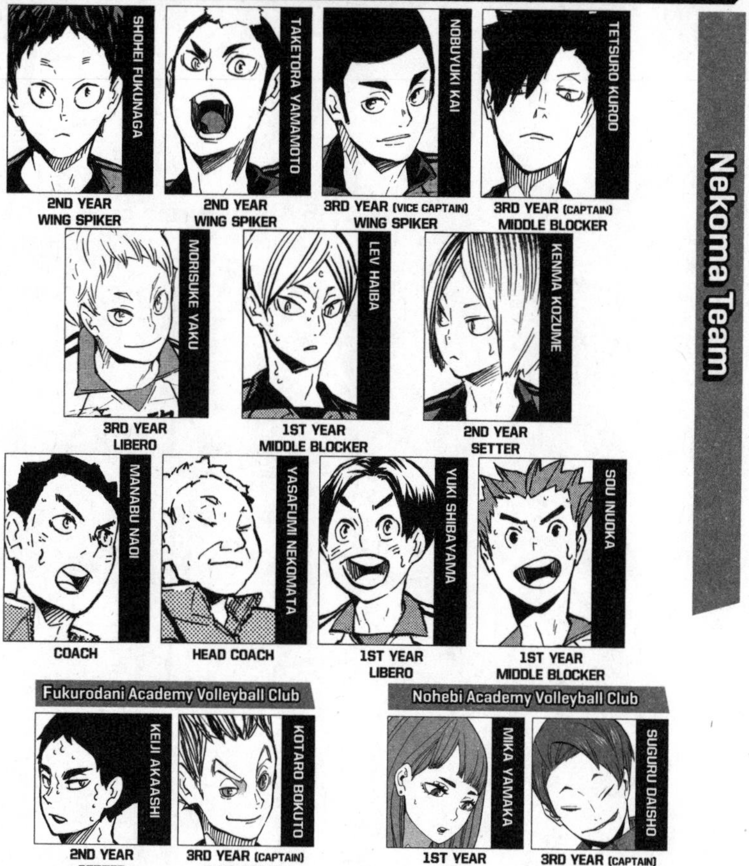
Nekoma Team
SHOHEI FUKUNAGA
2ND YEAR
WING SPIKER
TAKETORA YAMAMOTO
2ND YEAR
WING SPIKER
NOBUYUKI KAI
3RD YEAR (VICE CAPTAIN)
WING SPIKER
TETSURO KUROO
3RD YEAR (CAPTAIN)
MIDDLE BLOCKER
MORISUKE YAKU
3RD YEAR
LIBERO
LEV HAIBA
1ST YEAR
MIDDLE BLOCKER
KENMA KOZUME
2ND YEAR
SETTER
MANABU NAOI
COACH
YASAFUMI NEKOMATA
HEAD COACH
YUKI SHIBAYAMA
1ST YEAR
LIBERO
SOU INUOKA
1ST YEAR
MIDDLE BLOCKER
Fukurodani Academy Volleyball Club
KEIJI AKAASHI
2ND YEAR
SETTER
KOTARO BOKUTO
3RD YEAR (CAPTAIN)
WING SPIKER
Nohebi Academy Volleyball Club
MIKA YAMAKA
1ST YEAR
LIBERO
SUGURU DAISHO
3RD YEAR (CAPTAIN)
WING SPIKER

Ever since he saw the legendary player known as "the Little Giant" compete at the national volleyball finals, Shoyo Hinata has been aiming to be the best volleyball player ever! He decides to join the volleyball club at his middle school and gets to play in an official tournament during his third year. His team is crushed by a team led by volleyball prodigy Tobio Kageyama, also known as "the King of the Court." Swearing revenge on Kageyama, Hinata graduates middle school and enters Karasuno High School, the school where the Little Giant played. However, upon joining the club, he finds out that Kageyama is there too! The two of them bicker constantly, but they bring out the best in each other's talents and become a powerful combo. It's day 3 of the Spring Tournament, and the Dumpster Battle is in full swing! Kenma's plan to trap Hinata in a birdcage has been foiled by Kageyama's beautifully high-arcing four set. But Kenma quickly adjusts and counters their move with one of his own—building a wall with Inuoka and Lev! Nekoma also brings out rookie Teshiro and his ceiling serve, but with Hinata's save leading to the decisive point, Karasuno wins set 2! The third and final set begins, and both teams give it their utmost, enjoying every minute. Kenma and Hinata play all out, and Kenma even lets slip that he's having fun...!

HAIKYU!!

37 THE PARTY'S OVER

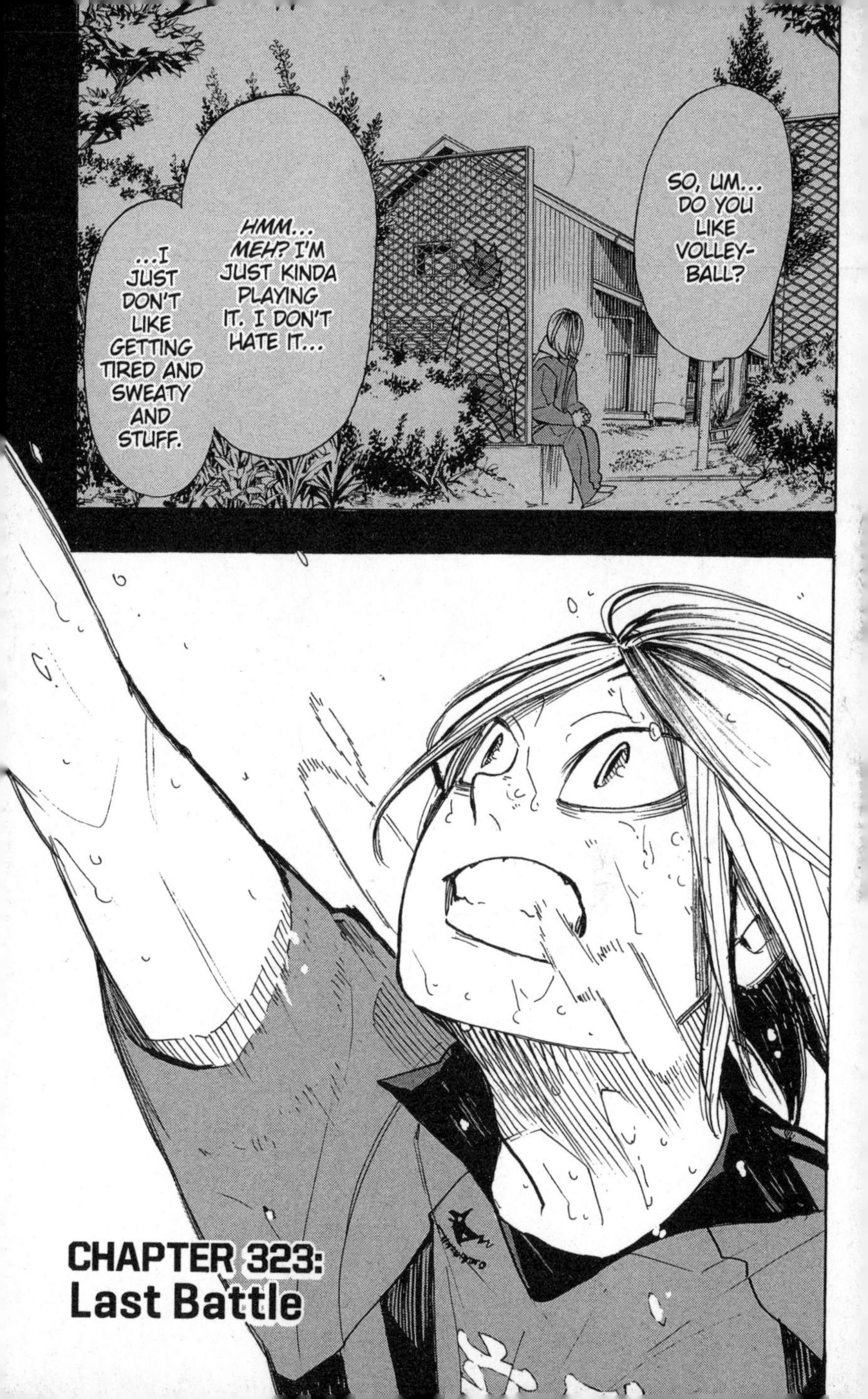
SO, UM... DO YOU LIKE VOLLEY-BALL?
HMM... MEH? I'M JUST KINDA PLAYING IT. I DON'T HATE IT...
...I JUST DON'T LIKE GETTING TIRED AND SWEATY AND STUFF.

CHAPTER 323: Last Battle

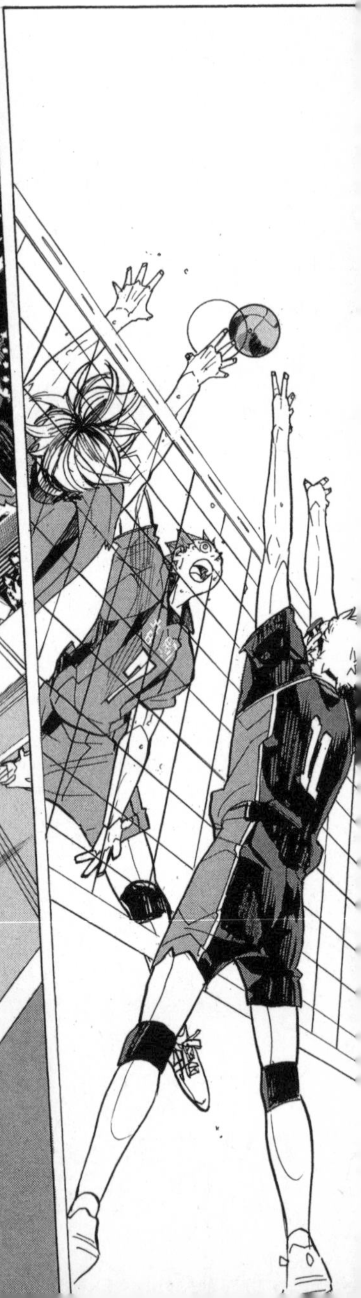
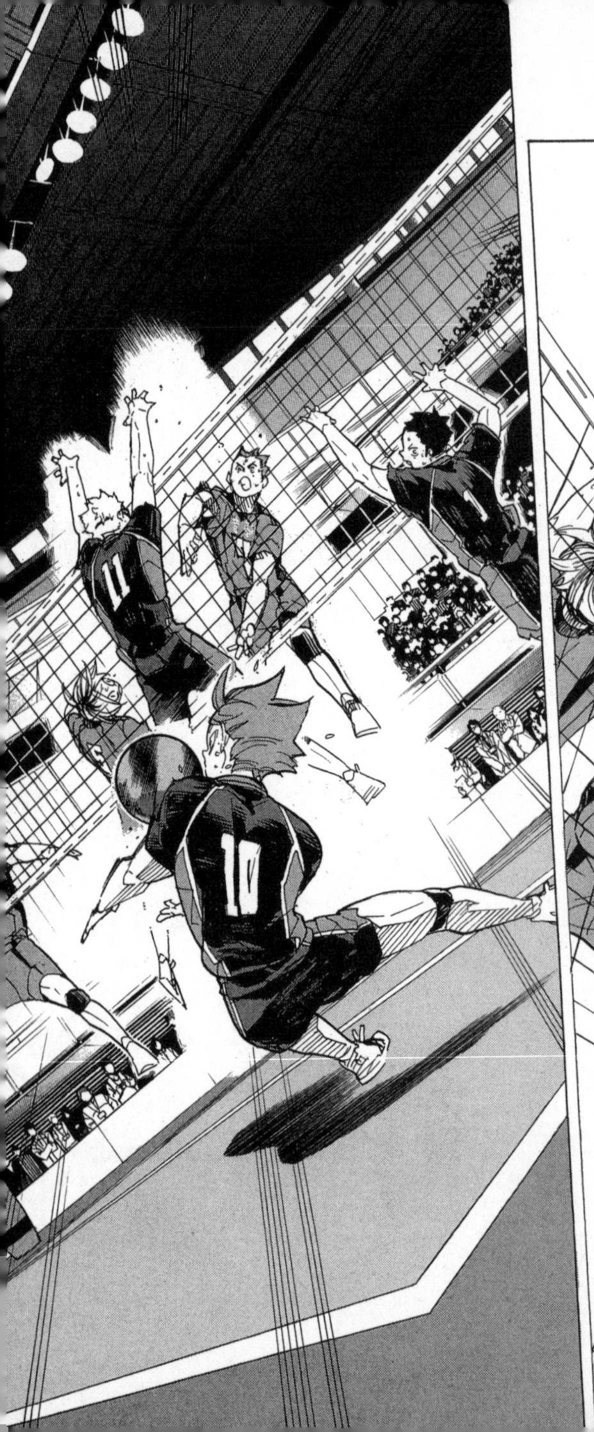

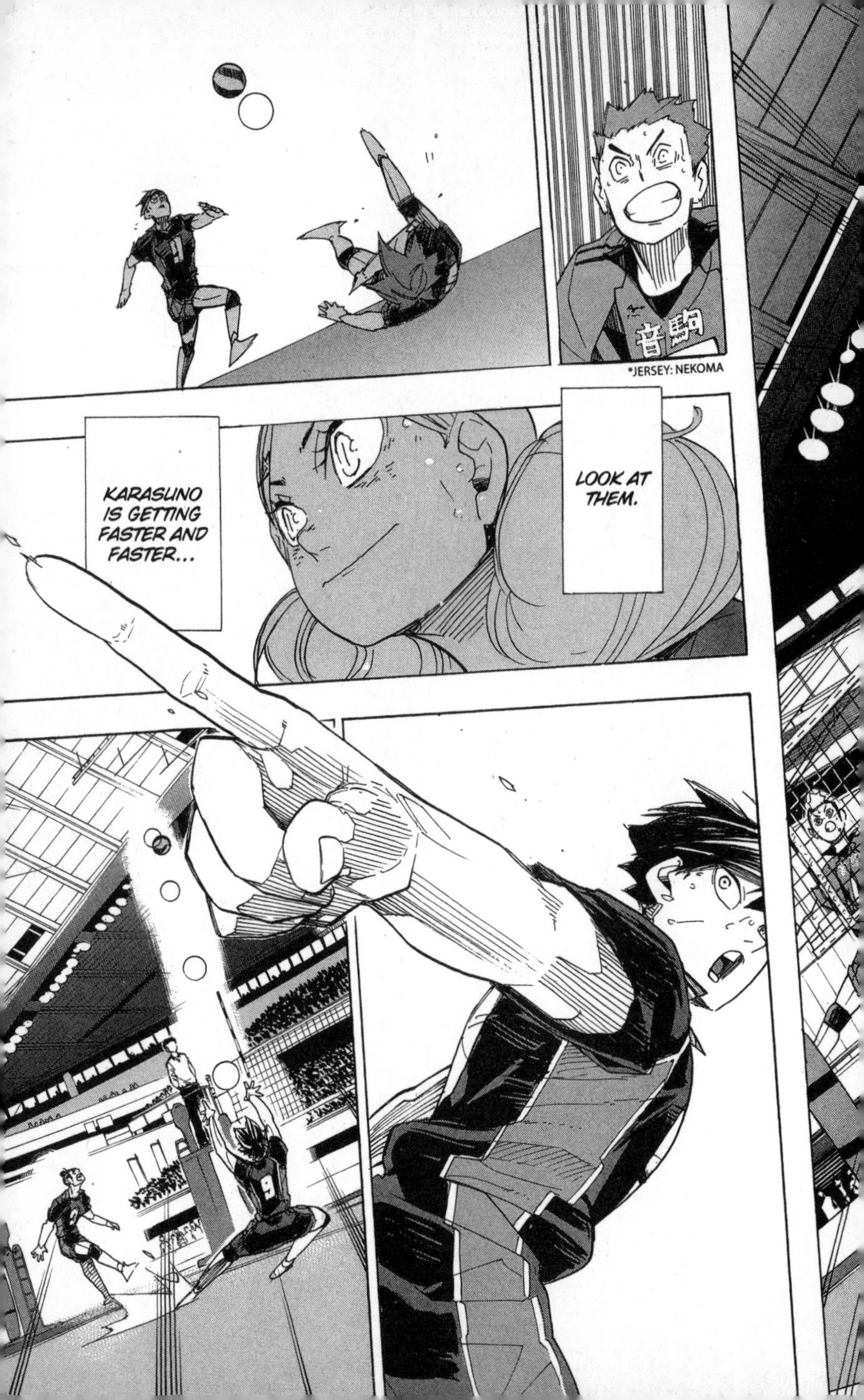
音駒
*JERSEY: NEKOMA
LOOK AT THEM.
KARASUNO IS GETTING FASTER AND FASTER...

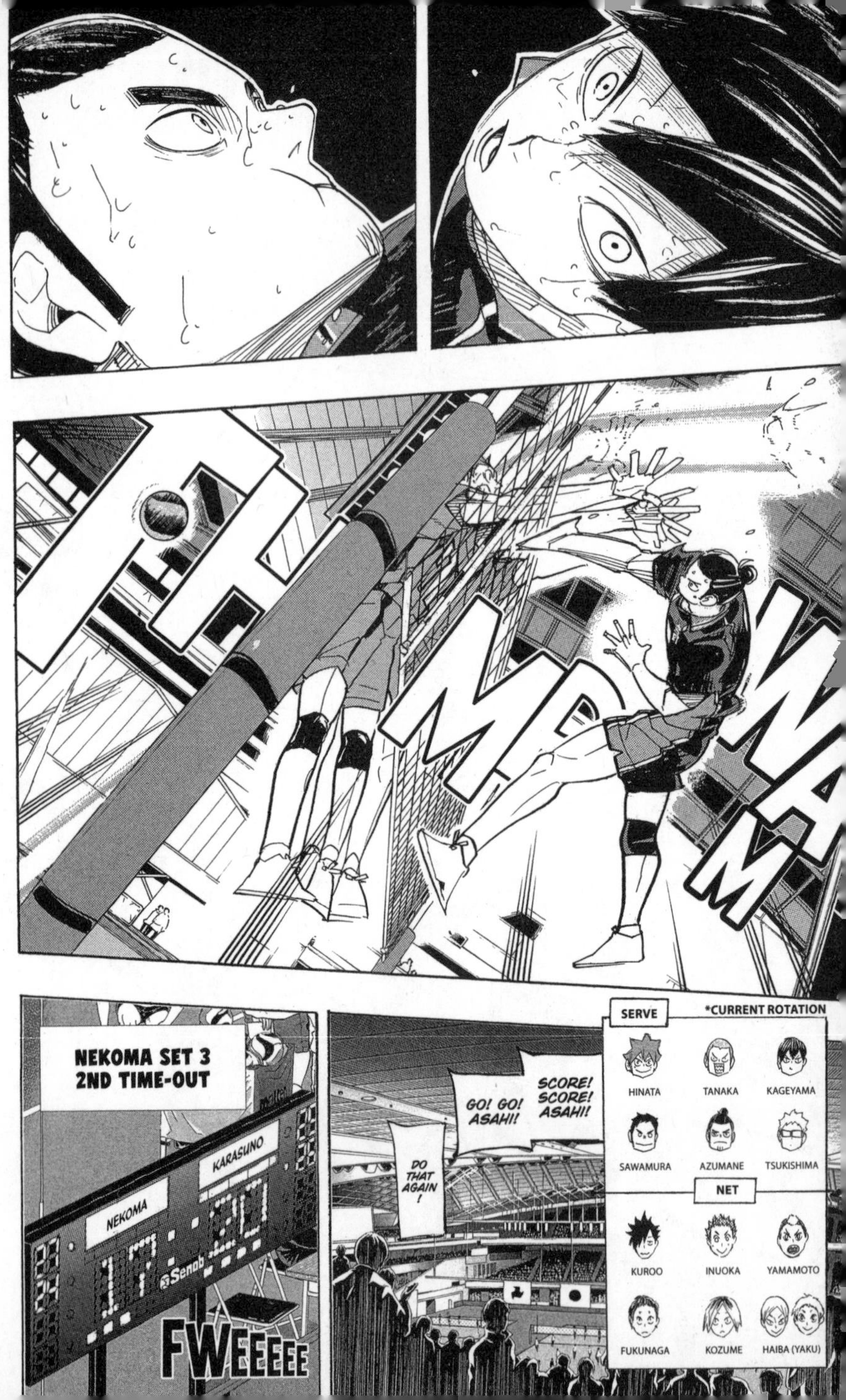
SERVE
*CURRENT ROTATION
HINATA
TANAKA
KAGEYAMA
SAWAMURA
AZUMANE
TSUKISHIMA
NET
KUROO
INUOKA
YAMAMOTO
FUKUNAGA
KOZUME
HAIBA (YAKU)
SCORE! SCORE! ASAHI!
GO! GO! ASAHI!
DO THAT AGAIN!
NEKOMA SET 3 2ND TIME-OUT
KARASUNO
NEKOMA
FWEEEEE

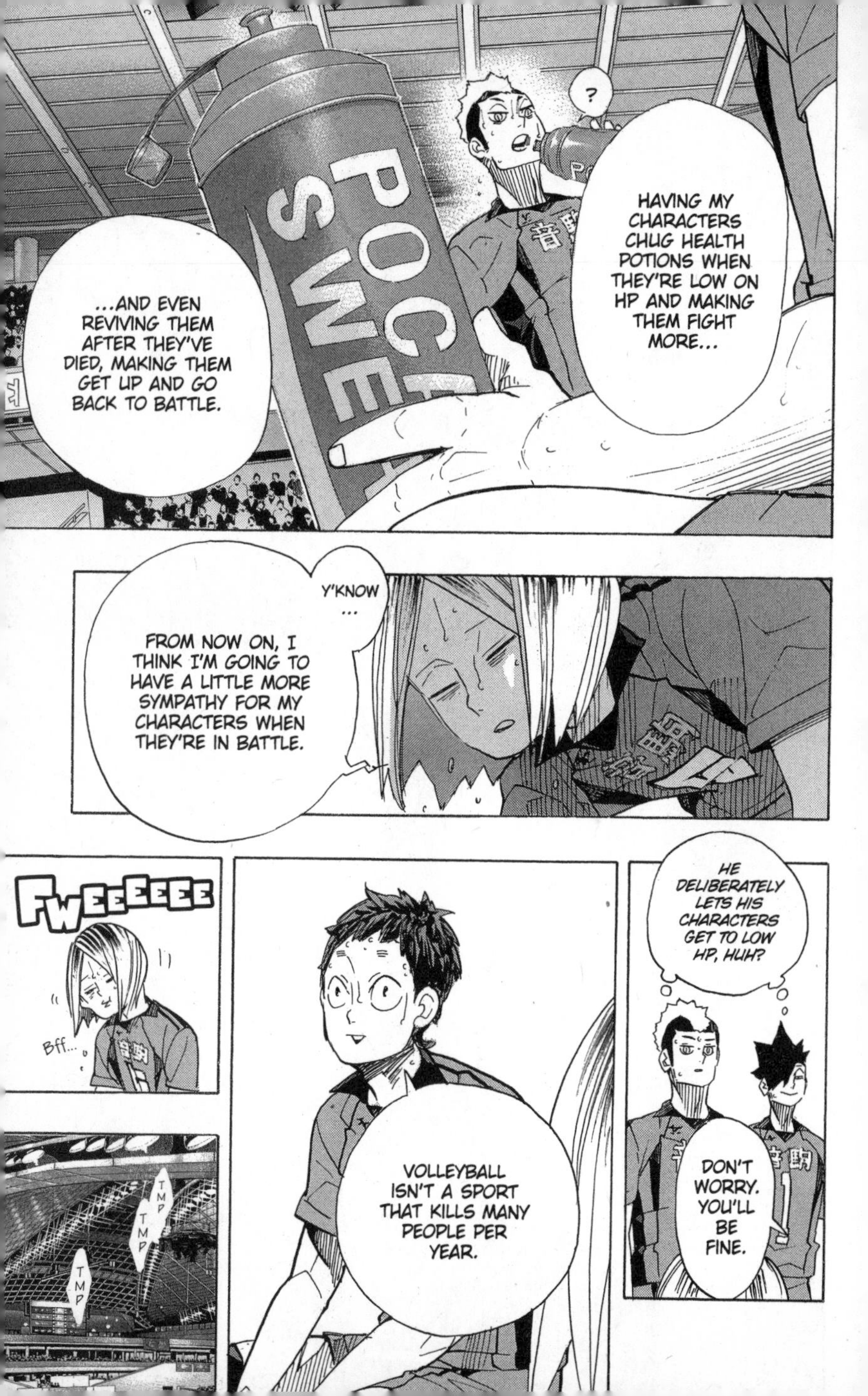
?
HAVING MY CHARACTERS CHUG HEALTH POTIONS WHEN THEY'RE LOW ON HP AND MAKING THEM FIGHT MORE...
...AND EVEN REVIVING THEM AFTER THEY'VE DIED, MAKING THEM GET UP AND GO BACK TO BATTLE.
Y'KNOW ...
FROM NOW ON, I THINK I'M GOING TO HAVE A LITTLE MORE SYMPATHY FOR MY CHARACTERS WHEN THEY'RE IN BATTLE.
HE DELIBERATELY LETS HIS CHARACTERS GET TO LOW HP, HUH?
DON'T WORRY. YOU'LL BE FINE.
VOLLEYBALL ISN'T A SPORT THAT KILLS MANY PEOPLE PER YEAR.
FWEEEEEE
Bff...
TMP
TMP
TMP

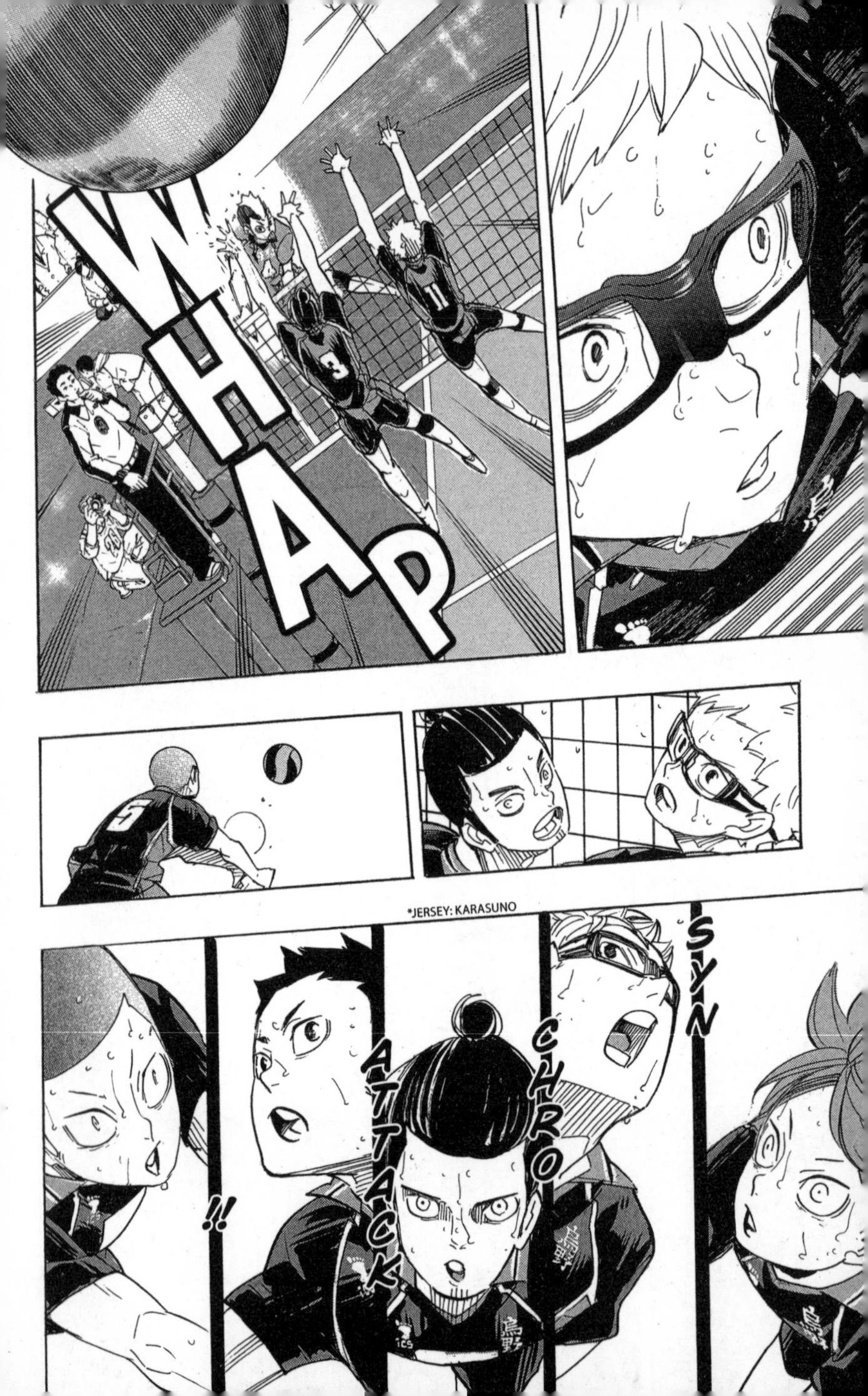
WHAP
*JERSEY: KARASUNO
SYNCHRO ATTACK
!!

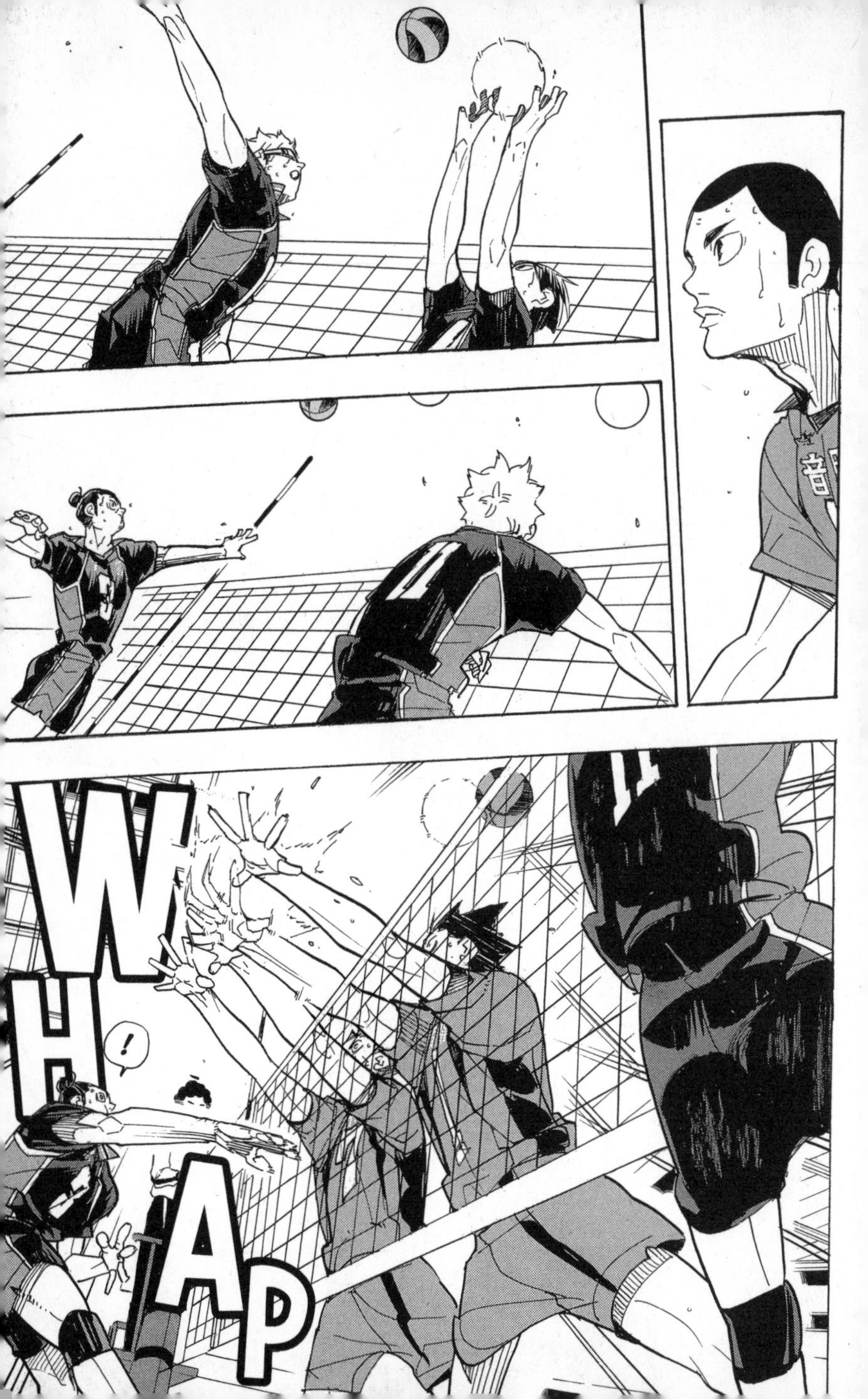
!
WHAP

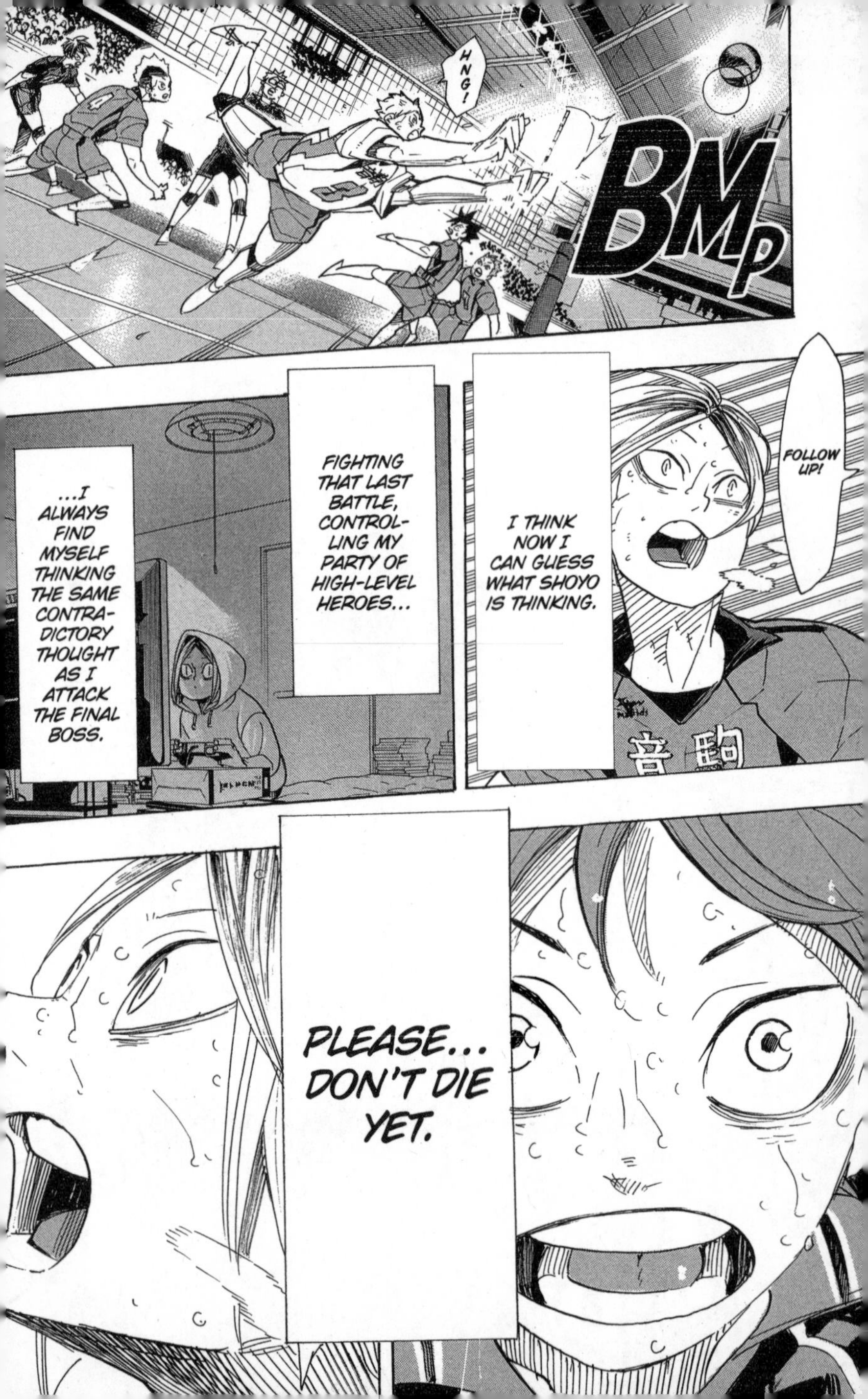
HNG!
BMP
FOLLOW UP!
I THINK NOW I CAN GUESS WHAT SHOYO IS THINKING.
音駒
FIGHTING THAT LAST BATTLE, CONTROLLING MY PARTY OF HIGH-LEVEL HEROES...
...I ALWAYS FIND MYSELF THINKING THE SAME CONTRADICTORY THOUGHT AS I ATTACK THE FINAL BOSS.
PLEASE... DON'T DIE YET.

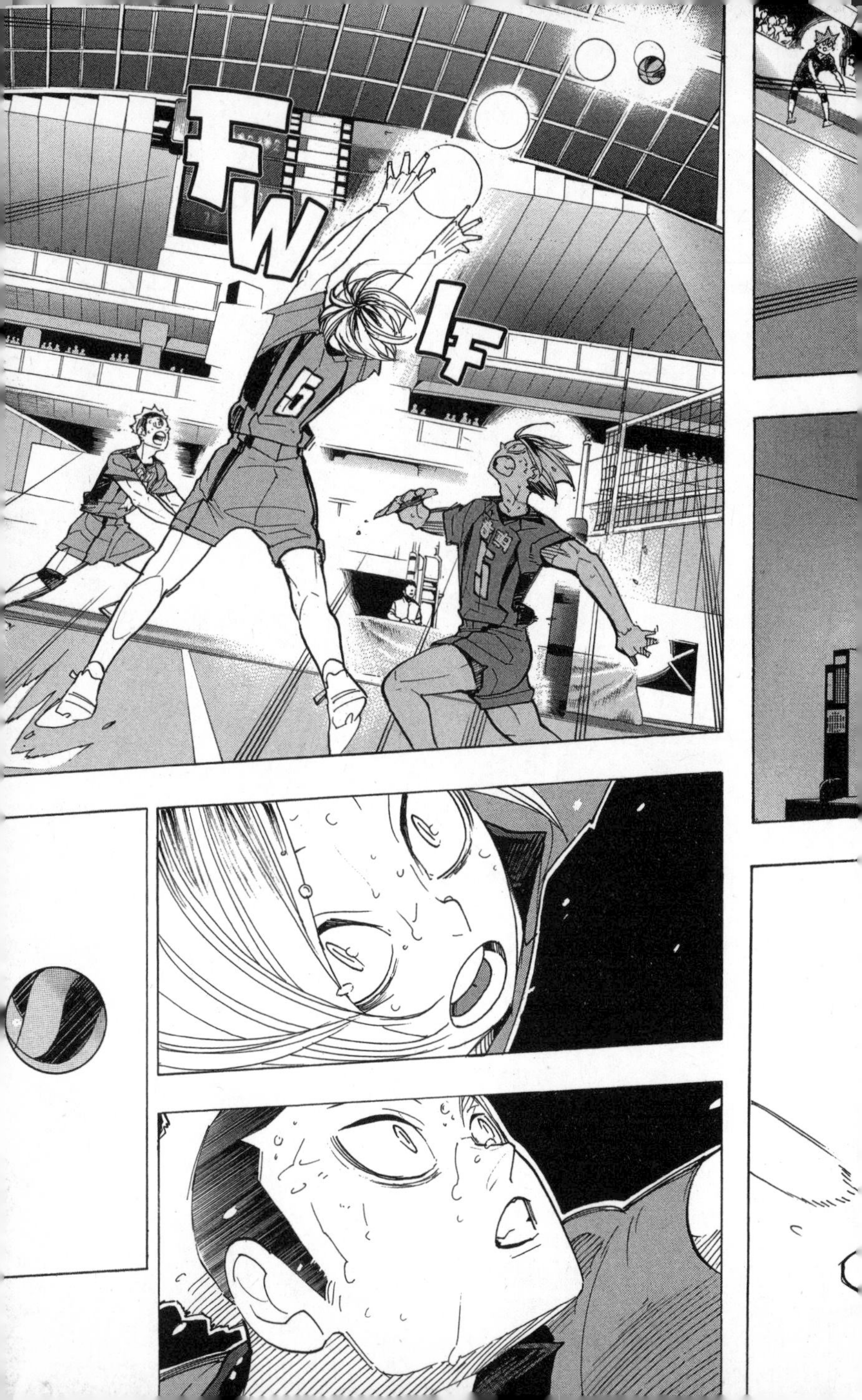
FWIF

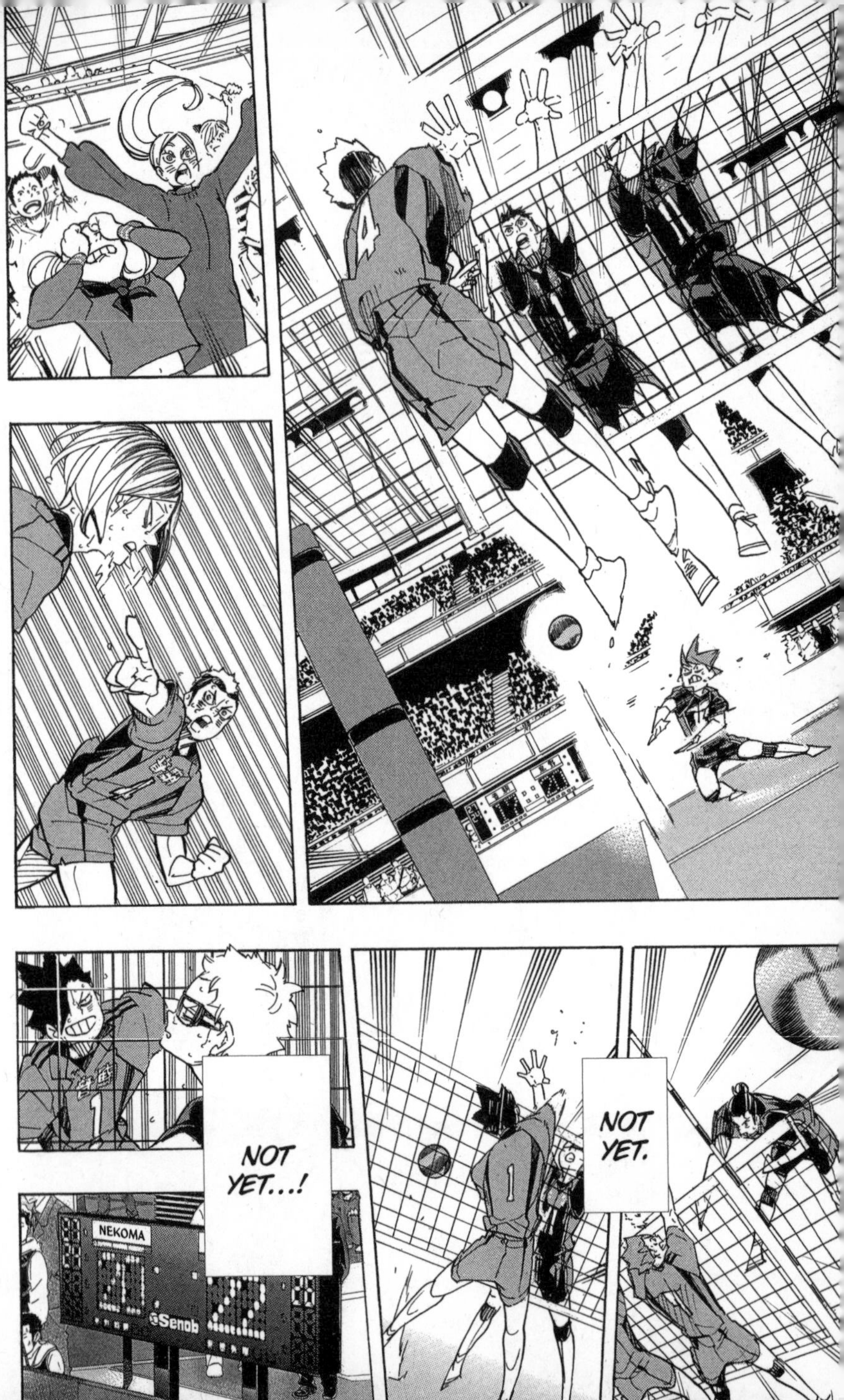
NOT YET.
NOT YET...!
NEKOMA
Senob

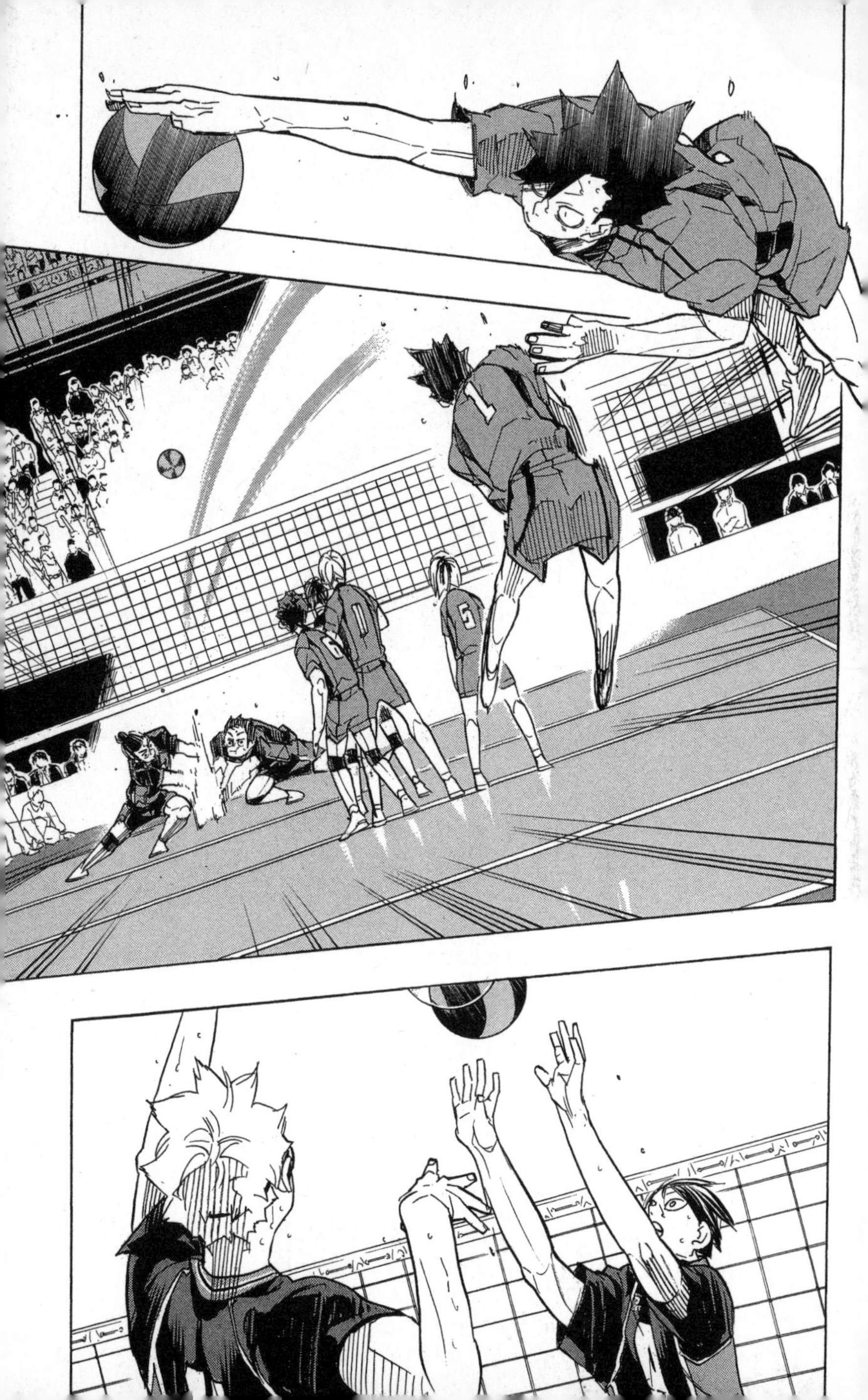

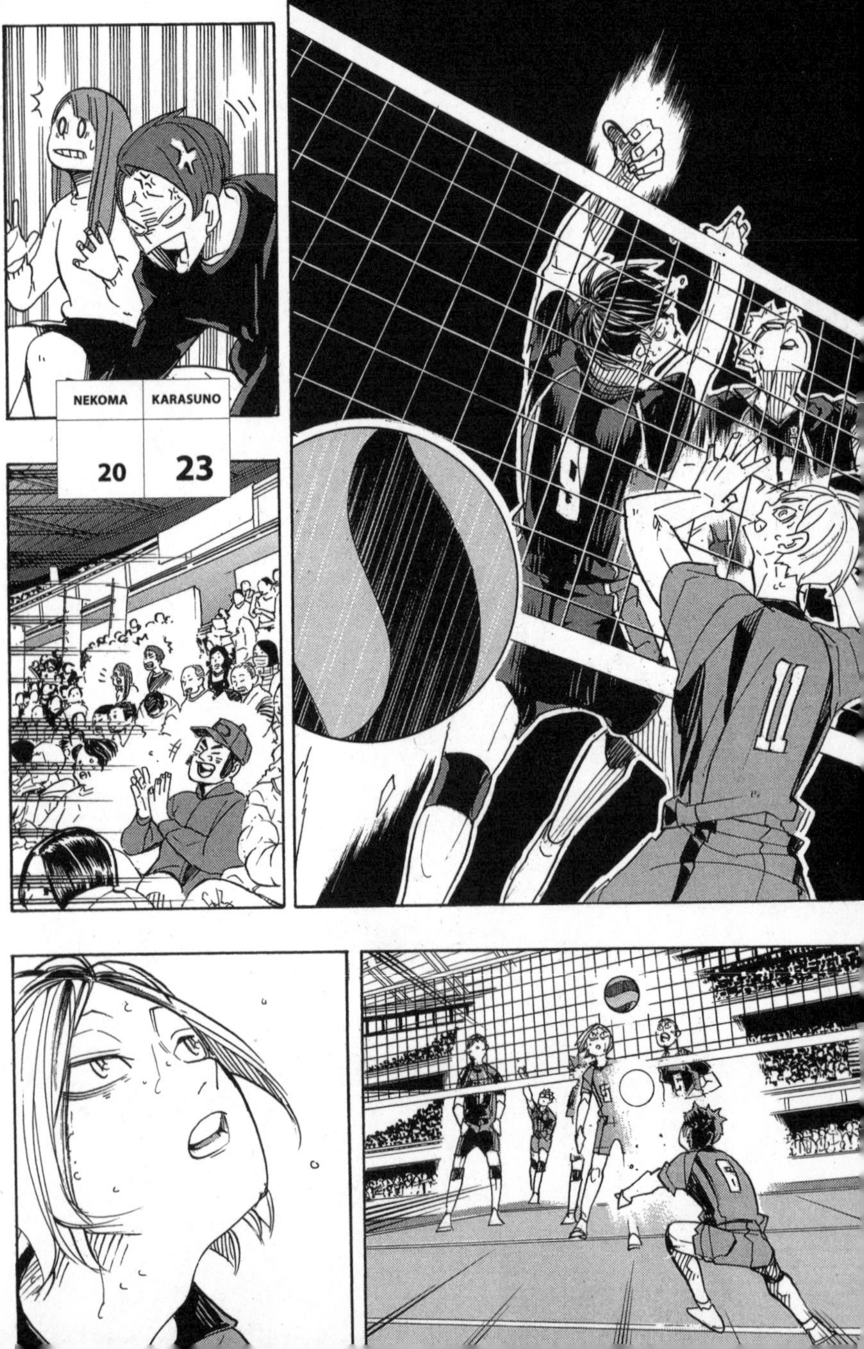
NEKOMA
20
KARASUNO
23

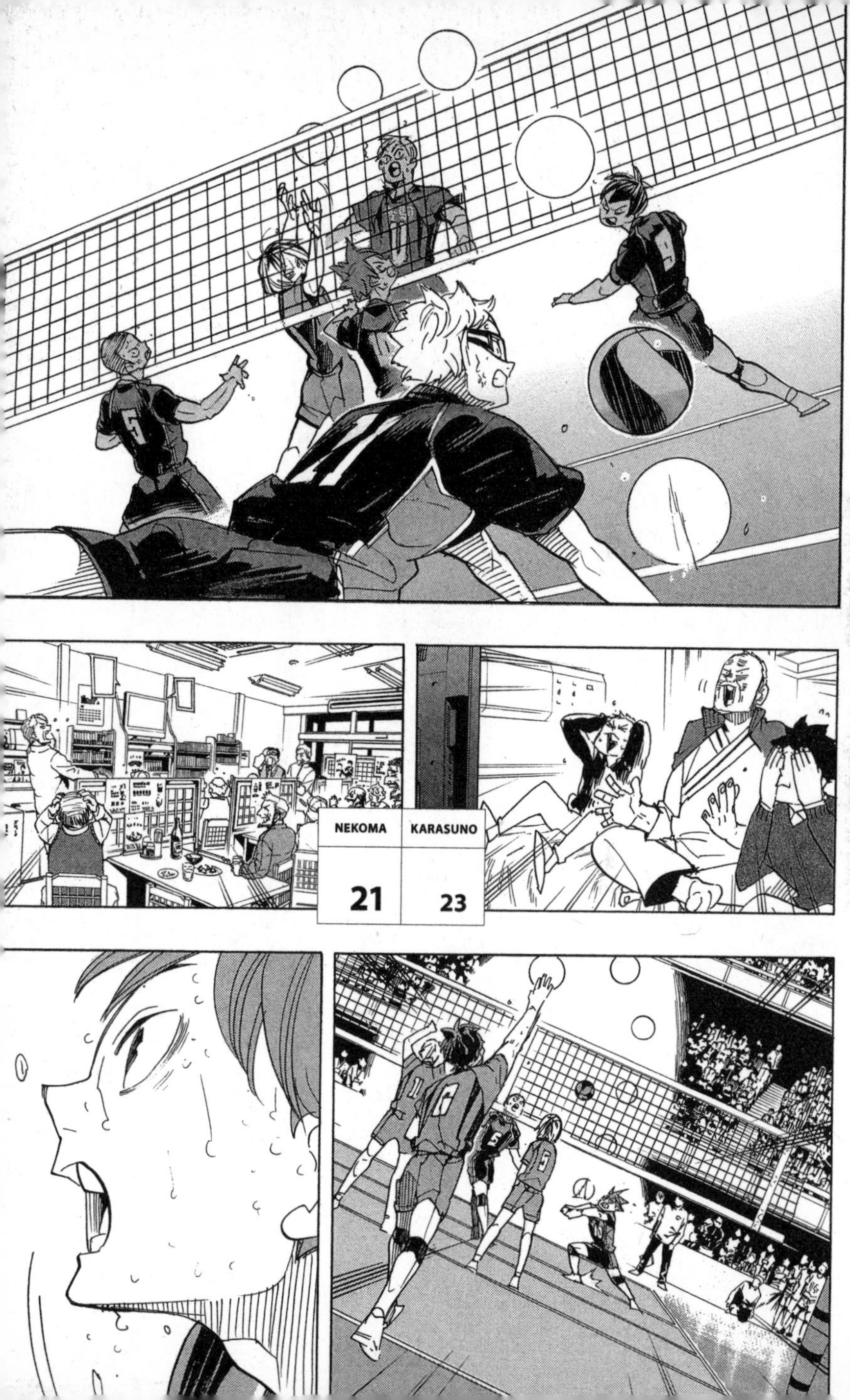
NEKOMA
KARASUNO
21
23

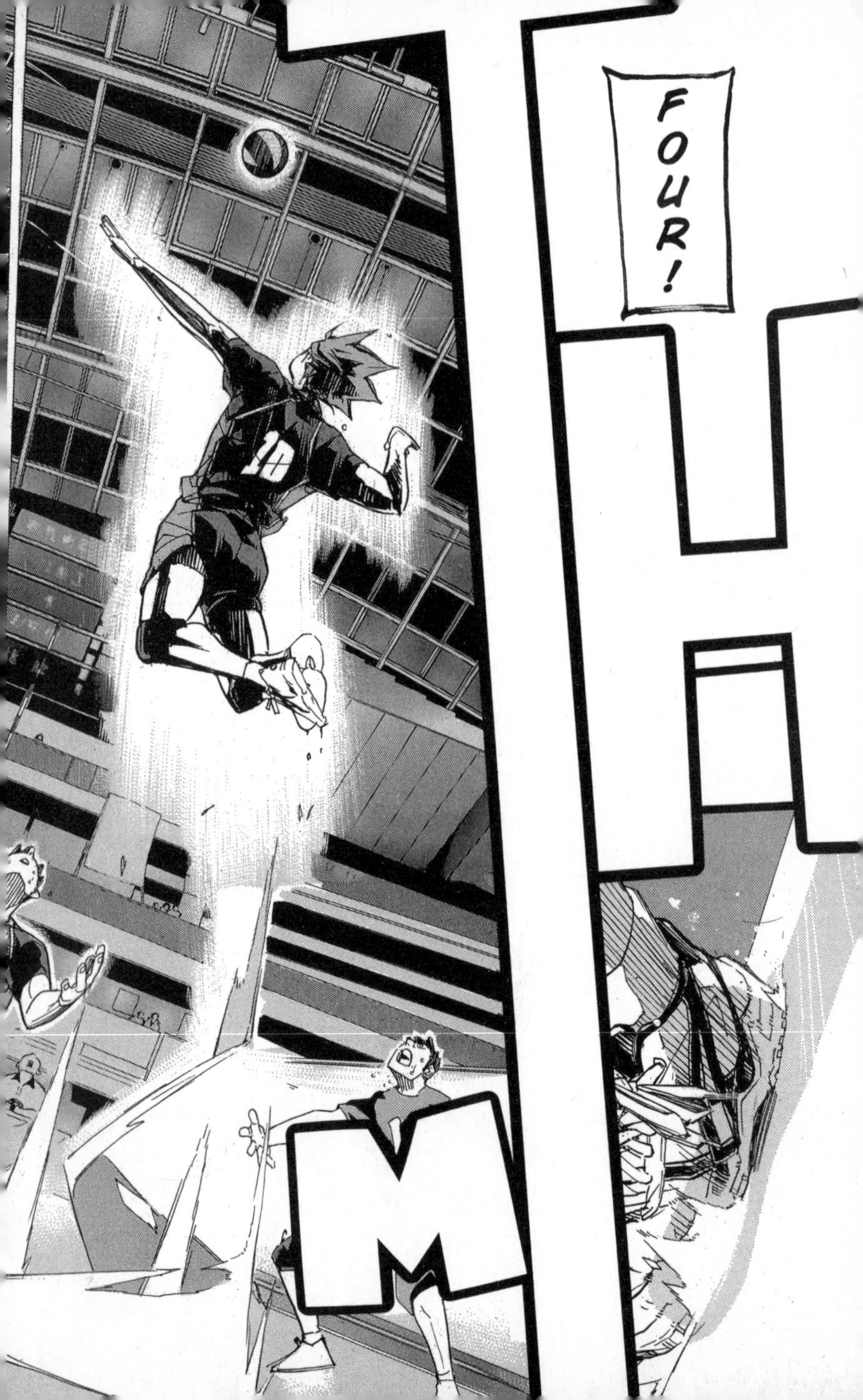
FOUR!

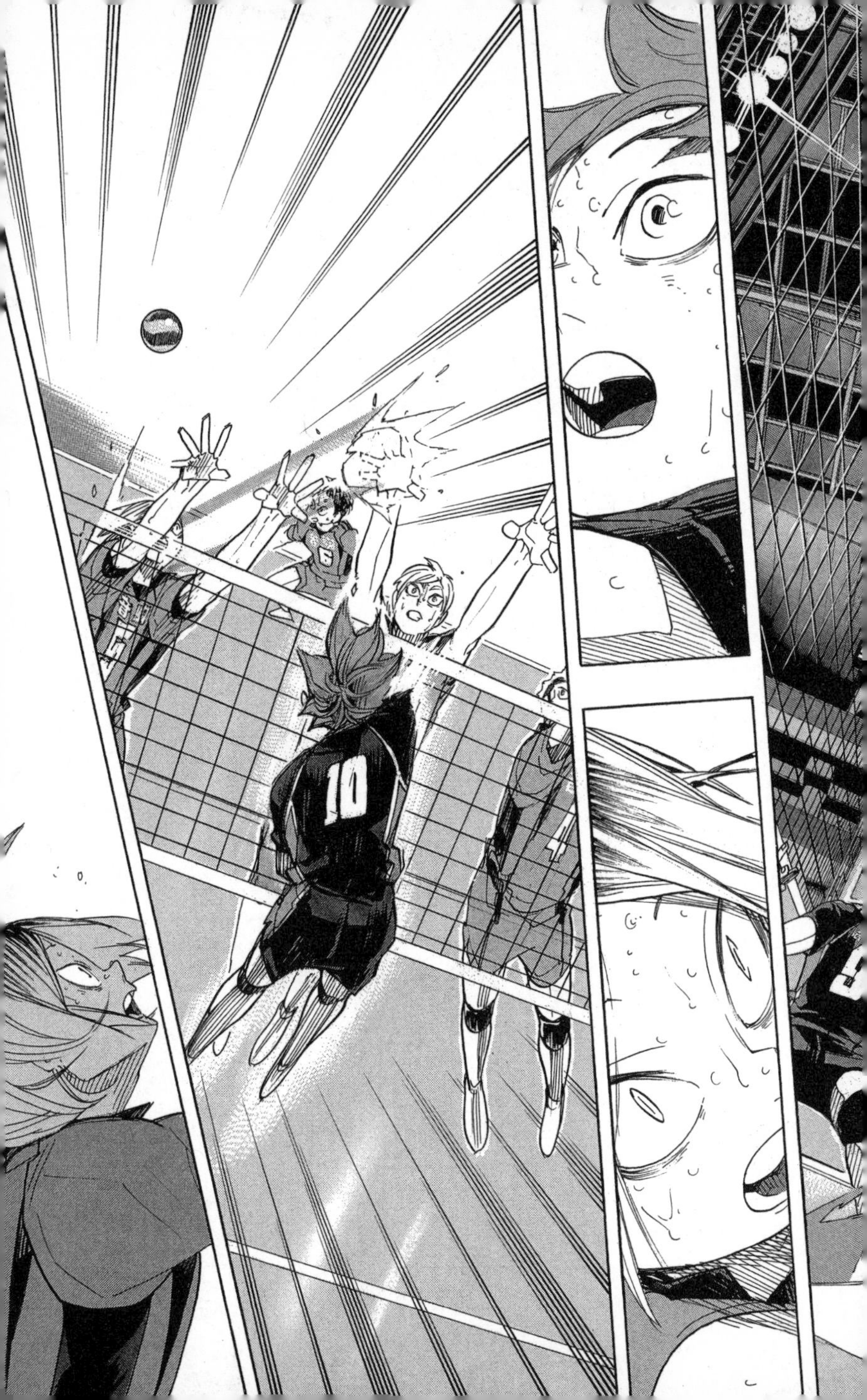

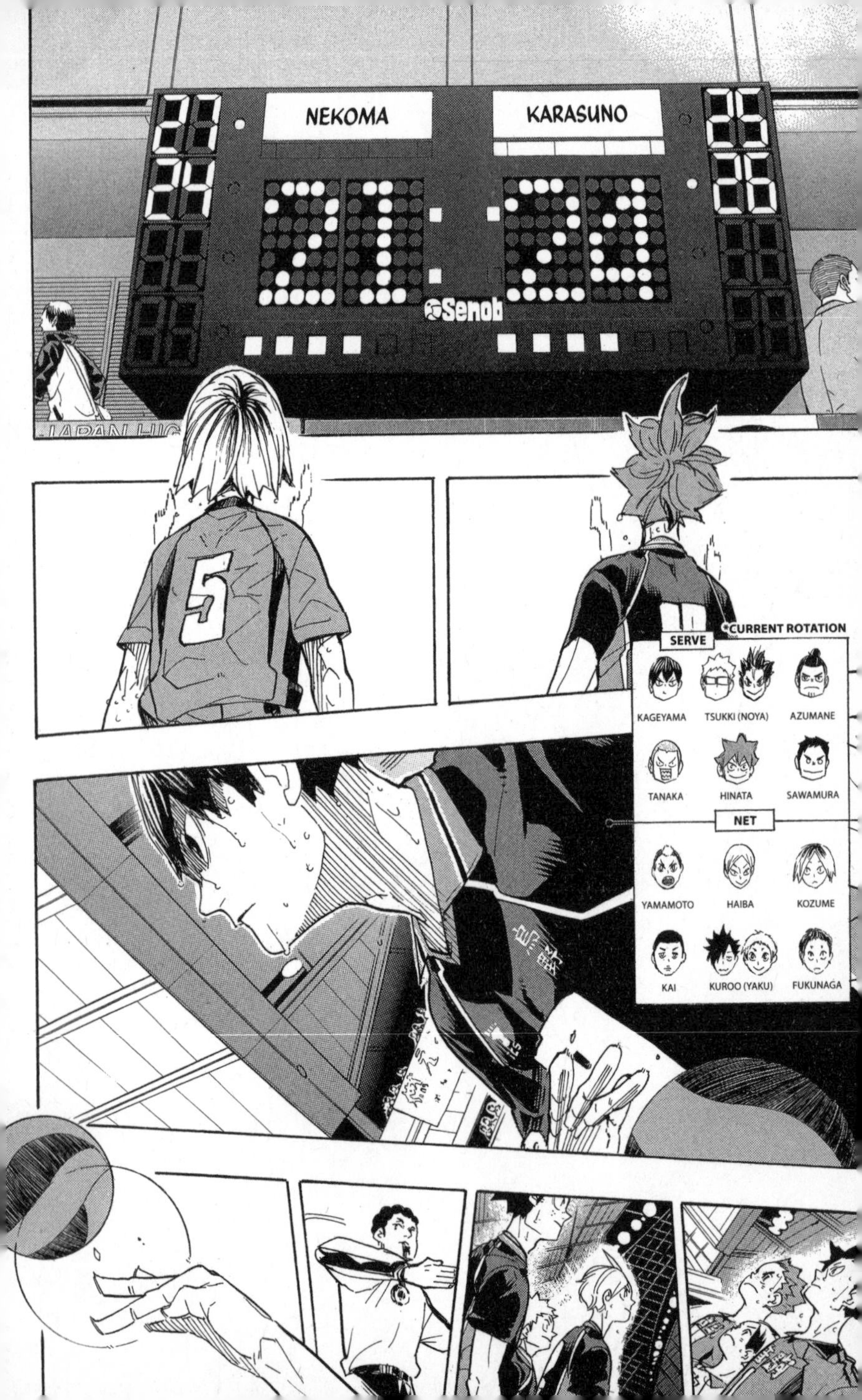
NEKOMA
KARASUNO
Senob
*CURRENT ROTATION
SERVE
KAGEYAMA
TSUKKI (NOYA)
AZUMANE
TANAKA
HINATA
SAWAMURA
NET
YAMAMOTO
HAIBA
KOZUME
KAI
KUROO (YAKU)
FUKUNAGA

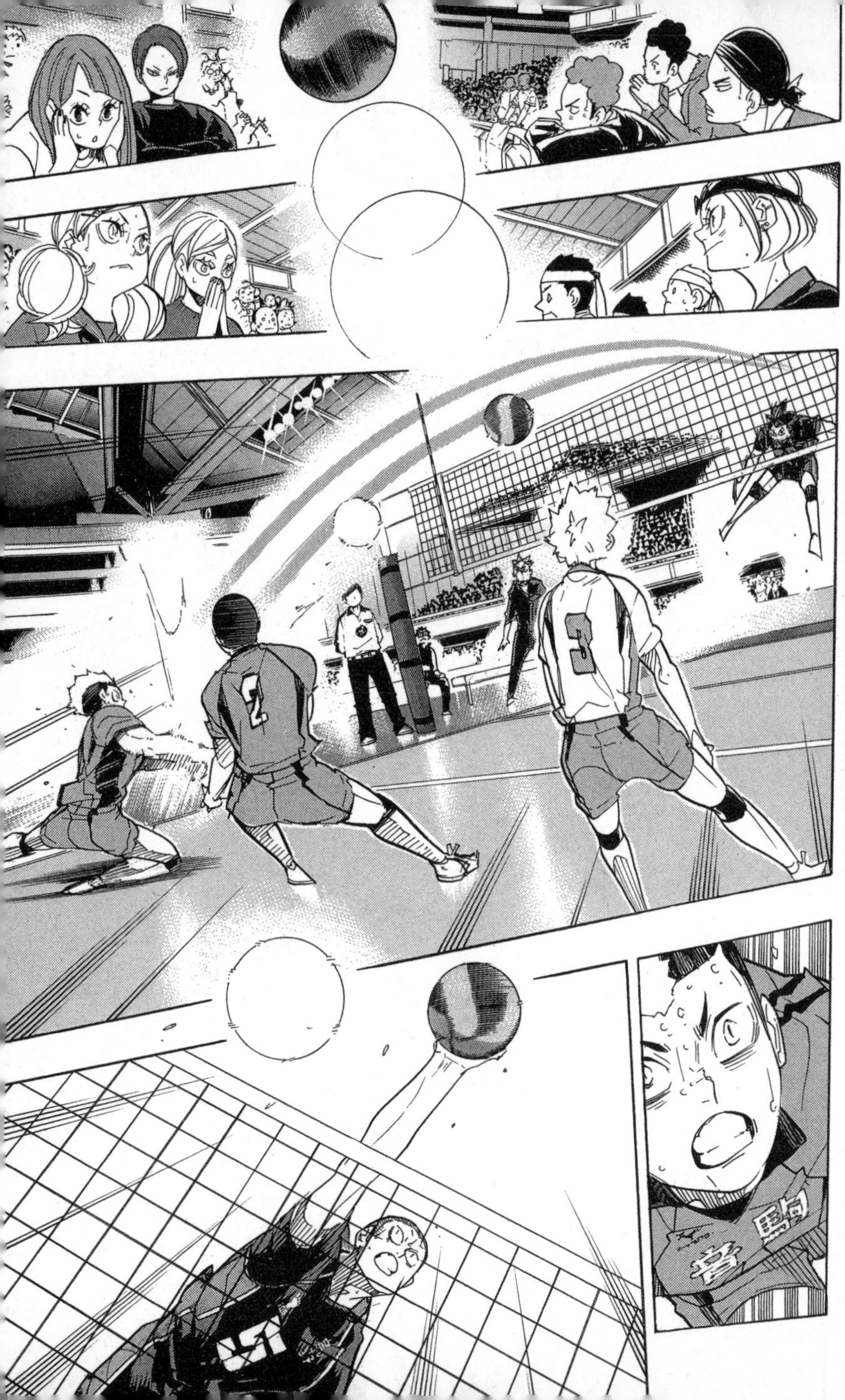

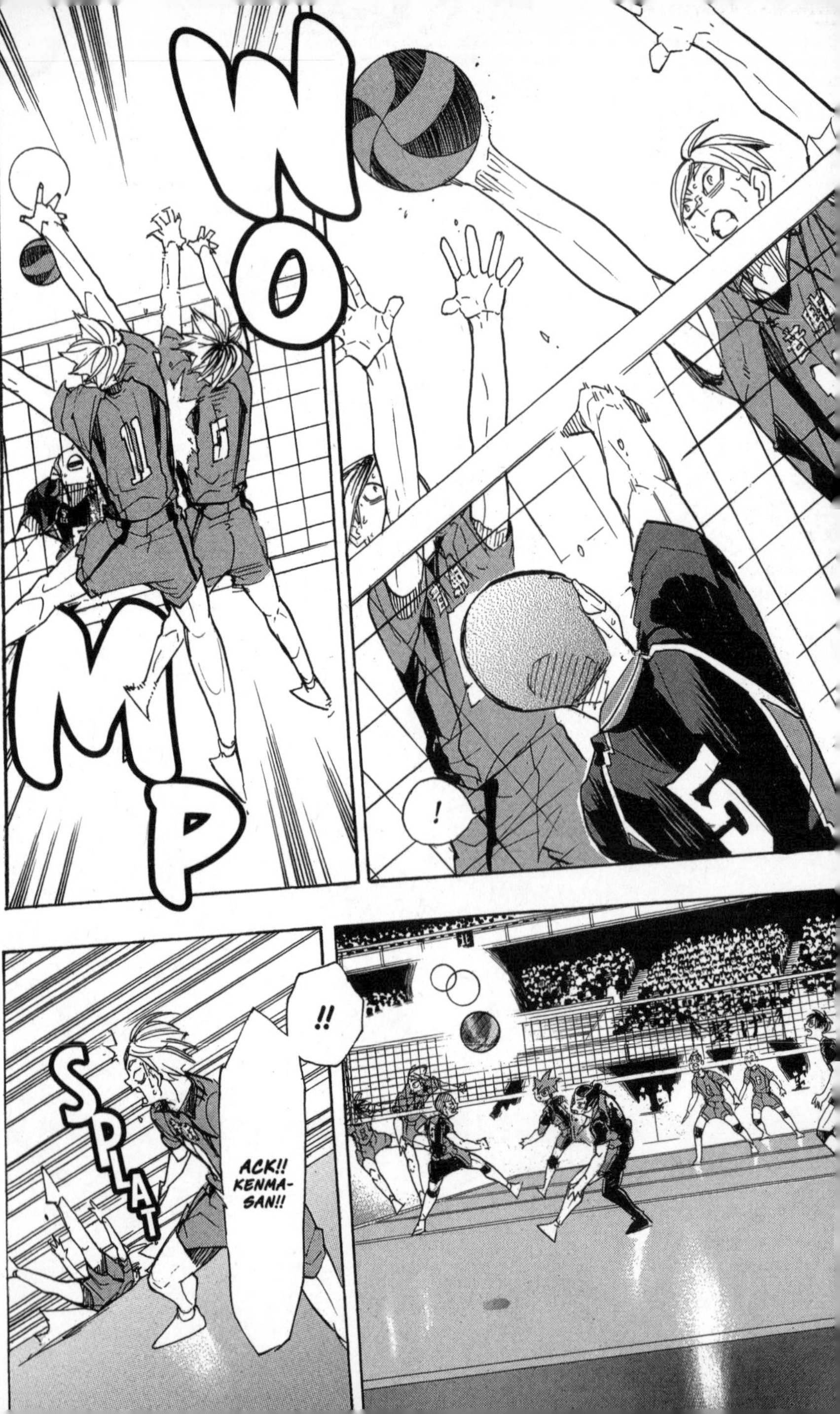
!
WOMP
!!
ACK!! KENMA-SAN!!
SPLAT

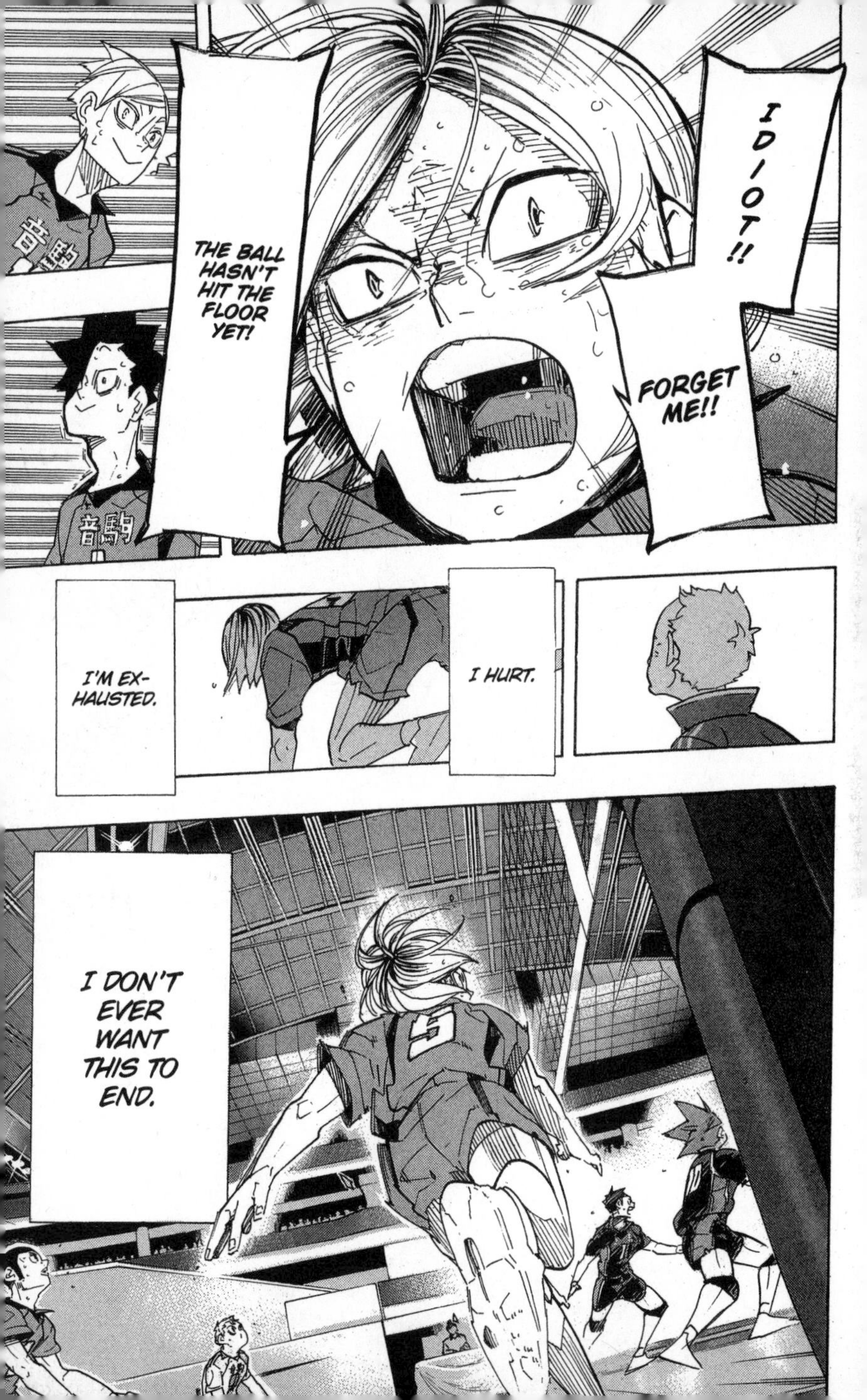
IDIOT!!
FORGET ME!!
THE BALL HASN'T HIT THE FLOOR YET!
I HURT.
I'M EX-HAUSTED.
I DON'T EVER WANT THIS TO END.

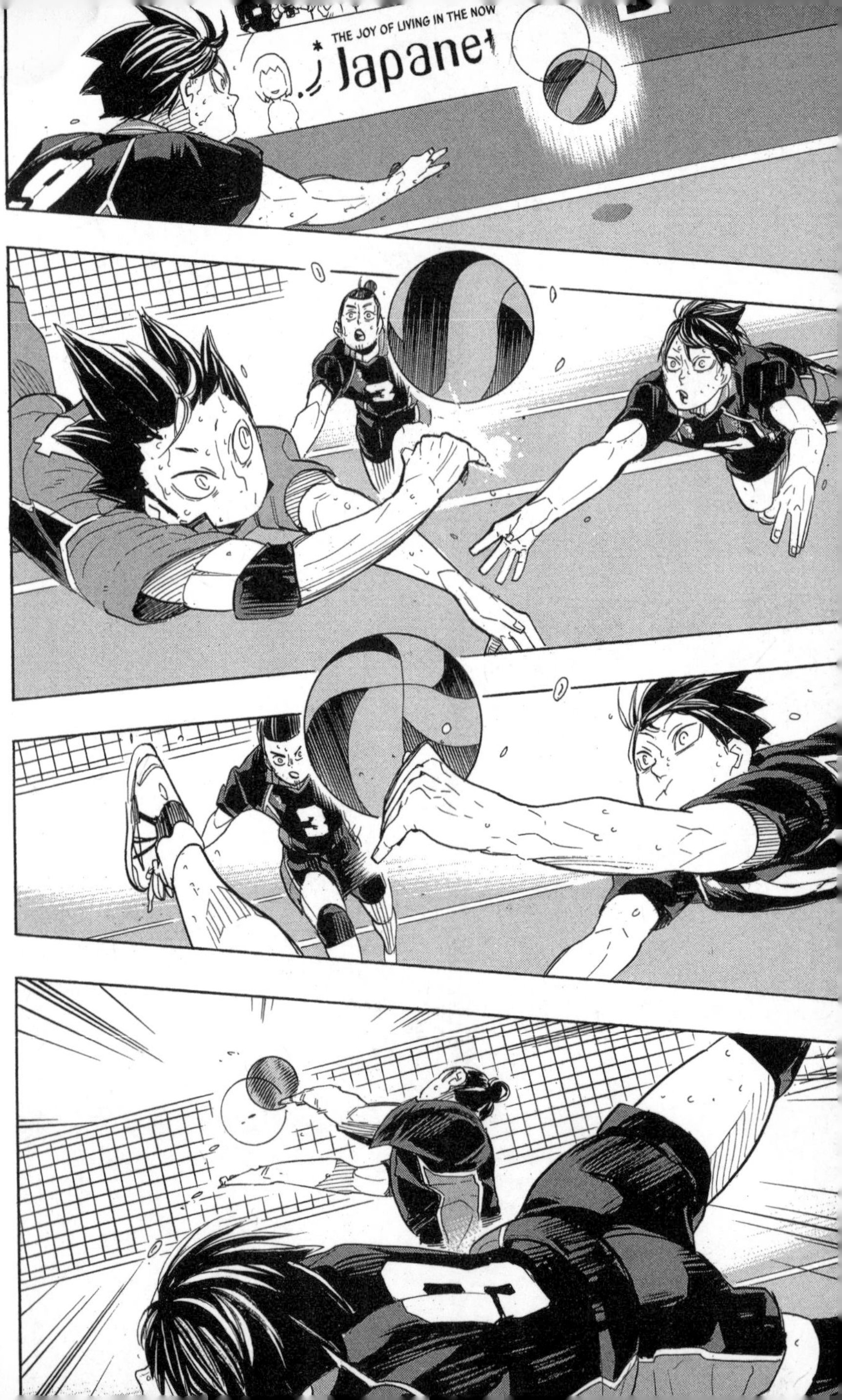
THE JOY OF LIVING IN THE NOW
Japane

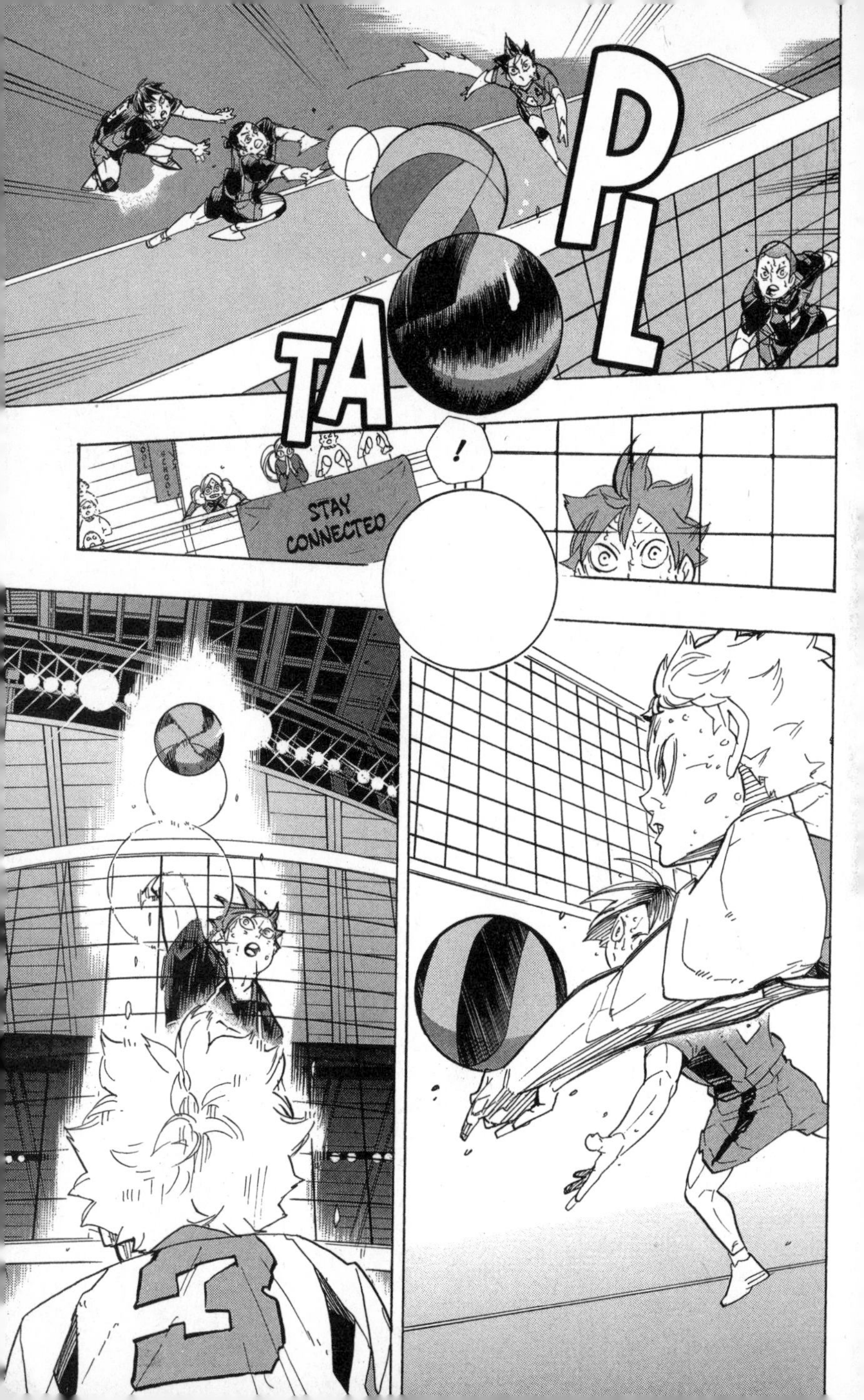

TAP
PL
STAY CONNECTED
!

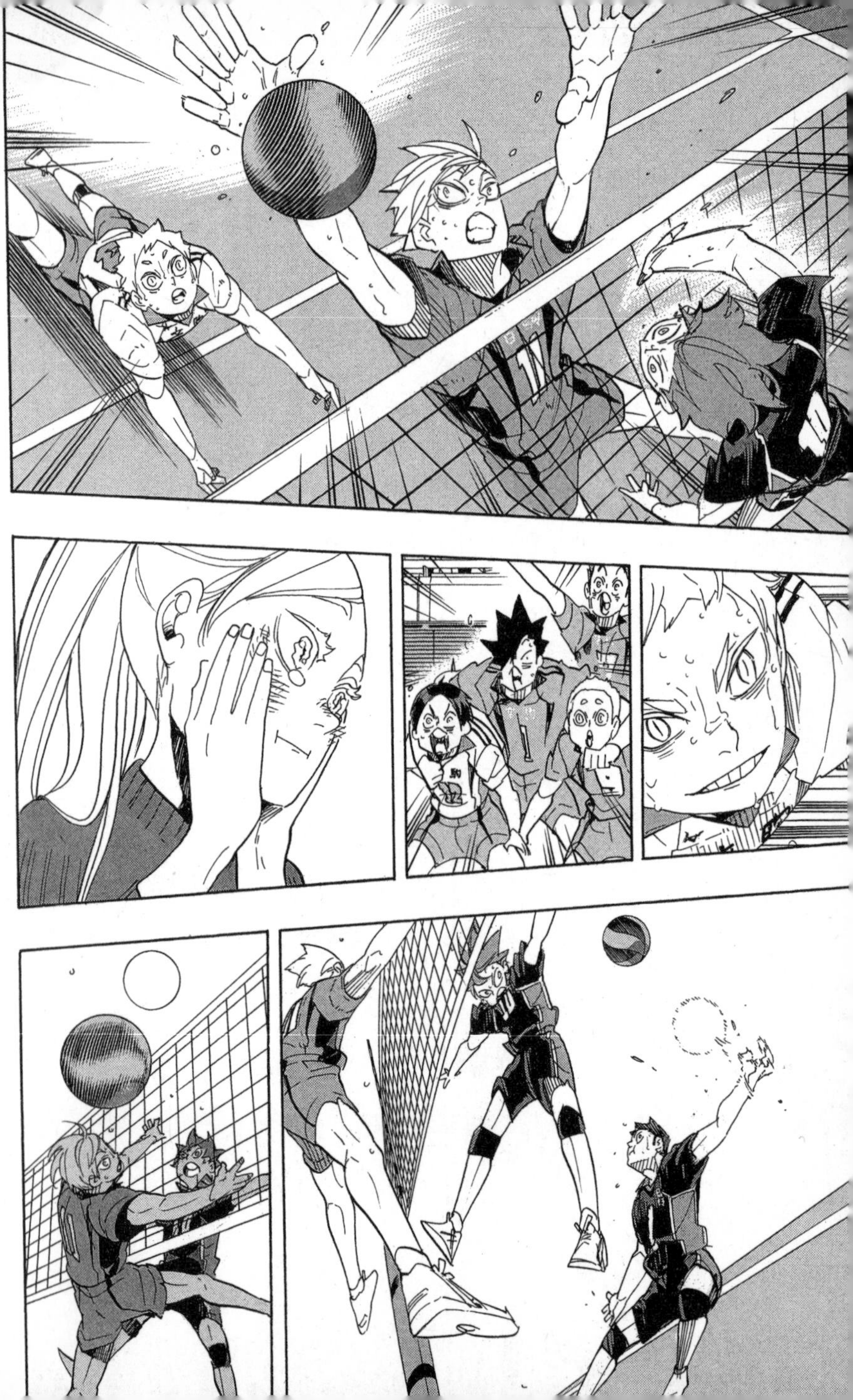

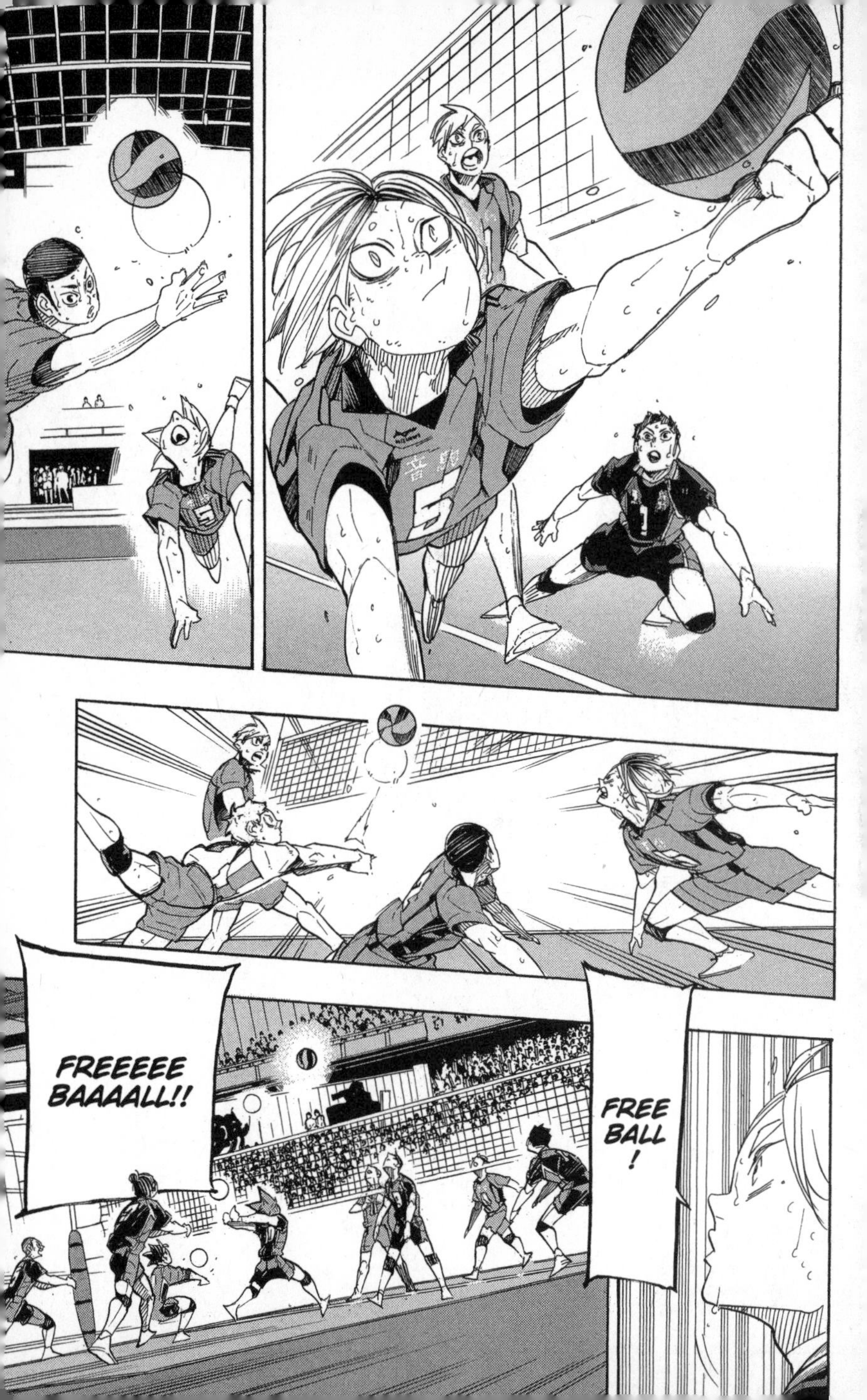
FREE BALL!
FREEEEE BAAAALL!!

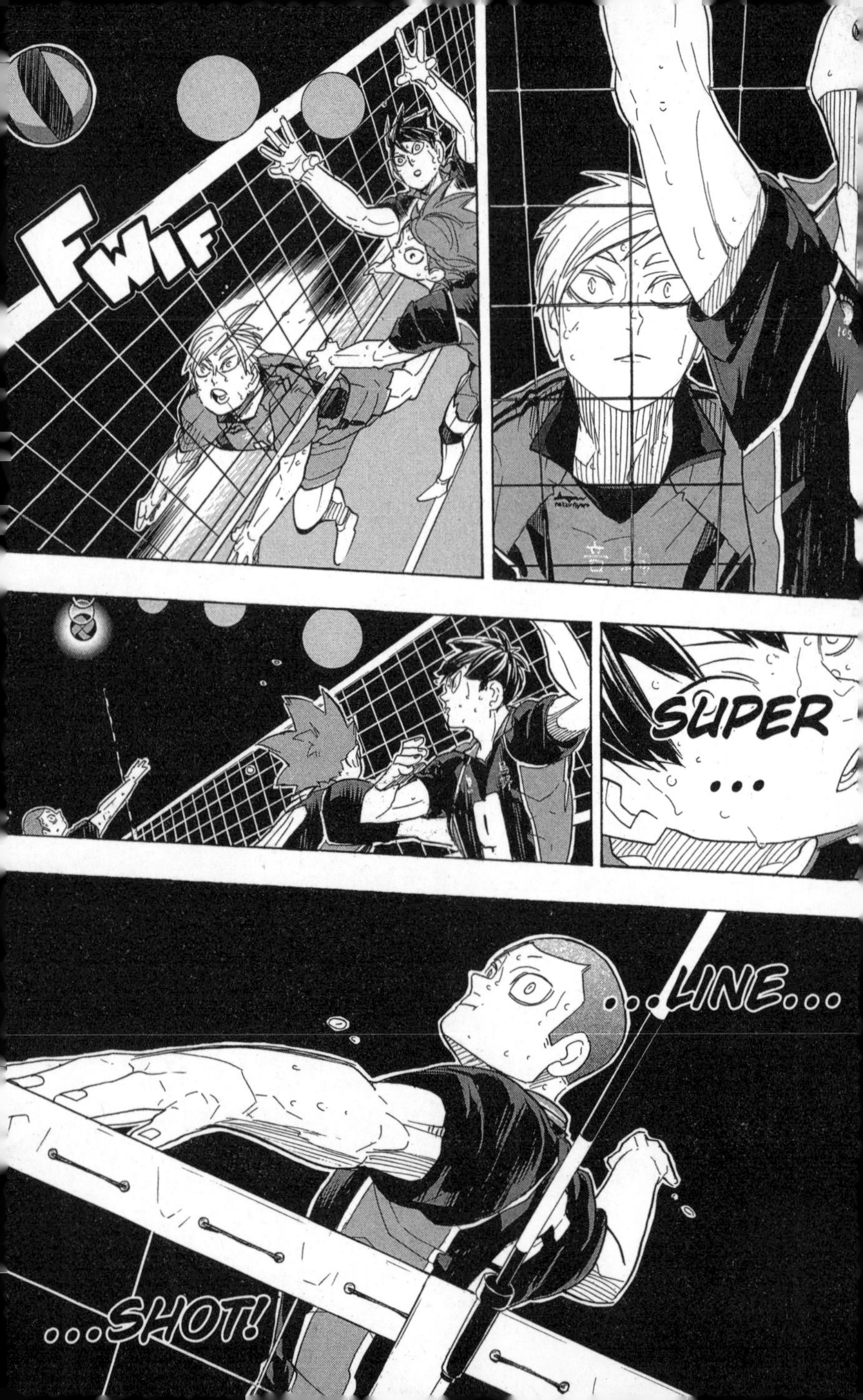
FWIF
SUPER ...
...LINE...
...SHOT!

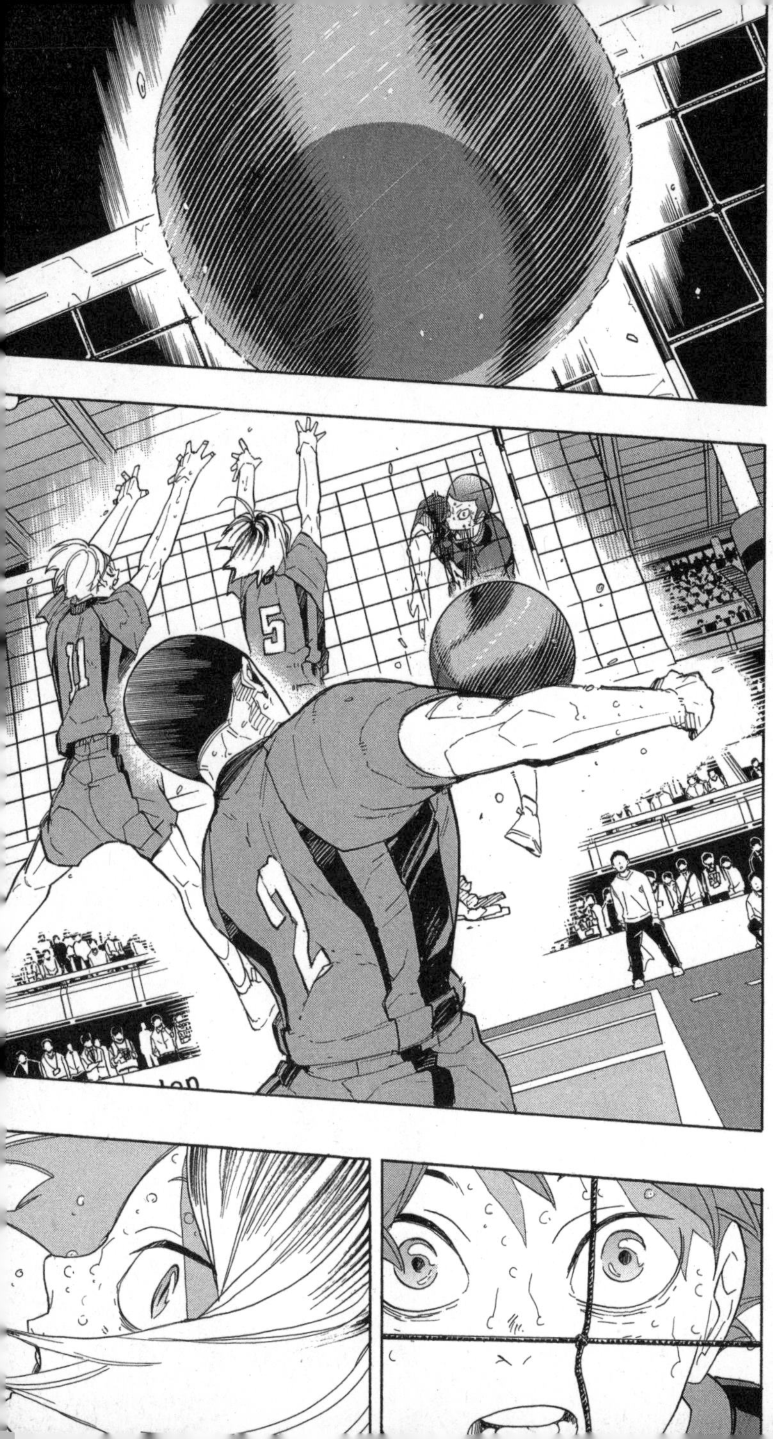

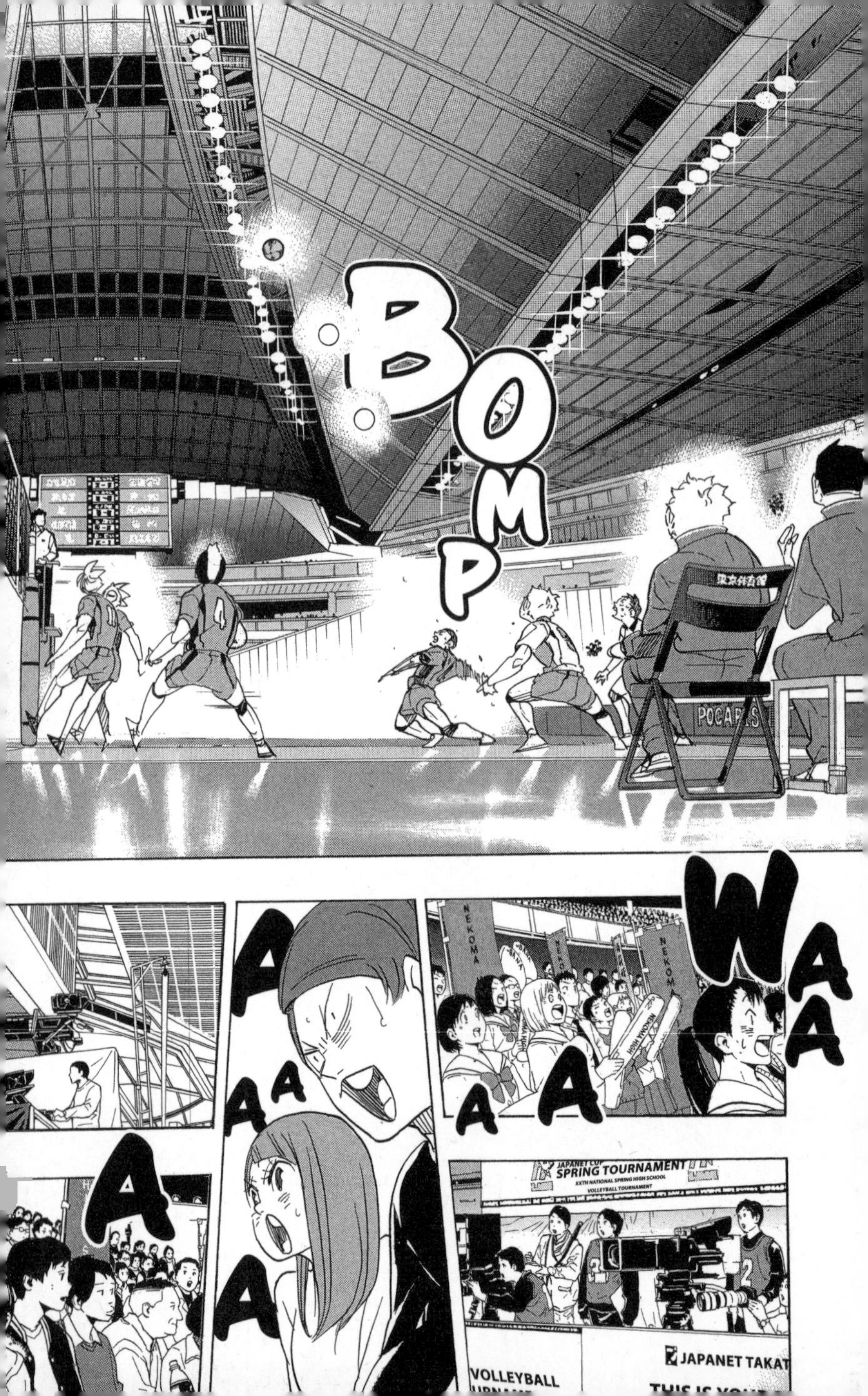
BOMP
POCARI S
NEKOMA
NEKOMA HIGH
WAAAAA
AAAAA
JAPANET CUP
SPRING TOURNAMENT
XXTH NATIONAL SPRING HIGH SCHOOL
VOLLEYBALL TOURNAMENT
JAPANET TAKAT
VOLLEYBALL
A-

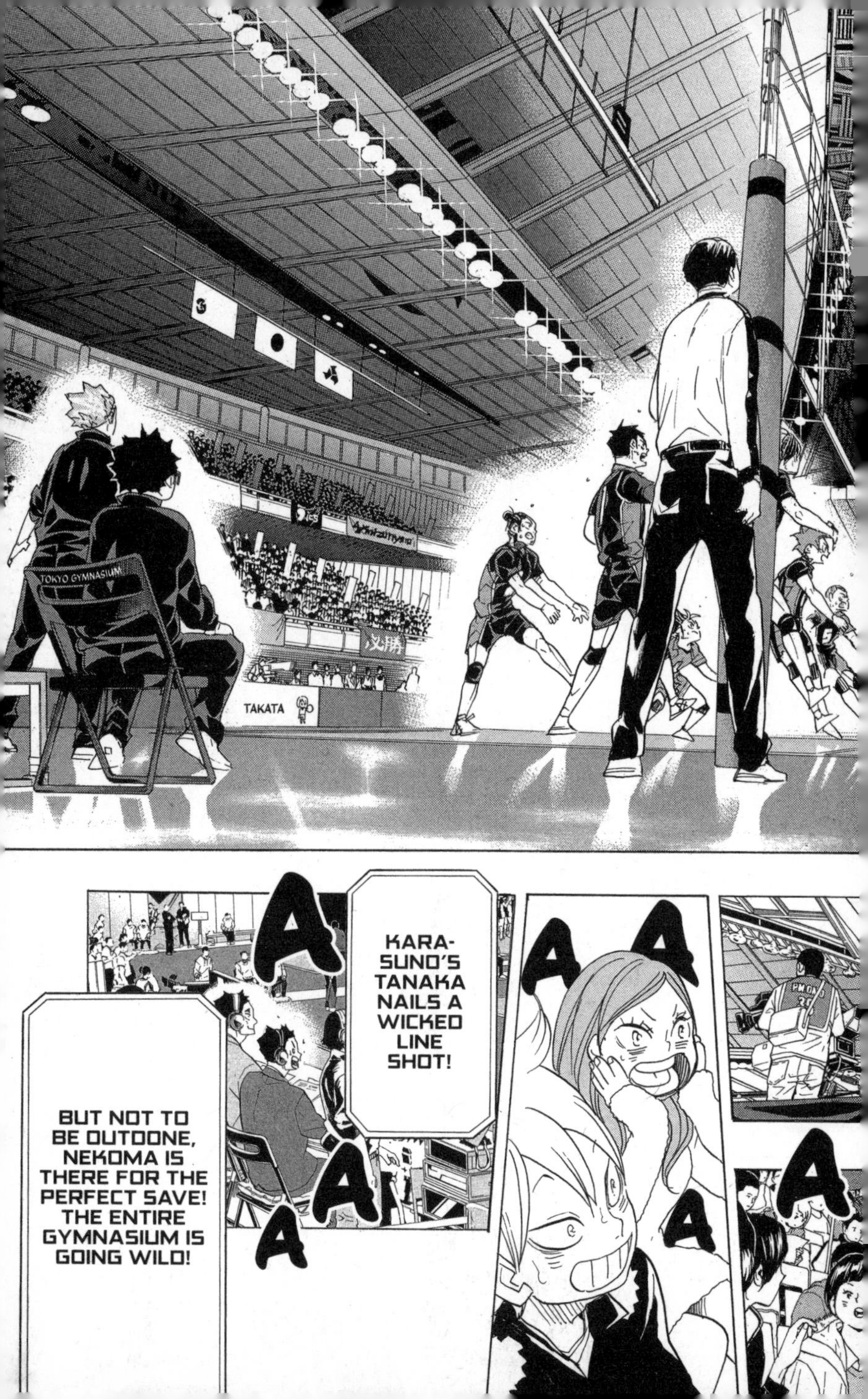
TOKYO GYMNASIUM
TAKATA
A
A
A
A
KARA-SUNO'S TANAKA NAILS A WICKED LINE SHOT!
A
A
A
BUT NOT TO BE OUTDONE, NEKOMA IS THERE FOR THE PERFECT SAVE! THE ENTIRE GYMNASIUM IS GOING WILD!

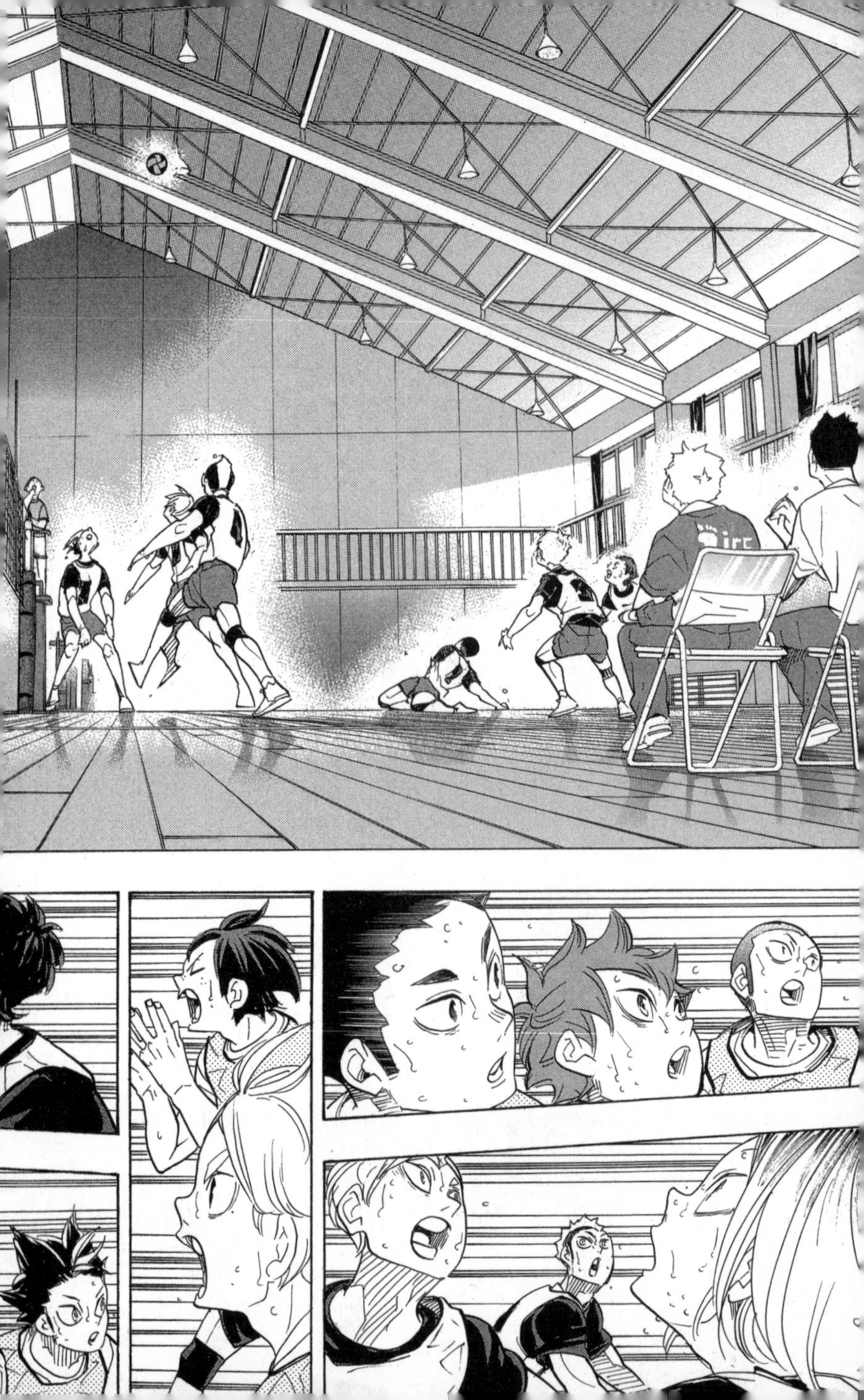

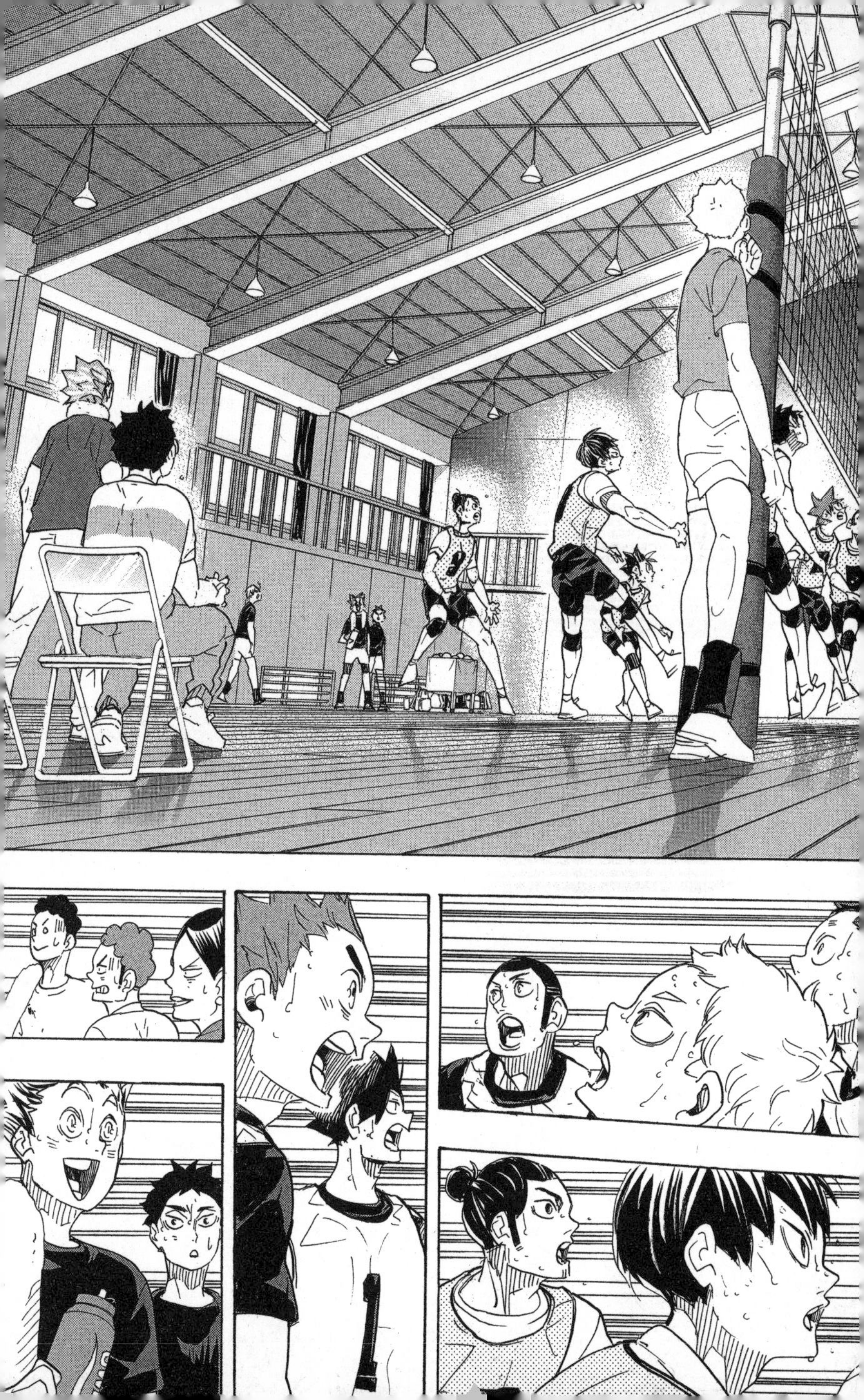

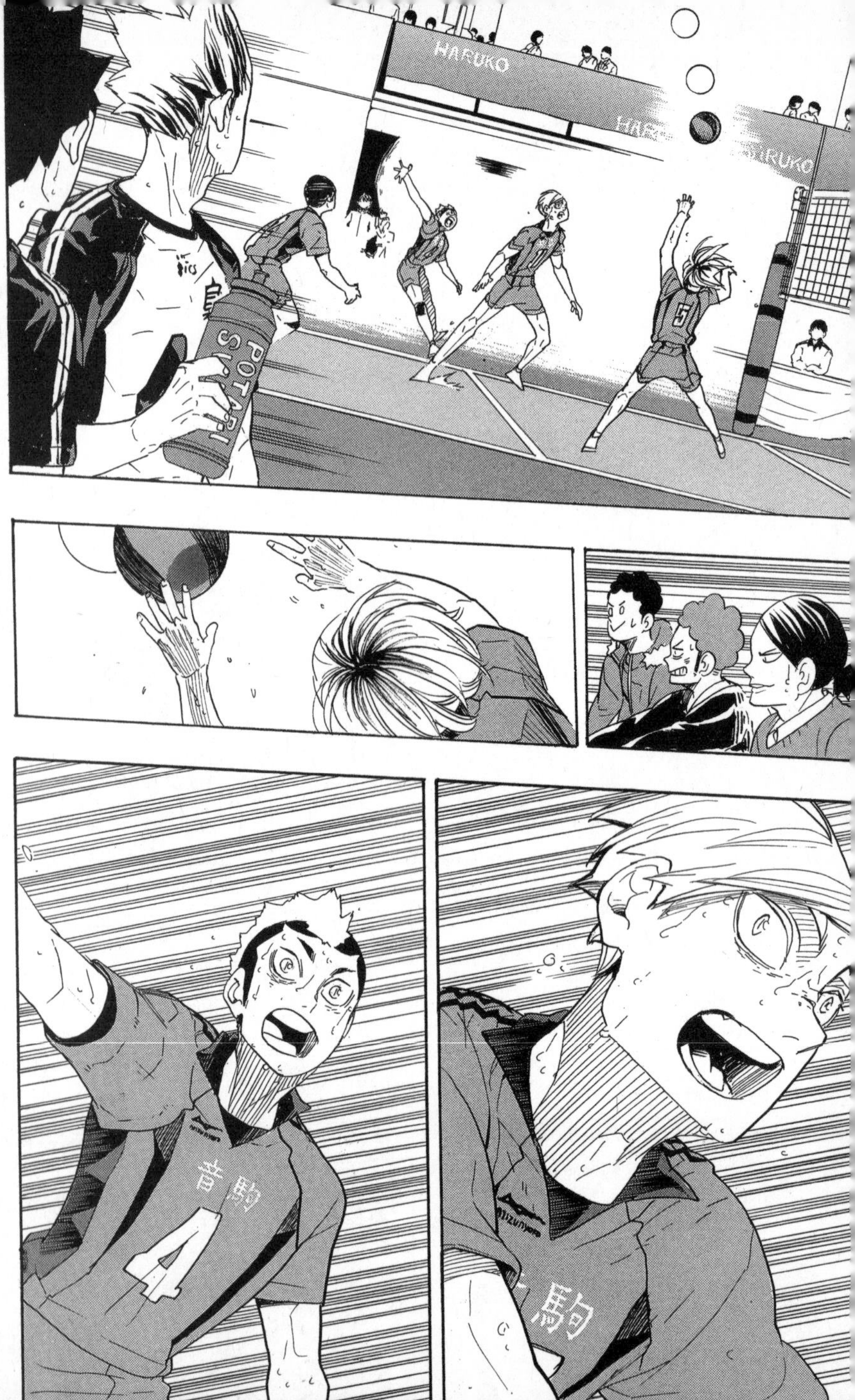
HARUKO
POTARI
音駒
4
音駒

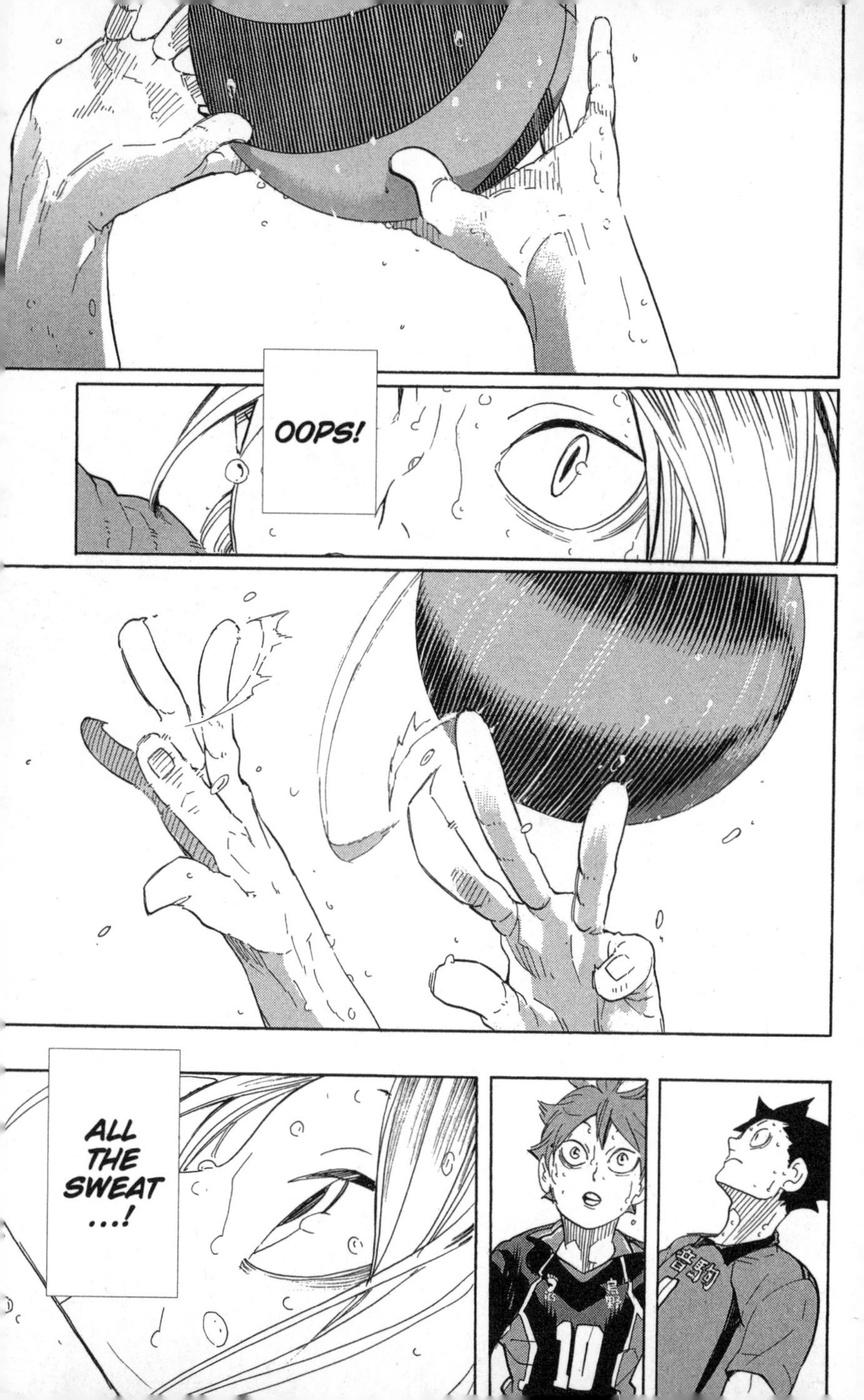
OOPS!
ALL THE SWEAT ...!

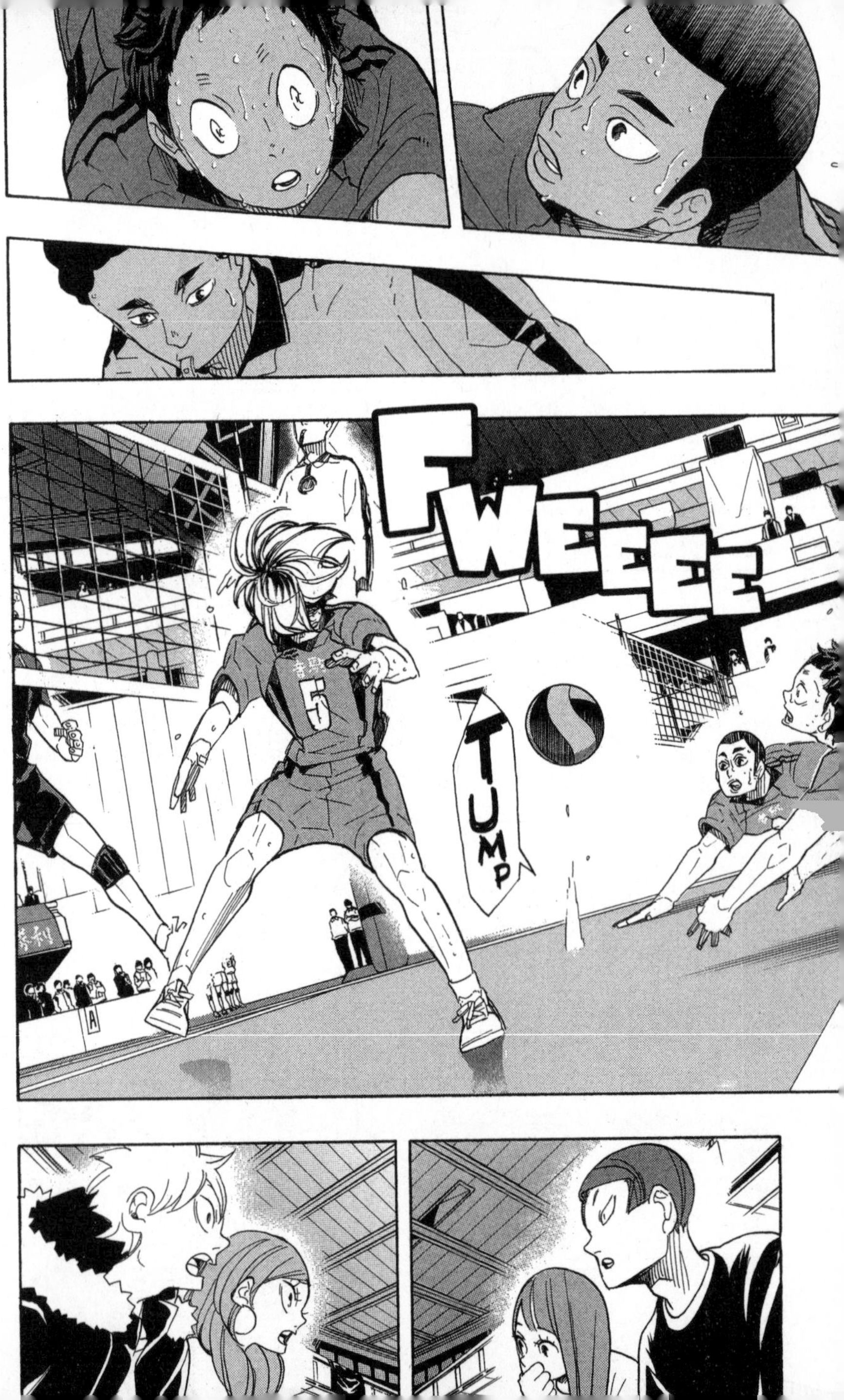
FWEEEE
TUMP

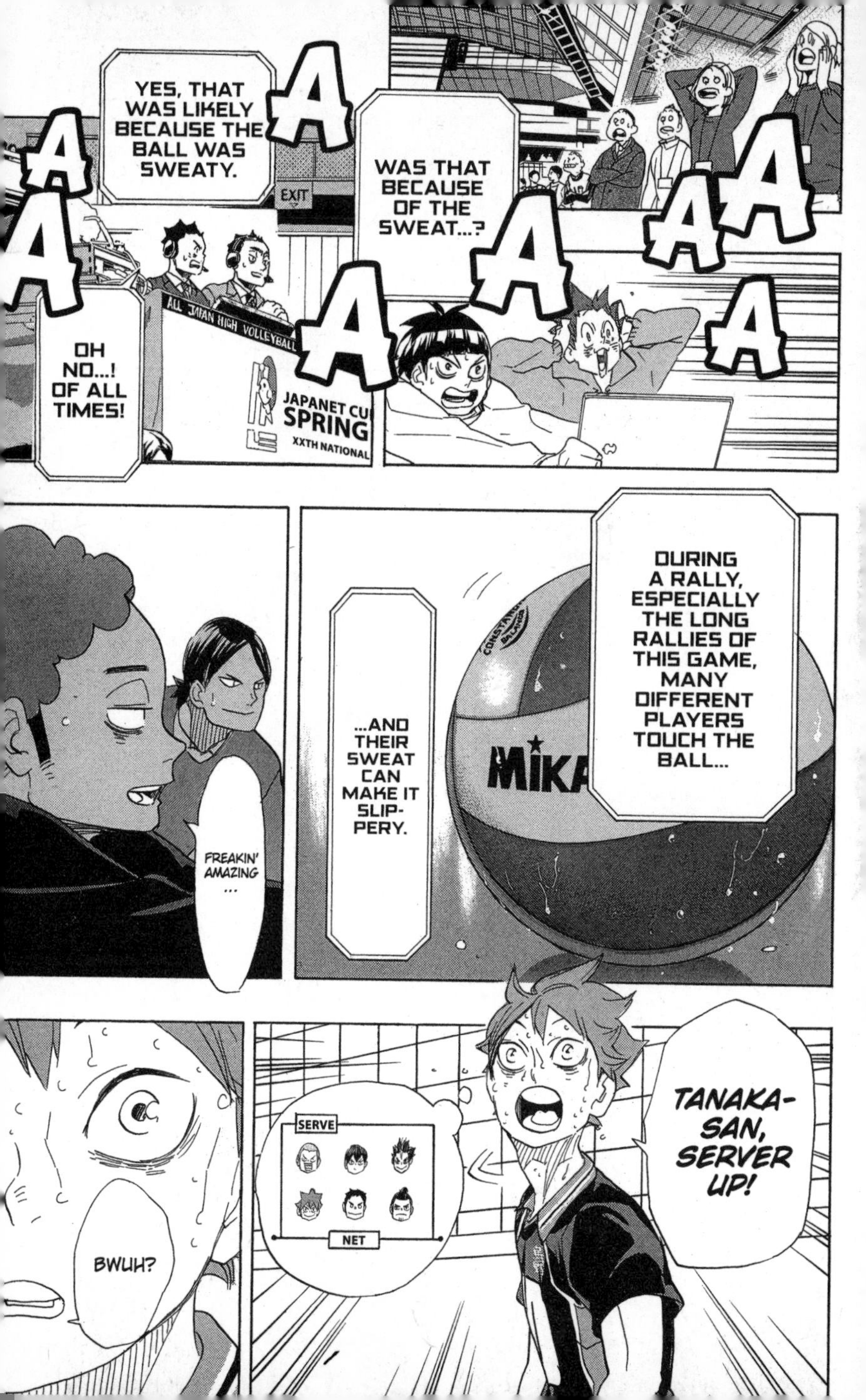
AAAAAAAA
WAS THAT BECAUSE OF THE SWEAT...?
YES, THAT WAS LIKELY BECAUSE THE BALL WAS SWEATY.
EXIT
ALL JAPAN HIGH VOLLEYBALL
JAPANET CU SPRING
XXTH NATIONAL
OH NO...! OF ALL TIMES!
DURING A RALLY, ESPECIALLY THE LONG RALLIES OF THIS GAME, MANY DIFFERENT PLAYERS TOUCH THE BALL...
...AND THEIR SWEAT CAN MAKE IT SLIP-PERY.
MIKA
FREAKIN' AMAZING ...
TANAKA-SAN, SERVER UP!
SERVE
NET
BWUH?

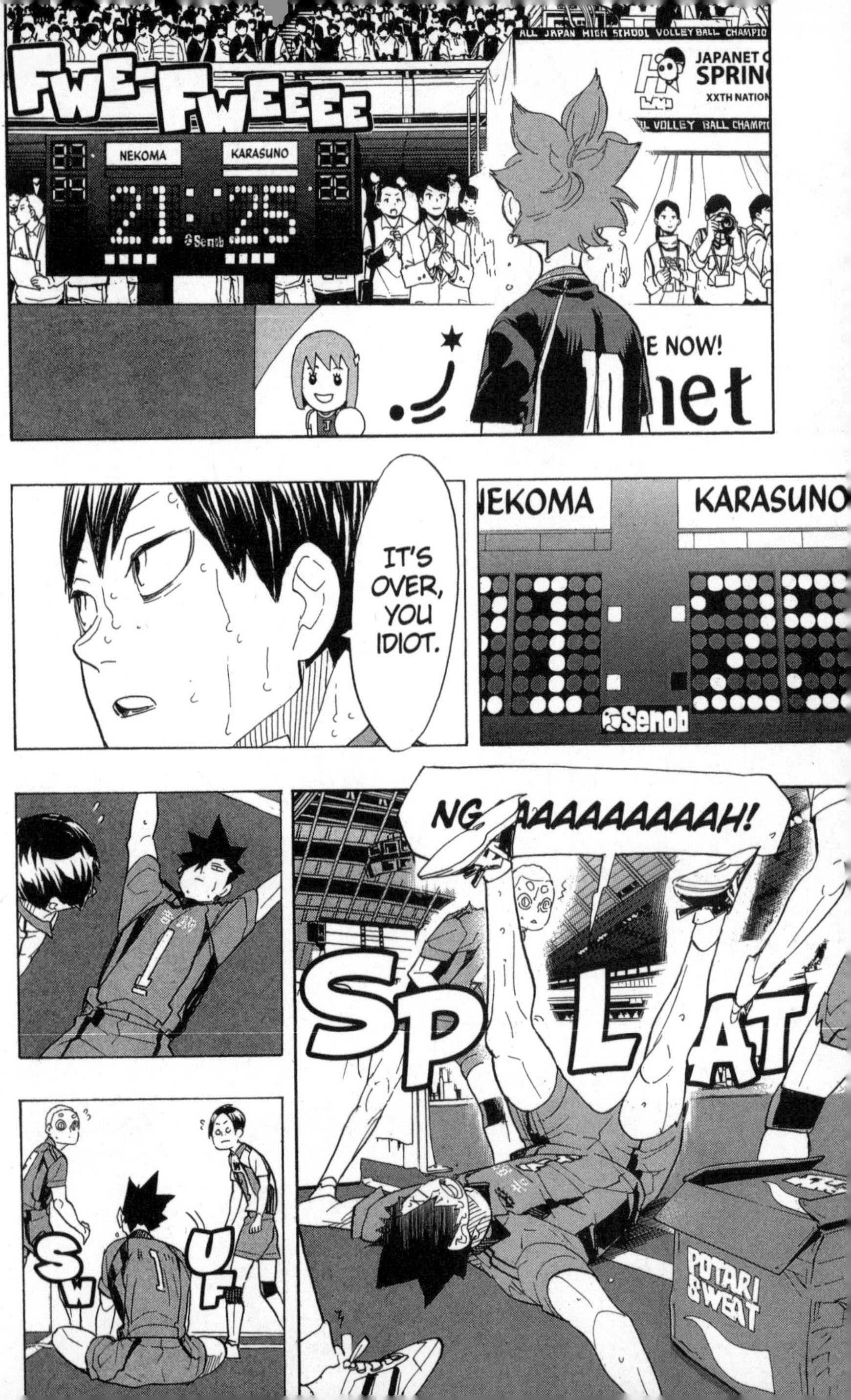
ALL JAPAN HIGH SCHOOL VOLLEYBALL CHAMPIO
JAPANET C
SPRING
XXTH NATION
FWE-FWEEEE
NEKOMA
KARASUNO
21 : 25
Senob
E NOW!
net
NEKOMA
KARASUNO
Senob
IT'S OVER, YOU IDIOT.
NG AAAAAAAAAAH!
SPLAT
POTARI SWEAT
SWUF

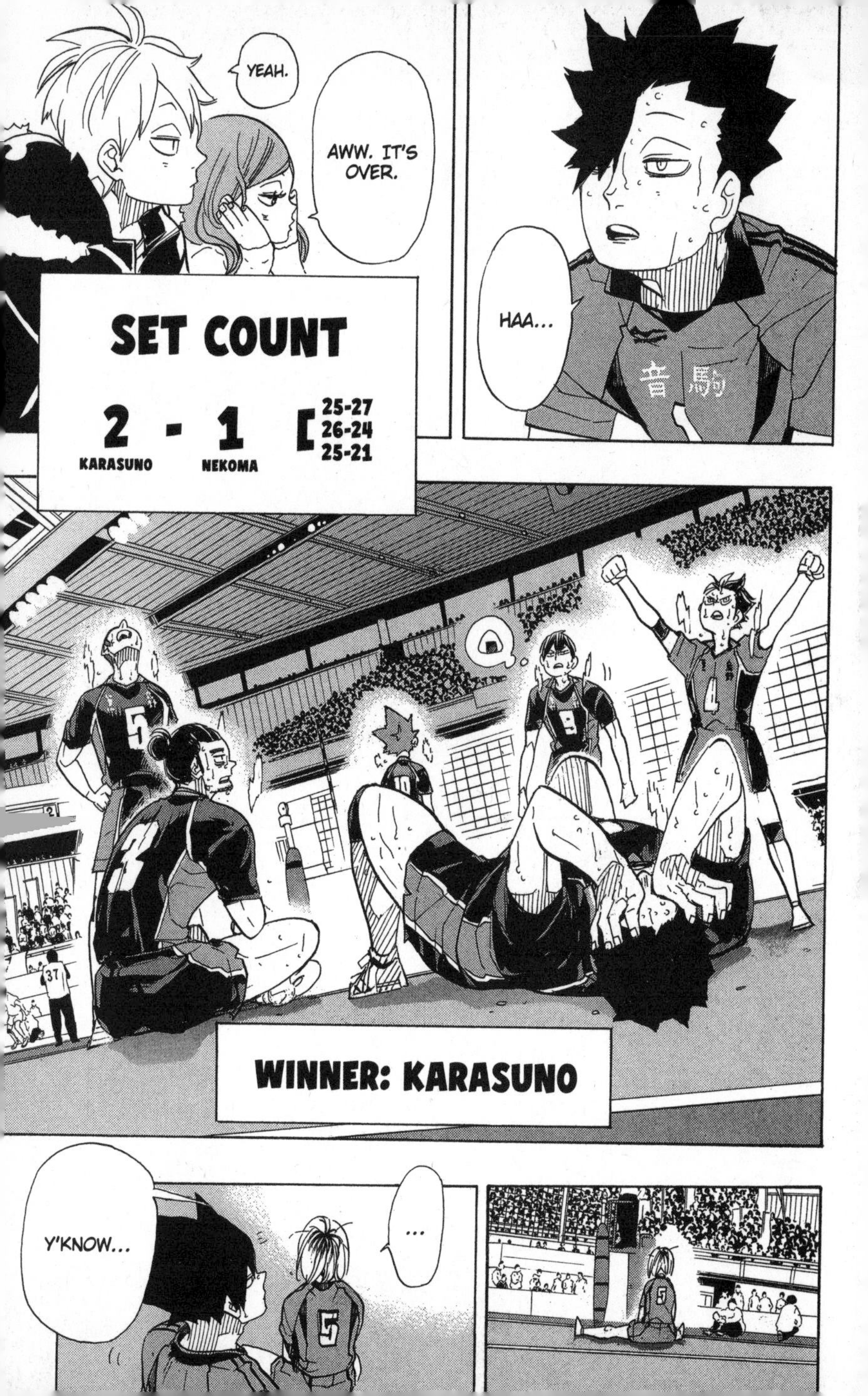
HAA...
AWW. IT'S OVER.
YEAH.
SET COUNT
2 - 1 [25-27 26-24 25-21
KARASUNO
NEKOMA
WINNER: KARASUNO
...
Y'KNOW...

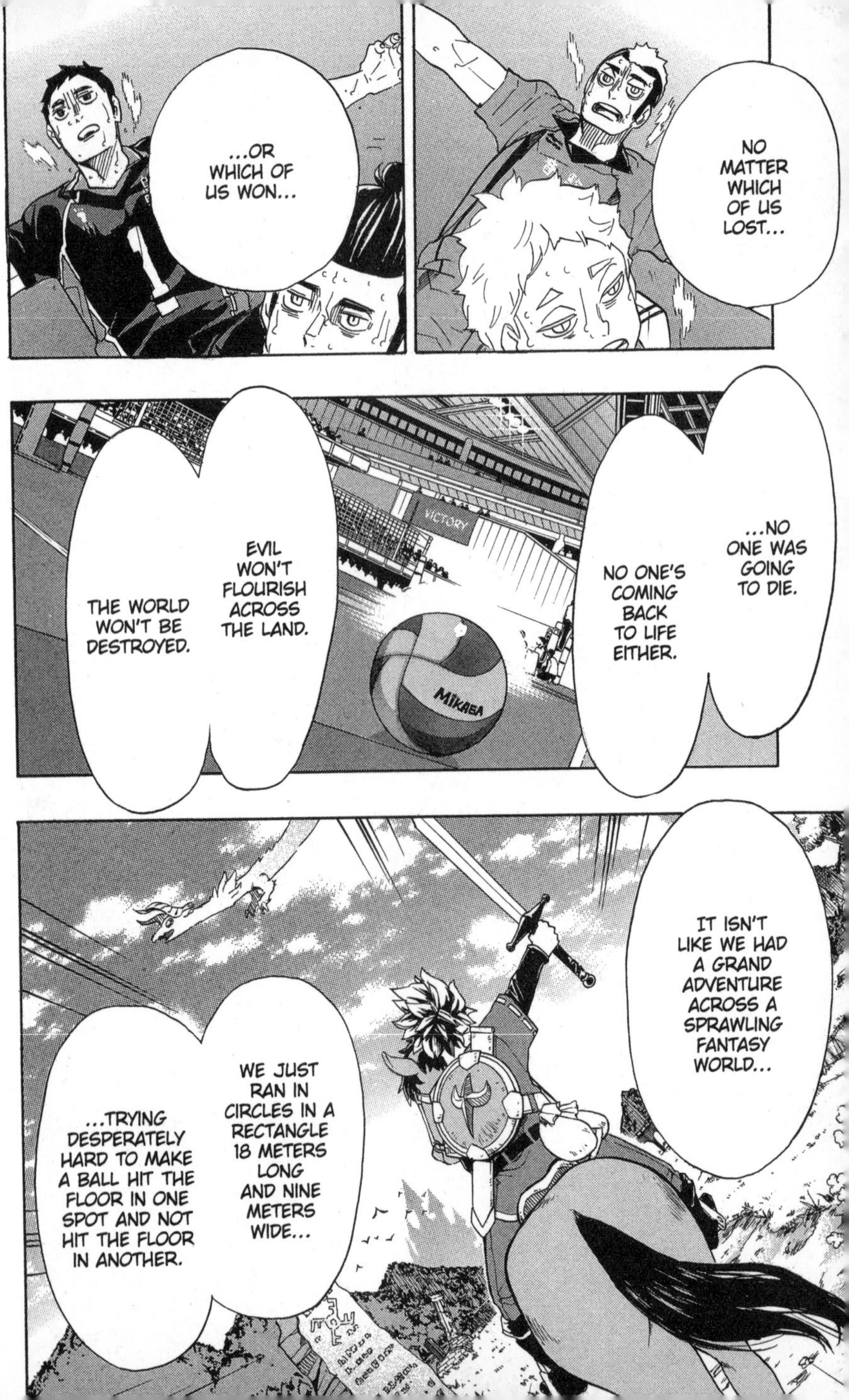
NO MATTER WHICH OF US LOST...
...OR WHICH OF US WON...
...NO ONE WAS GOING TO DIE.
NO ONE'S COMING BACK TO LIFE EITHER.
VICTORY
MIKASA
EVIL WON'T FLOURISH ACROSS THE LAND.
THE WORLD WON'T BE DESTROYED.
IT ISN'T LIKE WE HAD A GRAND ADVENTURE ACROSS A SPRAWLING FANTASY WORLD...
WE JUST RAN IN CIRCLES IN A RECTANGLE 18 METERS LONG AND NINE METERS WIDE...
...TRYING DESPERATELY HARD TO MAKE A BALL HIT THE FLOOR IN ONE SPOT AND NOT HIT THE FLOOR IN ANOTHER.

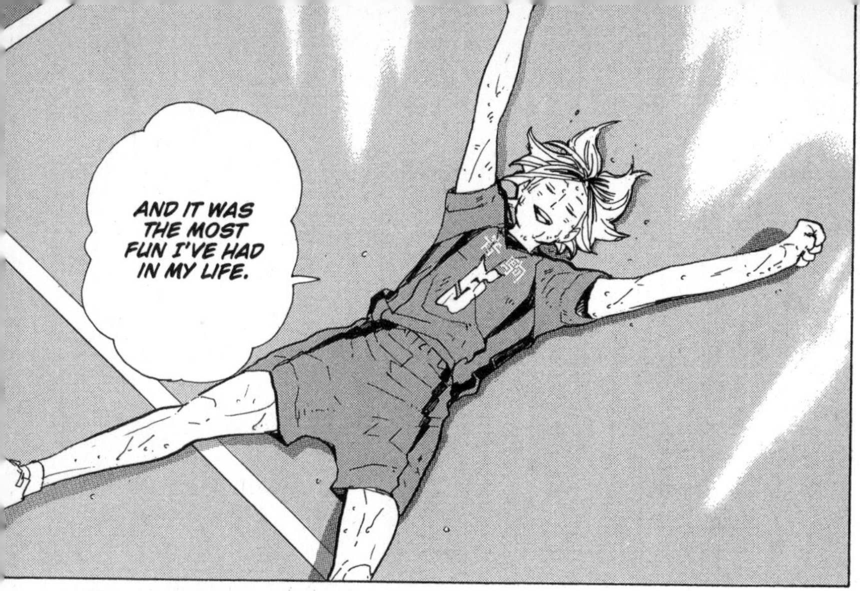
AND IT WAS THE MOST FUN I'VE HAD IN MY LIFE.

CHAPTER 324: The Party's Over

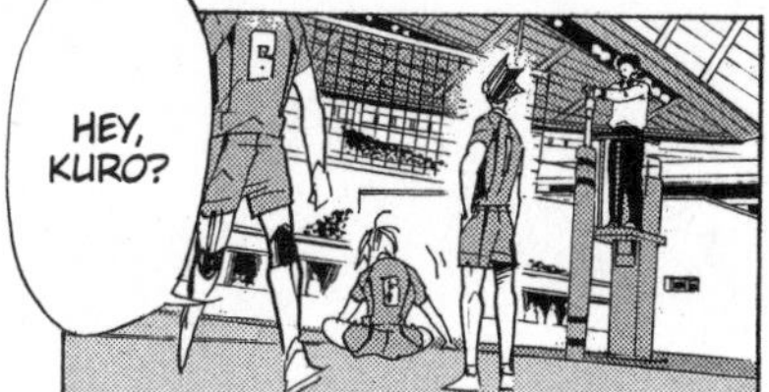
HEY, KURO?

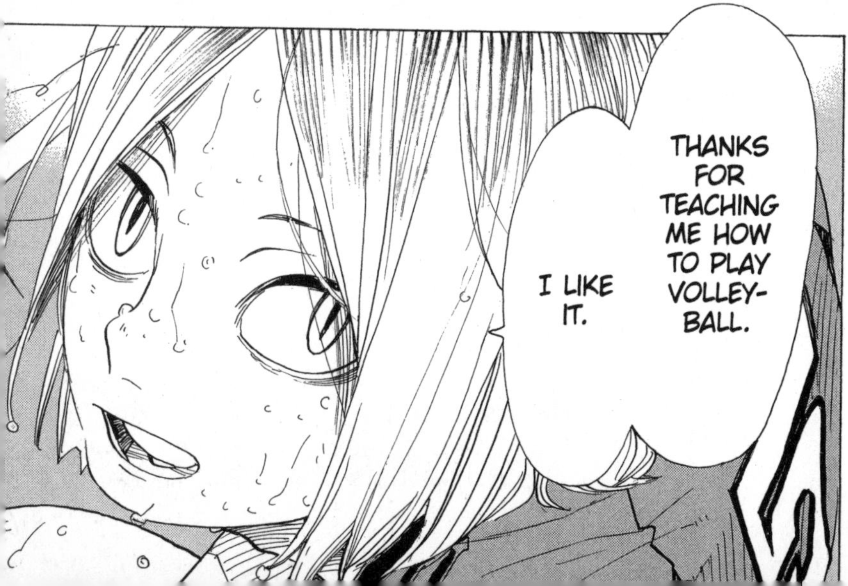
THANKS FOR TEACHING ME HOW TO PLAY VOLLEY-BALL.
I LIKE IT.

HAIKYU!!

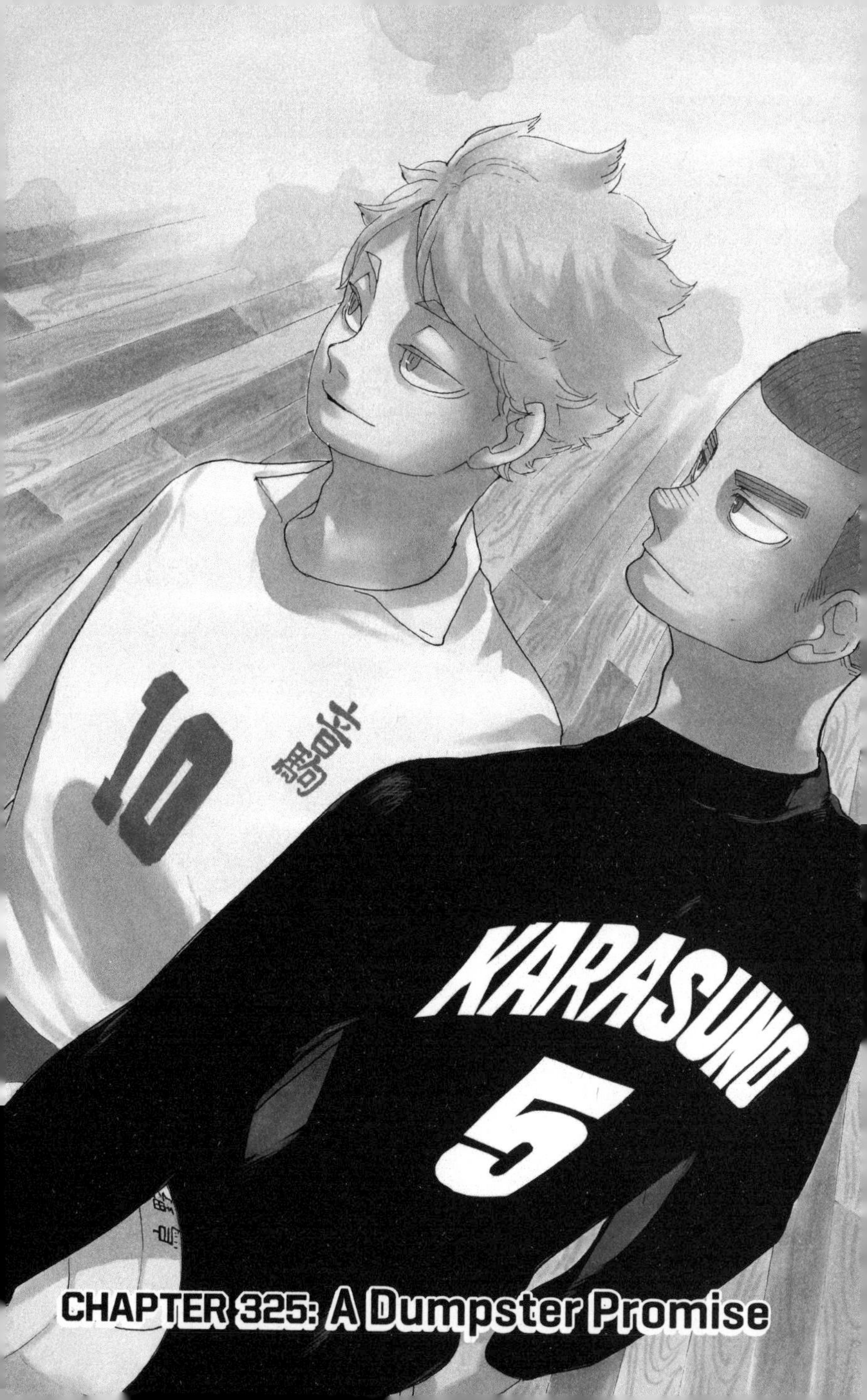
10
KARASUNO
5

CHAPTER 325: A Dumpster Promise

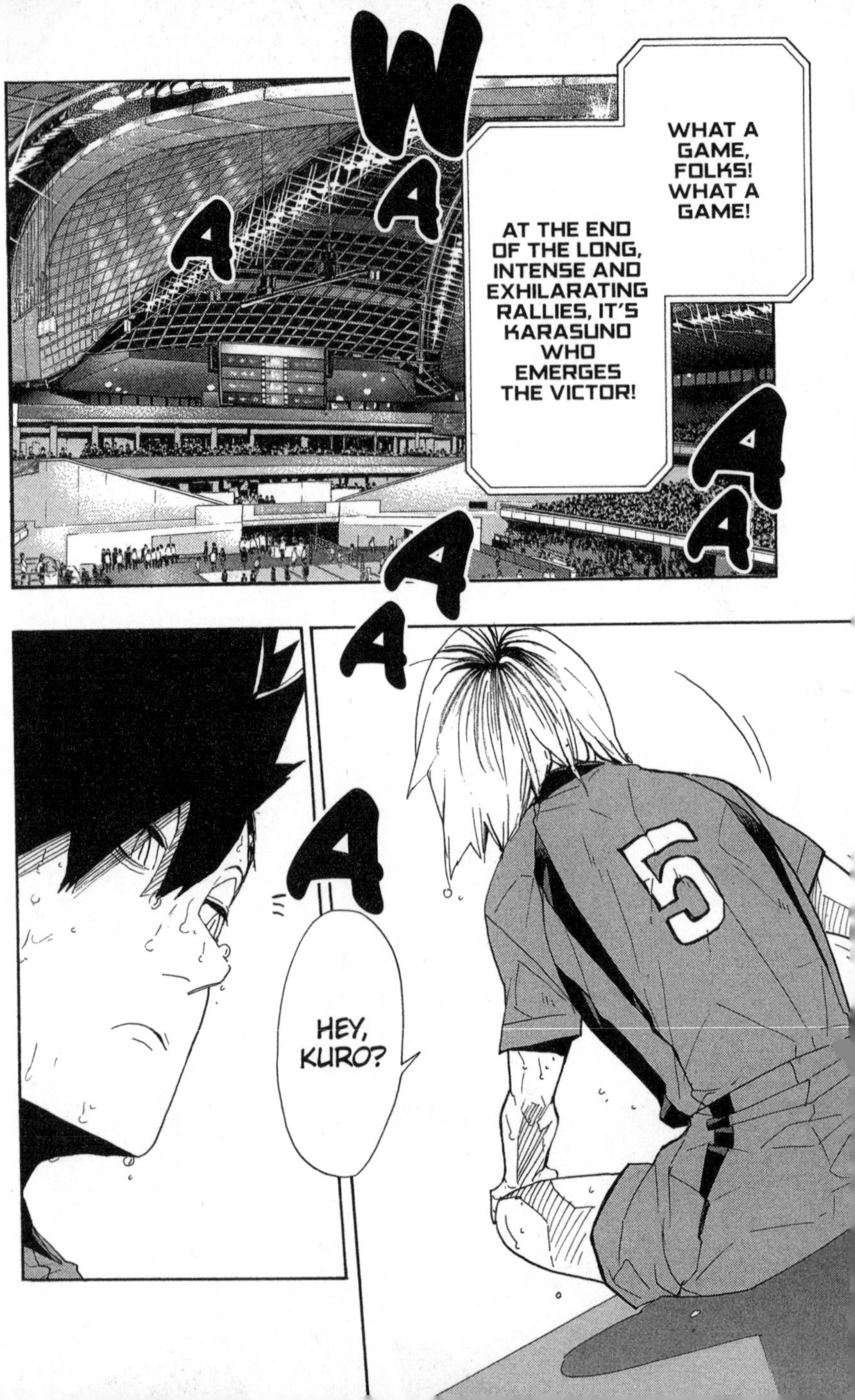
WHAT A GAME, FOLKS! WHAT A GAME!
AT THE END OF THE LONG, INTENSE AND EXHILARATING RALLIES, IT'S KARASUNO WHO EMERGES THE VICTOR!
WAAAAAAAA
HEY, KURO?

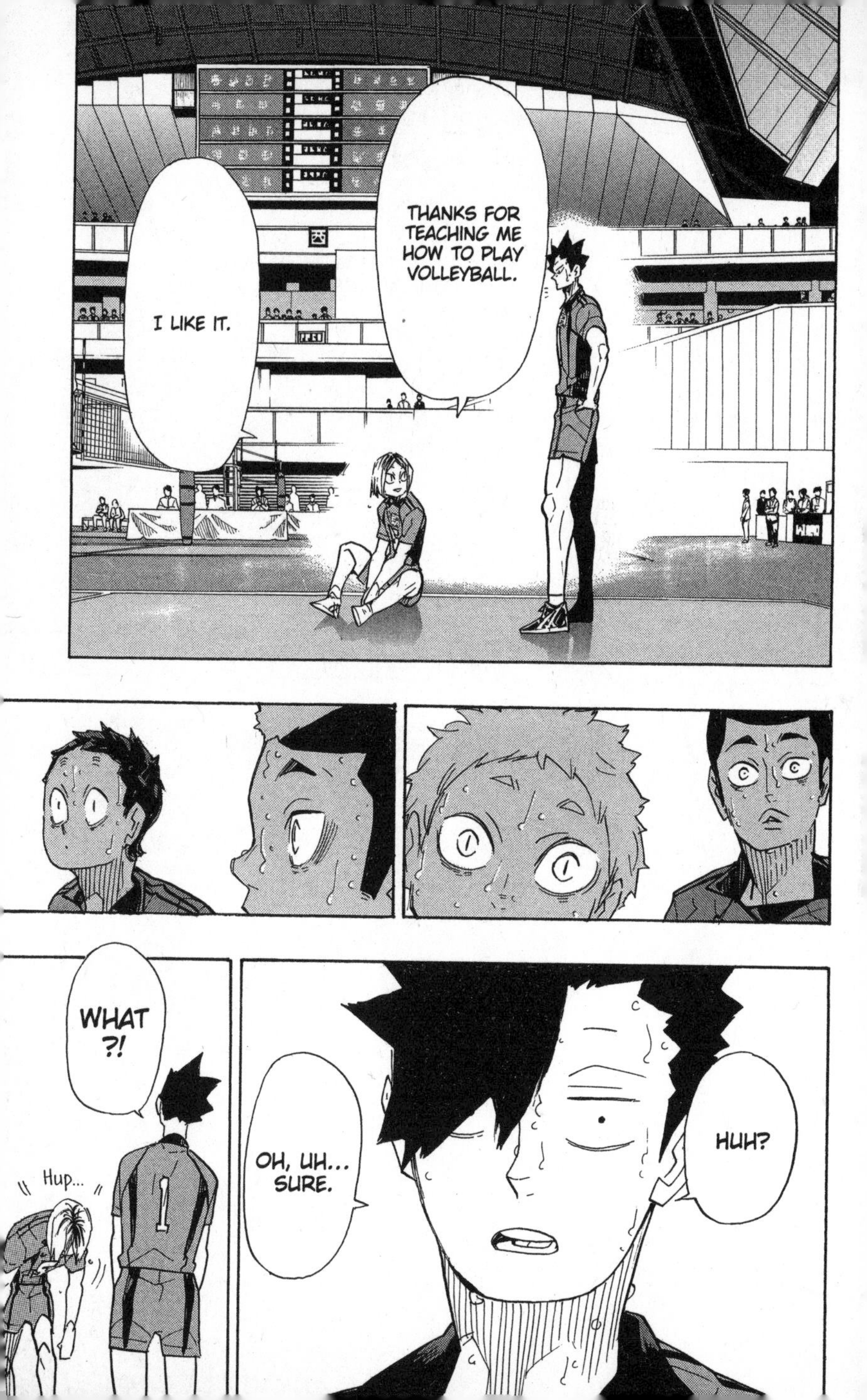
THANKS FOR TEACHING ME HOW TO PLAY VOLLEYBALL.
I LIKE IT.
HUH?
OH, UH... SURE.
WHAT ?!
Hup...

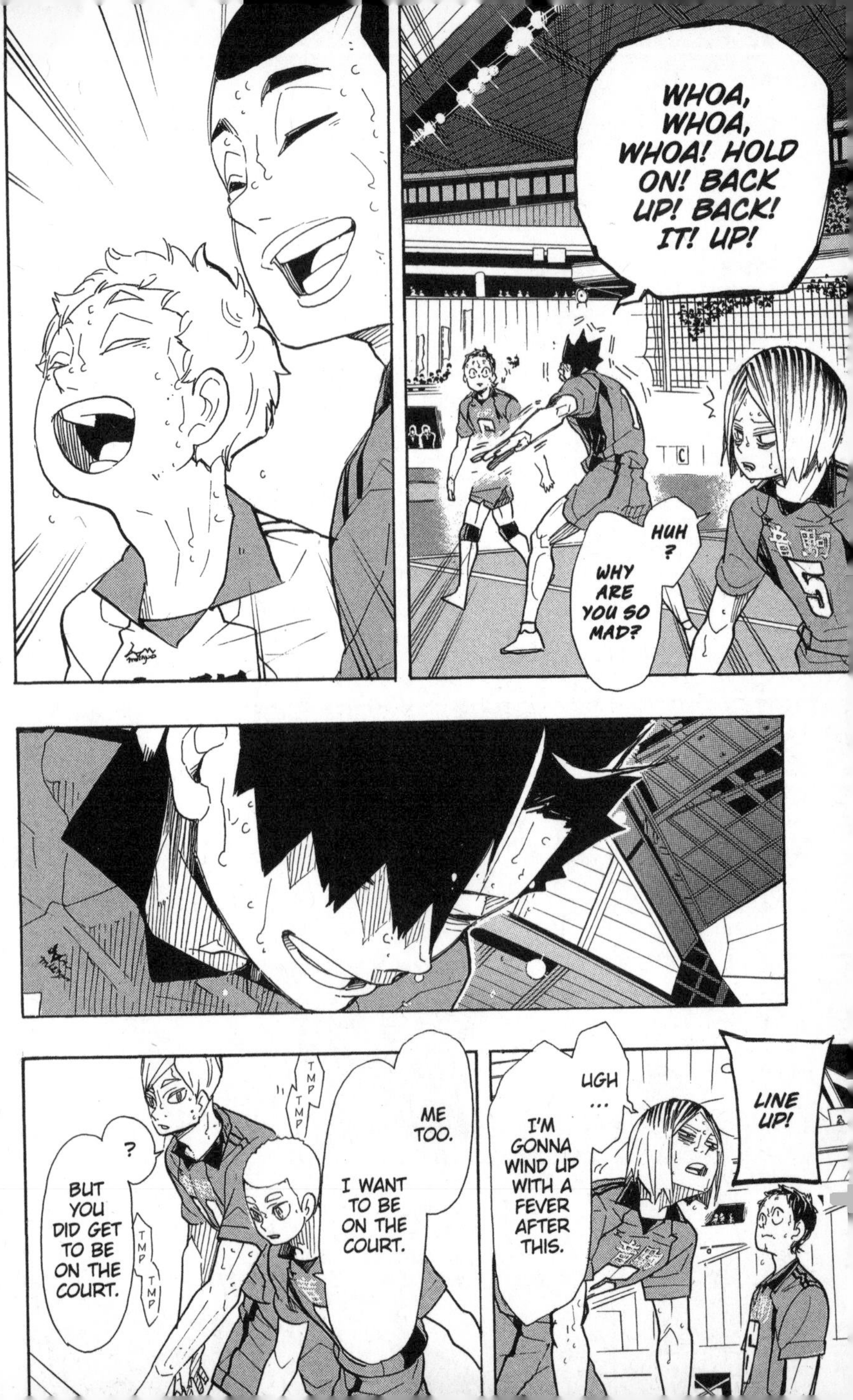
WHOA, WHOA, WHOA! HOLD ON! BACK UP! BACK! IT! UP!
HUH?
WHY ARE YOU SO MAD?
LINE UP!
UGH...
I'M GONNA WIND UP WITH A FEVER AFTER THIS.
ME TOO.
I WANT TO BE ON THE COURT.
TMP TMP
?
BUT YOU DID GET TO BE ON THE COURT.
TMP TMP

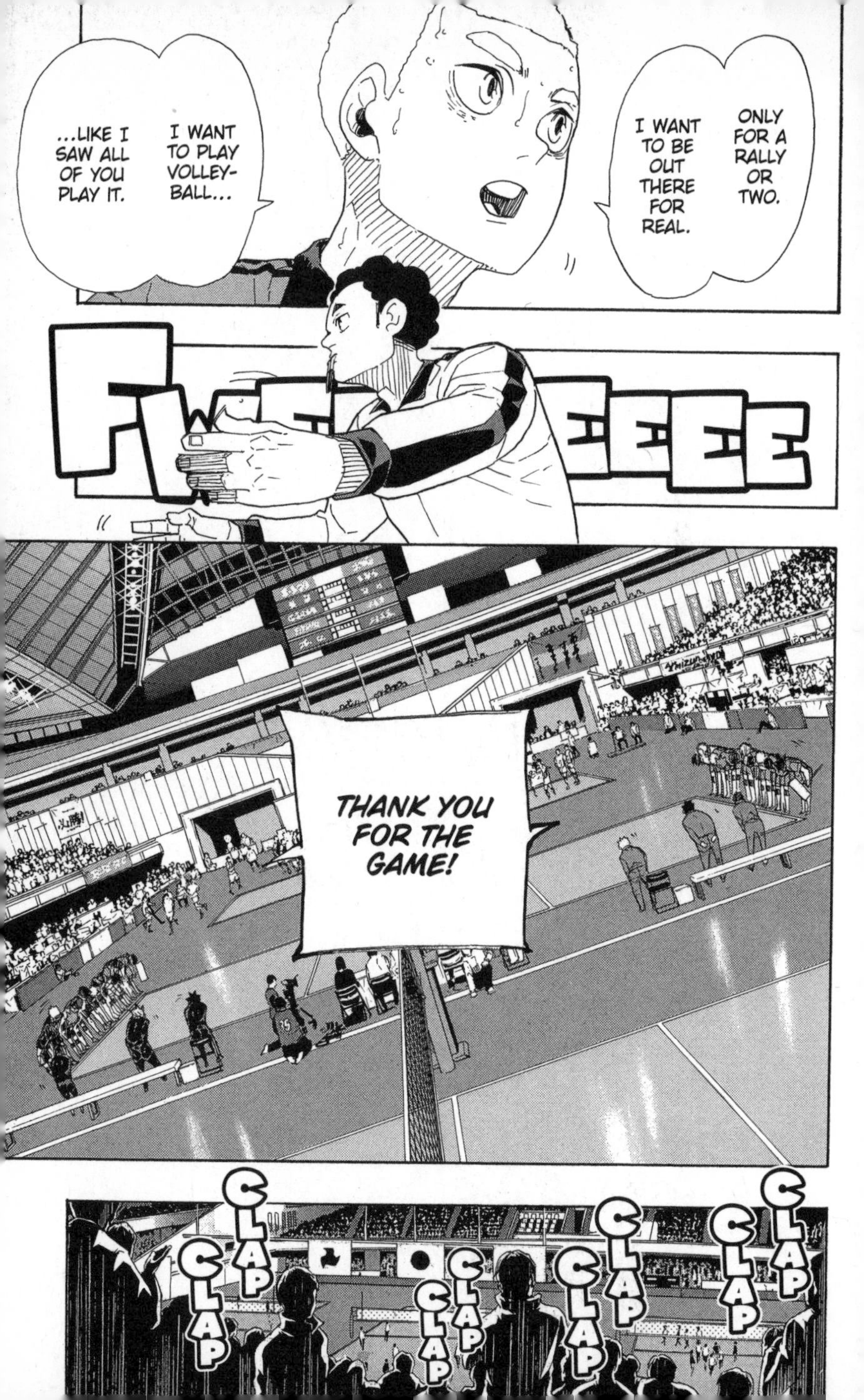
ONLY FOR A RALLY OR TWO.
I WANT TO BE OUT THERE FOR REAL.
I WANT TO PLAY VOLLEY-BALL...
...LIKE I SAW ALL OF YOU PLAY IT.
FWEEEE
THANK YOU FOR THE GAME!
CLAP CLAP CLAP CLAP CLAP CLAP CLAP CLAP

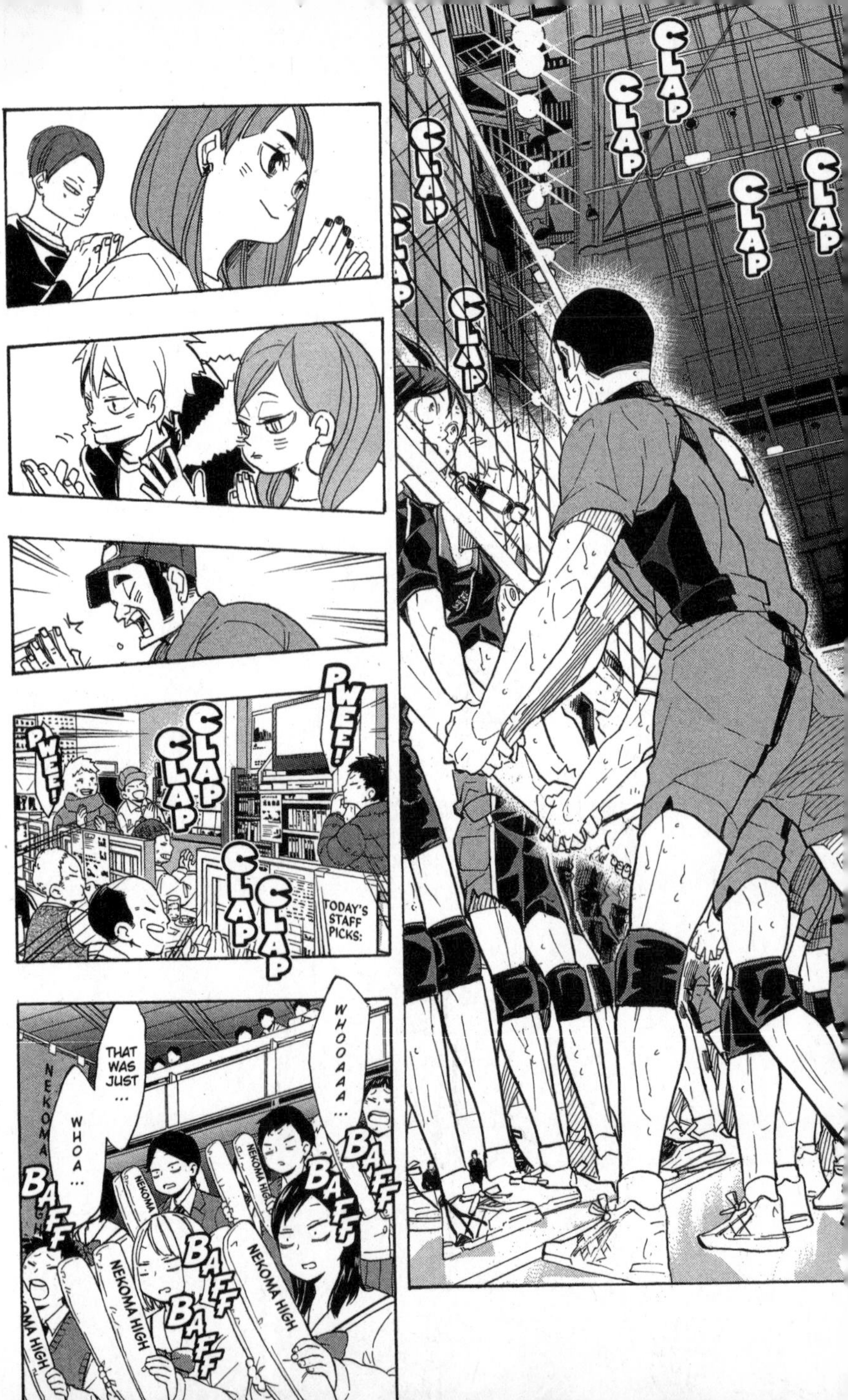

CLAP
CLAP
CLAP
CLAP
CLAP
CLAP
PWEE!
CLAP
CLAP
CLAP
CLAP
PWEE!
TODAY'S STAFF PICKS:
WHOOAAA...
BAFF
BAFF
BAFF
THAT WAS JUST...
WHOA...
NEKOMA HIGH
NEKOMA
NEKOMA HIGH
BAFF
BAFF
NEKOMA HIGH
BAFF
NEKOMA HIGH

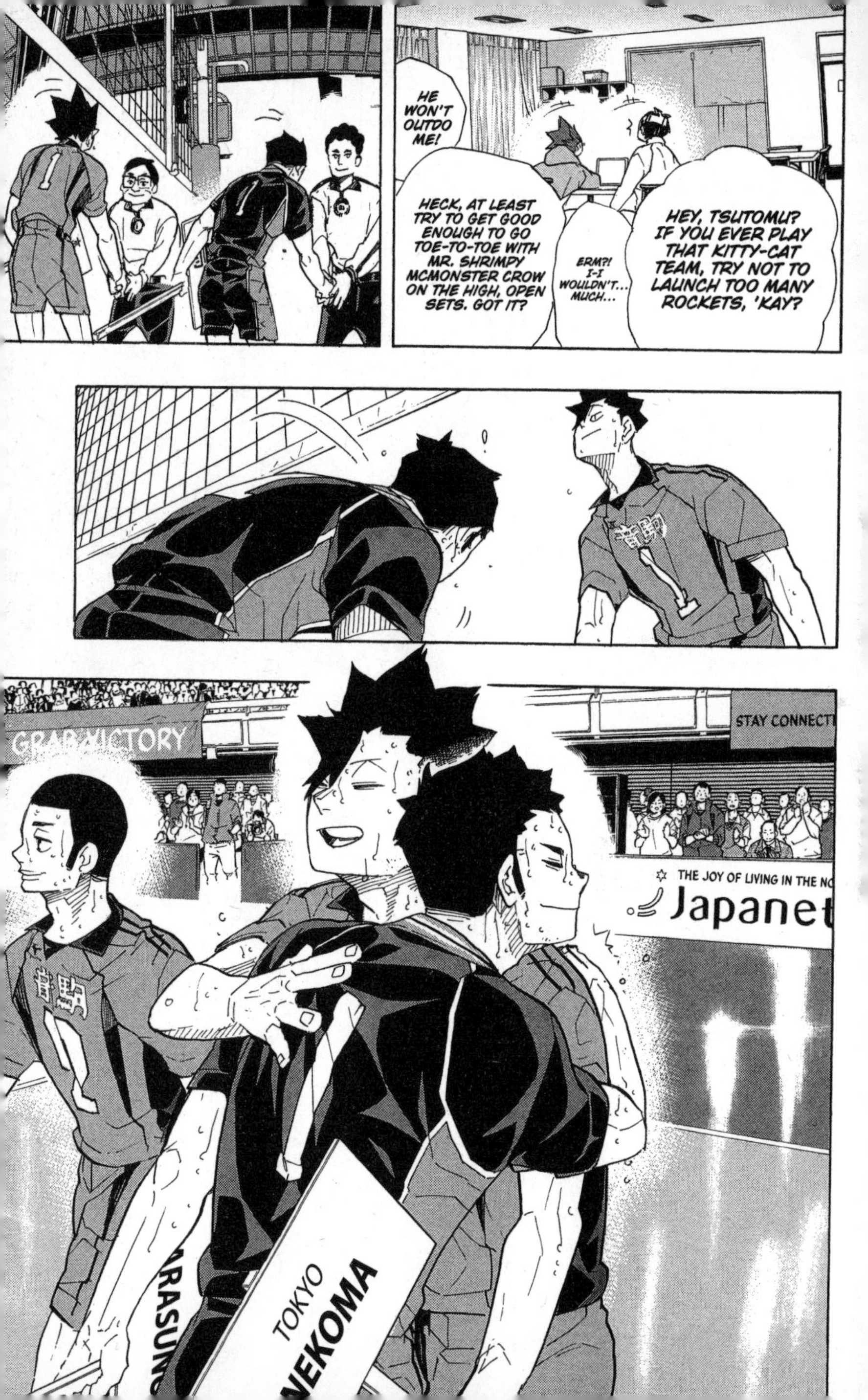
HEY, TSUTOMU? IF YOU EVER PLAY THAT KITTY-CAT TEAM, TRY NOT TO LAUNCH TOO MANY ROCKETS, 'KAY?
ERM?! I-I WOULDN'T... MUCH...
HECK, AT LEAST TRY TO GET GOOD ENOUGH TO GO TOE-TO-TOE WITH MR. SHRIMPY MCMONSTER CROW ON THE HIGH, OPEN SETS. GOT IT?
HE WON'T OUTDO ME!
STAY CONNECT
GRAB VICTORY
THE JOY OF LIVING IN THE NO
Japanet
TOKYO
NEKOMA
ARASUNO

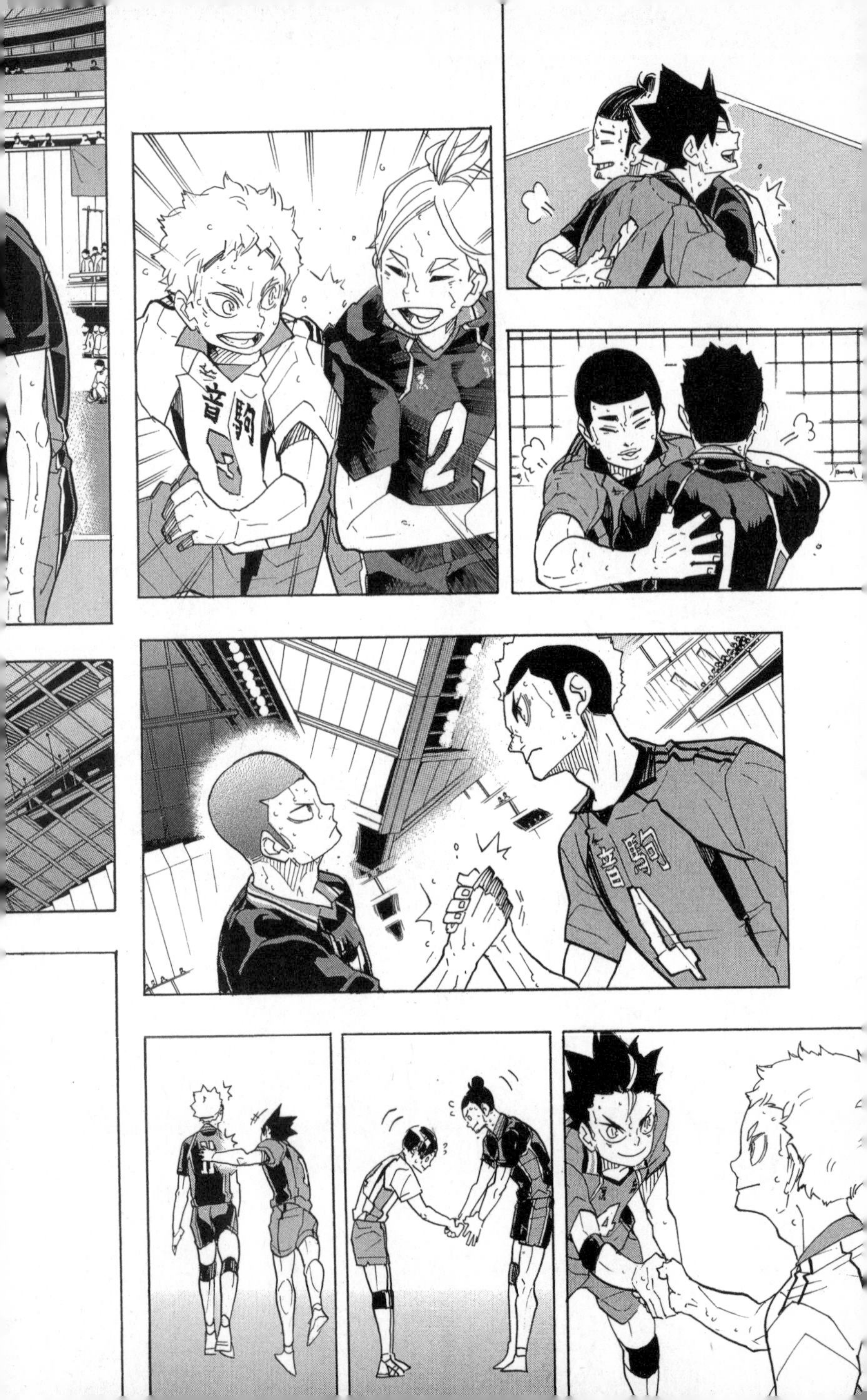
音駒
音駒

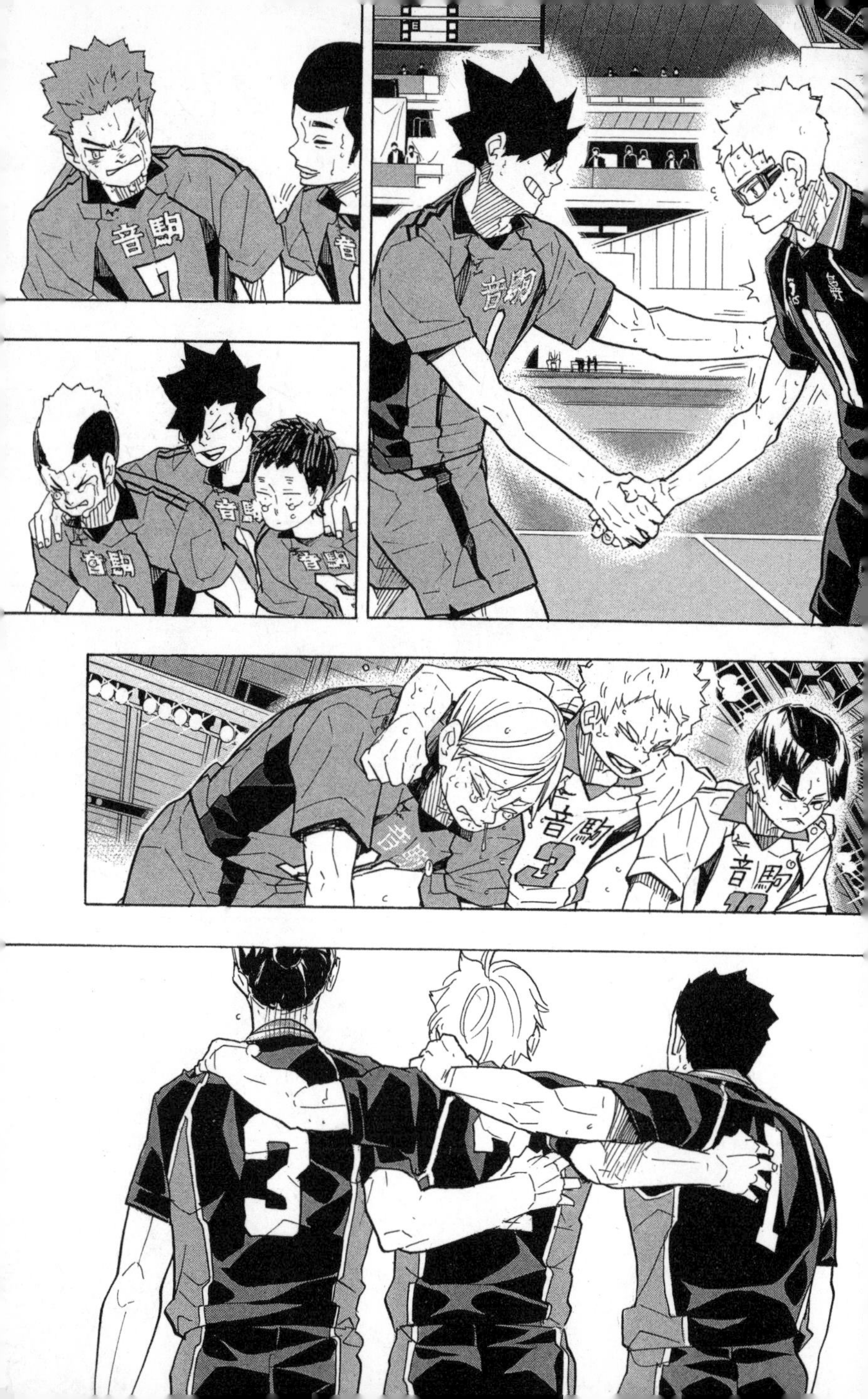

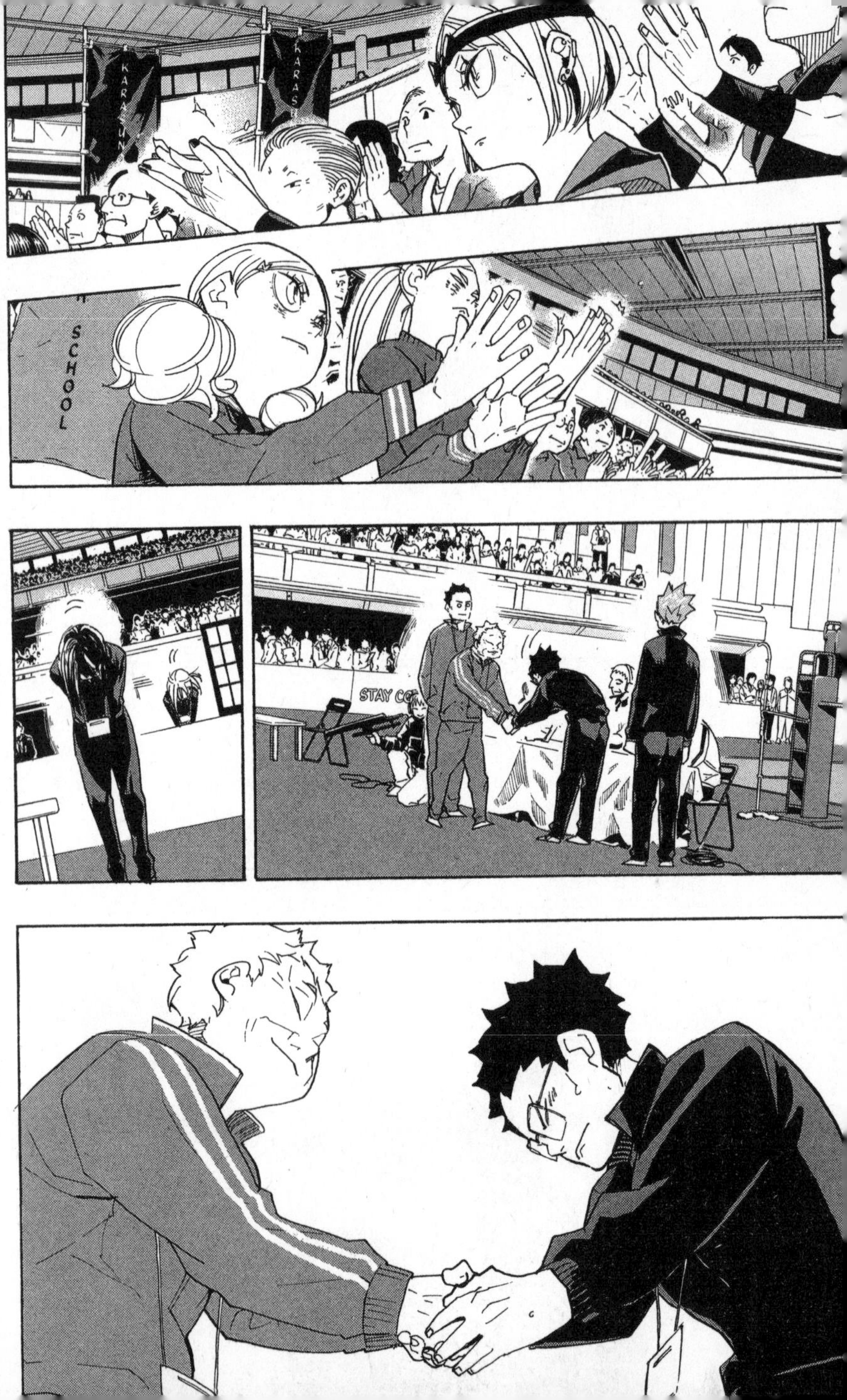
KARASUN
SCHOOL
STAY CO

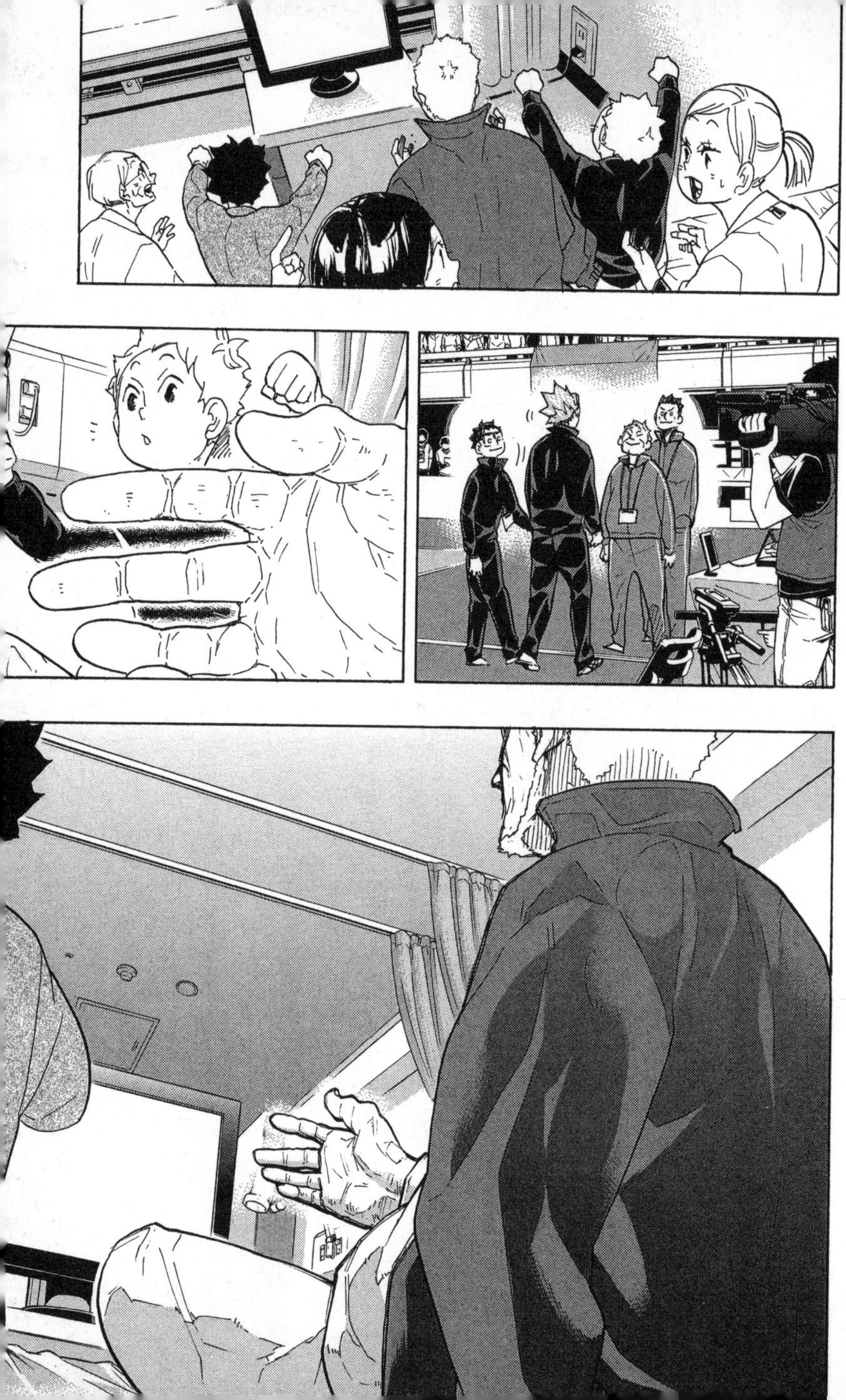

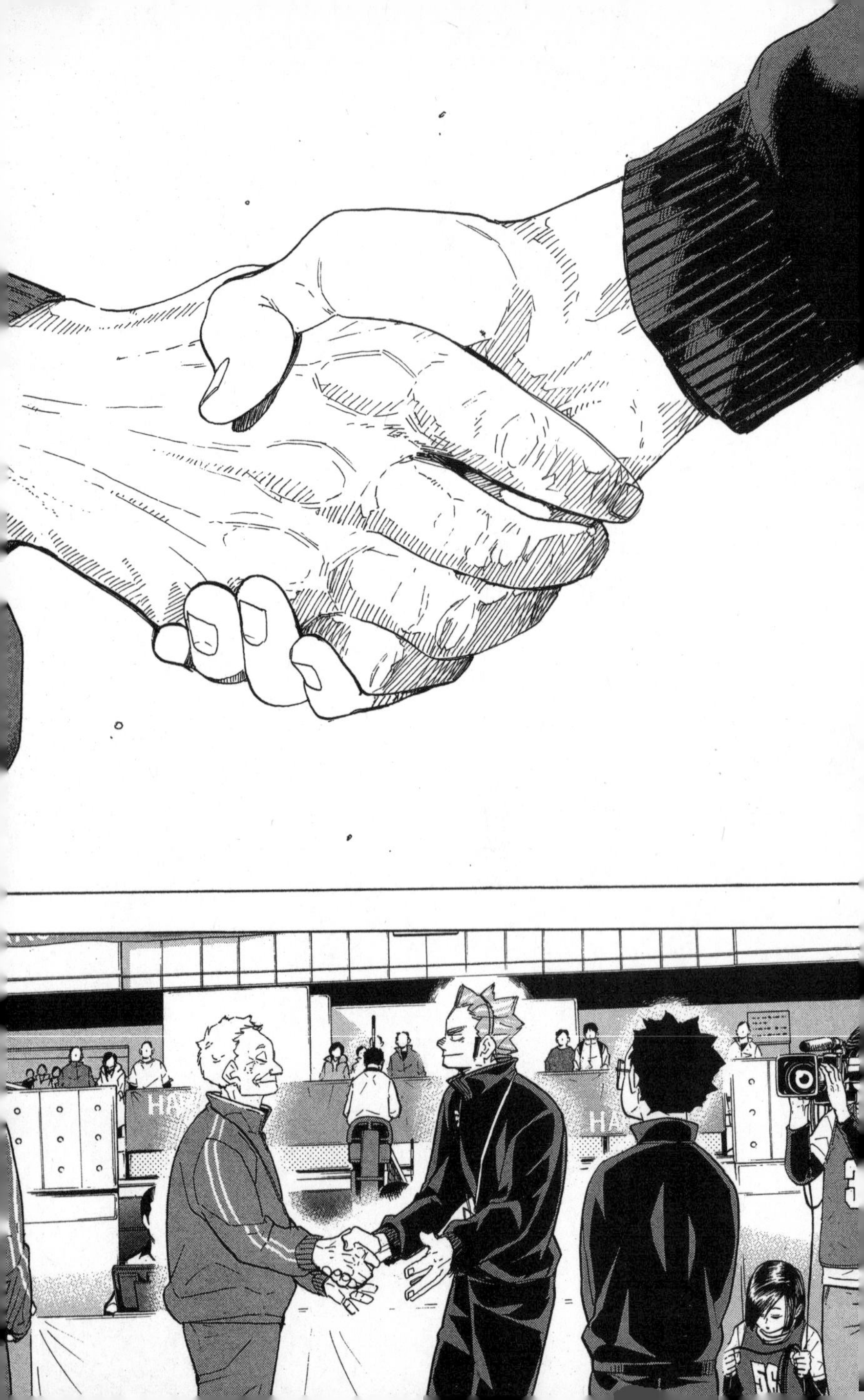

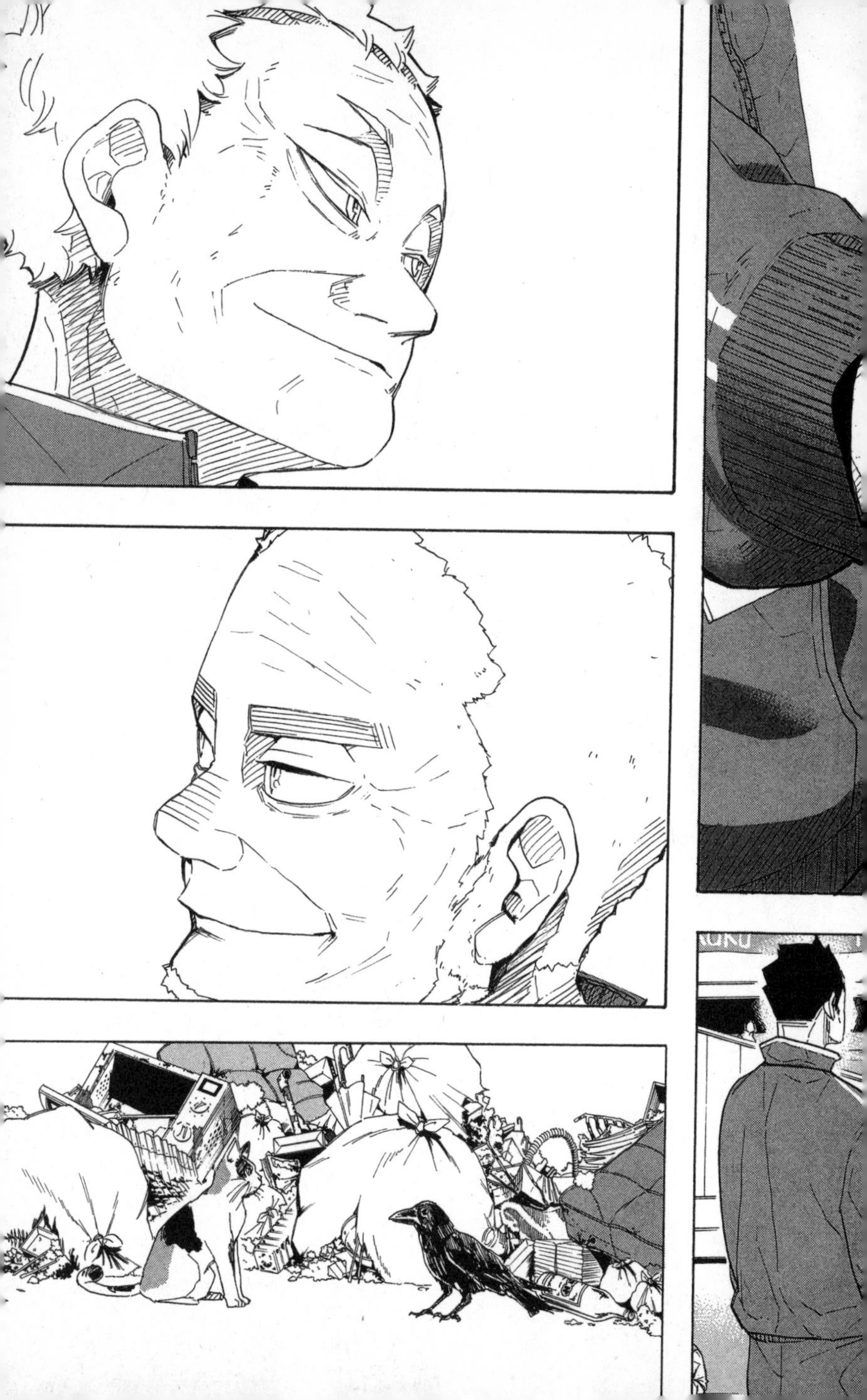

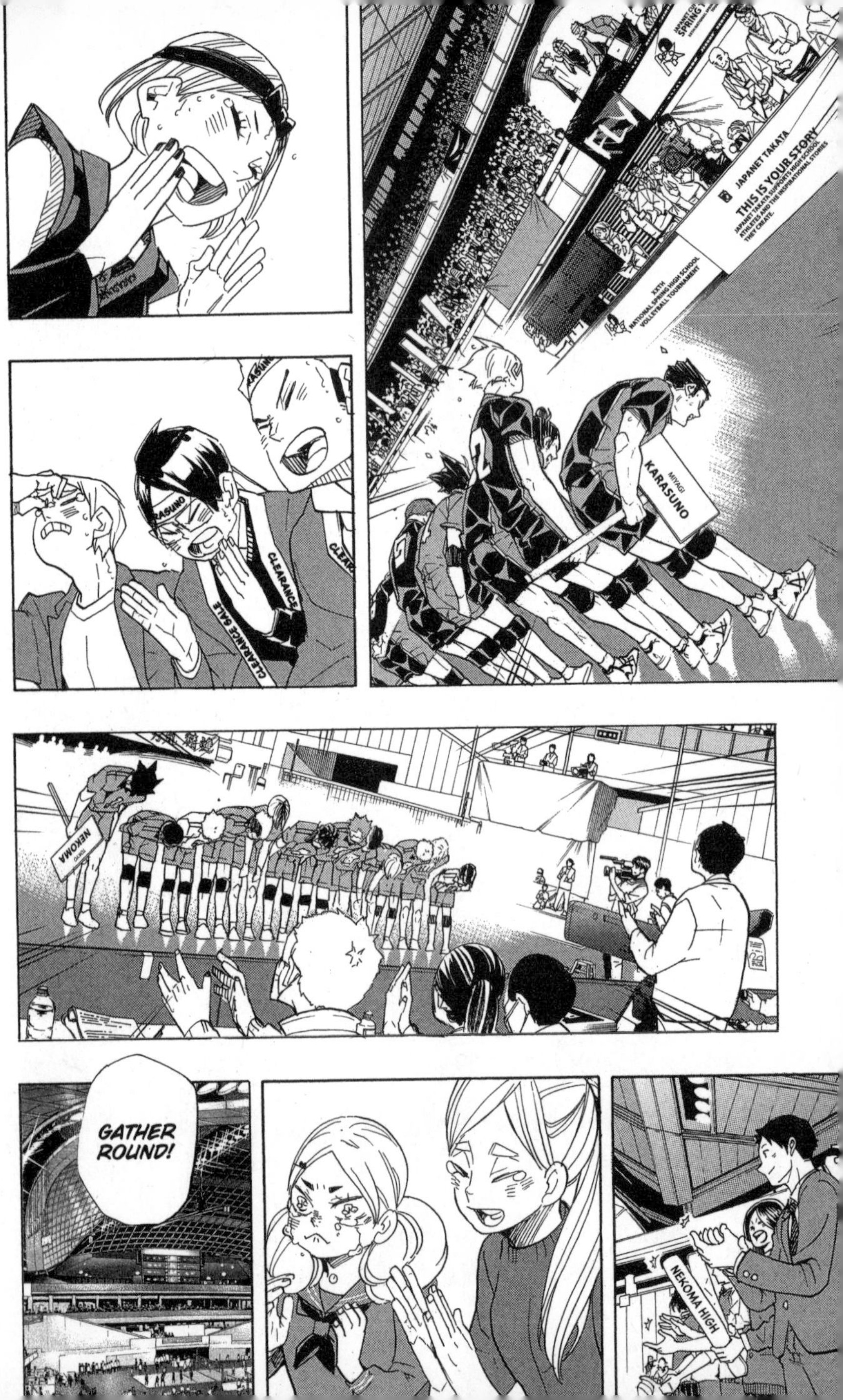
JAPANET TAKATA
THIS IS YOUR STORY
JAPANET TAKATA SUPPORTS HIGH SCHOOL ATHLETES AND THE INSPIRATIONAL STORIES THEY CREATE.
XXTH NATIONAL SPRING HIGH SCHOOL VOLLEYBALL TOURNAMENT
MIYAGI
KARASUNO
CLEARANCE SALE
NEKOMA
NEKOMA HIGH
GATHER ROUND!

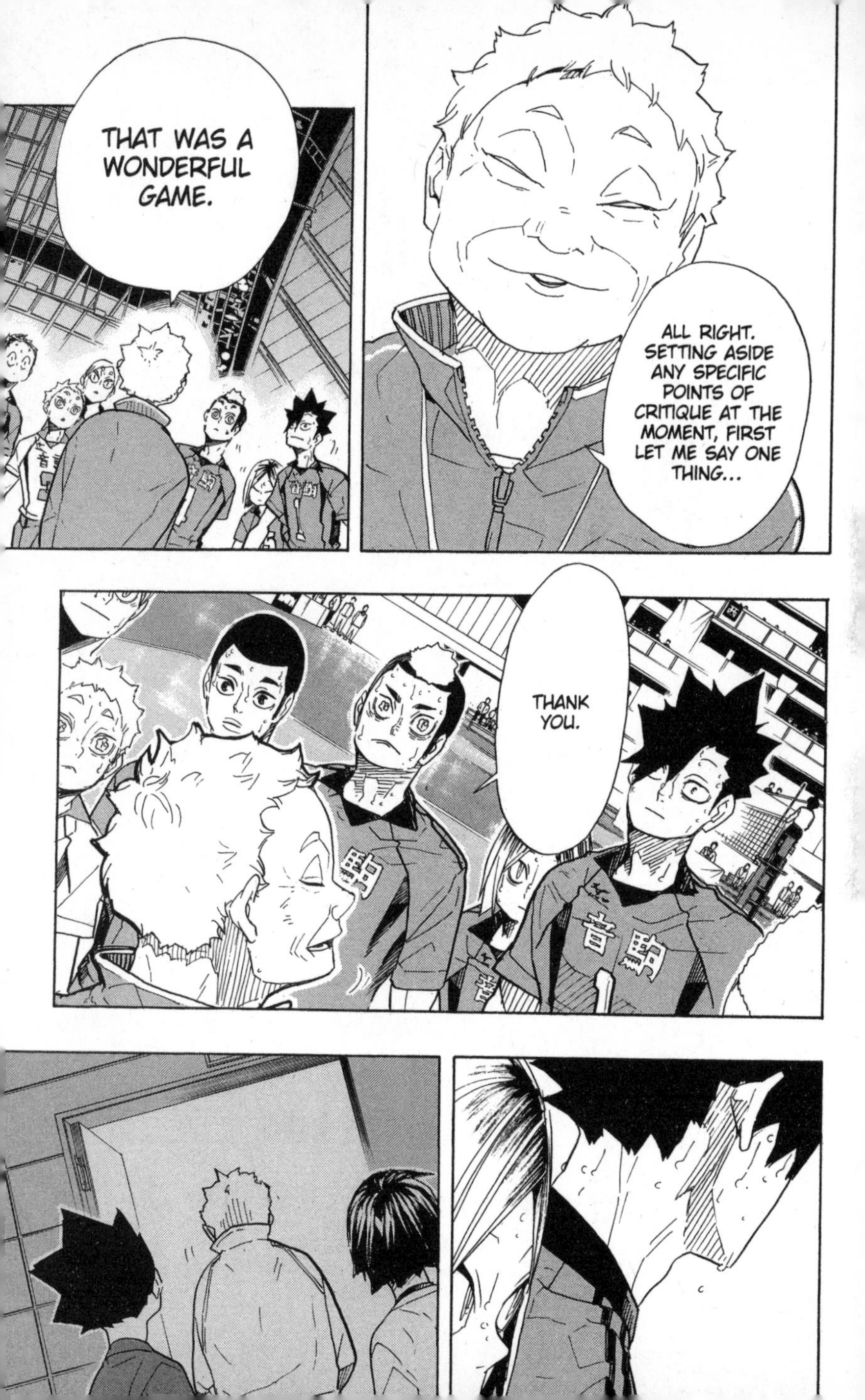
ALL RIGHT. SETTING ASIDE ANY SPECIFIC POINTS OF CRITIQUE AT THE MOMENT, FIRST LET ME SAY ONE THING...
THAT WAS A WONDERFUL GAME.
THANK YOU.

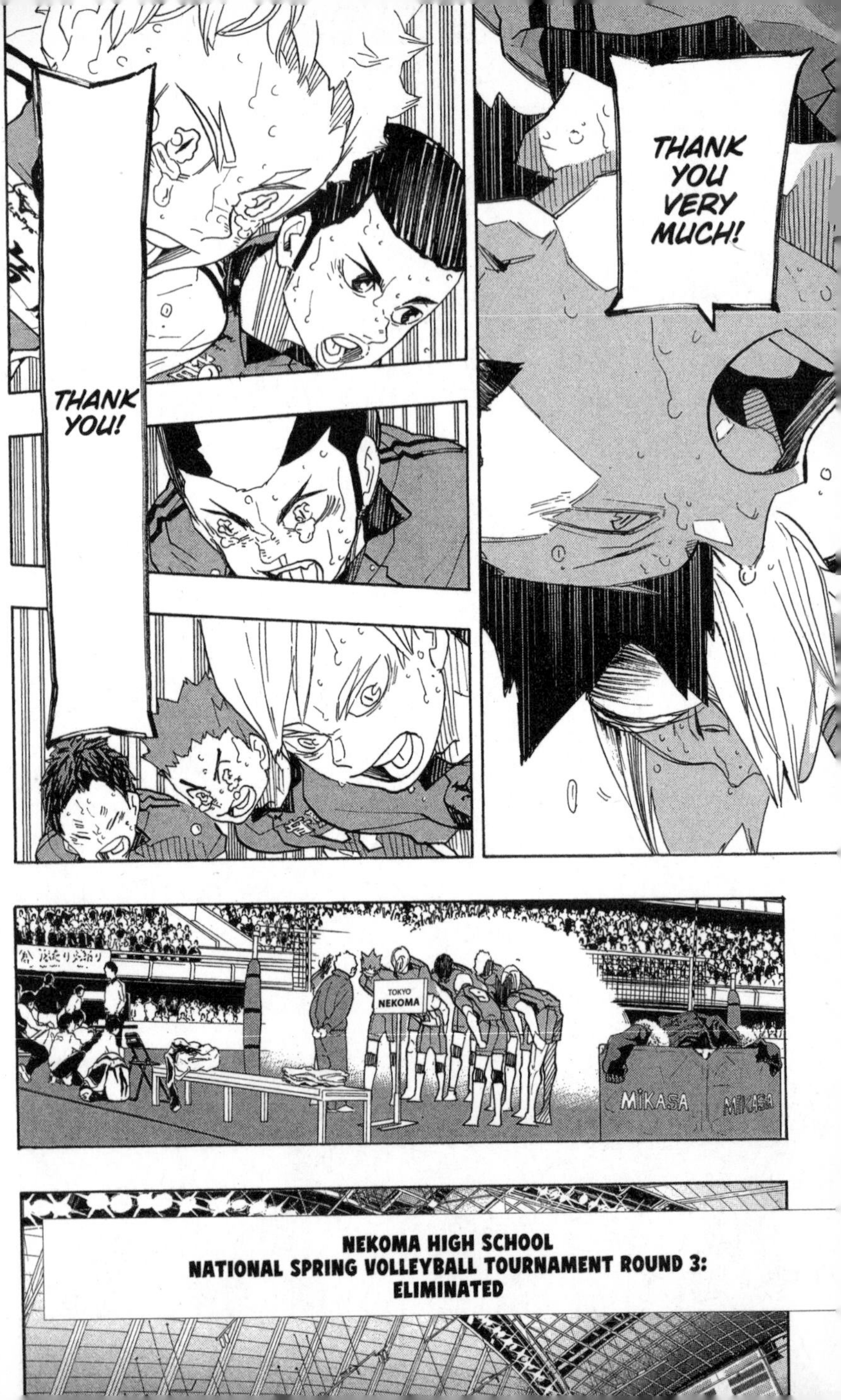
THANK YOU VERY MUCH!
THANK YOU!
TOKYO NEKOMA
MIKASA
MIKASA
NEKOMA HIGH SCHOOL
NATIONAL SPRING VOLLEYBALL TOURNAMENT ROUND 3:
ELIMINATED

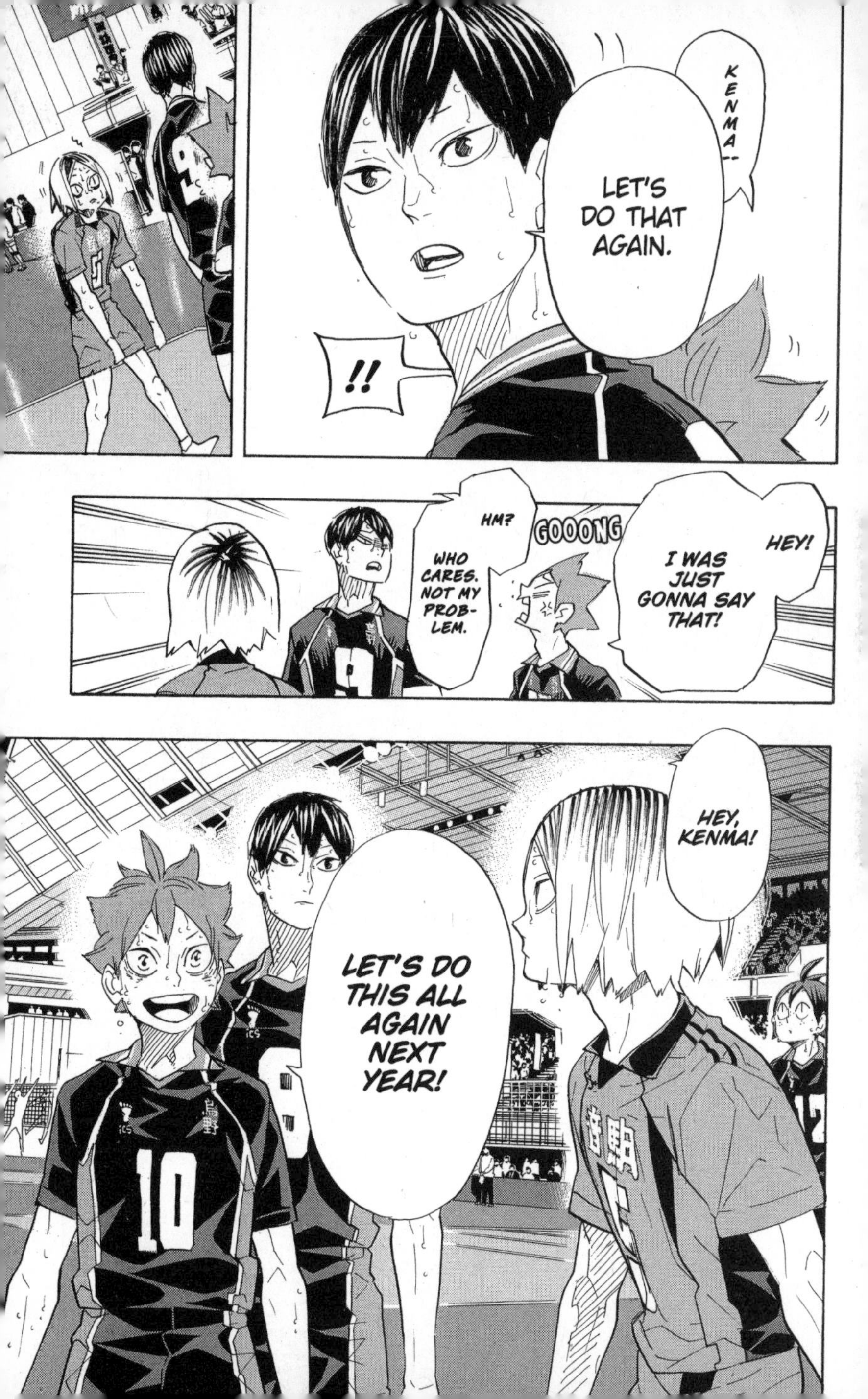
KENMA--
LET'S DO THAT AGAIN.
!!
HEY! I WAS JUST GONNA SAY THAT!
GOOONG
HM? WHO CARES. NOT MY PROBLEM.
HEY, KENMA!
LET'S DO THIS ALL AGAIN NEXT YEAR!

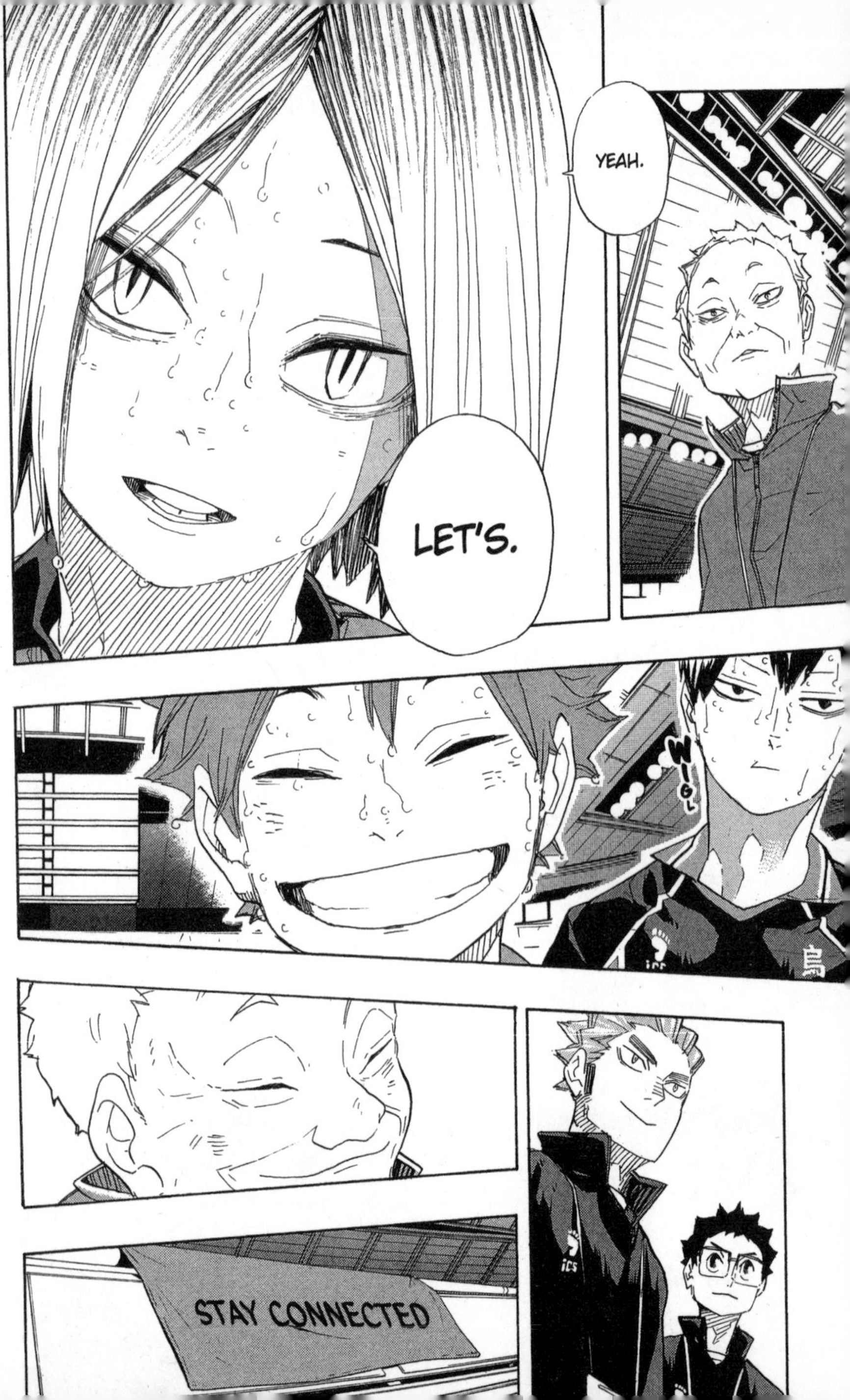
YEAH.
LET'S.
WIGL
STAY CONNECTED

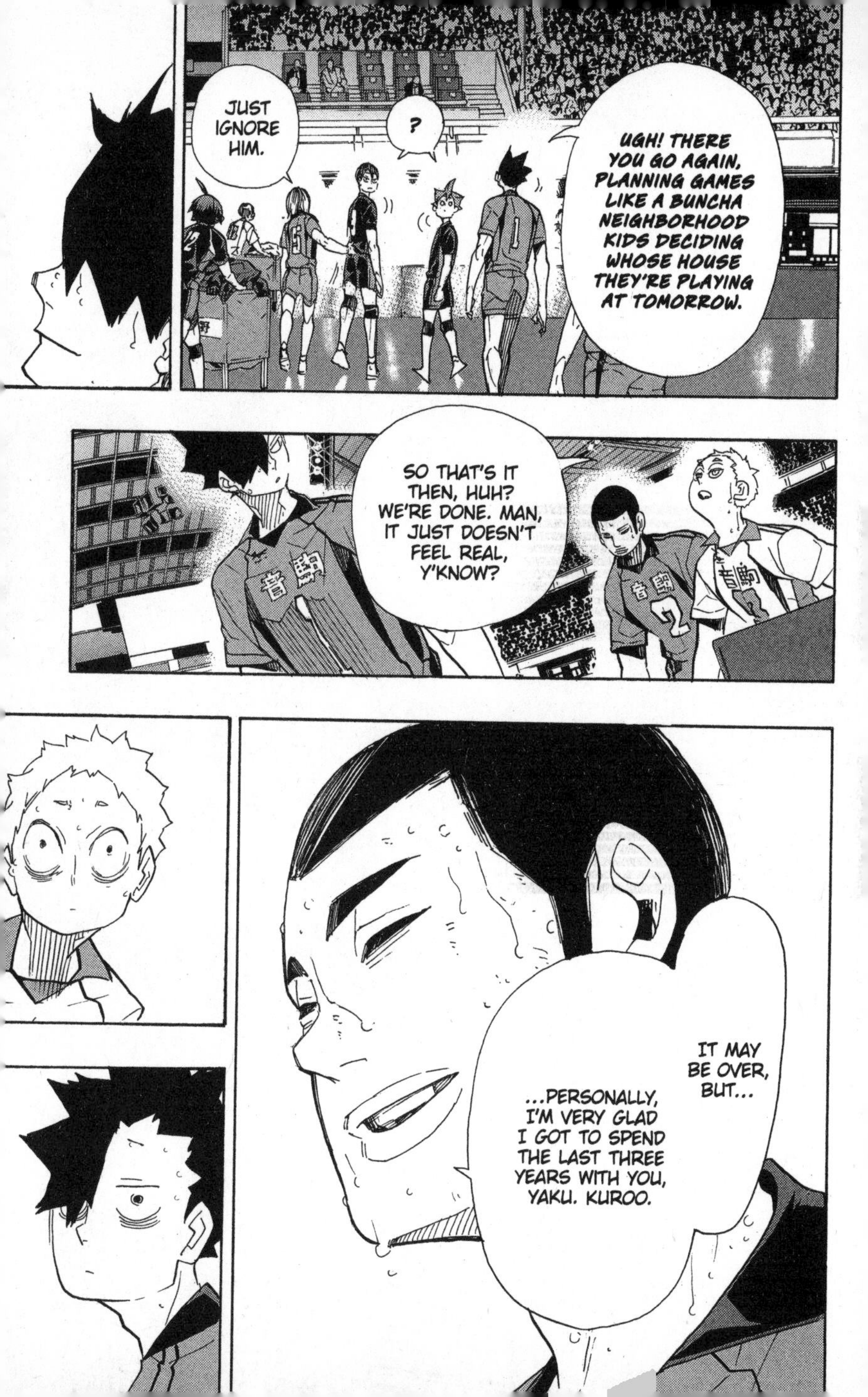
UGH! THERE YOU GO AGAIN, PLANNING GAMES LIKE A BUNCHA NEIGHBORHOOD KIDS DECIDING WHOSE HOUSE THEY'RE PLAYING AT TOMORROW.
?
JUST IGNORE HIM.
SO THAT'S IT THEN, HUH? WE'RE DONE. MAN, IT JUST DOESN'T FEEL REAL, Y'KNOW?
IT MAY BE OVER, BUT...
...PERSONALLY, I'M VERY GLAD I GOT TO SPEND THE LAST THREE YEARS WITH YOU, YAKU. KUROO.

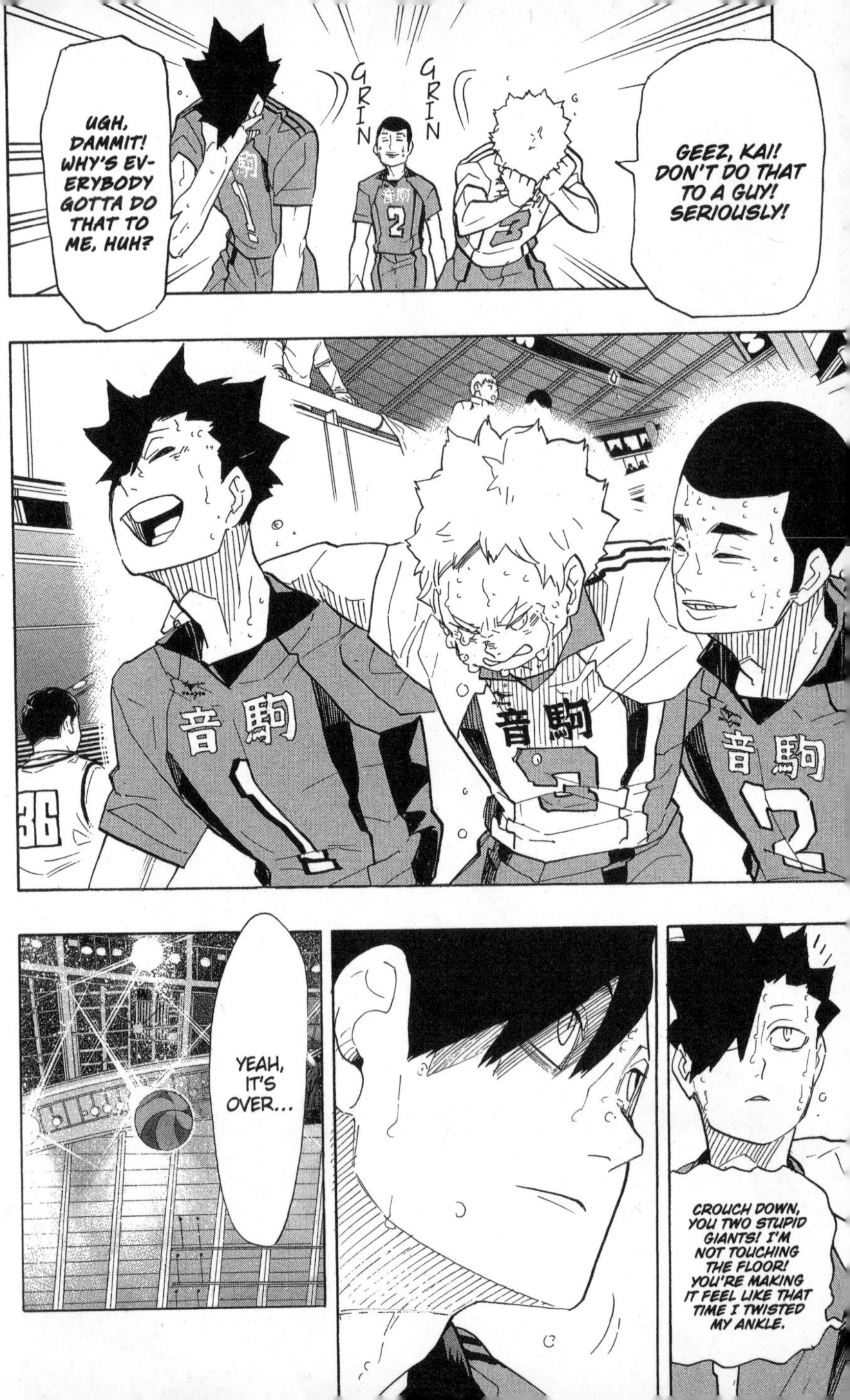
GEEZ, KAI! DON'T DO THAT TO A GUY! SERIOUSLY!
GRIN
GRIN
UGH, DAMMIT! WHY'S EV-ERYBODY GOTTA DO THAT TO ME, HUH?
CROUCH DOWN, YOU TWO STUPID GIANTS! I'M NOT TOUCHING THE FLOOR! YOU'RE MAKING IT FEEL LIKE THAT TIME I TWISTED MY ANKLE.
YEAH, IT'S OVER...

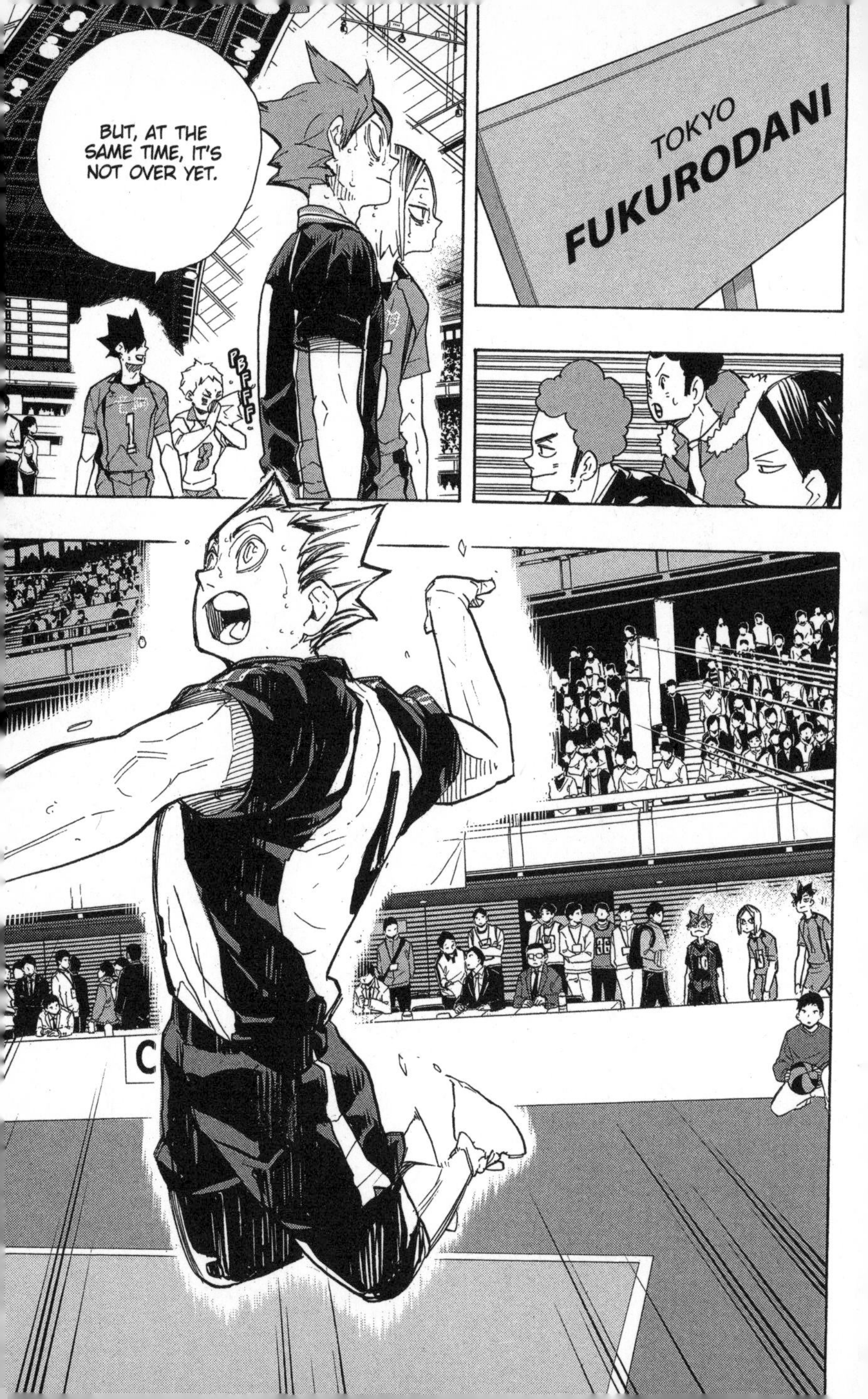
TOKYO
FUKURODANI
BUT, AT THE SAME TIME, IT'S NOT OVER YET.
PBFFF

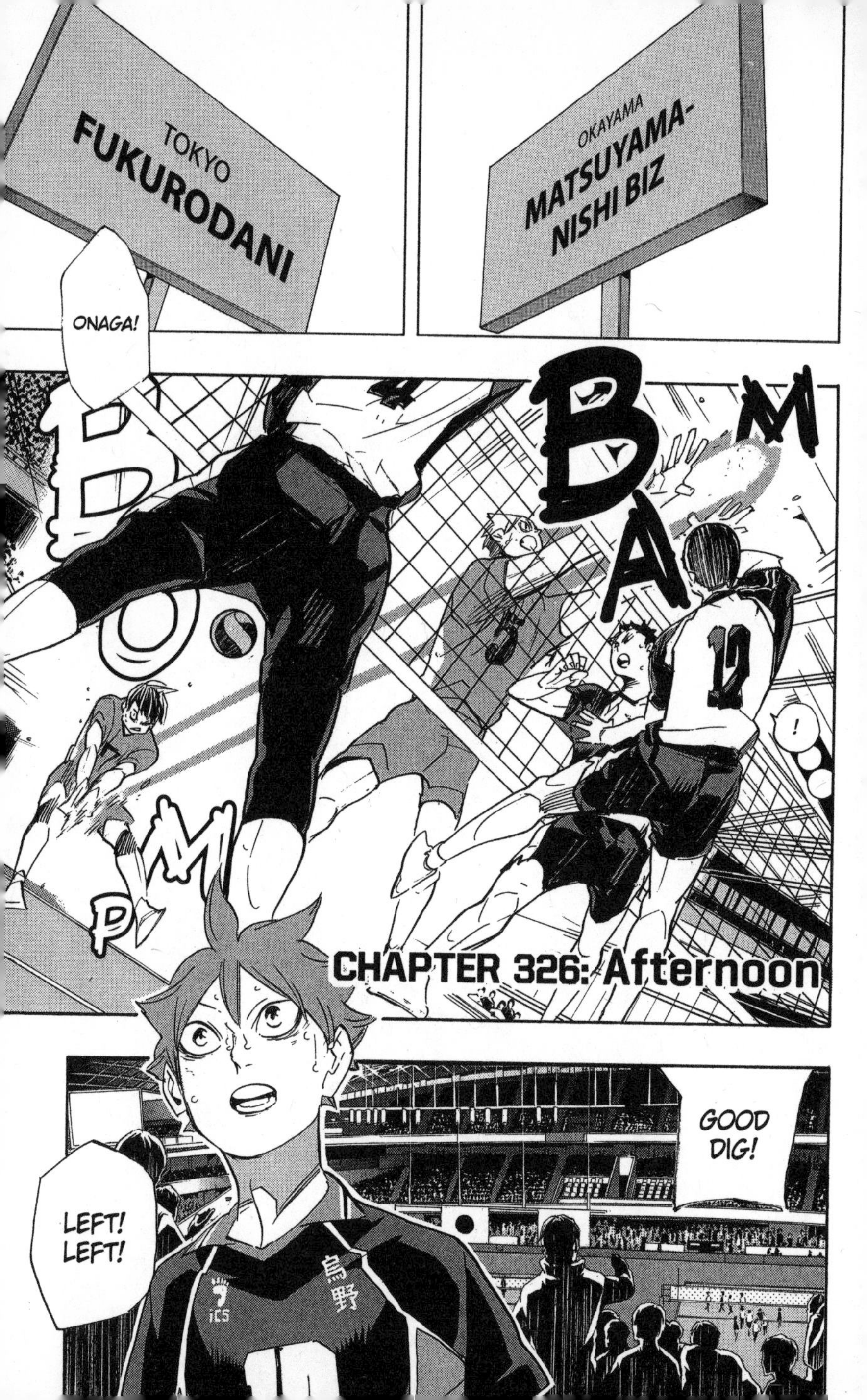
OKAYAMA
MATSUYAMA-NISHI BIZ
TOKYO
FUKURODANI
ONAGA!
BAM
!
CHAPTER 326: Afternoon
GOOD DIG!
LEFT! LEFT!

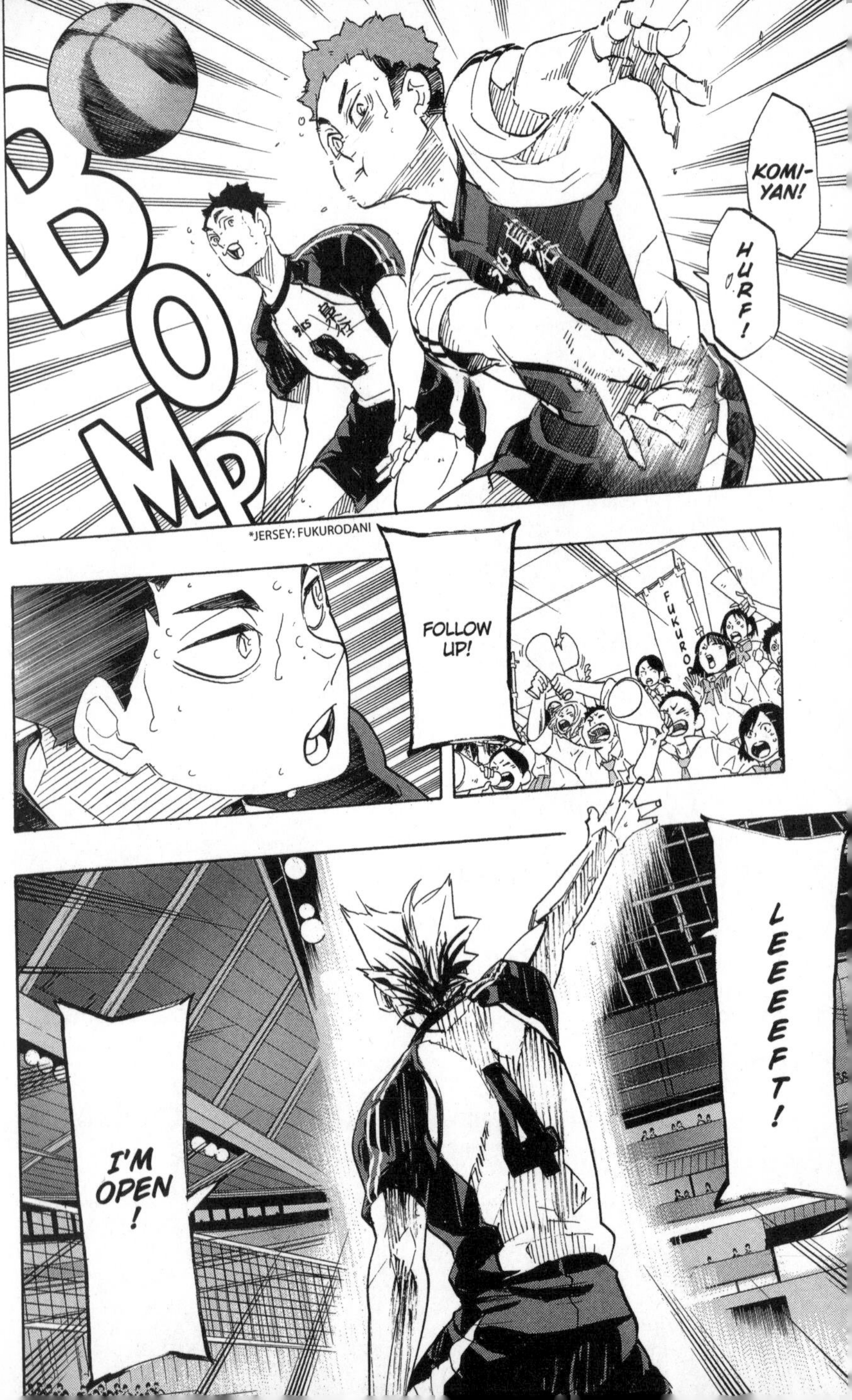
KOMI-YAN!
HURF!
BOMP
*JERSEY: FUKURODANI
FUKURO
FOLLOW UP!
LEEEEEFT!
I'M OPEN!

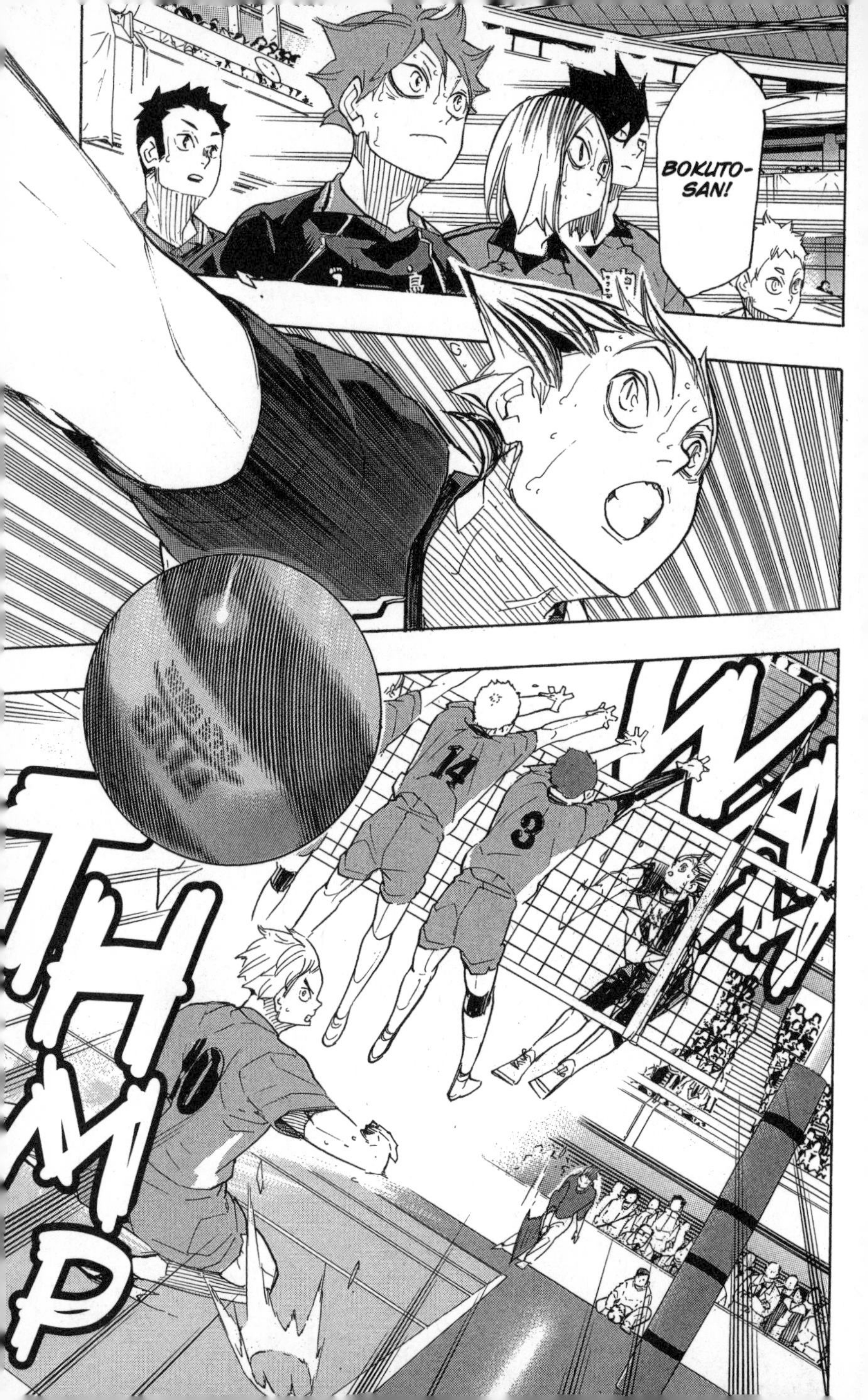
BOKUTO-SAN!
WAM
THUMP

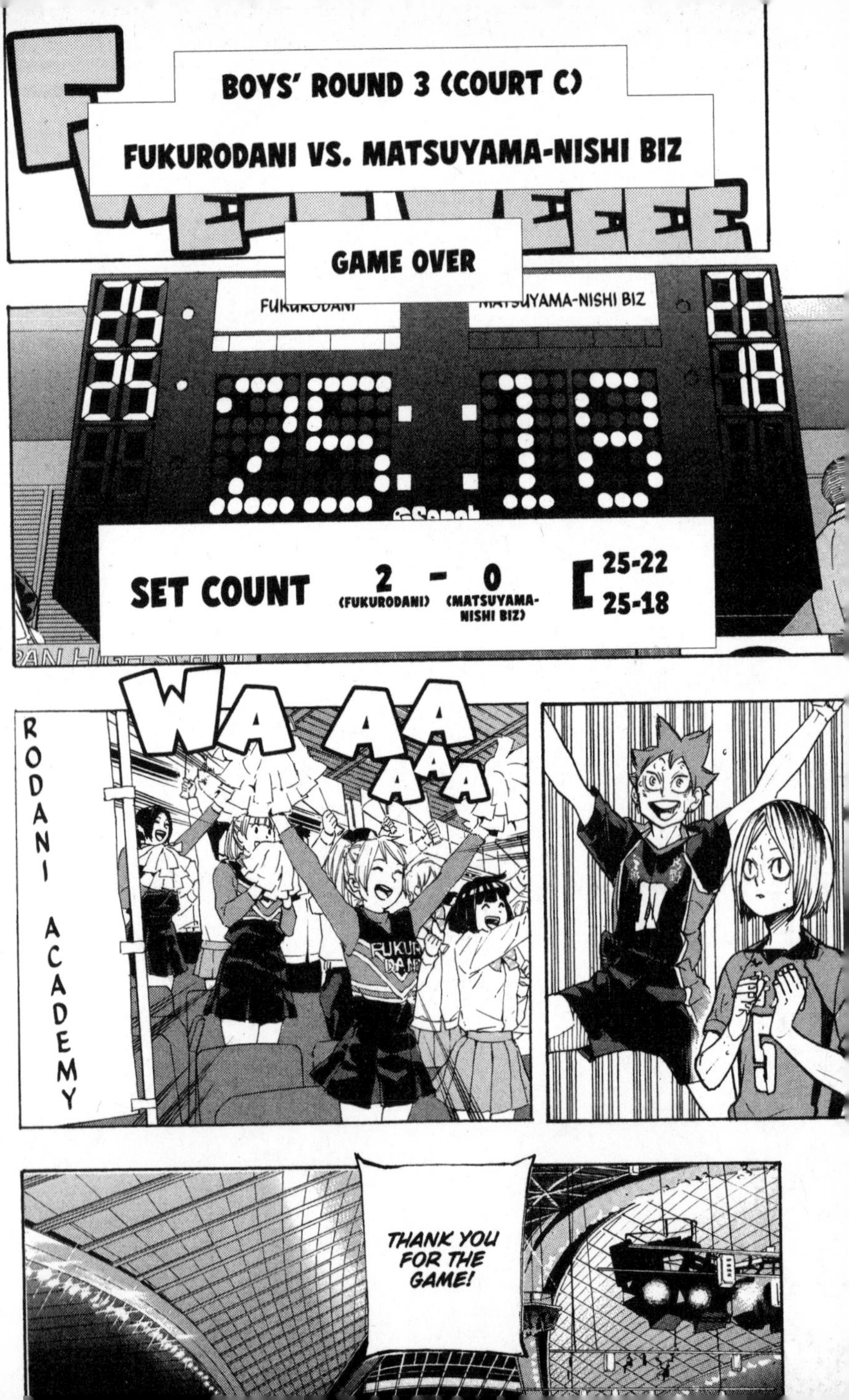
BOYS' ROUND 3 (COURT C)
FUKURODANI VS. MATSUYAMA-NISHI BIZ
GAME OVER
SET COUNT 2 - 0 (FUKURODANI) (MATSUYAMA-NISHI BIZ) 25-22 25-18
WAAAAA
RODANI ACADEMY
THANK YOU FOR THE GAME!

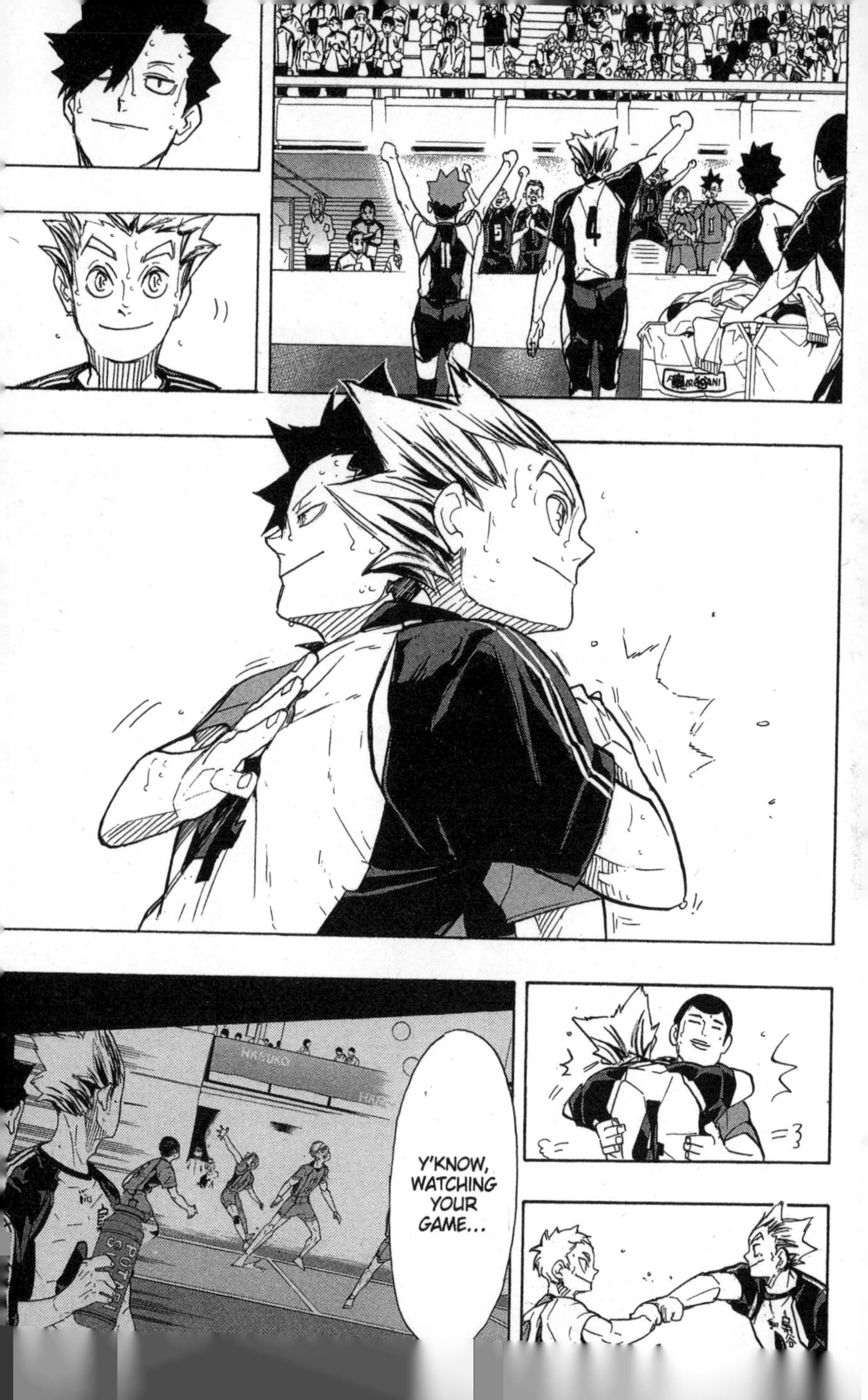

Y'KNOW, WATCHING YOUR GAME...

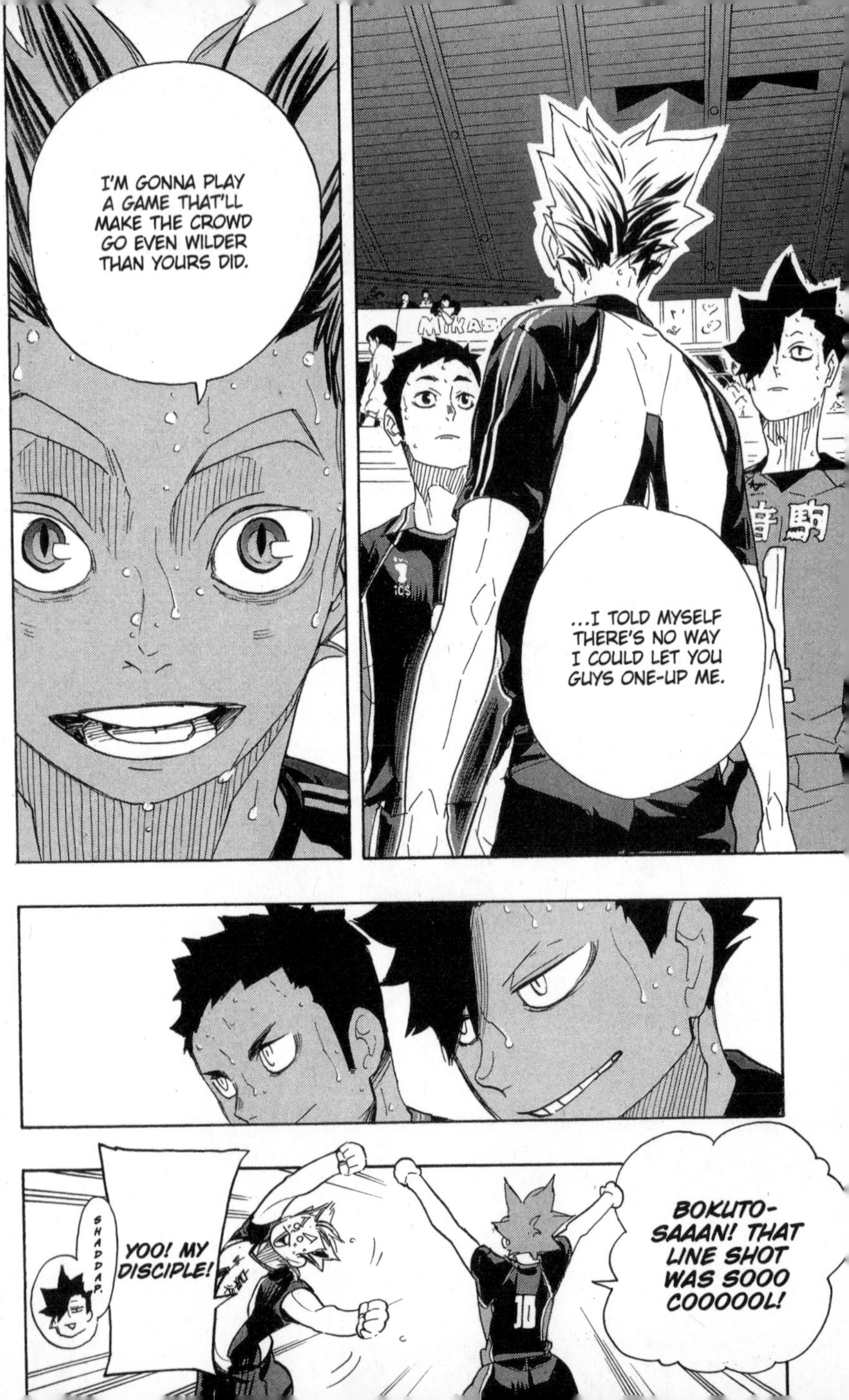
...I TOLD MYSELF THERE'S NO WAY I COULD LET YOU GUYS ONE-UP ME.
I'M GONNA PLAY A GAME THAT'LL MAKE THE CROWD GO EVEN WILDER THAN YOURS DID.
BOKUTO-SAAAN! THAT LINE SHOT WAS SOOO COOOOOL!
YOO! MY DISCIPLE!
SHADDAP.

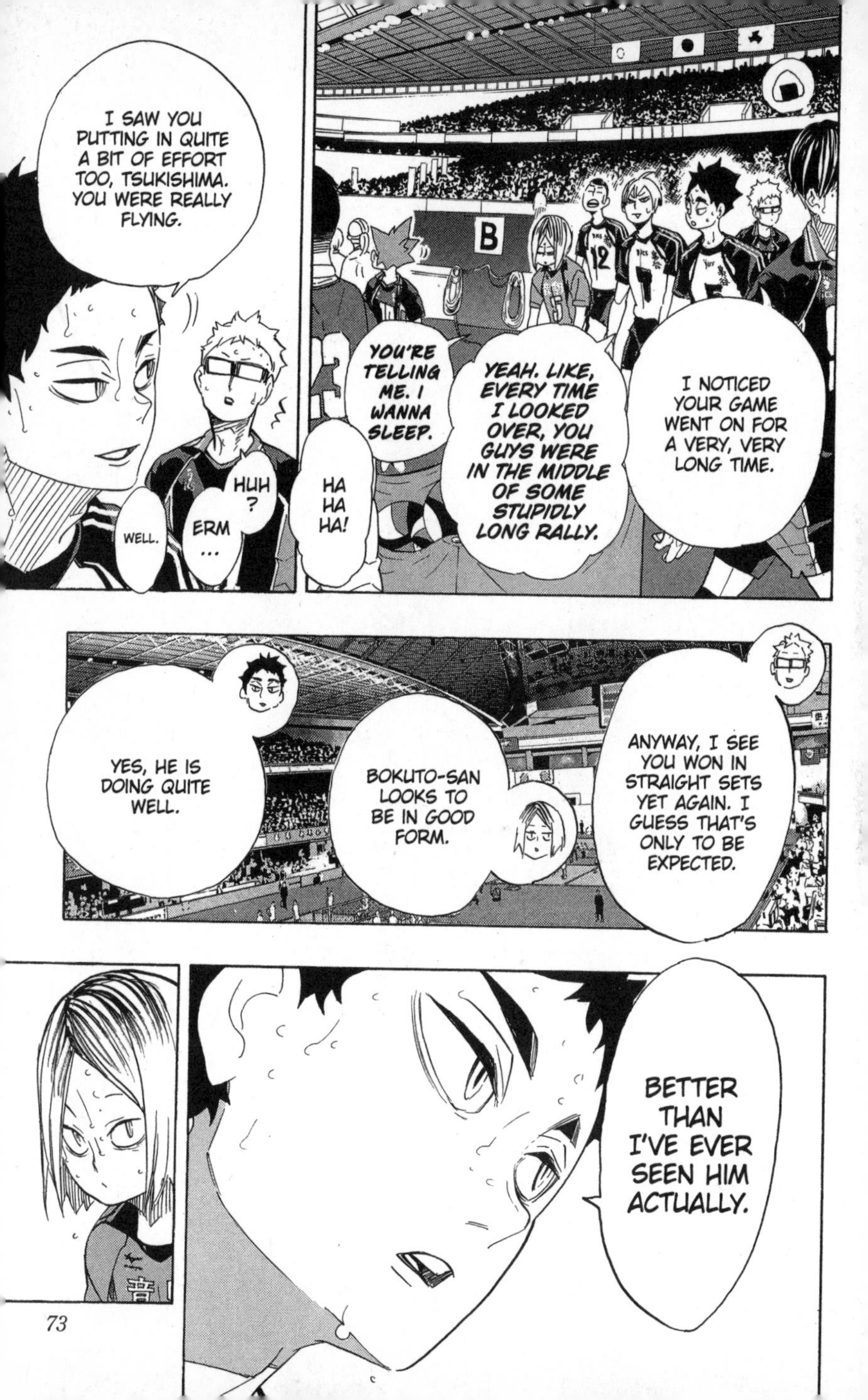
I NOTICED YOUR GAME WENT ON FOR A VERY, VERY LONG TIME.
YEAH. LIKE, EVERY TIME I LOOKED OVER, YOU GUYS WERE IN THE MIDDLE OF SOME STUPIDLY LONG RALLY.
YOU'RE TELLING ME. I WANNA SLEEP.
HA HA HA!
I SAW YOU PUTTING IN QUITE A BIT OF EFFORT TOO, TSUKISHIMA. YOU WERE REALLY FLYING.
HUH?
ERM...
WELL.
ANYWAY, I SEE YOU WON IN STRAIGHT SETS YET AGAIN. I GUESS THAT'S ONLY TO BE EXPECTED.
BOKUTO-SAN LOOKS TO BE IN GOOD FORM.
YES, HE IS DOING QUITE WELL.
BETTER THAN I'VE EVER SEEN HIM ACTUALLY.

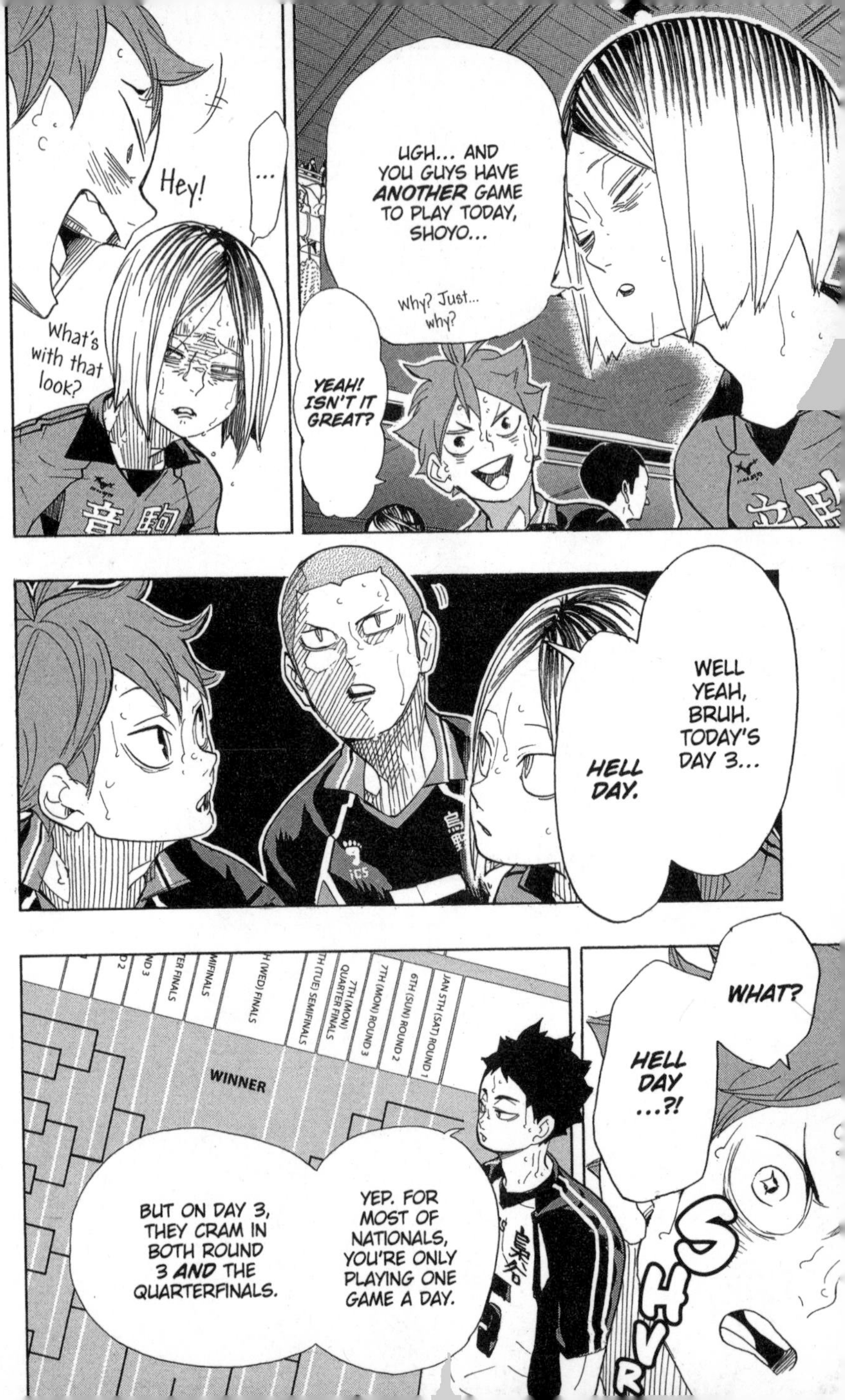
UGH... AND YOU GUYS HAVE ANOTHER GAME TO PLAY TODAY, SHOYO...
Why? Just... why?
YEAH! ISN'T IT GREAT?
...
Hey!
What's with that look?
WELL YEAH, BRUH. TODAY'S DAY 3...
HELL DAY.
WHAT?
HELL DAY ...?!
JAN 5TH (SAT) ROUND 1
6TH (SUN) ROUND 2
7TH (MON) ROUND 3
7TH (MON) QUARTER FINALS
TH (TUE) SEMIFINALS
H (WED) FINALS
WINNER
YEP. FOR MOST OF NATIONALS, YOU'RE ONLY PLAYING ONE GAME A DAY.
BUT ON DAY 3, THEY CRAM IN BOTH ROUND 3 AND THE QUARTERFINALS.

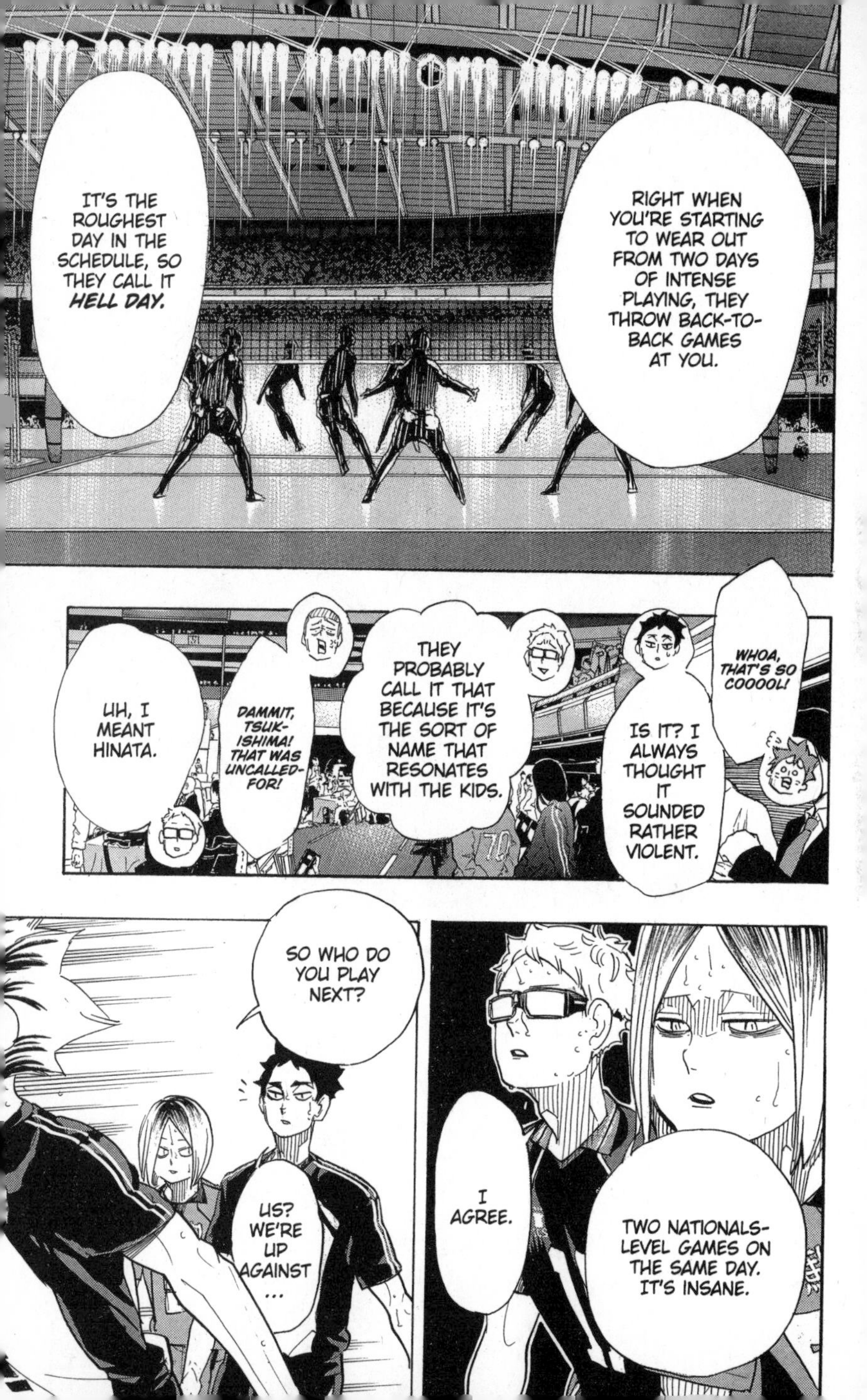
RIGHT WHEN YOU'RE STARTING TO WEAR OUT FROM TWO DAYS OF INTENSE PLAYING, THEY THROW BACK-TO-BACK GAMES AT YOU.
IT'S THE ROUGHEST DAY IN THE SCHEDULE, SO THEY CALL IT HELL DAY.
WHOA, THAT'S SO COOOOL!
IS IT? I ALWAYS THOUGHT IT SOUNDED RATHER VIOLENT.
THEY PROBABLY CALL IT THAT BECAUSE IT'S THE SORT OF NAME THAT RESONATES WITH THE KIDS.
DAMMIT, TSUKISHIMA! THAT WAS UNCALLED-FOR!
UH, I MEANT HINATA.
TWO NATIONALS-LEVEL GAMES ON THE SAME DAY. IT'S INSANE.
I AGREE.
SO WHO DO YOU PLAY NEXT?
US? WE'RE UP AGAINST ...

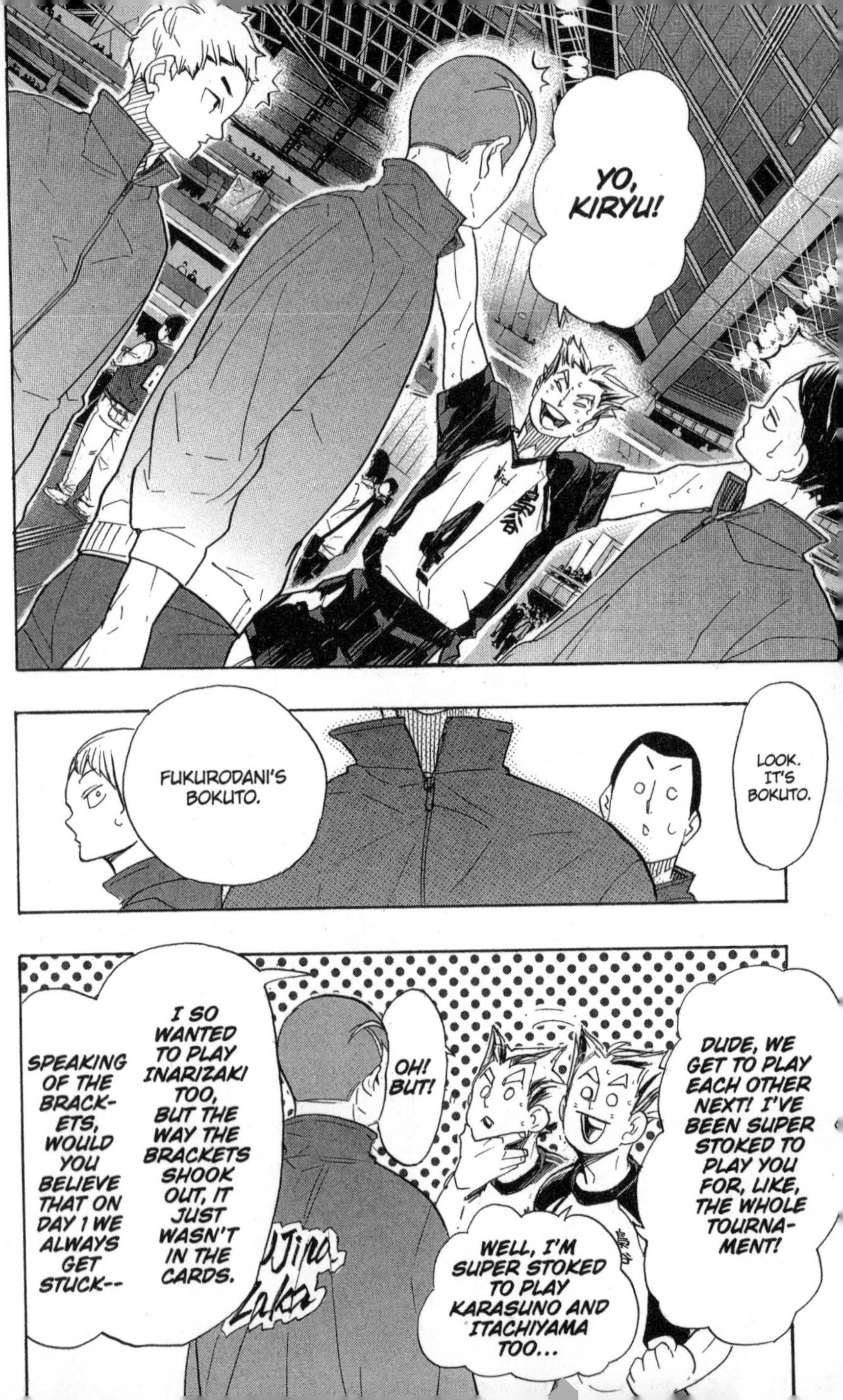
YO, KIRYU!
LOOK. IT'S BOKUTO.
FUKURODANI'S BOKUTO.
DUDE, WE GET TO PLAY EACH OTHER NEXT! I'VE BEEN SUPER STOKED TO PLAY YOU FOR, LIKE, THE WHOLE TOURNAMENT!
WELL, I'M SUPER STOKED TO PLAY KARASUNO AND ITACHIYAMA TOO...
OH! BUT!
I SO WANTED TO PLAY INARIZAKI TOO, BUT THE WAY THE BRACKETS SHOOK OUT, IT JUST WASN'T IN THE CARDS.
SPEAKING OF THE BRACKETS, WOULD YOU BELIEVE THAT ON DAY 1 WE ALWAYS GET STUCK--

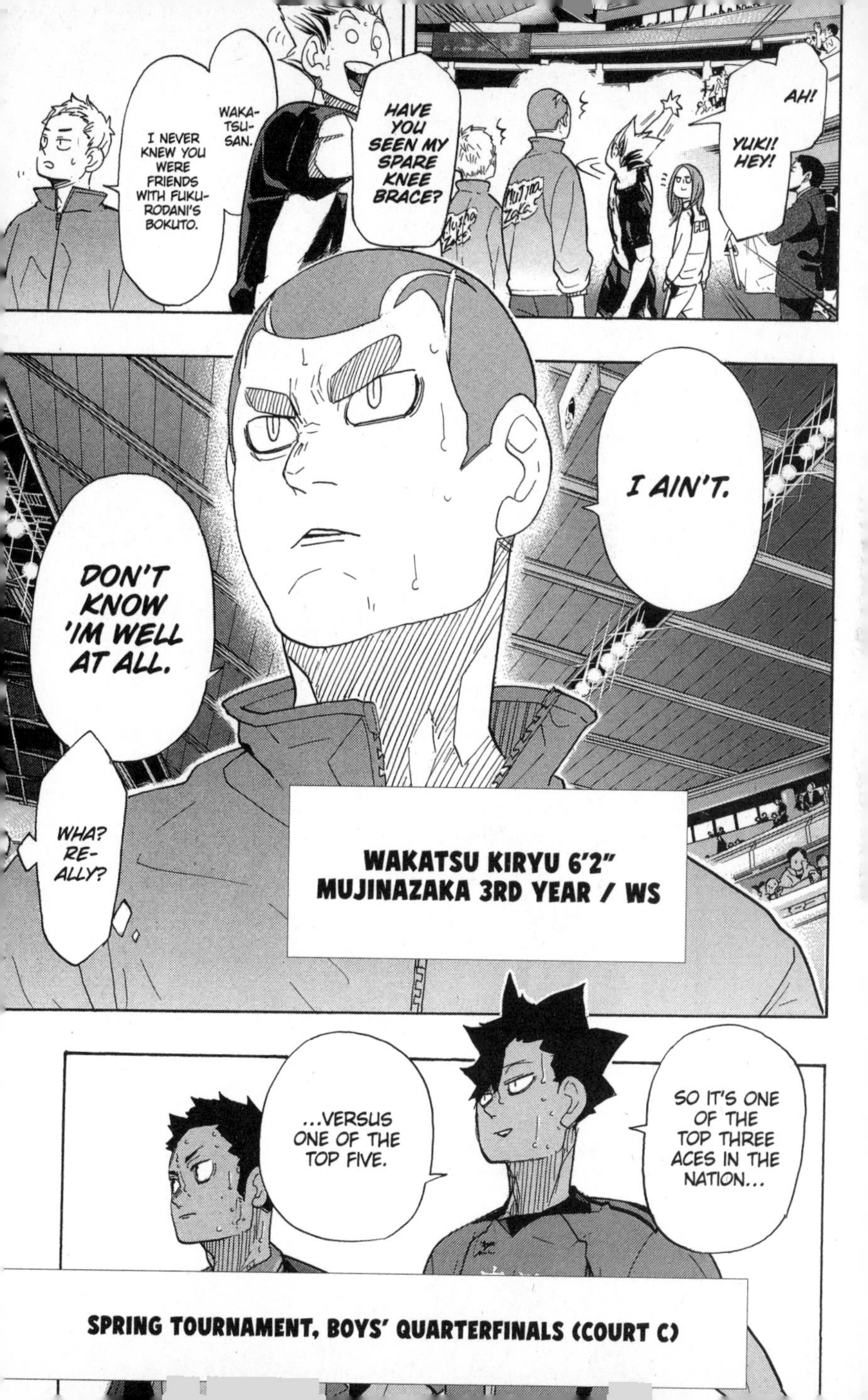
AH!
YUKI! HEY!
HAVE YOU SEEN MY SPARE KNEE BRACE?
WAKATSU-SAN.
I NEVER KNEW YOU WERE FRIENDS WITH FUKURODANI'S BOKUTO.
I AIN'T.
DON'T KNOW 'IM WELL AT ALL.
WHA? REALLY?
WAKATSU KIRYU 6'2"
MUJINAZAKA 3RD YEAR / WS
SO IT'S ONE OF THE TOP THREE ACES IN THE NATION...
...VERSUS ONE OF THE TOP FIVE.
SPRING TOURNAMENT, BOYS' QUARTERFINALS (COURT C)

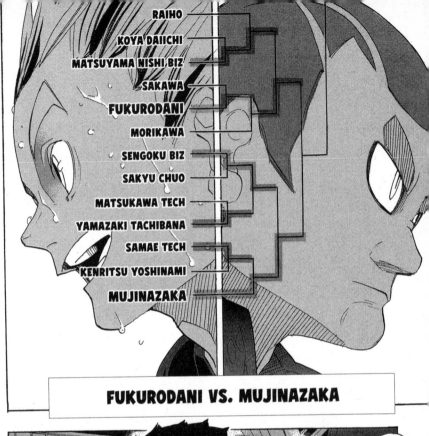

RAIHO
KOYA DAIICHI
MATSUYAMA NISHI BIZ
SAKAWA
FUKURODANI
MORIKAWA
SENGOKU BIZ
SAKYU CHUO
MATSUKAWA TECH
YAMAZAKI TACHIBANA
SAMAE TECH
KENRITSU YOSHINAMI
MUJINAZAKA

FUKURODANI VS. MUJINAZAKA

GOOD. GO SLEEP.

I AM GOING TO *SLEEP.*

OKAY!

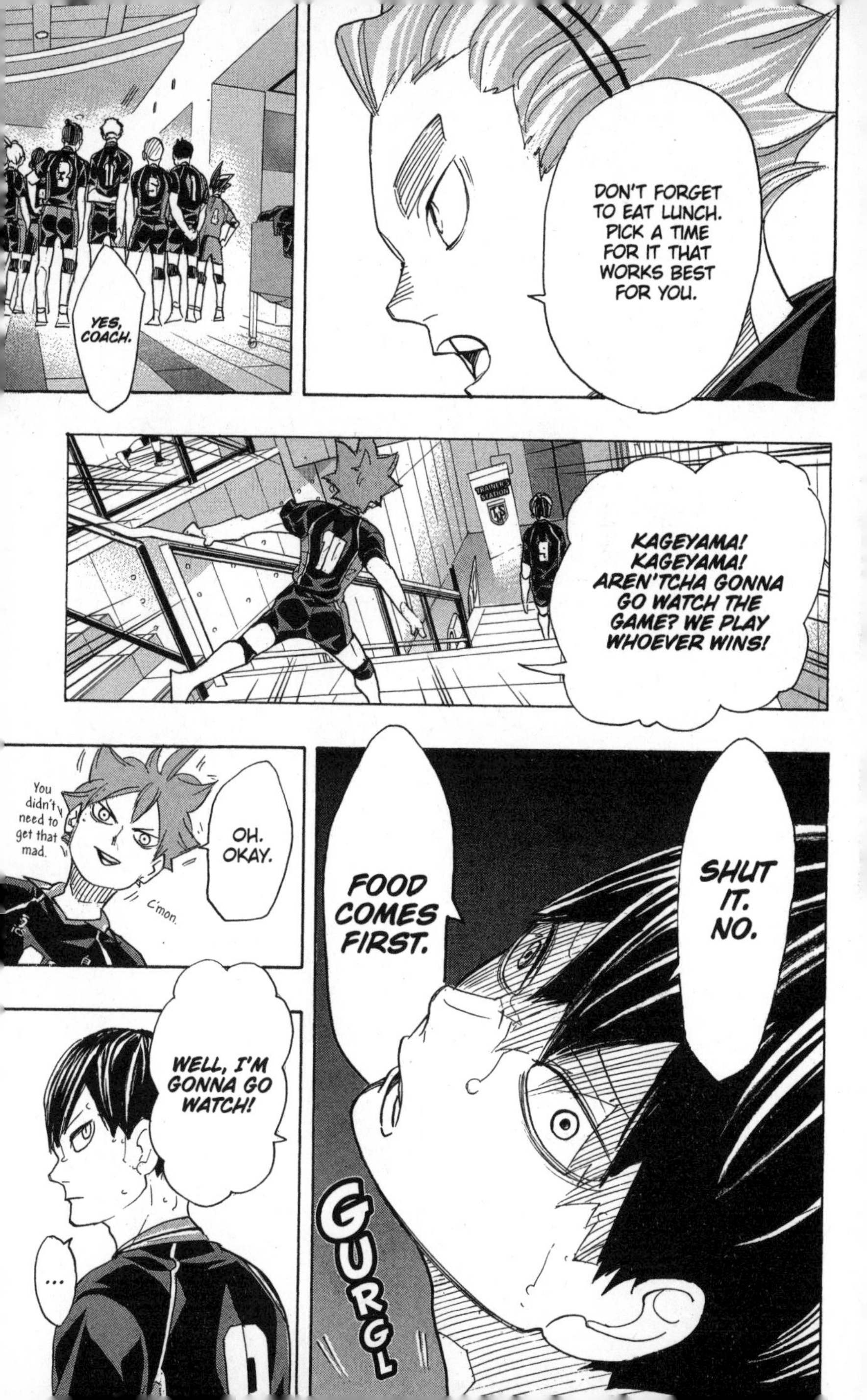
DON'T FORGET TO EAT LUNCH. PICK A TIME FOR IT THAT WORKS BEST FOR YOU.
YES, COACH.
KAGEYAMA! KAGEYAMA! AREN'TCHA GONNA GO WATCH THE GAME? WE PLAY WHOEVER WINS!
SHUT IT. NO.
FOOD COMES FIRST.
GURGL
OH. OKAY.
You didn't need to get that mad.
C'mon.
WELL, I'M GONNA GO WATCH!
...

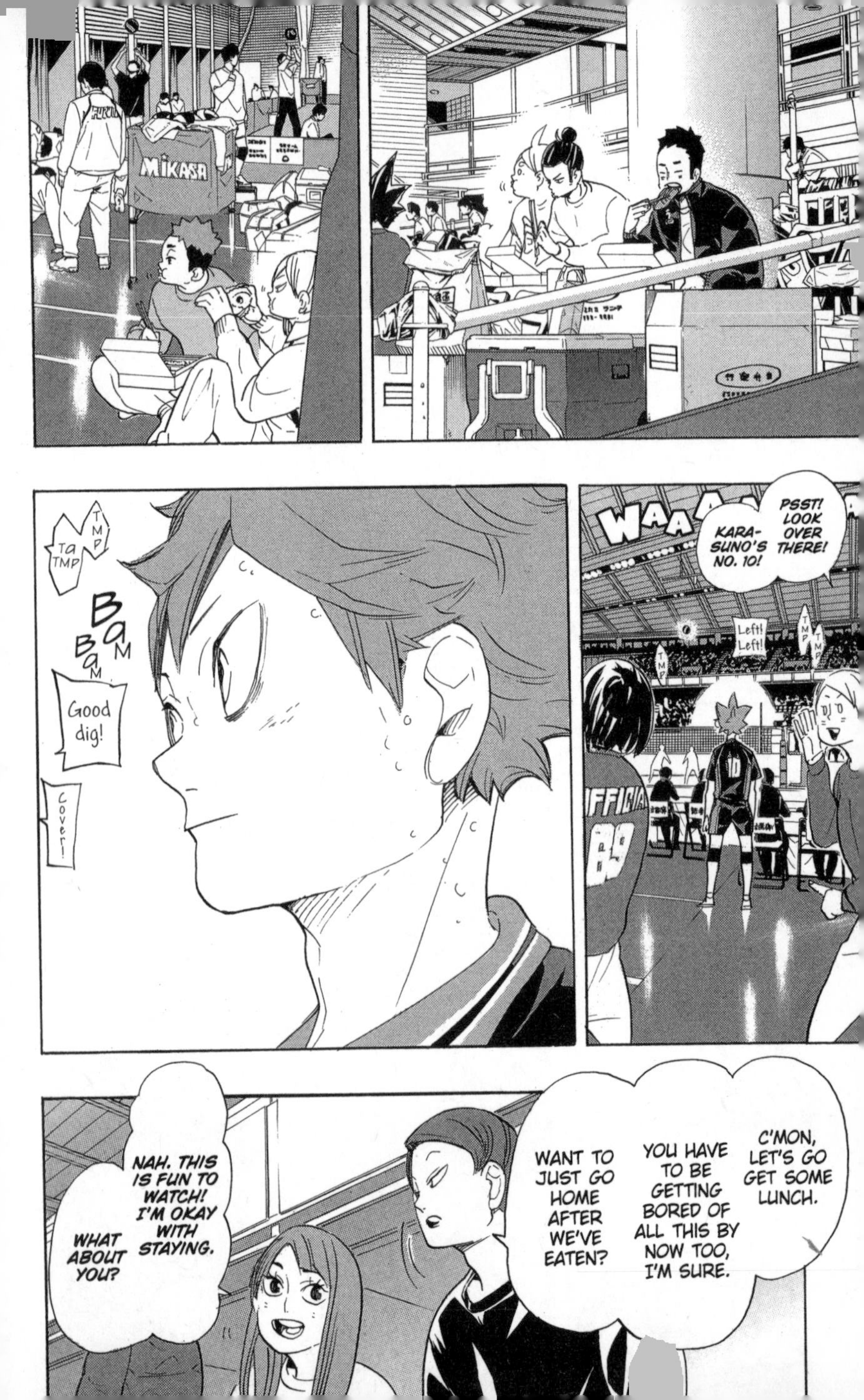
WAAA
PSST! LOOK OVER THERE!
KARA-SUNO'S NO. 10!
Left! Left!
TMP
TMP
TMP
TMP
Ta TMP
BaM
BaM
Good dig!
Cover!
C'MON, LET'S GO GET SOME LUNCH.
YOU HAVE TO BE GETTING BORED OF ALL THIS BY NOW TOO, I'M SURE.
WANT TO JUST GO HOME AFTER WE'VE EATEN?
NAH. THIS IS FUN TO WATCH! I'M OKAY WITH STAYING.
WHAT ABOUT YOU?

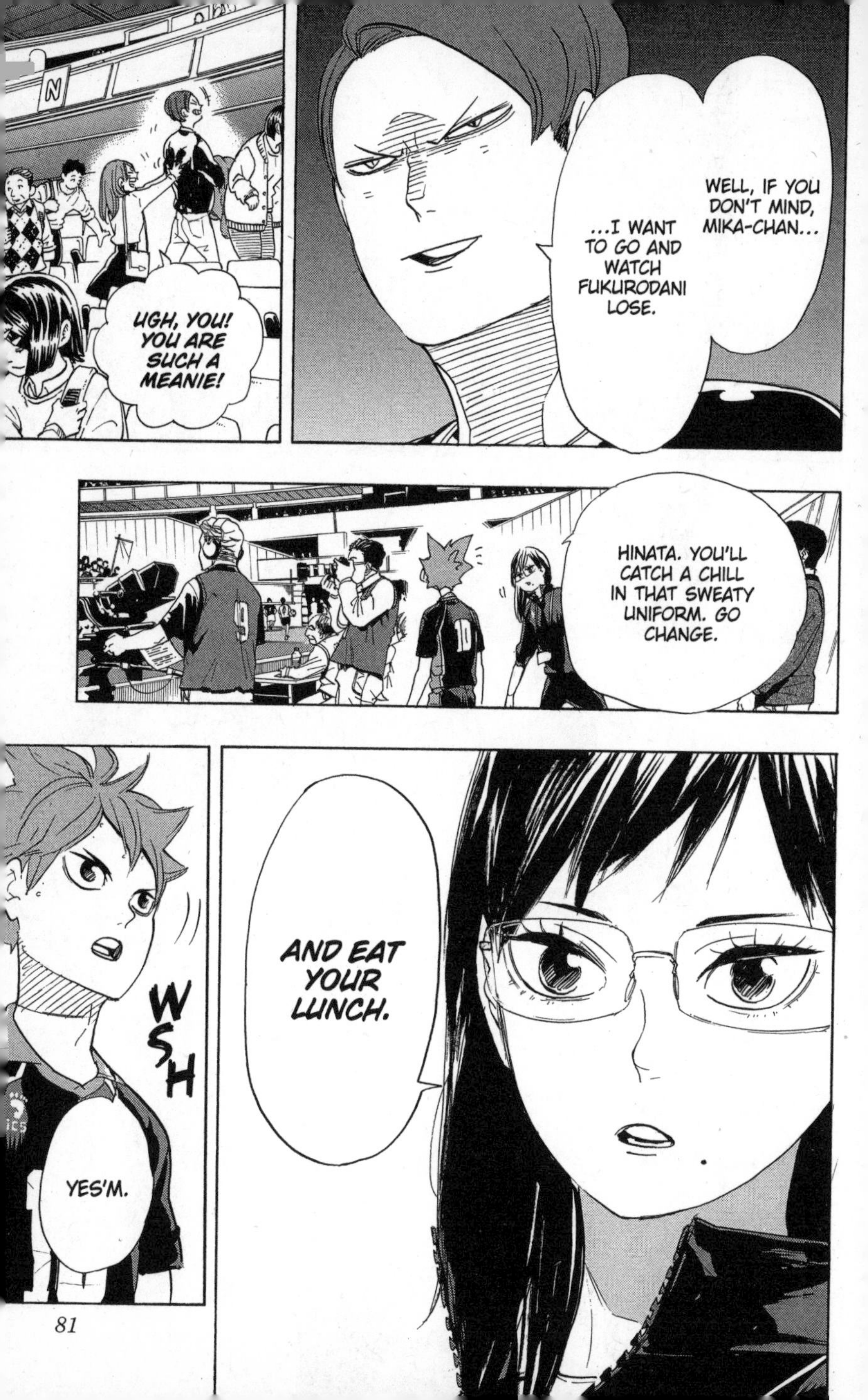
WELL, IF YOU DON'T MIND, MIKA-CHAN...
...I WANT TO GO AND WATCH FUKURODANI LOSE.
UGH, YOU! YOU ARE SUCH A MEANIE!
HINATA. YOU'LL CATCH A CHILL IN THAT SWEATY UNIFORM. GO CHANGE.
AND EAT YOUR LUNCH.
WSH
YES'M.

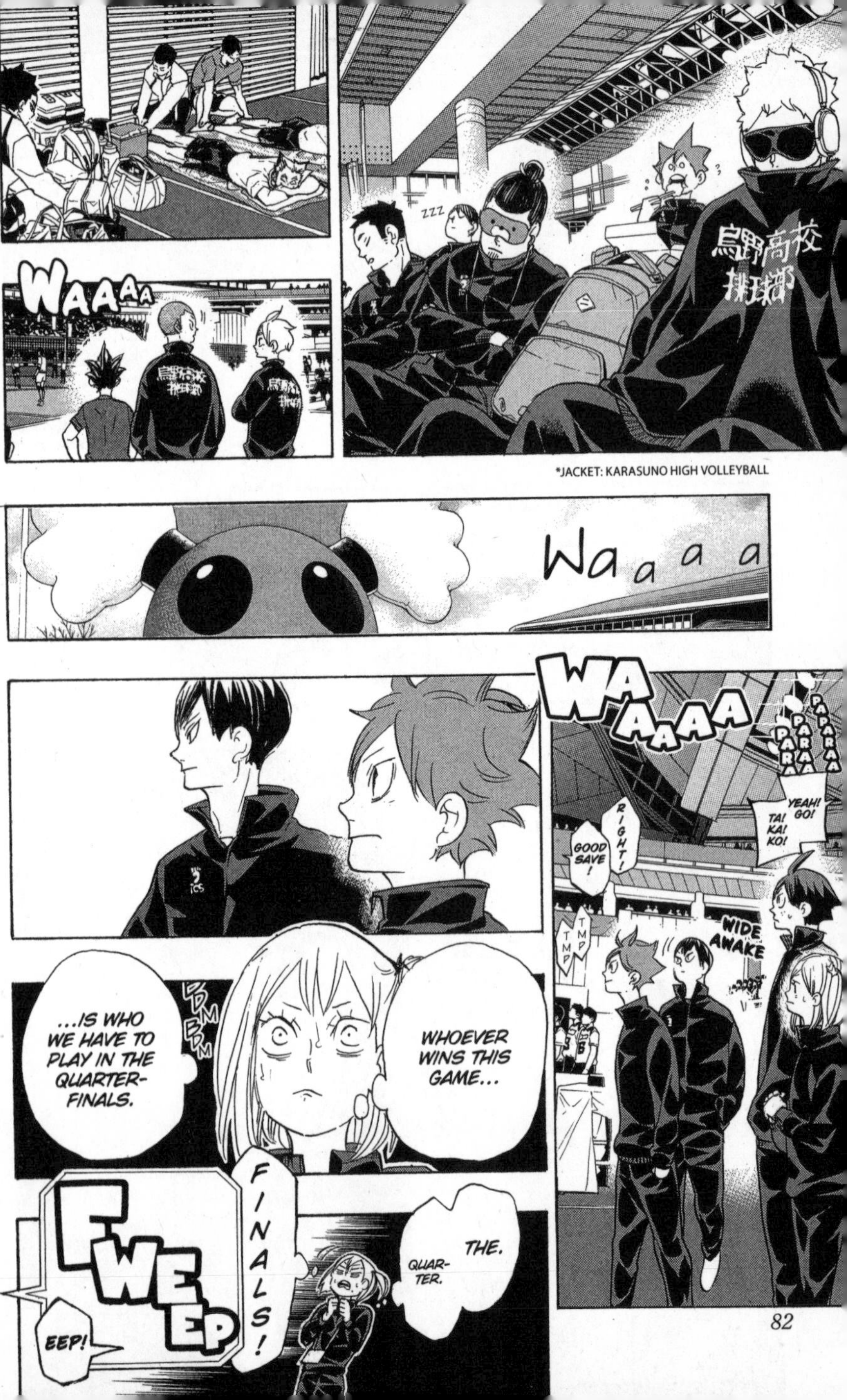
ZZZ
烏野高校
排球部
WAAAAA
*JACKET: KARASUNO HIGH VOLLEYBALL
Waaaaa
WAAAAAA
PARAPARAPARAA
PARAPARAPARAA
YEAH! GO!
TAI KA KO!
RIGHT!
GOOD SAVE!
WIDE AWAKE
TMP TMP
WHOEVER WINS THIS GAME...
BDM BDM
...IS WHO WE HAVE TO PLAY IN THE QUARTER-FINALS.
THE.
QUARTER.
FINALS!
FWEEP
EEP!

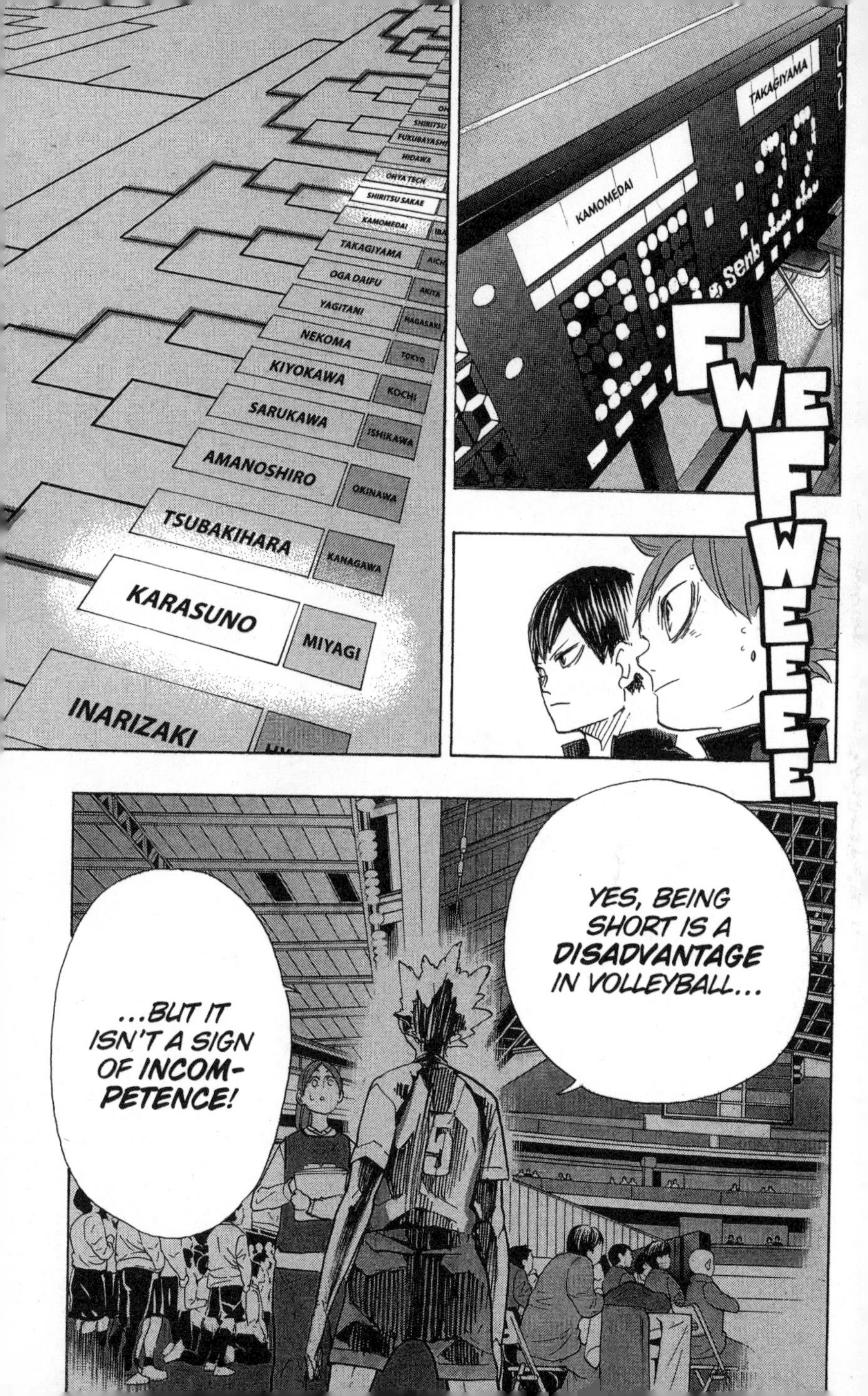
TAKAGIYAMA
KAMOMEDAI
FWEFWEEEE
SHIRITSU
FUKUBAYASHI
HIDAWA
OHYA TECH
SHIRITSU SAKAE
KAMOMEDAI
TAKAGIYAMA
OGA DAIFU
AKITA
YAGITANI
NAGASAKI
NEKOMA
TOKYO
KIYOKAWA
KOCHI
SARUKAWA
ISHIKAWA
AMANOSHIRO
OKINAWA
TSUBAKIHARA
KANAGAWA
KARASUNO
MIYAGI
INARIZAKI
YES, BEING SHORT IS A DISADVANTAGE IN VOLLEYBALL...
...BUT IT ISN'T A SIGN OF INCOMPETENCE!

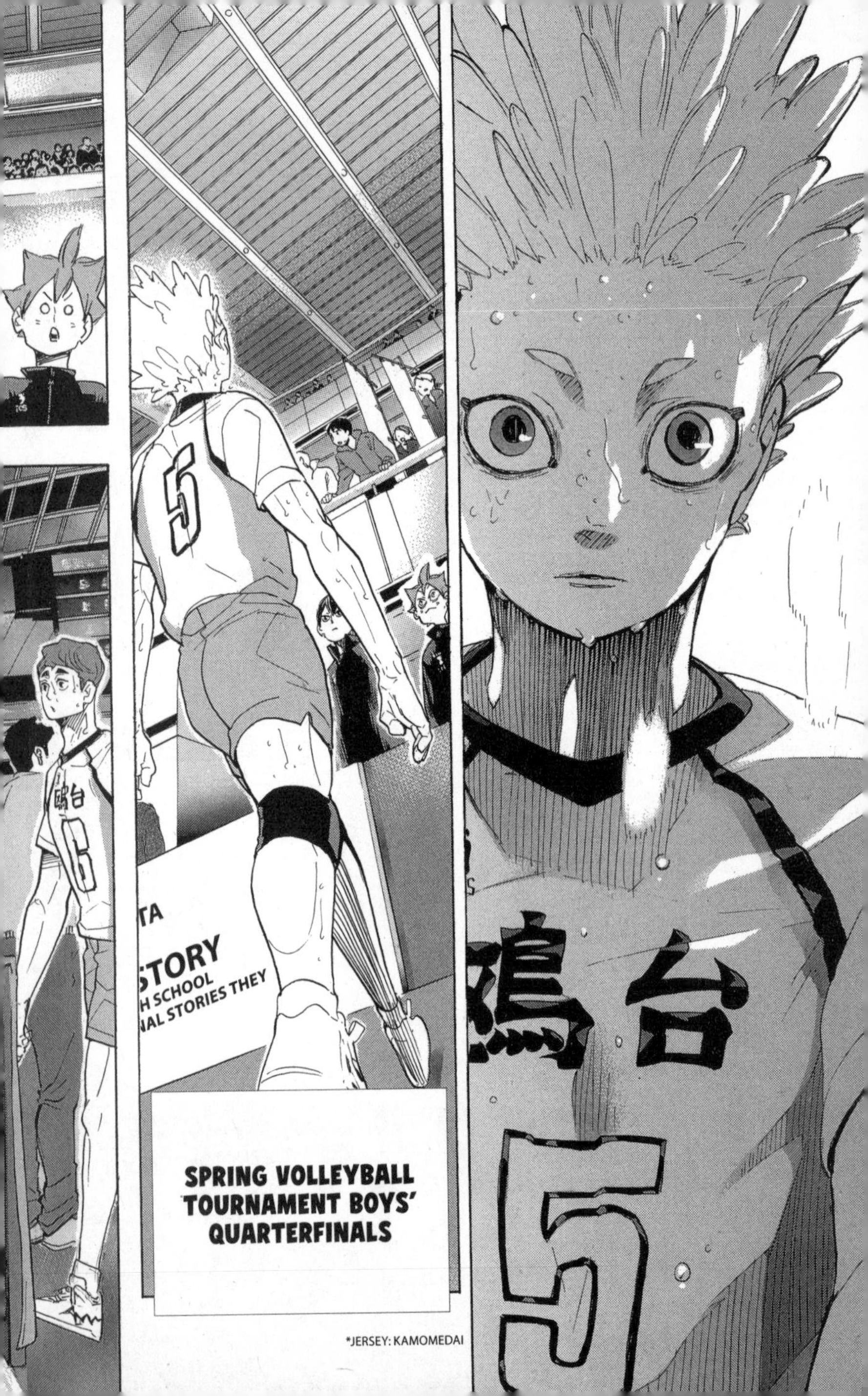
鴎台
*JERSEY: KAMOMEDAI
TA
STORY
H SCHOOL
NAL STORIES THEY
SPRING VOLLEYBALL TOURNAMENT BOYS' QUARTERFINALS

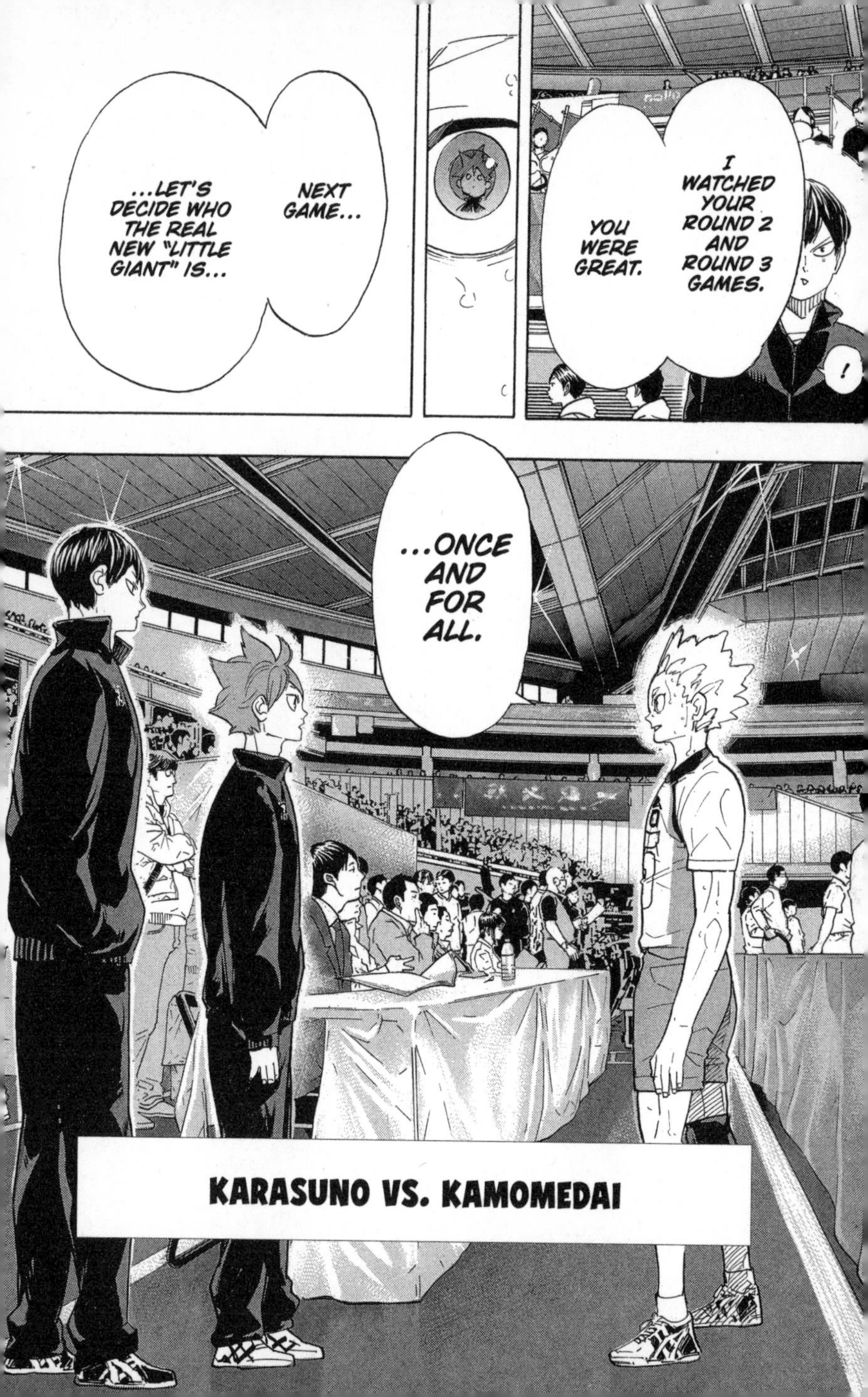
I WATCHED YOUR ROUND 2 AND ROUND 3 GAMES.
YOU WERE GREAT.
!
NEXT GAME...
...LET'S DECIDE WHO THE REAL NEW "LITTLE GIANT" IS...
...ONCE AND FOR ALL.
KARASUNO VS. KAMOMEDAI

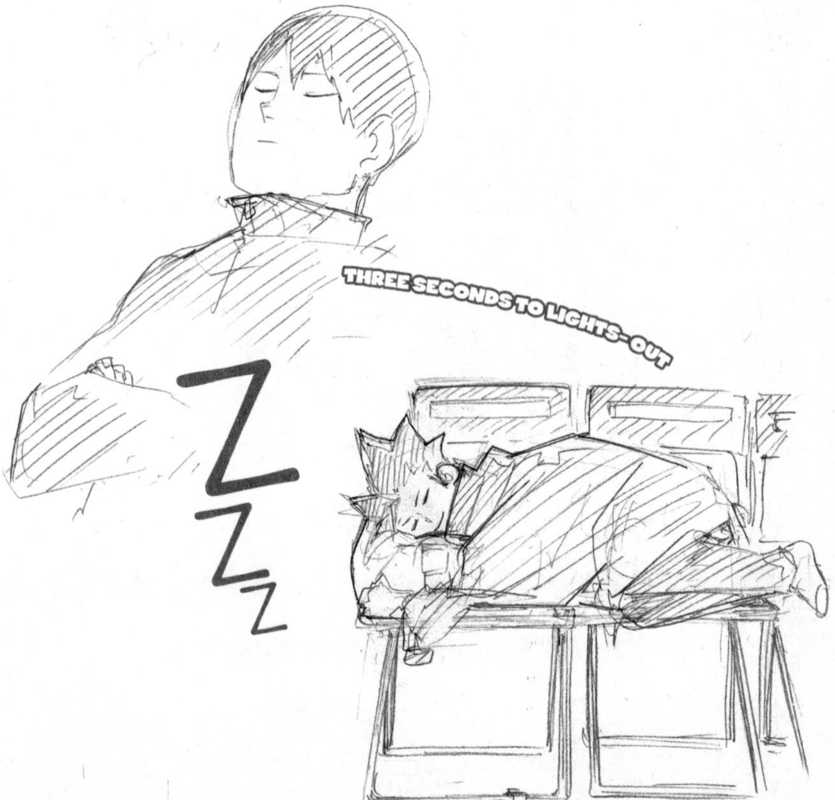
THREE SECONDS TO LIGHTS-OUT
ZZZ

CHAPTER 327: The Volleyball Bug

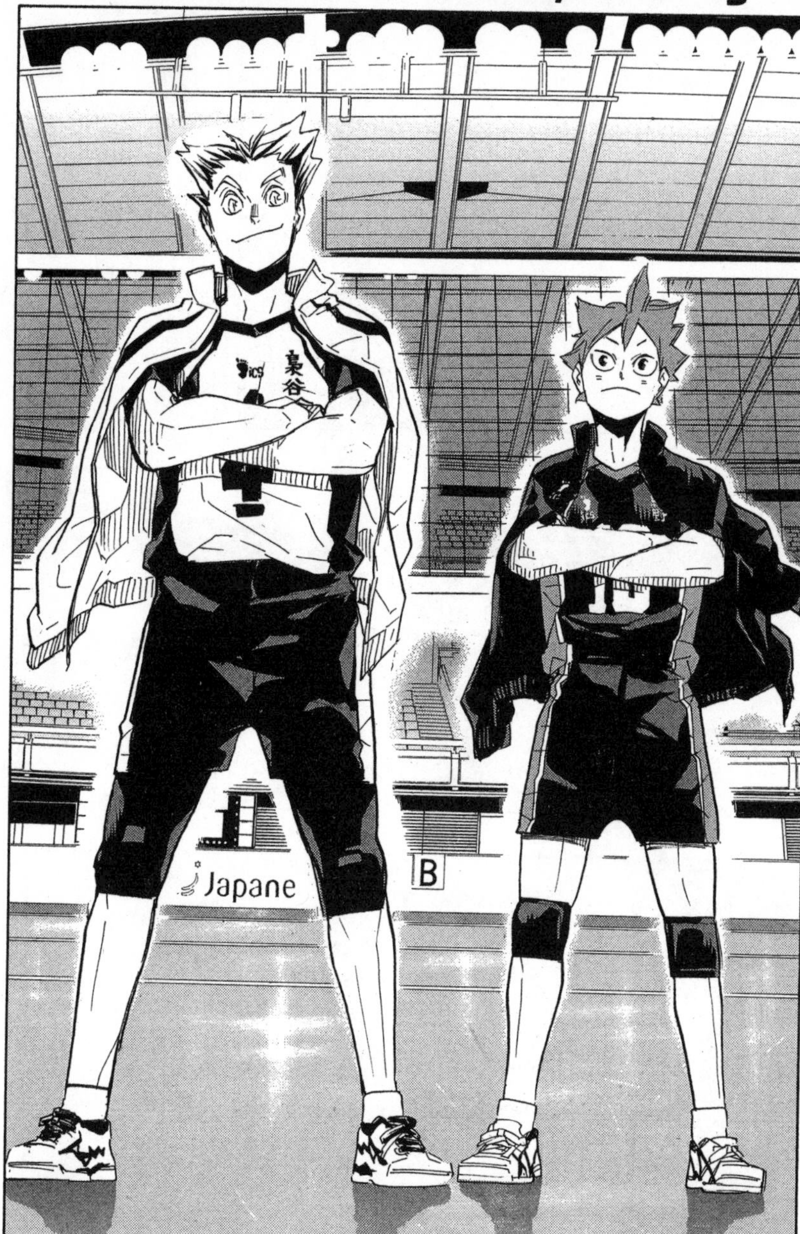

Japane
B

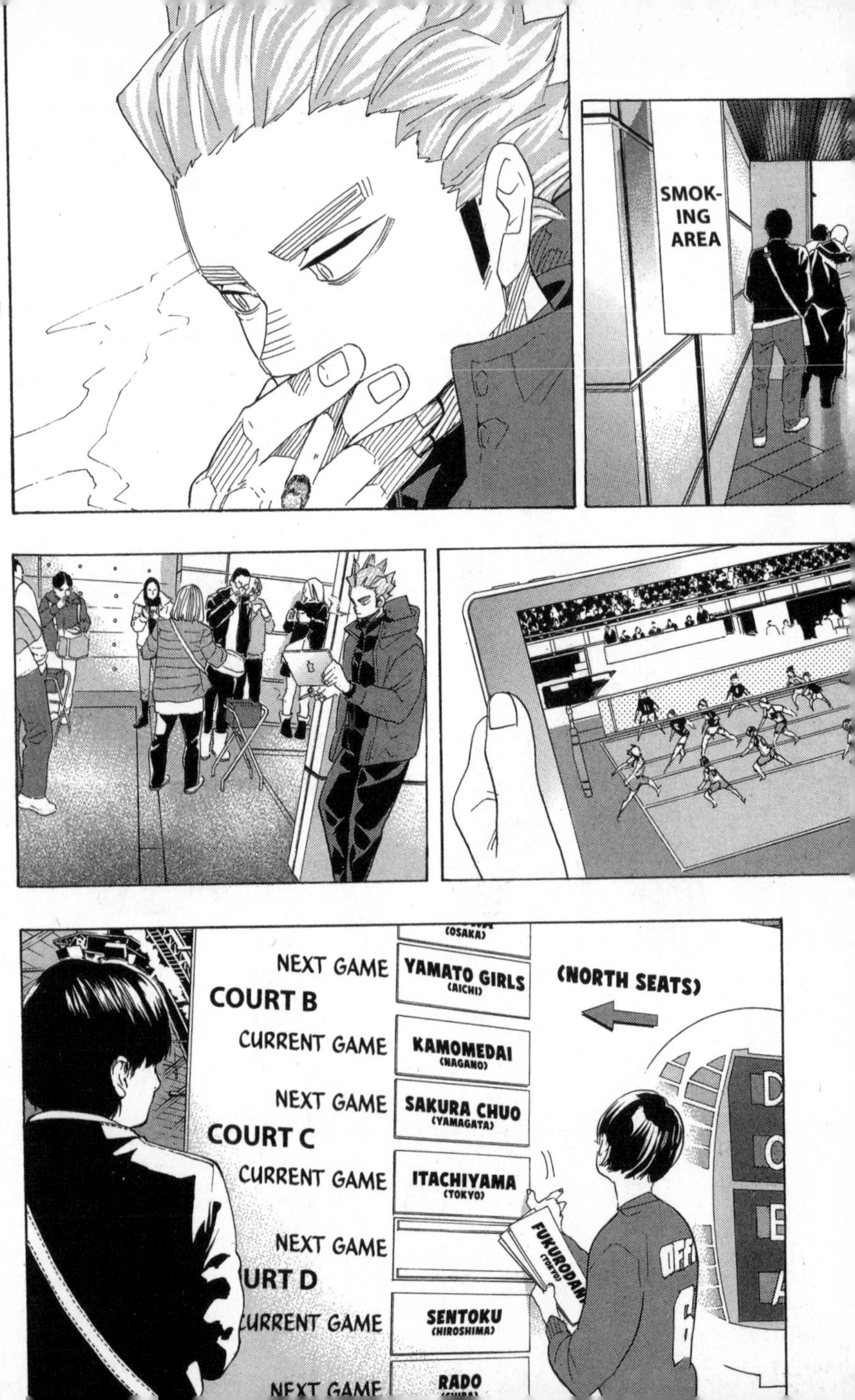
SMOKING AREA
(OSAKA)
NEXT GAME
YAMATO GIRLS
(AICHI)
COURT B
CURRENT GAME
KAMOMEDAI
(NAGANO)
NEXT GAME
SAKURA CHUO
(YAMAGATA)
COURT C
CURRENT GAME
ITACHIYAMA
(TOKYO)
NEXT GAME
URT D
URRENT GAME
SENTOKU
(HIROSHIMA)
NEXT GAME
RADO
(NORTH SEATS)
FUKURODANI
(TOKYO)

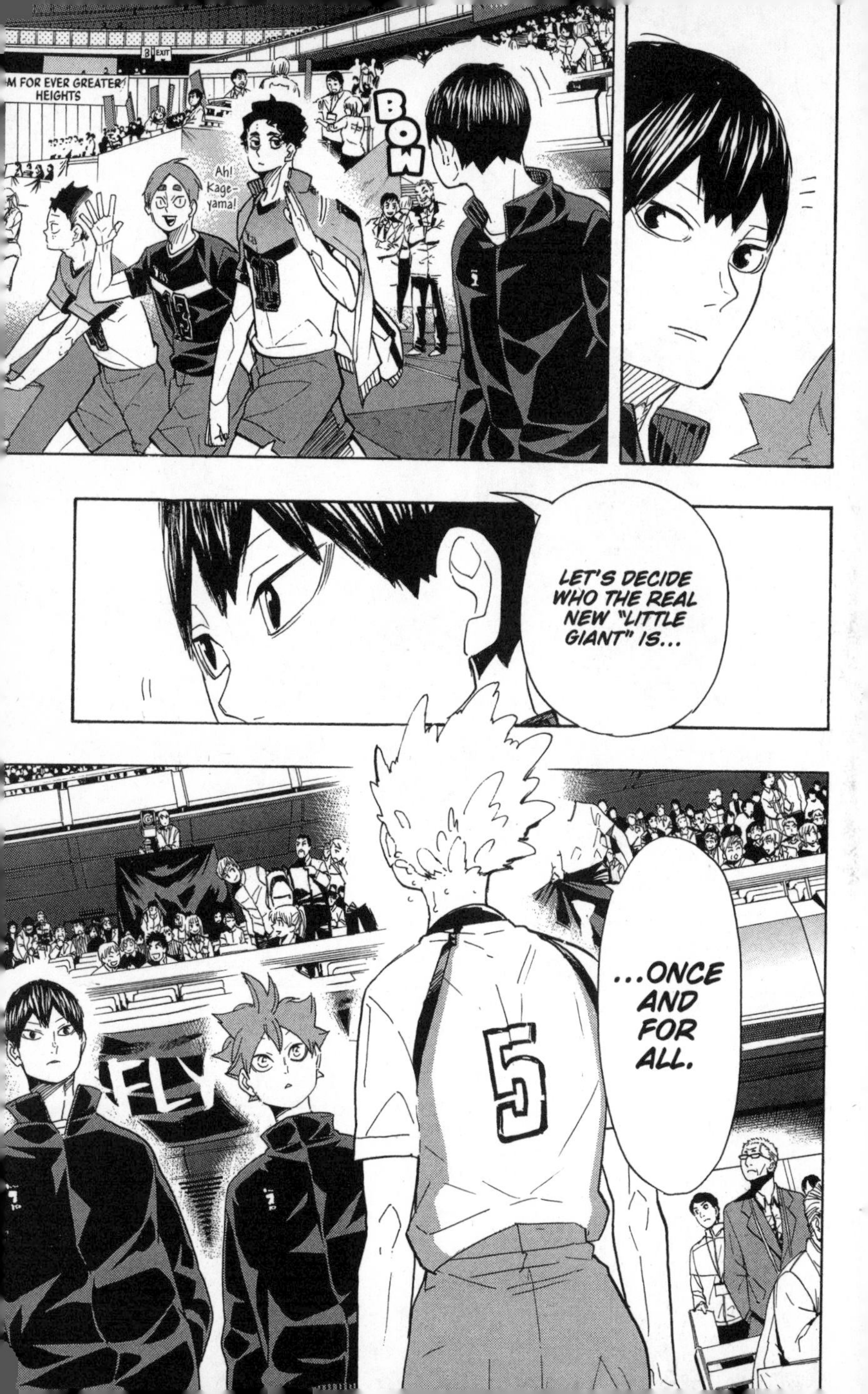
M FOR EVER GREATER HEIGHTS
B EXIT
BOW
Ah! Kage-yama!
LET'S DECIDE WHO THE REAL NEW "LITTLE GIANT" IS...
...ONCE AND FOR ALL.
FLY

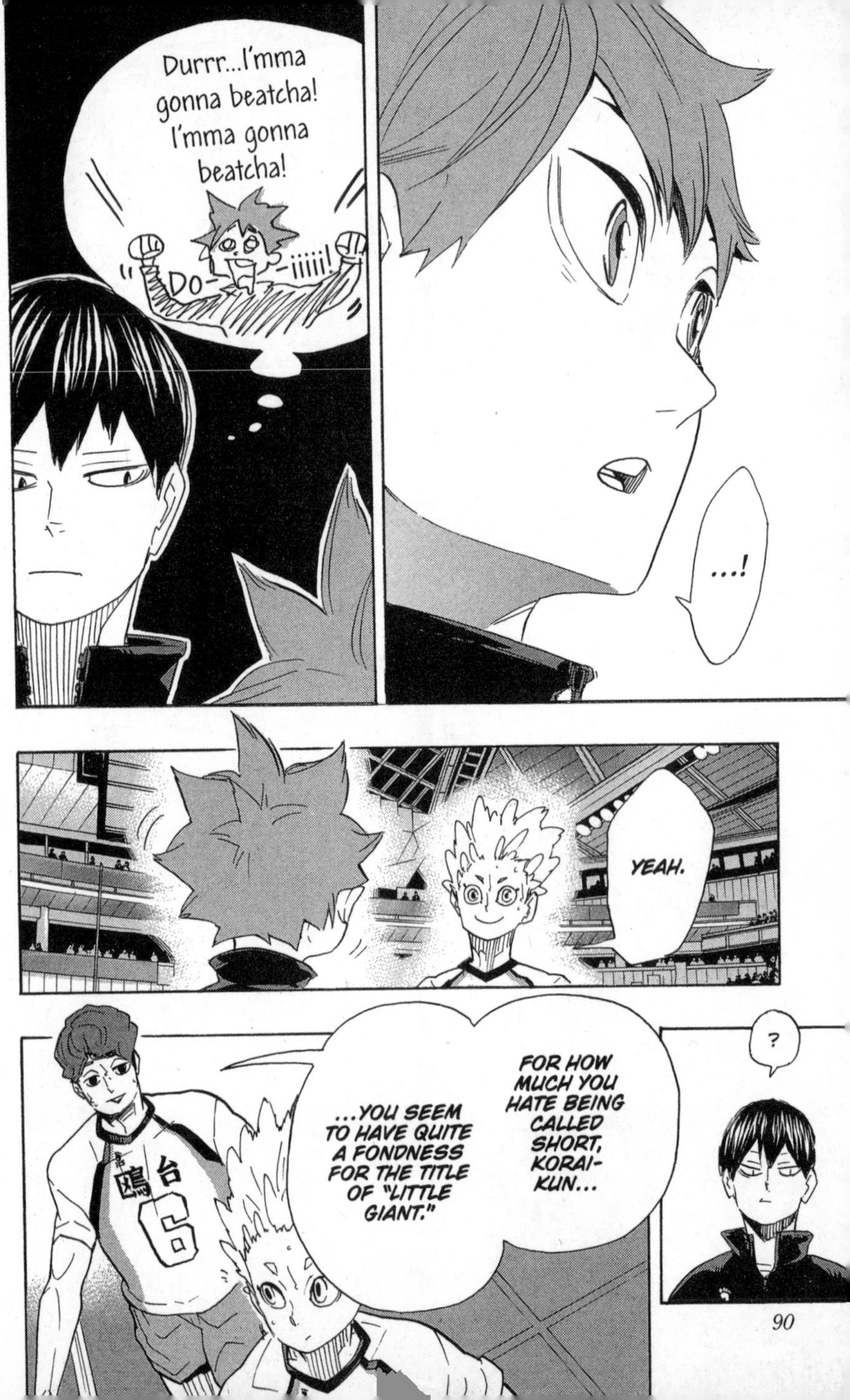

...!
Durrr...I'mma gonna beatcha! I'mma gonna beatcha!
"Do- -iiiii!"
YEAH.
?
FOR HOW MUCH YOU HATE BEING CALLED SHORT, KORAI-KUN...
...YOU SEEM TO HAVE QUITE A FONDNESS FOR THE TITLE OF "LITTLE GIANT."

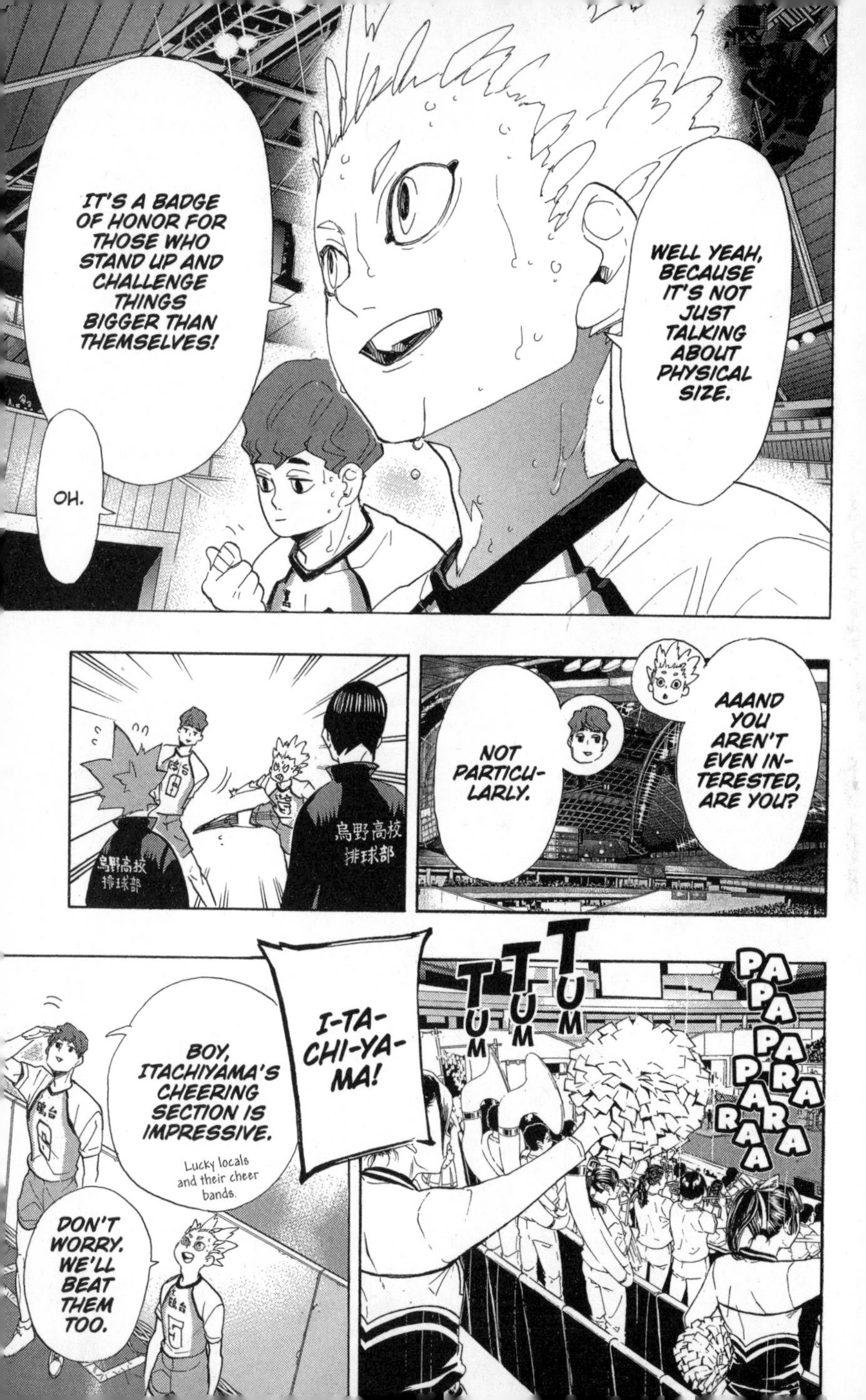
WELL YEAH, BECAUSE IT'S NOT JUST TALKING ABOUT PHYSICAL SIZE.
IT'S A BADGE OF HONOR FOR THOSE WHO STAND UP AND CHALLENGE THINGS BIGGER THAN THEMSELVES!
OH.
AAAND YOU AREN'T EVEN INTERESTED, ARE YOU?
NOT PARTICULARLY.
烏野高校 排球部
烏野高校 排球部
PAPAPAPARARARARAA
TUM TUM TUM
I-TA-CHI-YA-MA!
BOY, ITACHIYAMA'S CHEERING SECTION IS IMPRESSIVE.
Lucky locals and their cheer bands.
DON'T WORRY. WE'LL BEAT THEM TOO.

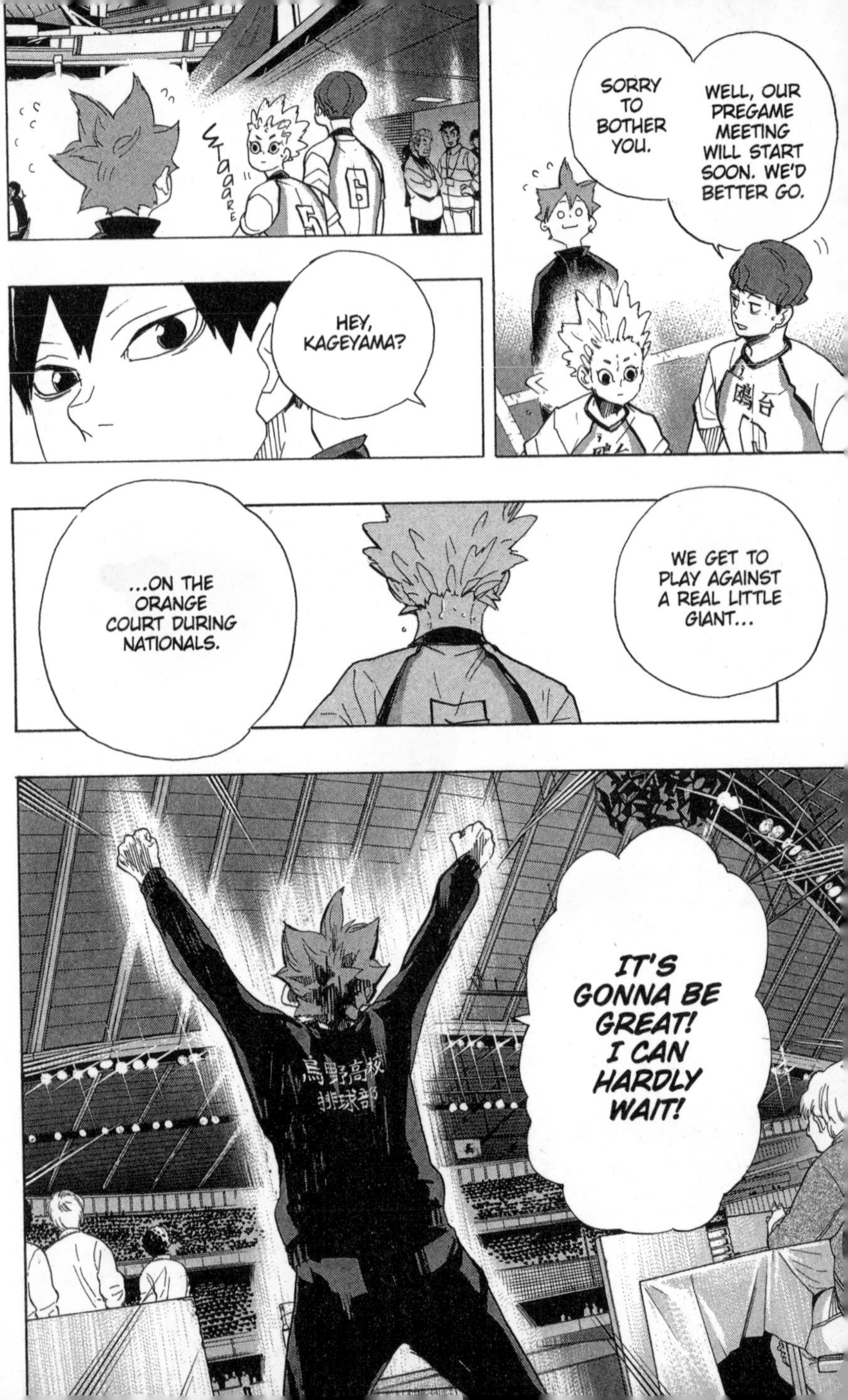
WELL, OUR PREGAME MEETING WILL START SOON. WE'D BETTER GO.
SORRY TO BOTHER YOU.
STAAARE
HEY, KAGEYAMA?
WE GET TO PLAY AGAINST A REAL LITTLE GIANT...
...ON THE ORANGE COURT DURING NATIONALS.
IT'S GONNA BE GREAT! I CAN HARDLY WAIT!

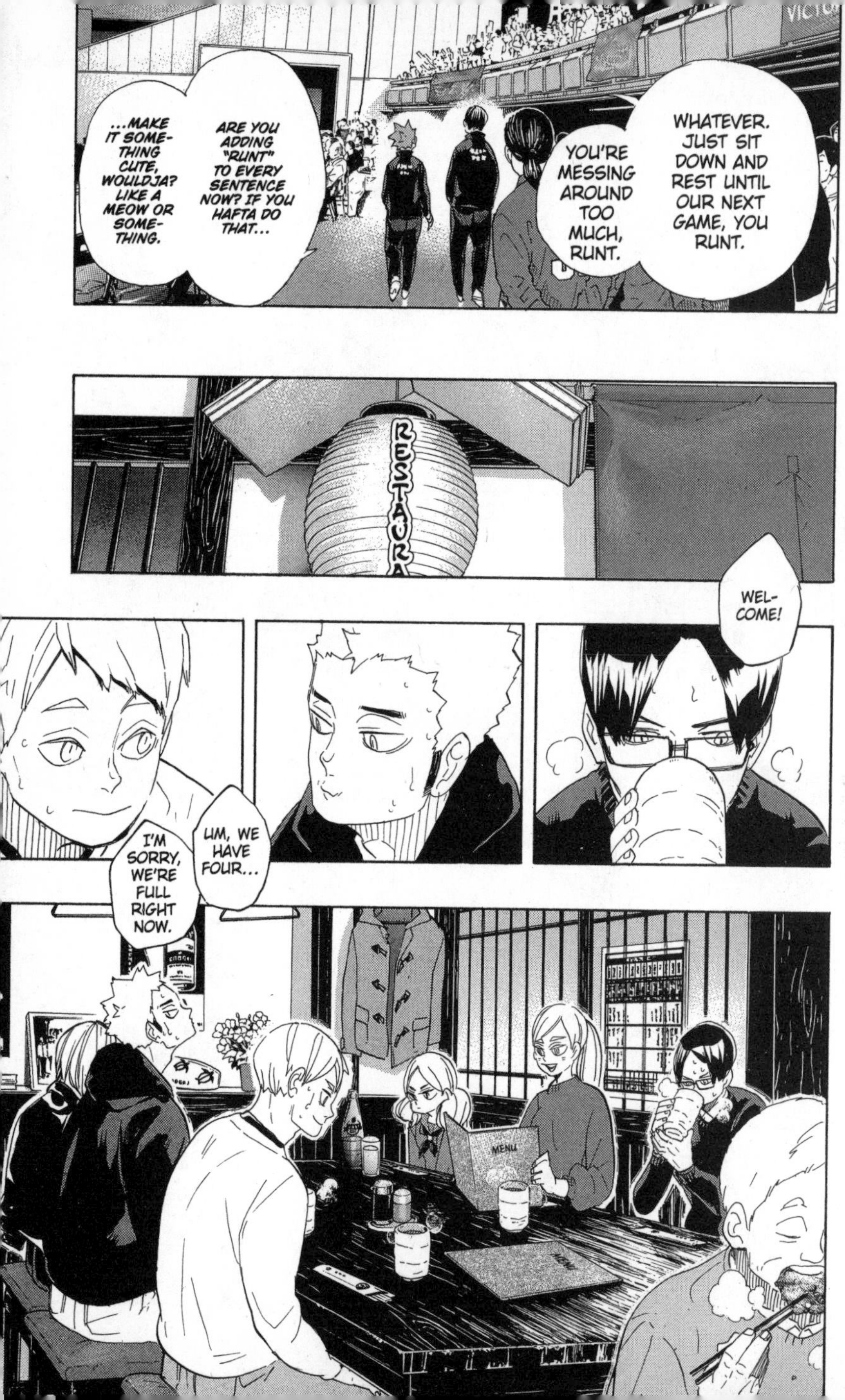
WHATEVER. JUST SIT DOWN AND REST UNTIL OUR NEXT GAME, YOU RUNT.
YOU'RE MESSING AROUND TOO MUCH, RUNT.
ARE YOU ADDING "RUNT" TO EVERY SENTENCE NOW? IF YOU HAFTA DO THAT...
...MAKE IT SOMETHING CUTE, WOULDJA? LIKE A MEOW OR SOMETHING.
RESTAURA
WEL-COME!
UM, WE HAVE FOUR...
I'M SORRY, WE'RE FULL RIGHT NOW.
MENU

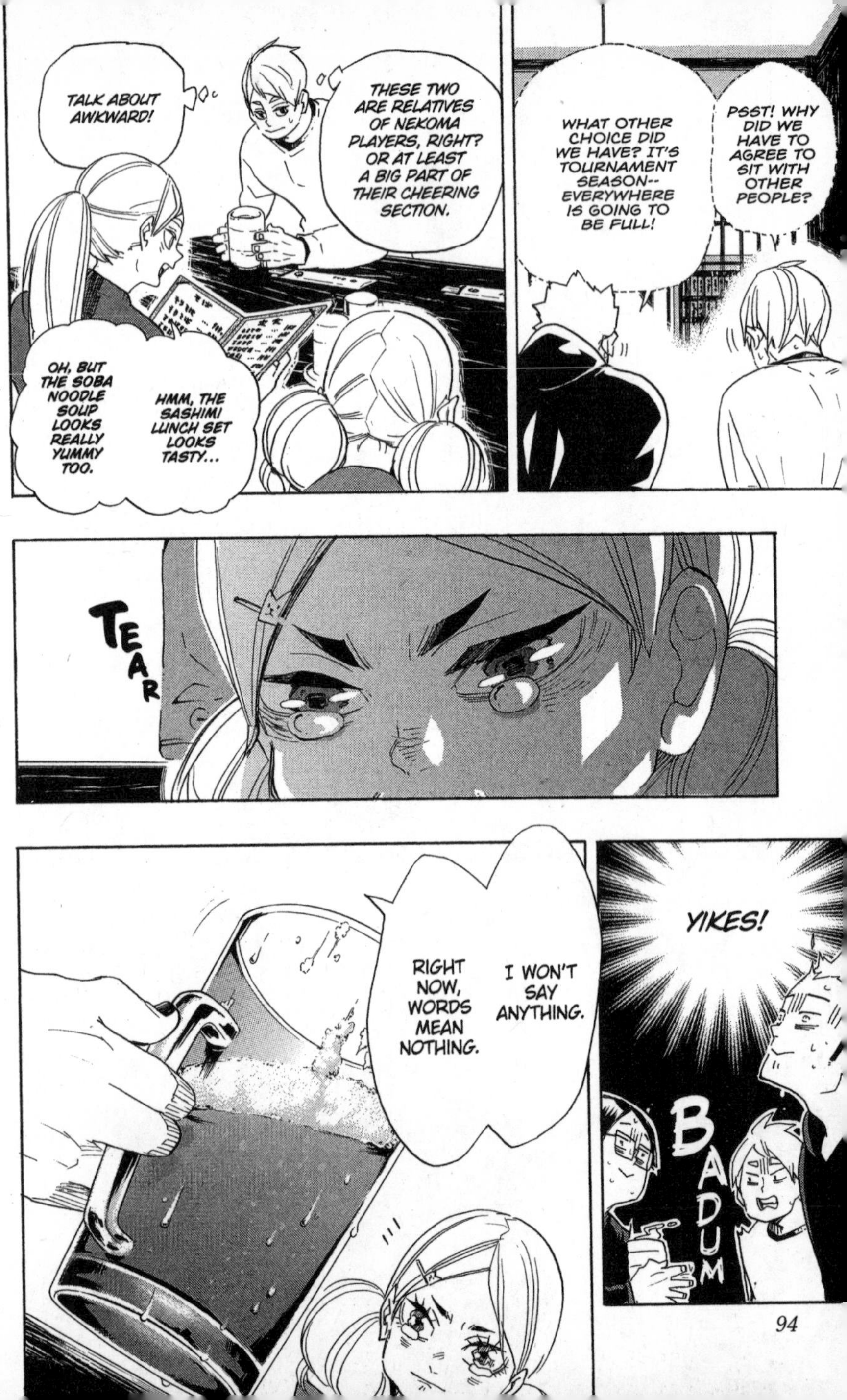
PSST! WHY DID WE HAVE TO AGREE TO SIT WITH OTHER PEOPLE?
WHAT OTHER CHOICE DID WE HAVE? IT'S TOURNAMENT SEASON-- EVERYWHERE IS GOING TO BE FULL!
THESE TWO ARE RELATIVES OF NEKOMA PLAYERS, RIGHT? OR AT LEAST A BIG PART OF THEIR CHEERING SECTION.
TALK ABOUT AWKWARD!
HMM, THE SASHIMI LUNCH SET LOOKS TASTY...
OH, BUT THE SOBA NOODLE SOUP LOOKS REALLY YUMMY TOO.
TEAR
YIKES!
BADUM
I WON'T SAY ANYTHING.
RIGHT NOW, WORDS MEAN NOTHING.

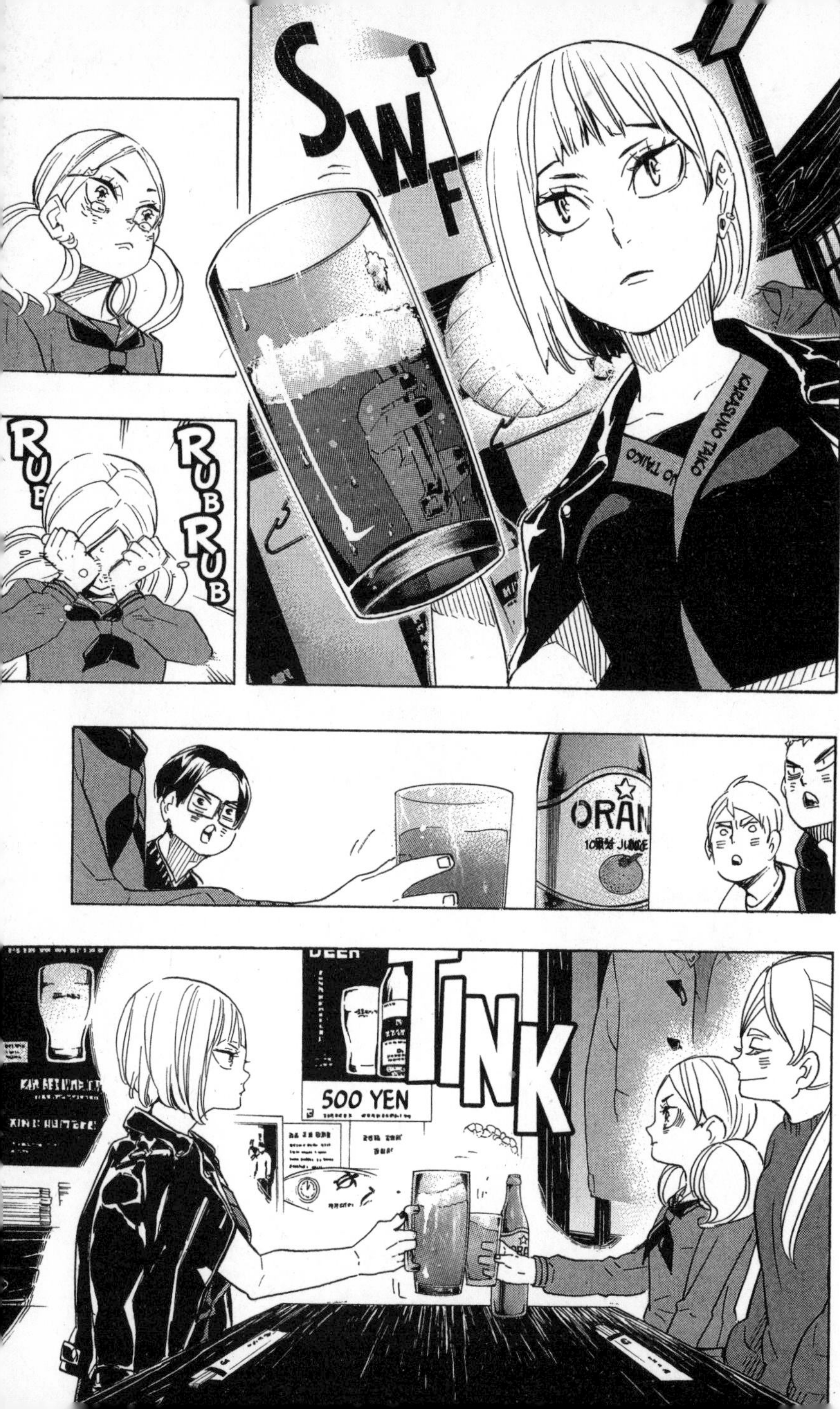
SWF
KARASUNO TAIKO
RUB
RUB RUB RUB
TINK
500 YEN

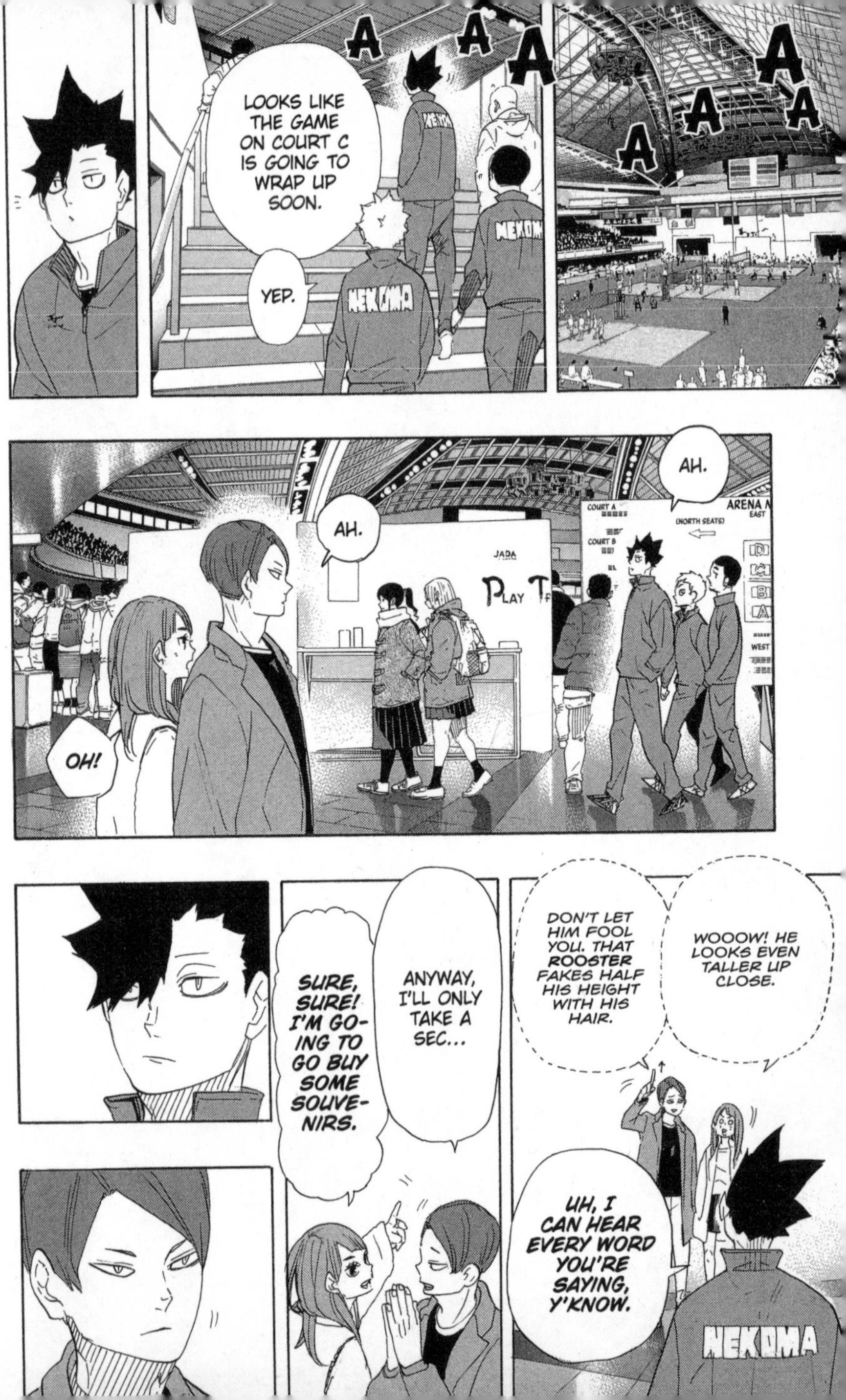
A A A A A A A
LOOKS LIKE THE GAME ON COURT C IS GOING TO WRAP UP SOON.
YEP.
AH.
COURT A
COURT B
(NORTH SEATS)
EAST
WEST
JADA
AH.
OH!
WOOOW! HE LOOKS EVEN TALLER UP CLOSE.
DON'T LET HIM FOOL YOU. THAT ROOSTER FAKES HALF HIS HEIGHT WITH HIS HAIR.
UH, I CAN HEAR EVERY WORD YOU'RE SAYING, Y'KNOW.
ANYWAY, I'LL ONLY TAKE A SEC...
SURE, SURE! I'M GOING TO GO BUY SOME SOUVENIRS.

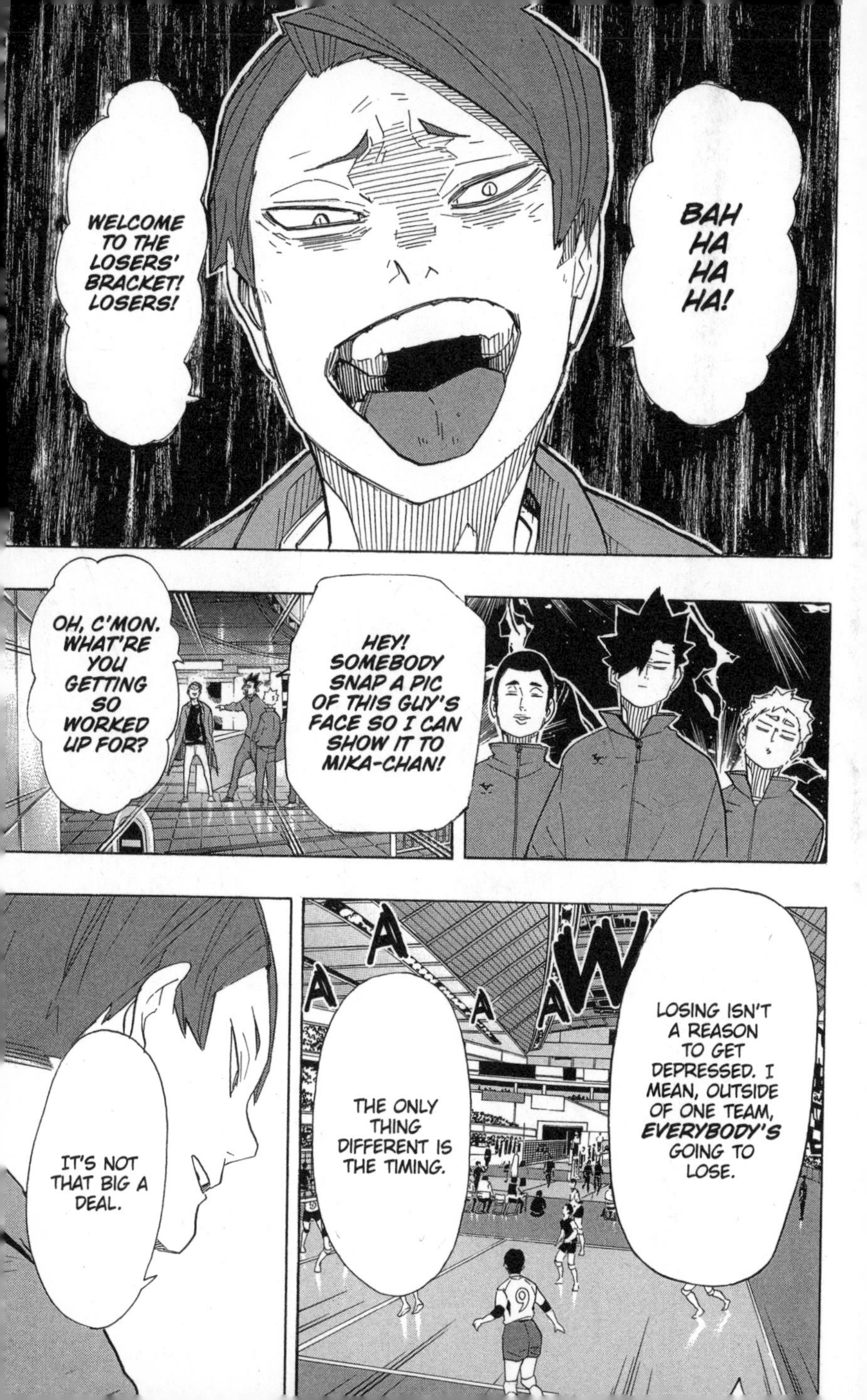
BAH HA HA HA!
WELCOME TO THE LOSERS' BRACKET! LOSERS!
HEY! SOMEBODY SNAP A PIC OF THIS GUY'S FACE SO I CAN SHOW IT TO MIKA-CHAN!
OH, C'MON. WHAT'RE YOU GETTING SO WORKED UP FOR?
LOSING ISN'T A REASON TO GET DEPRESSED. I MEAN, OUTSIDE OF ONE TEAM, **EVERYBODY'S** GOING TO LOSE.
THE ONLY THING DIFFERENT IS THE TIMING.
IT'S NOT THAT BIG A DEAL.

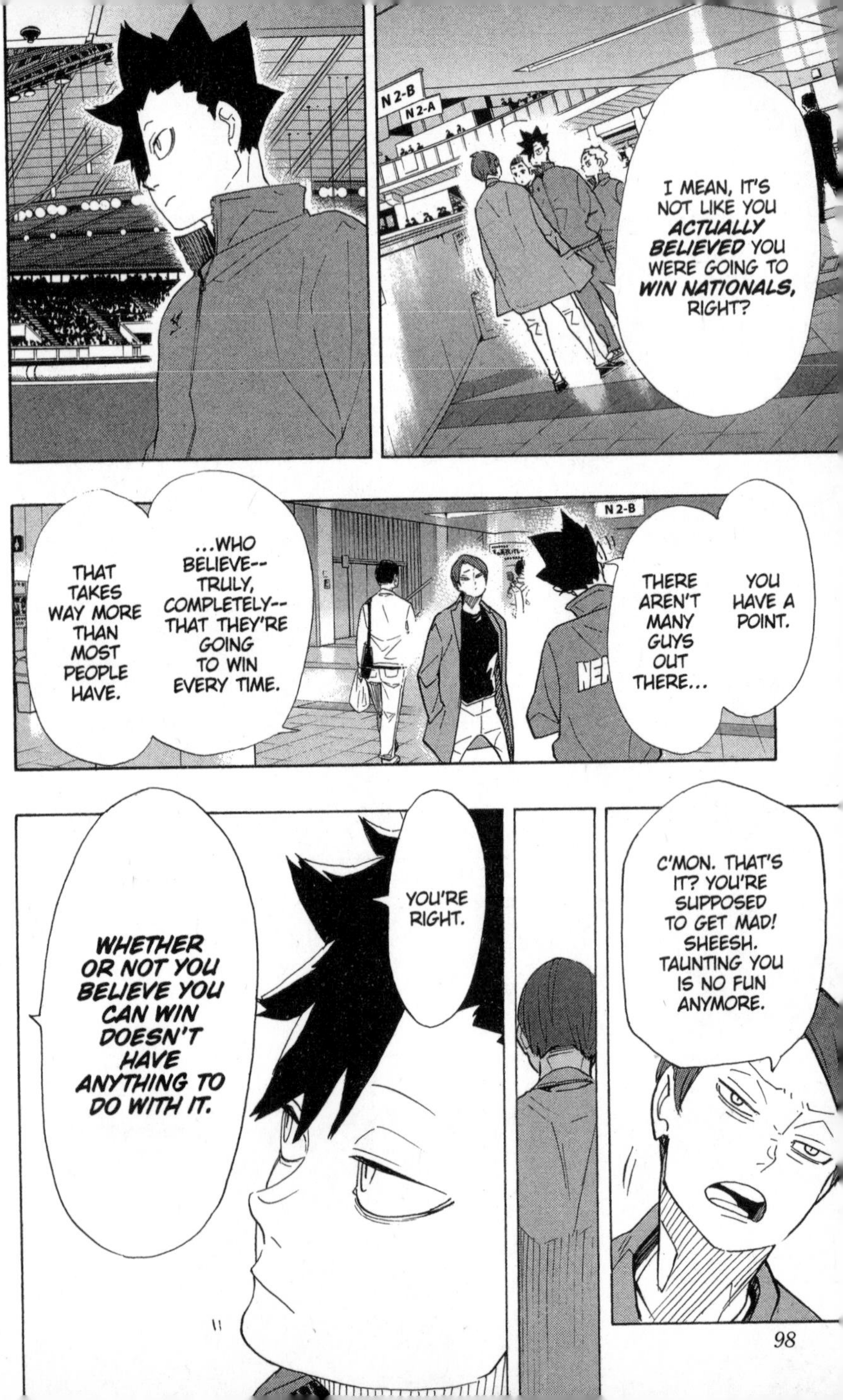
I MEAN, IT'S NOT LIKE YOU ACTUALLY BELIEVED YOU WERE GOING TO WIN NATIONALS, RIGHT?
N 2-B
N 2-A
YOU HAVE A POINT.
THERE AREN'T MANY GUYS OUT THERE...
...WHO BELIEVE--TRULY, COMPLETELY--THAT THEY'RE GOING TO WIN EVERY TIME.
THAT TAKES WAY MORE THAN MOST PEOPLE HAVE.
C'MON. THAT'S IT? YOU'RE SUPPOSED TO GET MAD! SHEESH. TAUNTING YOU IS NO FUN ANYMORE.
YOU'RE RIGHT.
WHETHER OR NOT YOU BELIEVE YOU CAN WIN DOESN'T HAVE ANYTHING TO DO WITH IT.

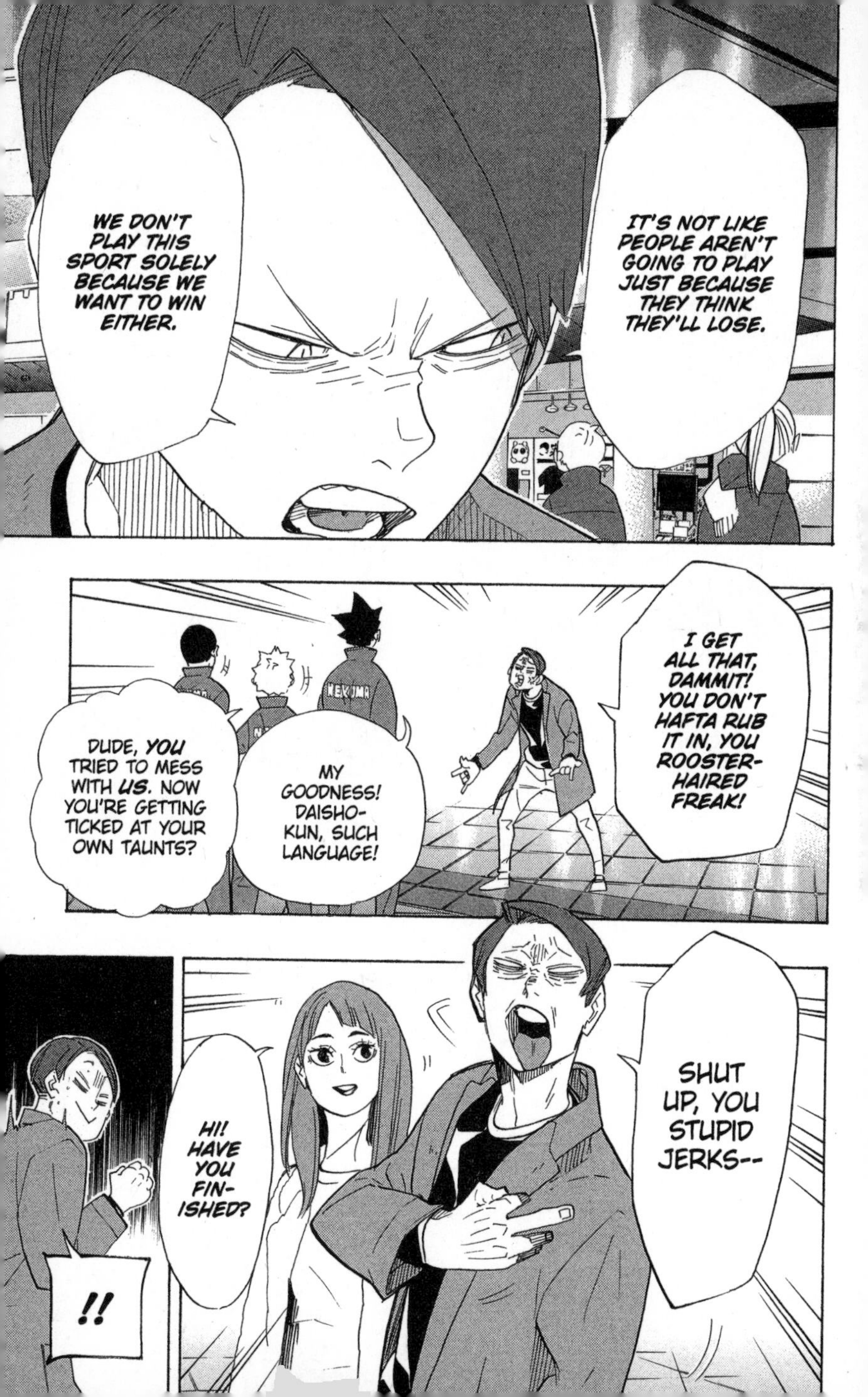
IT'S NOT LIKE PEOPLE AREN'T GOING TO PLAY JUST BECAUSE THEY THINK THEY'LL LOSE.
WE DON'T PLAY THIS SPORT SOLELY BECAUSE WE WANT TO WIN EITHER.
I GET ALL THAT, DAMMIT! YOU DON'T HAFTA RUB IT IN, YOU ROOSTER-HAIRED FREAK!
MY GOODNESS! DAISHO-KUN, SUCH LANGUAGE!
DUDE, *YOU* TRIED TO MESS WITH *US*. NOW YOU'RE GETTING TICKED AT YOUR OWN TAUNTS?
NEKOMA
SHUT UP, YOU STUPID JERKS--
HI! HAVE YOU FIN-ISHED?
!!

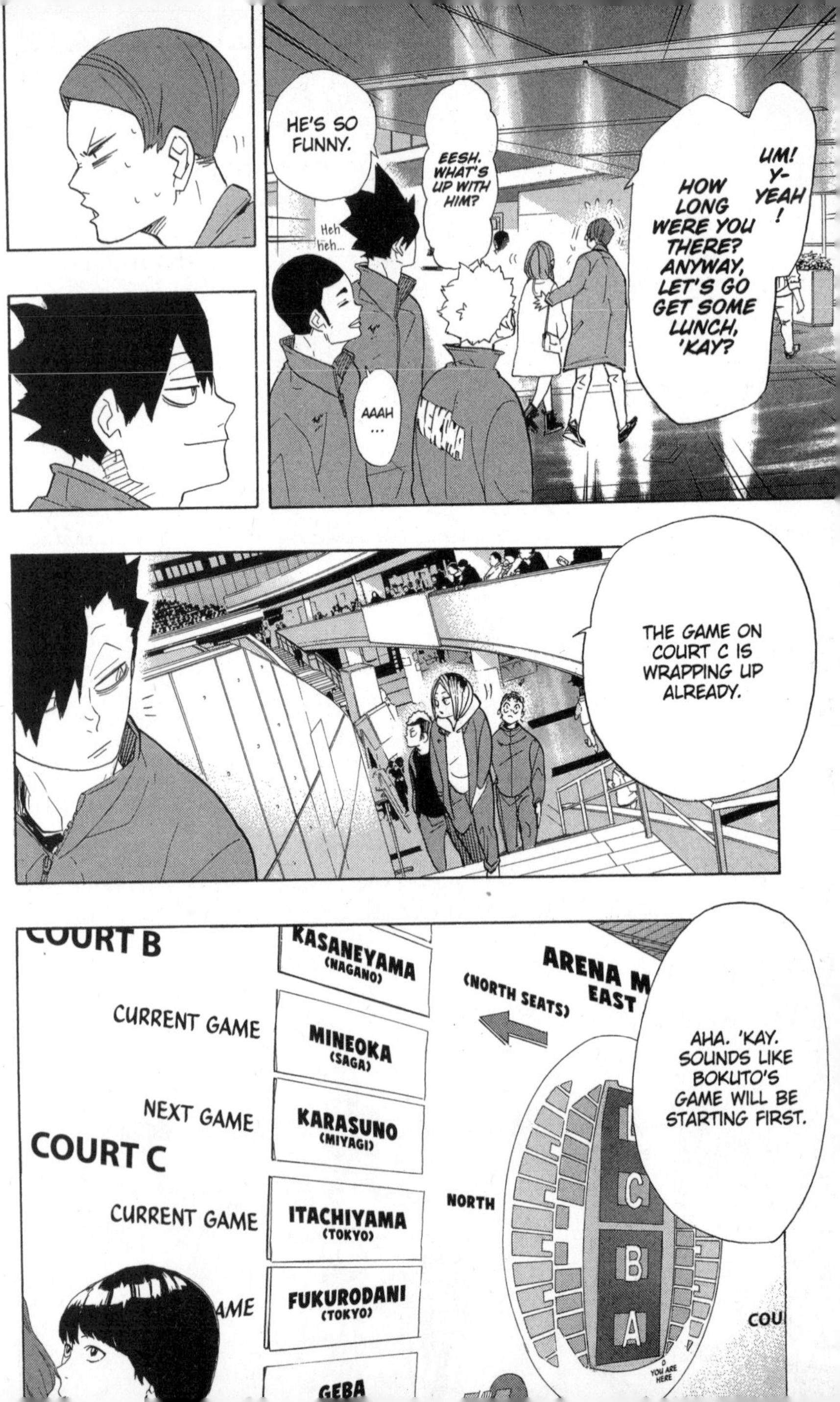
UM! Y-YEAH!
HOW LONG WERE YOU THERE? ANYWAY, LET'S GO GET SOME LUNCH, 'KAY?
EESH. WHAT'S UP WITH HIM?
HE'S SO FUNNY.
Heh heh...
AAAH...
THE GAME ON COURT C IS WRAPPING UP ALREADY.
AHA. 'KAY. SOUNDS LIKE BOKUTO'S GAME WILL BE STARTING FIRST.
ARENA M
EAST
(NORTH SEATS)
COURT B
KASANEYAMA (NAGANO)
CURRENT GAME
MINEOKA (SAGA)
NEXT GAME
KARASUNO (MIYAGI)
COURT C
CURRENT GAME
ITACHIYAMA (TOKYO)
AME
FUKURODANI (TOKYO)
GEBA
NORTH
C
B
A
YOU ARE HERE
COU

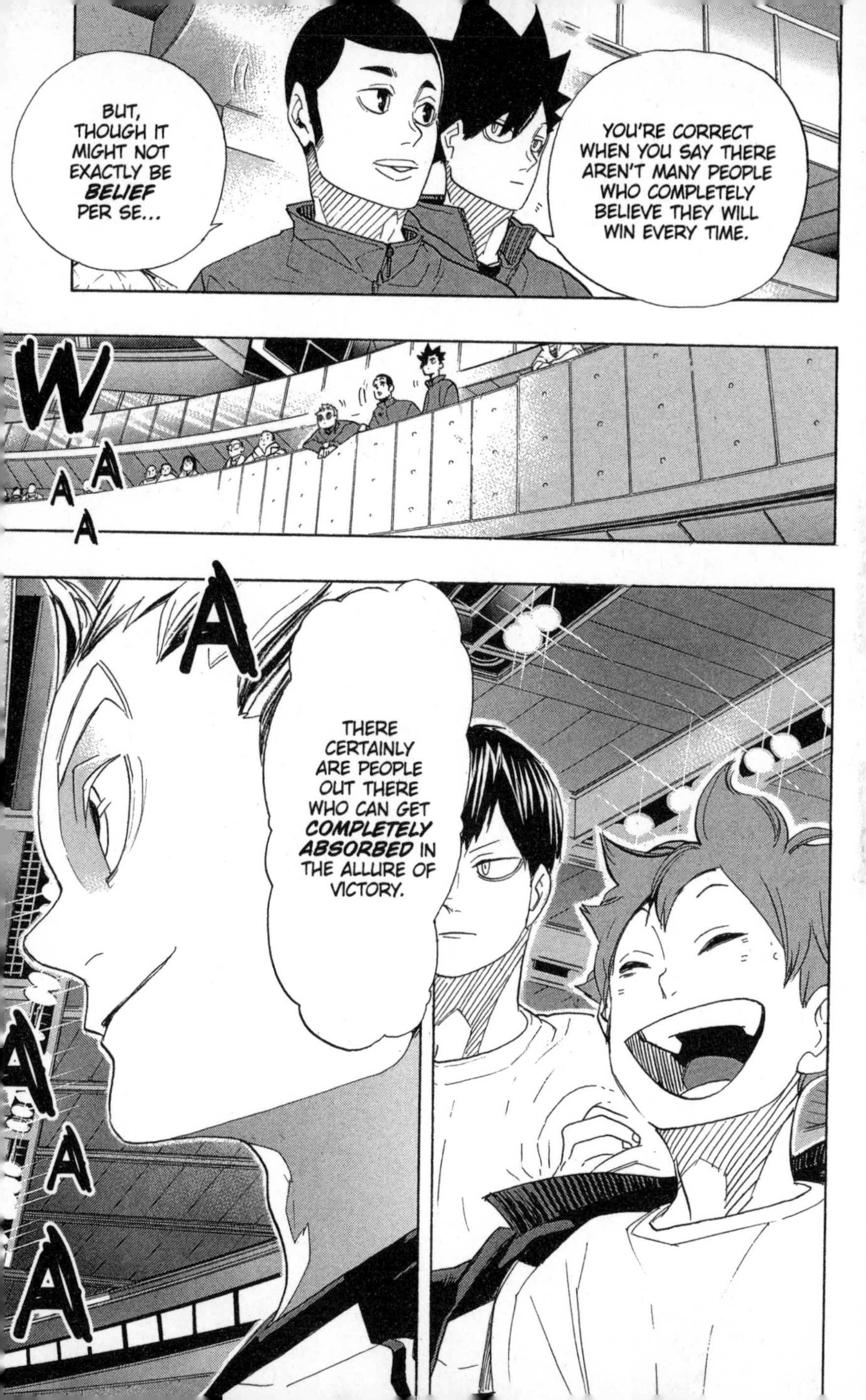
YOU'RE CORRECT WHEN YOU SAY THERE AREN'T MANY PEOPLE WHO COMPLETELY BELIEVE THEY WILL WIN EVERY TIME.
BUT, THOUGH IT MIGHT NOT EXACTLY BE BELIEF PER SE...
WAAA
A
THERE CERTAINLY ARE PEOPLE OUT THERE WHO CAN GET COMPLETELY ABSORBED IN THE ALLURE OF VICTORY.
AAAAA

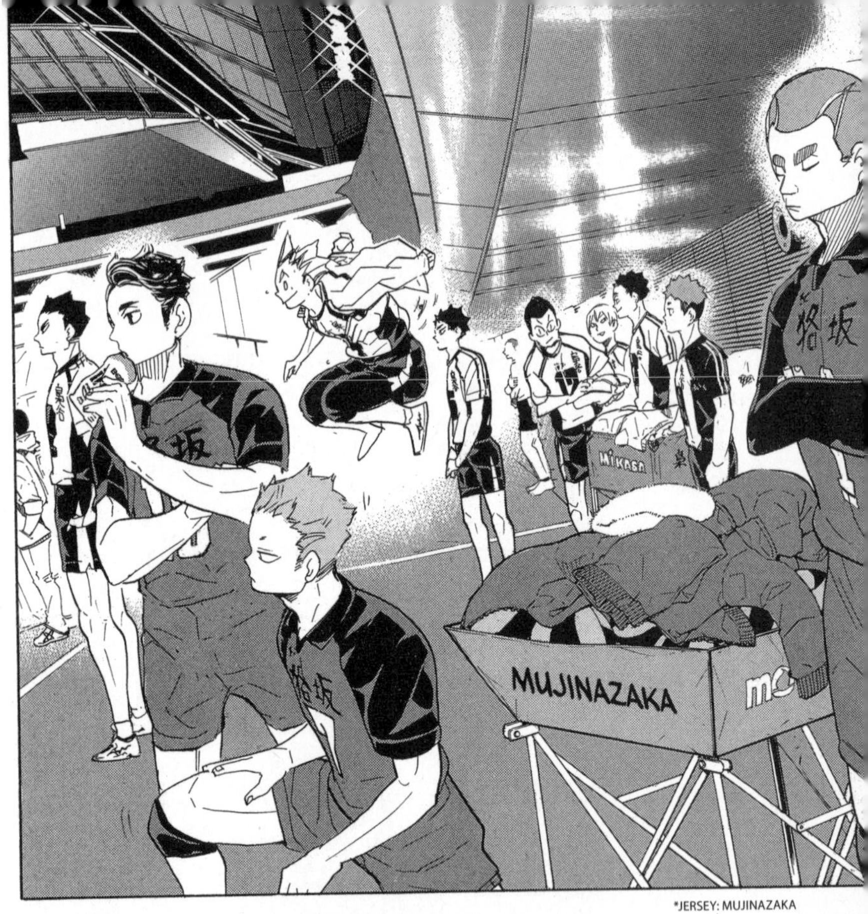
MUJINAZAKA

*JERSEY: MUJINAZAKA

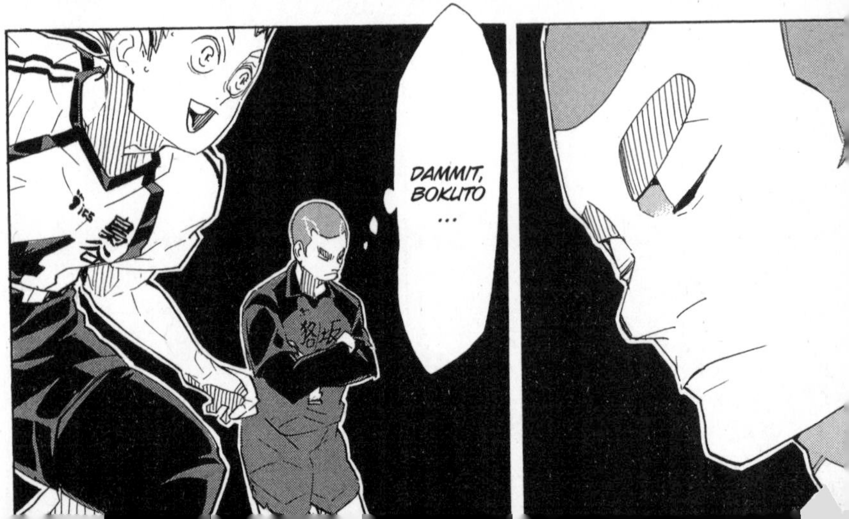
DAMMIT, BOKUTO ...

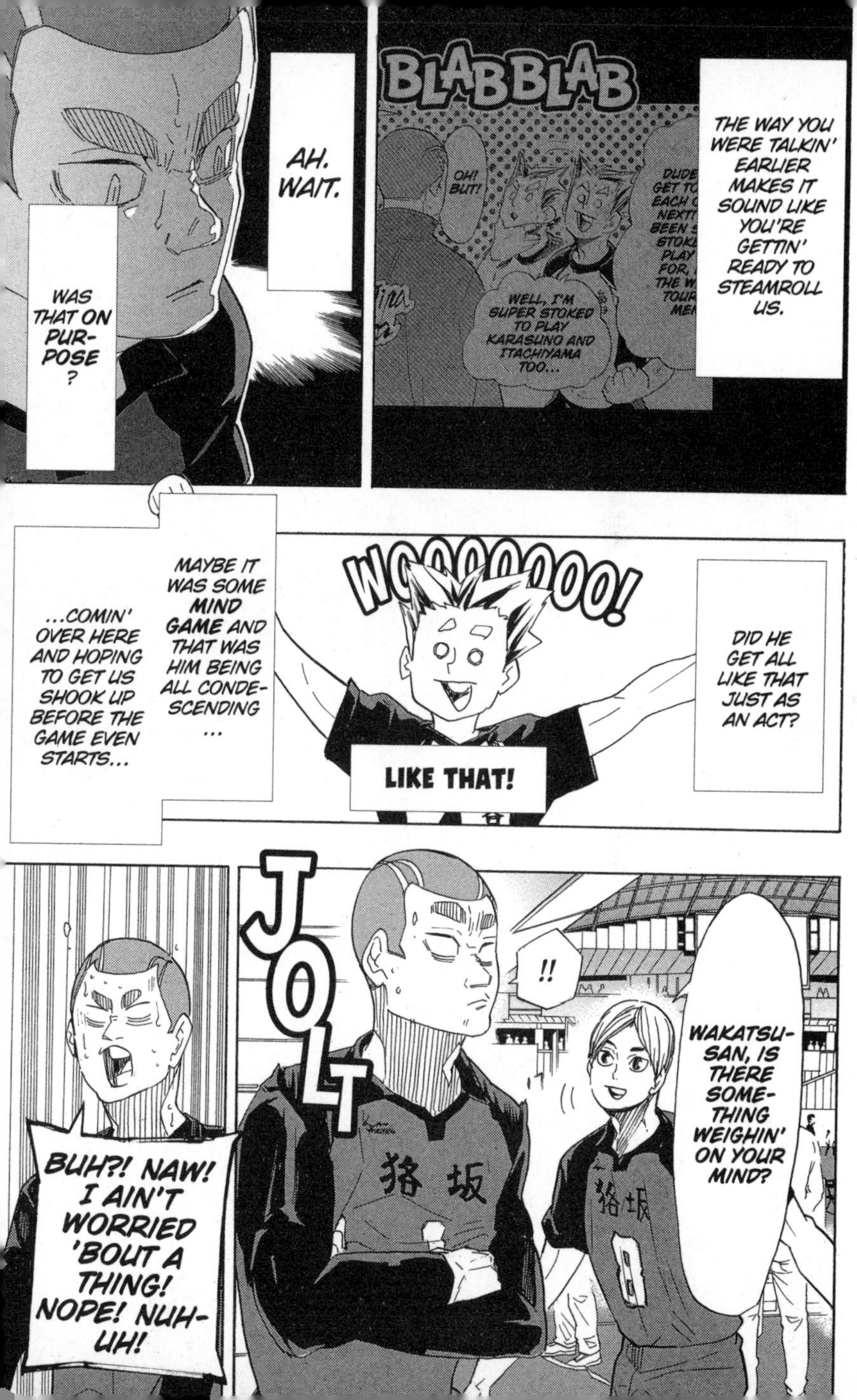
THE WAY YOU WERE TALKIN' EARLIER MAKES IT SOUND LIKE YOU'RE GETTIN' READY TO STEAMROLL US.
BLABBLAB
OH! BUT!
WELL, I'M SUPER STOKED TO PLAY KARASUNO AND ITACHIYAMA TOO...
AH. WAIT.
WAS THAT ON PURPOSE?
DID HE GET ALL LIKE THAT JUST AS AN ACT?
WOOOOOOOO!
LIKE THAT!
MAYBE IT WAS SOME MIND GAME AND THAT WAS HIM BEING ALL CONDESCENDING...
...COMIN' OVER HERE AND HOPING TO GET US SHOOK UP BEFORE THE GAME EVEN STARTS...
WAKATSU-SAN, IS THERE SOMETHING WEIGHIN' ON YOUR MIND?
!!
JOLT
BUH?! NAW! I AIN'T WORRIED 'BOUT A THING! NOPE! NUH-UH!

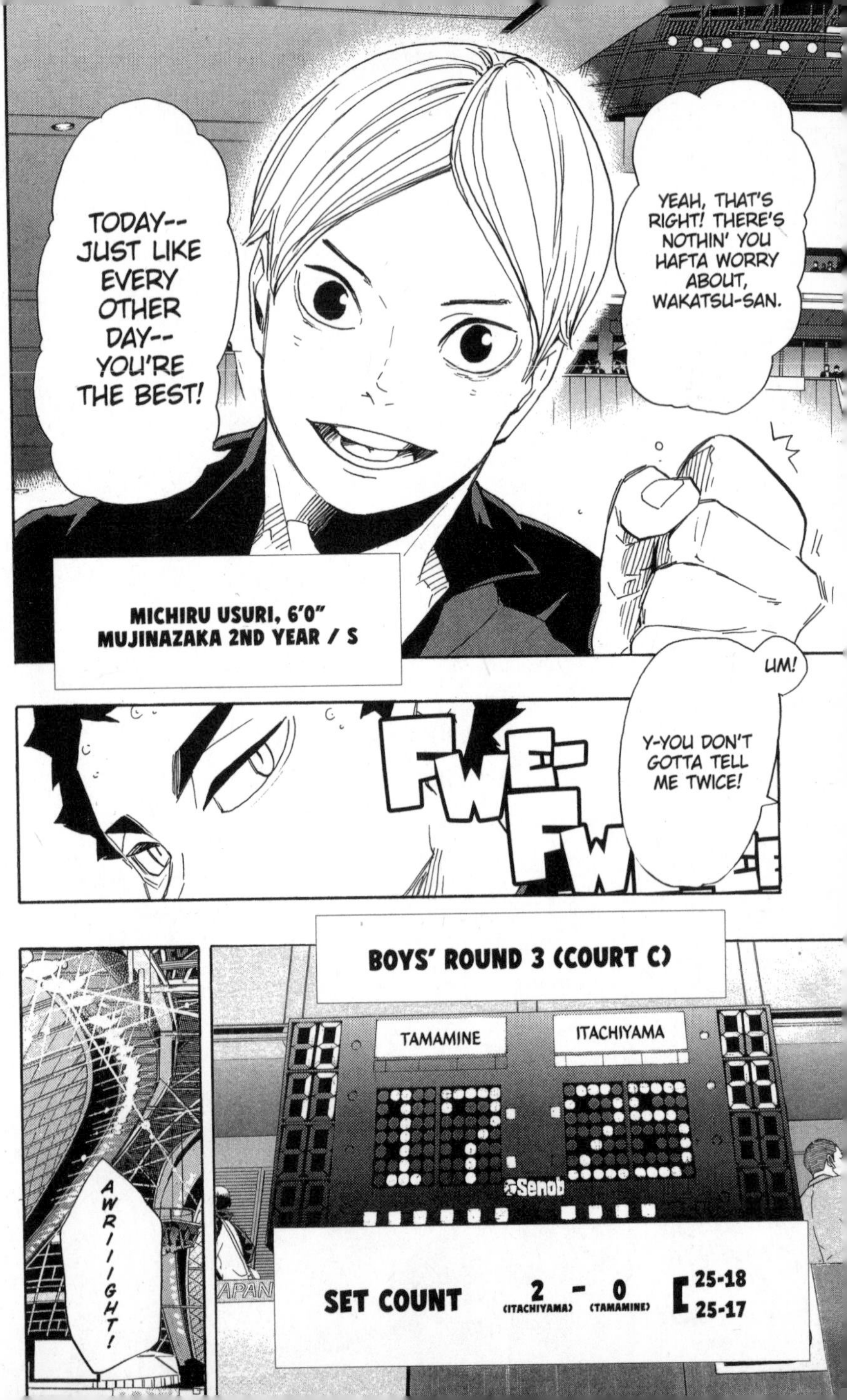
YEAH, THAT'S RIGHT! THERE'S NOTHIN' YOU HAFTA WORRY ABOUT, WAKATSU-SAN.
TODAY-- JUST LIKE EVERY OTHER DAY-- YOU'RE THE BEST!
MICHIRU USURI, 6'0"
MUJINAZAKA 2ND YEAR / S
UM!
Y-YOU DON'T GOTTA TELL ME TWICE!
FWE-
FW
BOYS' ROUND 3 (COURT C)
TAMAMINE
ITACHIYAMA
Senob
SET COUNT 2 (ITACHIYAMA) - 0 (TAMAMINE) [25-18 25-17
AWRIIIGHT!

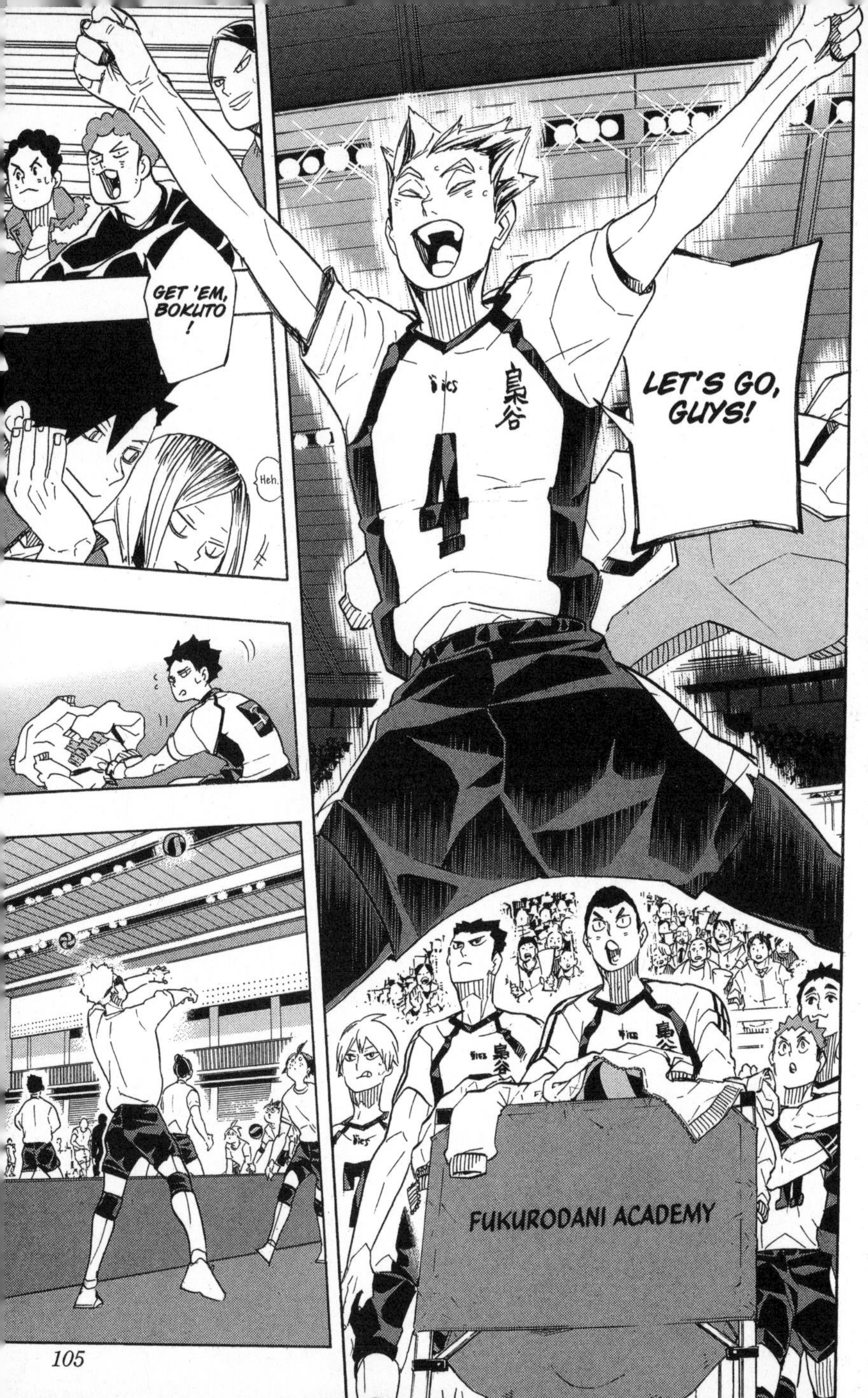
LET'S GO, GUYS!
FUKURODANI ACADEMY
GET 'EM, BOKUTO!
Heh.

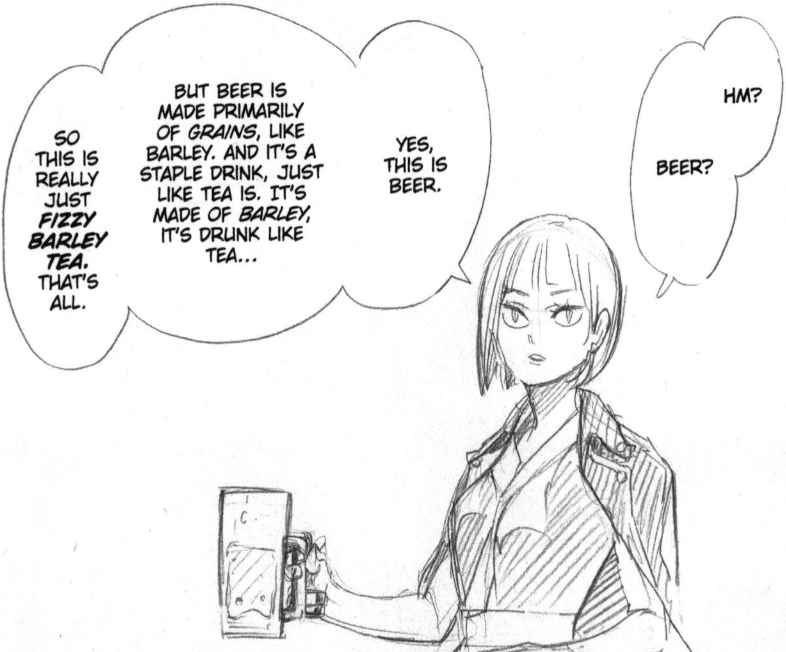
HM?
BEER?
YES, THIS IS BEER.
BUT BEER IS MADE PRIMARILY OF *GRAINS*, LIKE BARLEY. AND IT'S A STAPLE DRINK, JUST LIKE TEA IS. IT'S MADE OF *BARLEY*, IT'S DRUNK LIKE TEA...
SO THIS IS REALLY JUST **FIZZY BARLEY TEA.** THAT'S ALL.

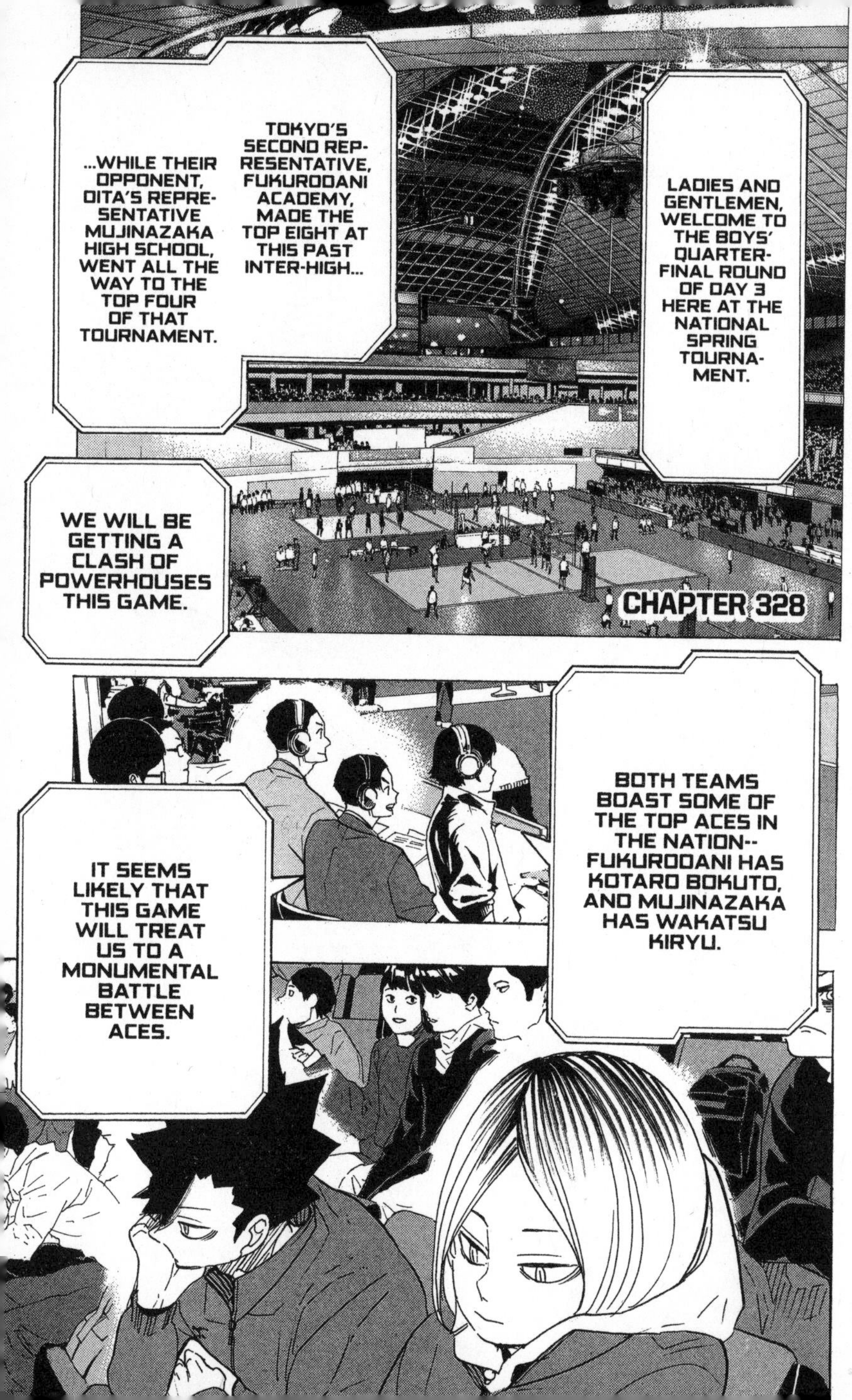
LADIES AND GENTLEMEN, WELCOME TO THE BOYS' QUARTER-FINAL ROUND OF DAY 3 HERE AT THE NATIONAL SPRING TOURNAMENT.
TOKYO'S SECOND REPRESENTATIVE, FUKURODANI ACADEMY, MADE THE TOP EIGHT AT THIS PAST INTER-HIGH...
...WHILE THEIR OPPONENT, OITA'S REPRESENTATIVE MUJINAZAKA HIGH SCHOOL, WENT ALL THE WAY TO THE TOP FOUR OF THAT TOURNAMENT.
WE WILL BE GETTING A CLASH OF POWERHOUSES THIS GAME.
CHAPTER 328
BOTH TEAMS BOAST SOME OF THE TOP ACES IN THE NATION-- FUKURODANI HAS KOTARO BOKUTO, AND MUJINAZAKA HAS WAKATSU KIRYU.
IT SEEMS LIKELY THAT THIS GAME WILL TREAT US TO A MONUMENTAL BATTLE BETWEEN ACES.

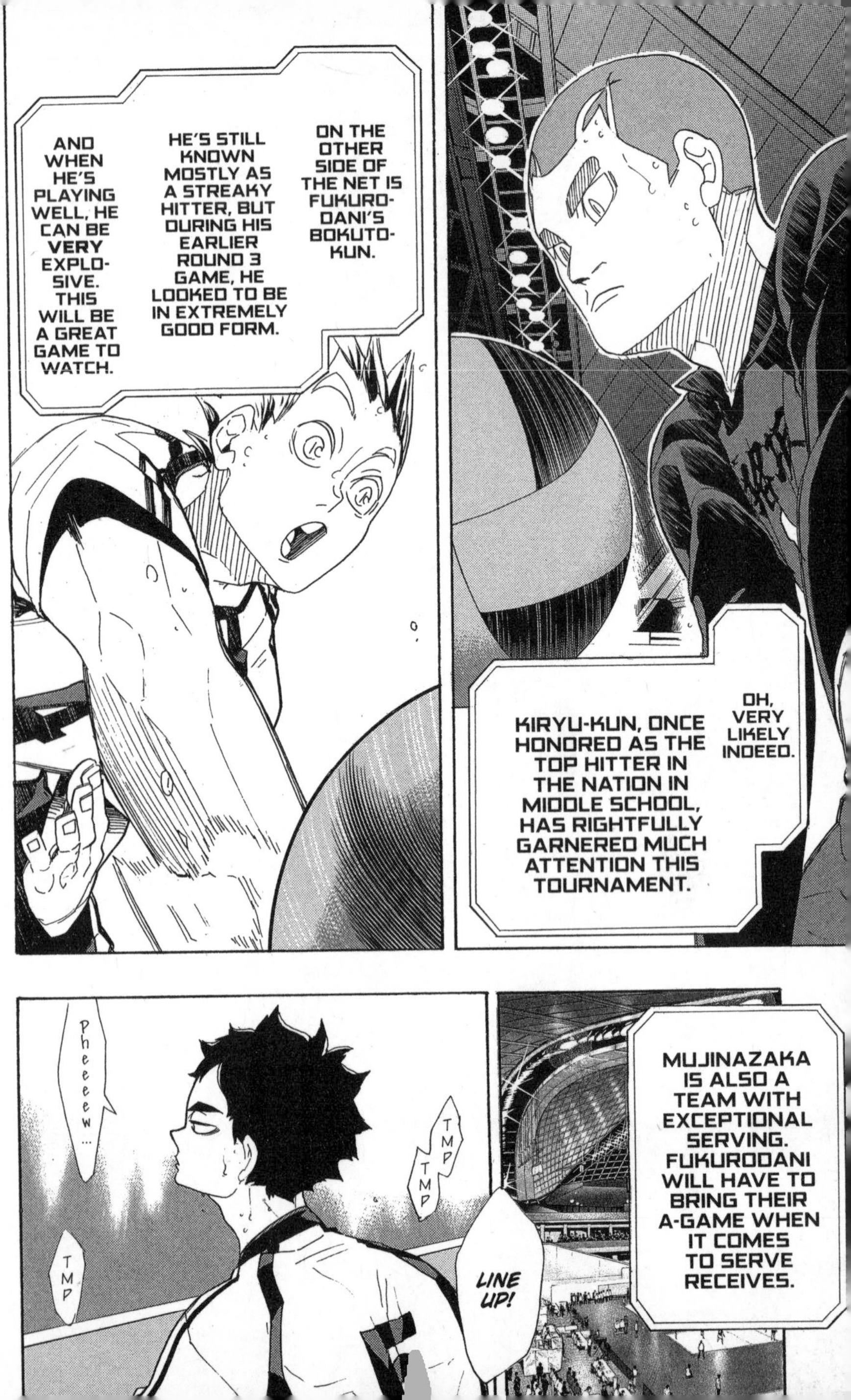
OH, VERY LIKELY INDEED.
KIRYU-KUN, ONCE HONORED AS THE TOP HITTER IN THE NATION IN MIDDLE SCHOOL, HAS RIGHTFULLY GARNERED MUCH ATTENTION THIS TOURNAMENT.
ON THE OTHER SIDE OF THE NET IS FUKURODANI'S BOKUTO-KUN.
HE'S STILL KNOWN MOSTLY AS A STREAKY HITTER, BUT DURING HIS EARLIER ROUND 3 GAME, HE LOOKED TO BE IN EXTREMELY GOOD FORM.
AND WHEN HE'S PLAYING WELL, HE CAN BE **VERY** EXPLOSIVE. THIS WILL BE A GREAT GAME TO WATCH.
MUJINAZAKA IS ALSO A TEAM WITH EXCEPTIONAL SERVING. FUKURODANI WILL HAVE TO BRING THEIR A-GAME WHEN IT COMES TO SERVE RECEIVES.
LINE UP!
TMP TMP
Pheeeew...
TMP

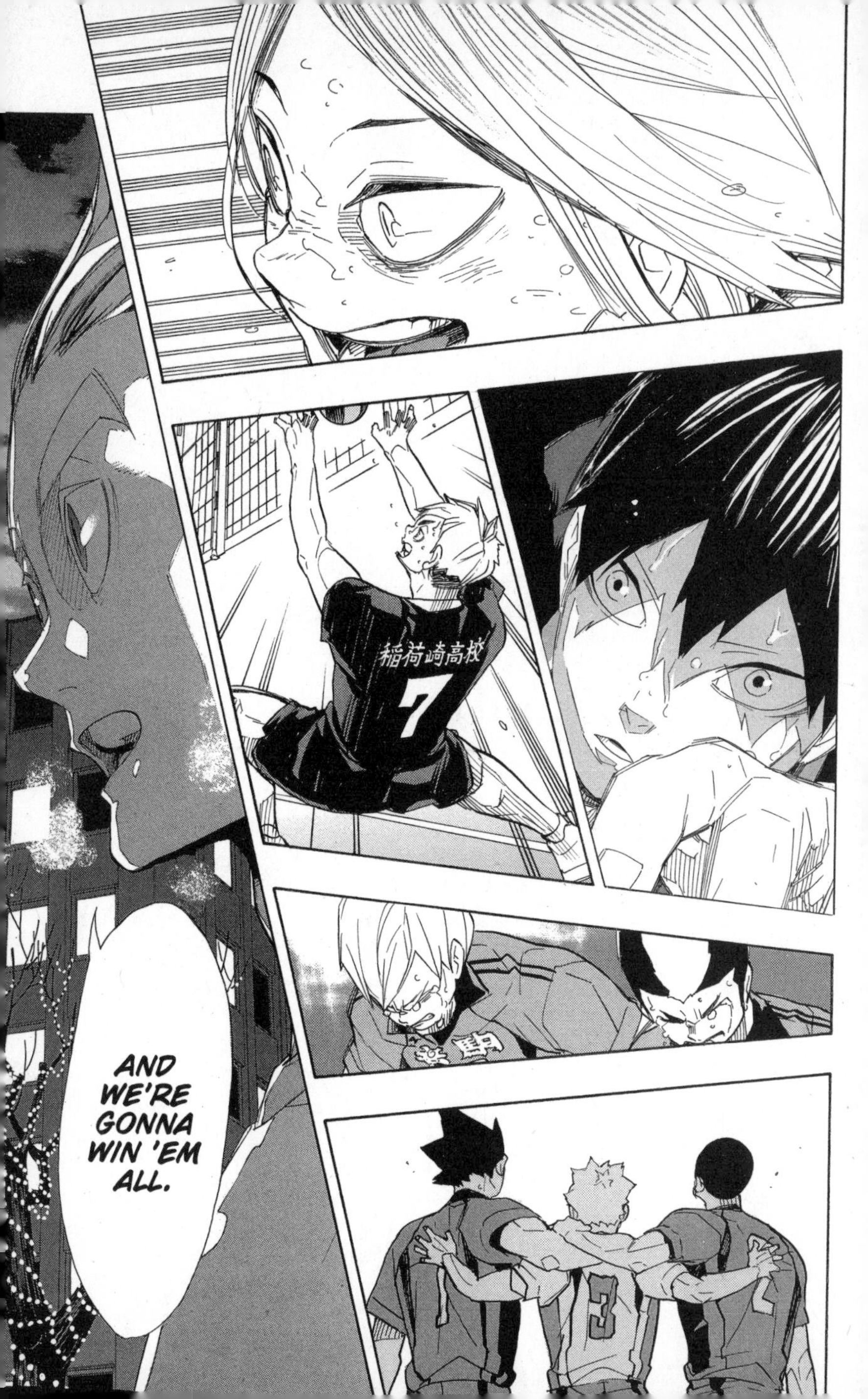
稲荷崎高校
7
AND WE'RE GONNA WIN 'EM ALL.
3

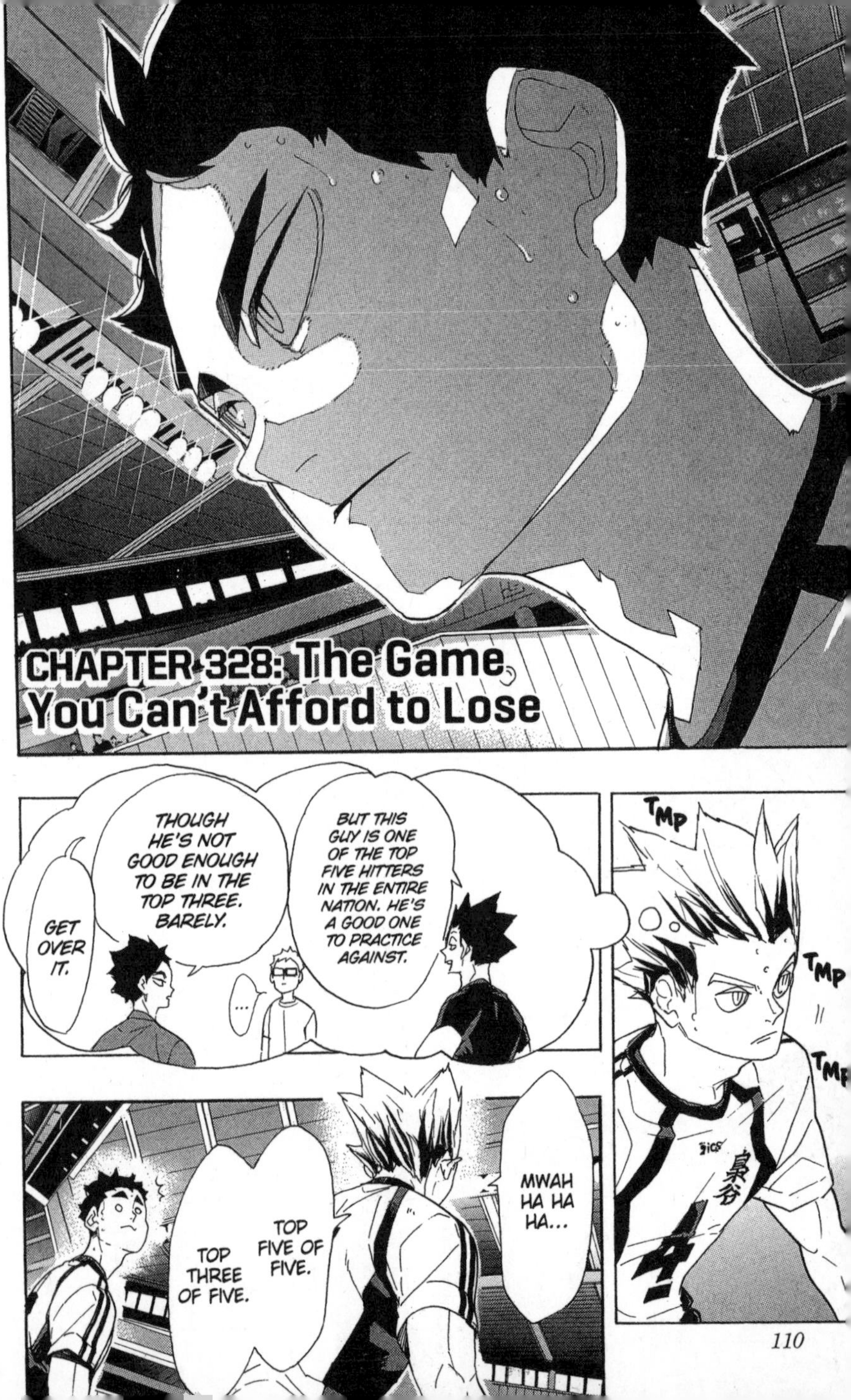
CHAPTER 328: The Game You Can't Afford to Lose
TMP
TMP
TMP
BUT THIS GUY IS ONE OF THE TOP FIVE HITTERS IN THE ENTIRE NATION. HE'S A GOOD ONE TO PRACTICE AGAINST.
THOUGH HE'S NOT GOOD ENOUGH TO BE IN THE TOP THREE. BARELY.
...
GET OVER IT.
MWAH HA HA HA...
TOP FIVE OF FIVE.
TOP THREE OF FIVE.

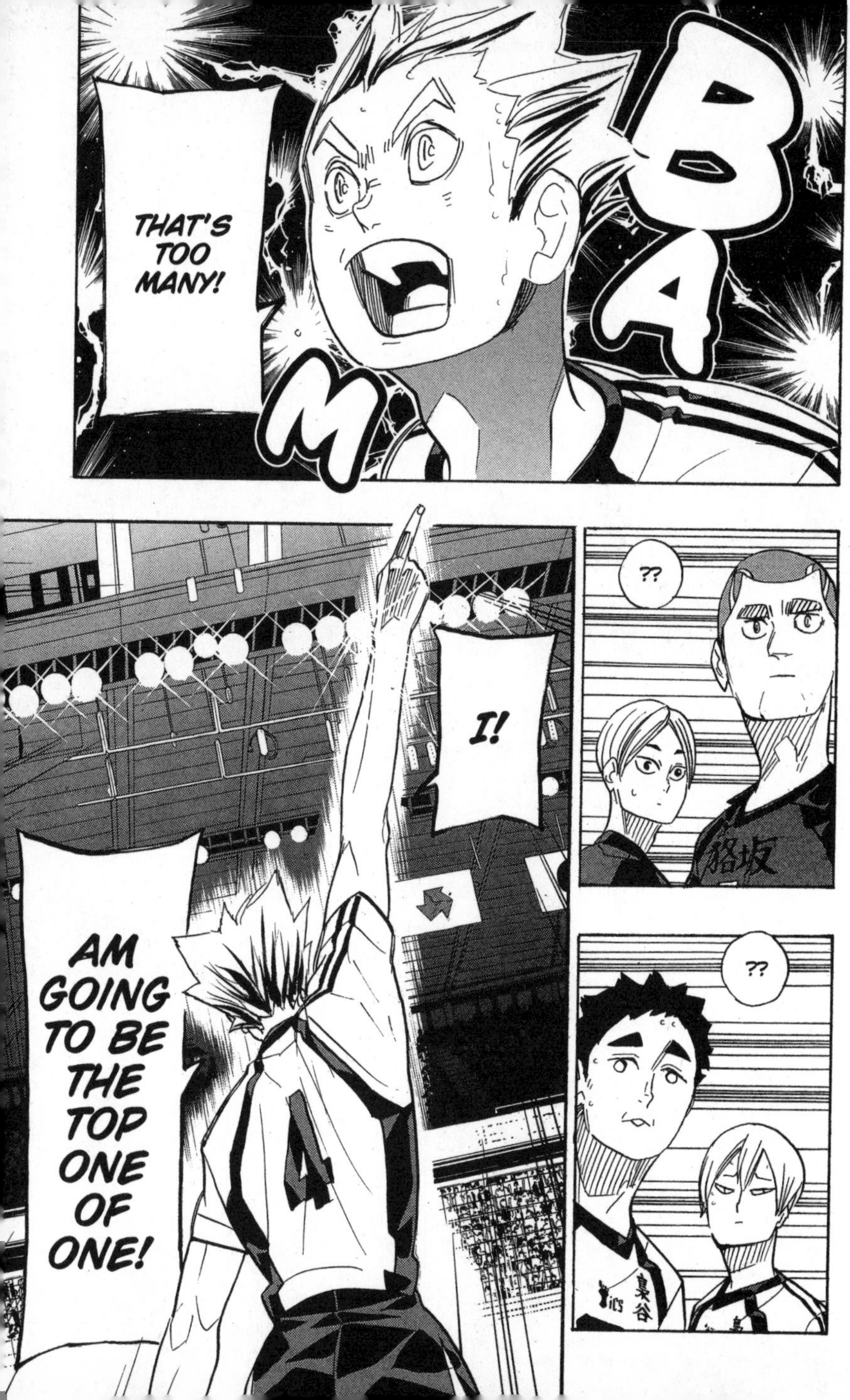
BAM
THAT'S TOO MANY!
??
??
I!
AM GOING TO BE THE TOP ONE OF ONE!

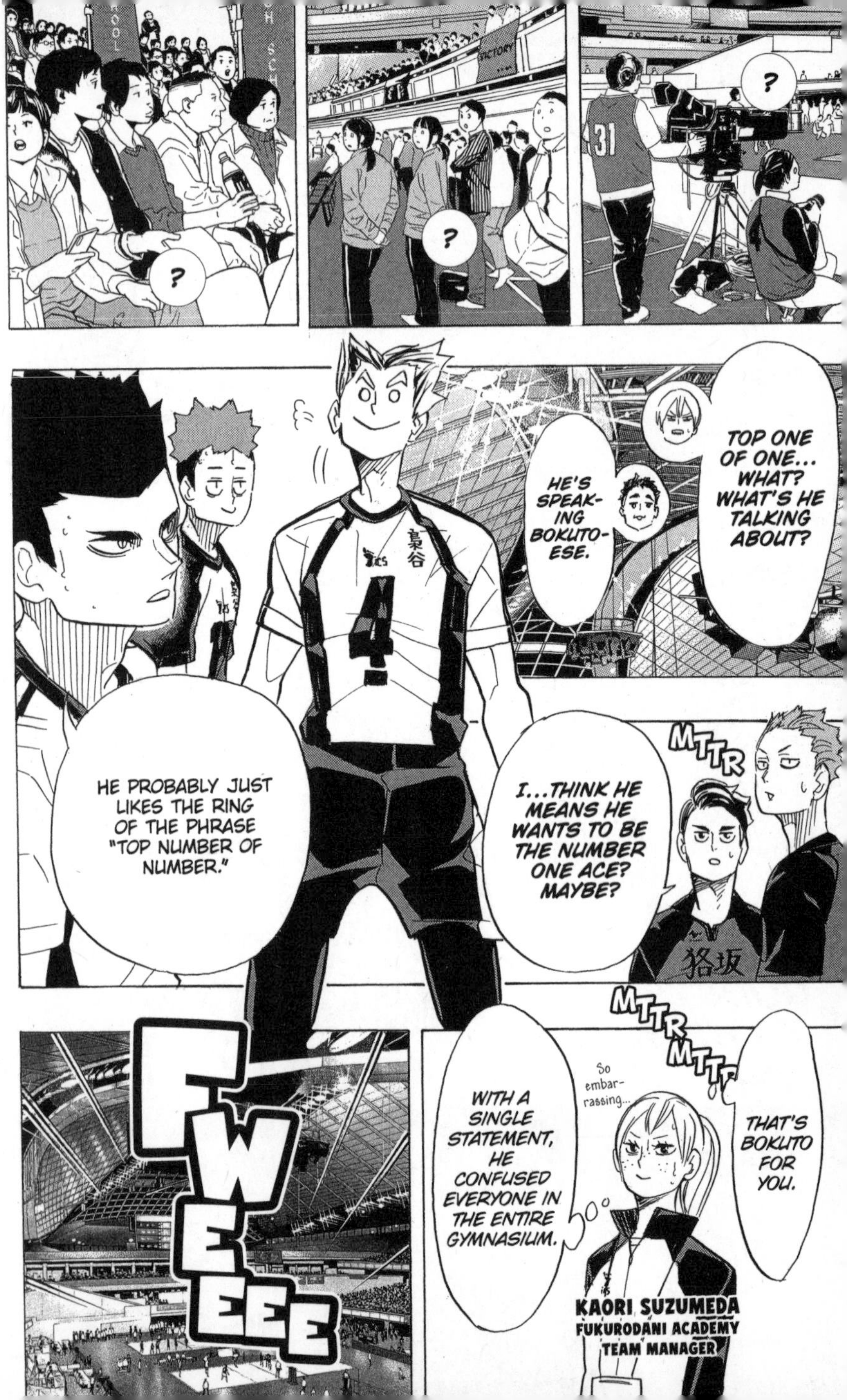
?
?
?
TOP ONE OF ONE... WHAT? WHAT'S HE TALKING ABOUT?
HE'S SPEAK-ING BOKUTO-ESE.
MTTR
I...THINK HE MEANS HE WANTS TO BE THE NUMBER ONE ACE? MAYBE?
HE PROBABLY JUST LIKES THE RING OF THE PHRASE "TOP NUMBER OF NUMBER."
MTTR MTTR
THAT'S BOKUTO FOR YOU.
So embar-rassing...
WITH A SINGLE STATEMENT, HE CONFUSED EVERYONE IN THE ENTIRE GYMNASIUM.
KAORI SUZUMEDA
FUKURODANI ACADEMY
TEAM MANAGER
FWEEEE

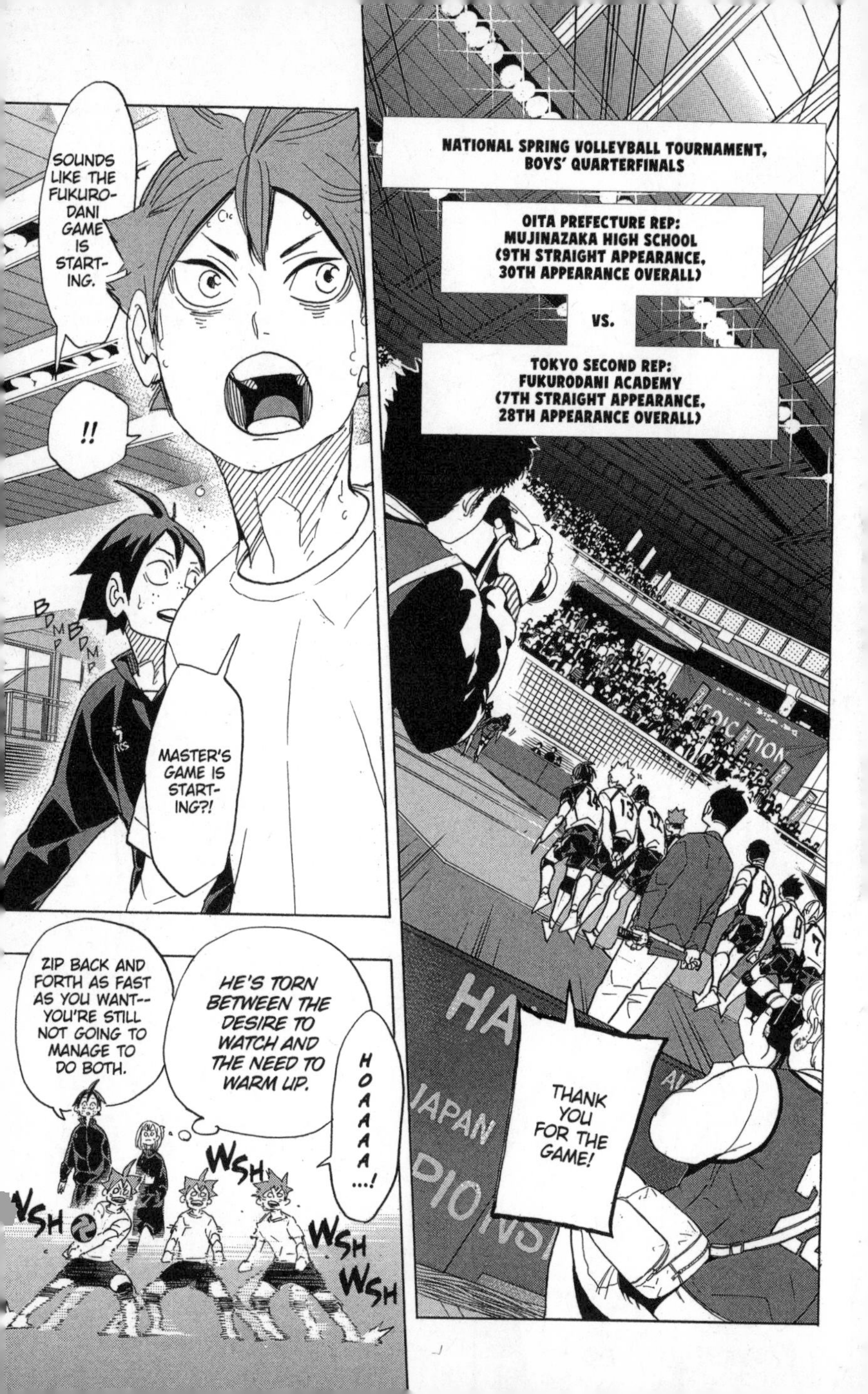
NATIONAL SPRING VOLLEYBALL TOURNAMENT, BOYS' QUARTERFINALS
OITA PREFECTURE REP: MUJINAZAKA HIGH SCHOOL (9TH STRAIGHT APPEARANCE, 30TH APPEARANCE OVERALL)
VS.
TOKYO SECOND REP: FUKURODANI ACADEMY (7TH STRAIGHT APPEARANCE, 28TH APPEARANCE OVERALL)
THANK YOU FOR THE GAME!
SOUNDS LIKE THE FUKURODANI GAME IS STARTING.
!!
BDMP BDMP
MASTER'S GAME IS STARTING?!
HOAAAAA...!
HE'S TORN BETWEEN THE DESIRE TO WATCH AND THE NEED TO WARM UP.
ZIP BACK AND FORTH AS FAST AS YOU WANT--YOU'RE STILL NOT GOING TO MANAGE TO DO BOTH.
WSH
WSH
WSH
WSH

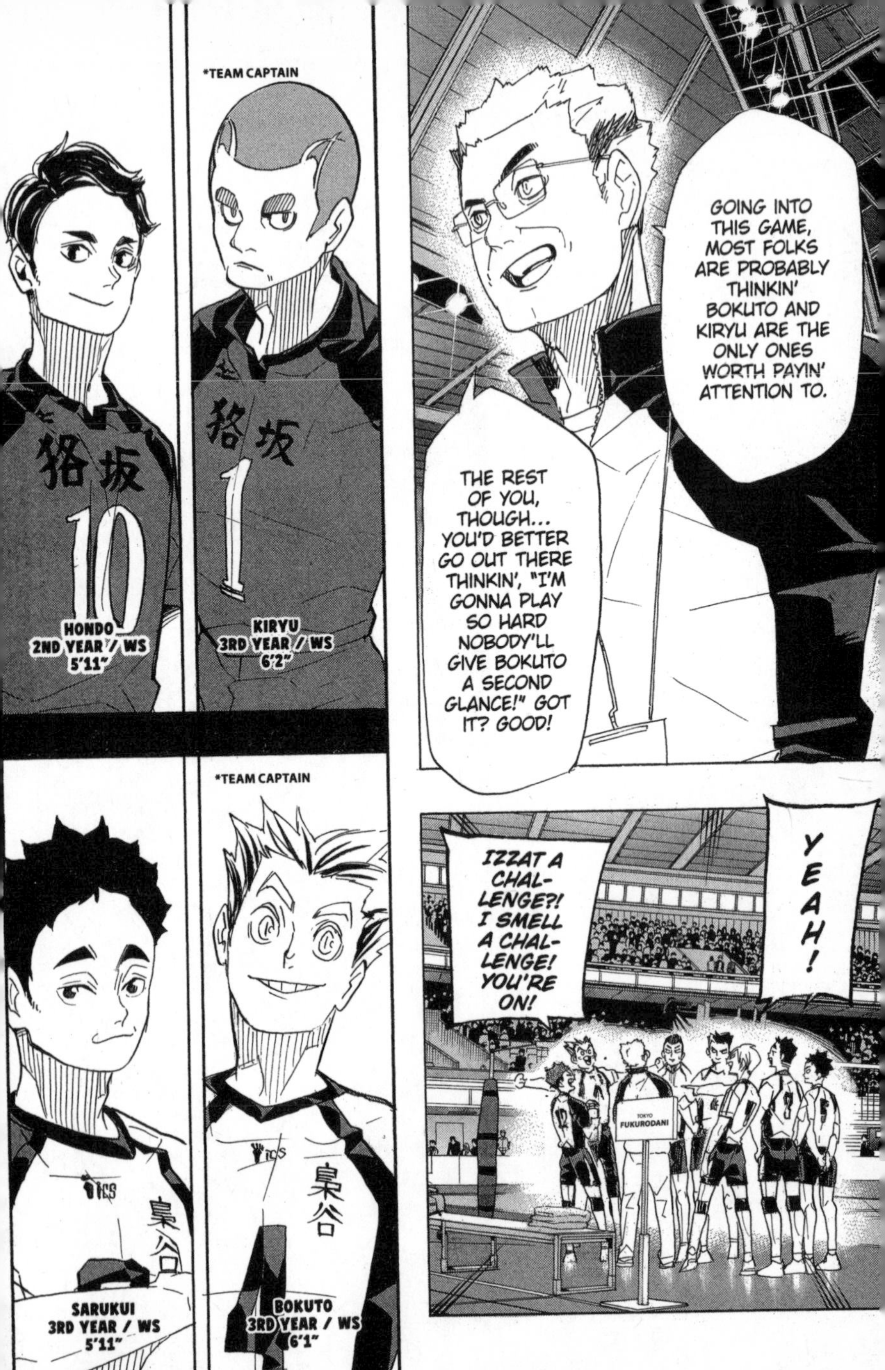
GOING INTO THIS GAME, MOST FOLKS ARE PROBABLY THINKIN' BOKUTO AND KIRYU ARE THE ONLY ONES WORTH PAYIN' ATTENTION TO.
THE REST OF YOU, THOUGH... YOU'D BETTER GO OUT THERE THINKIN', "I'M GONNA PLAY SO HARD NOBODY'LL GIVE BOKUTO A SECOND GLANCE!" GOT IT? GOOD!
*TEAM CAPTAIN
KIRYU
3RD YEAR / WS
6'2"
HONDO
2ND YEAR / WS
5'11"
YEAH!
IZZAT A CHAL-LENGE?! I SMELL A CHAL-LENGE! YOU'RE ON!
TOKYO
FUKURODANI
*TEAM CAPTAIN
BOKUTO
3RD YEAR / WS
6'1"
SARUKUI
3RD YEAR / WS
5'11"

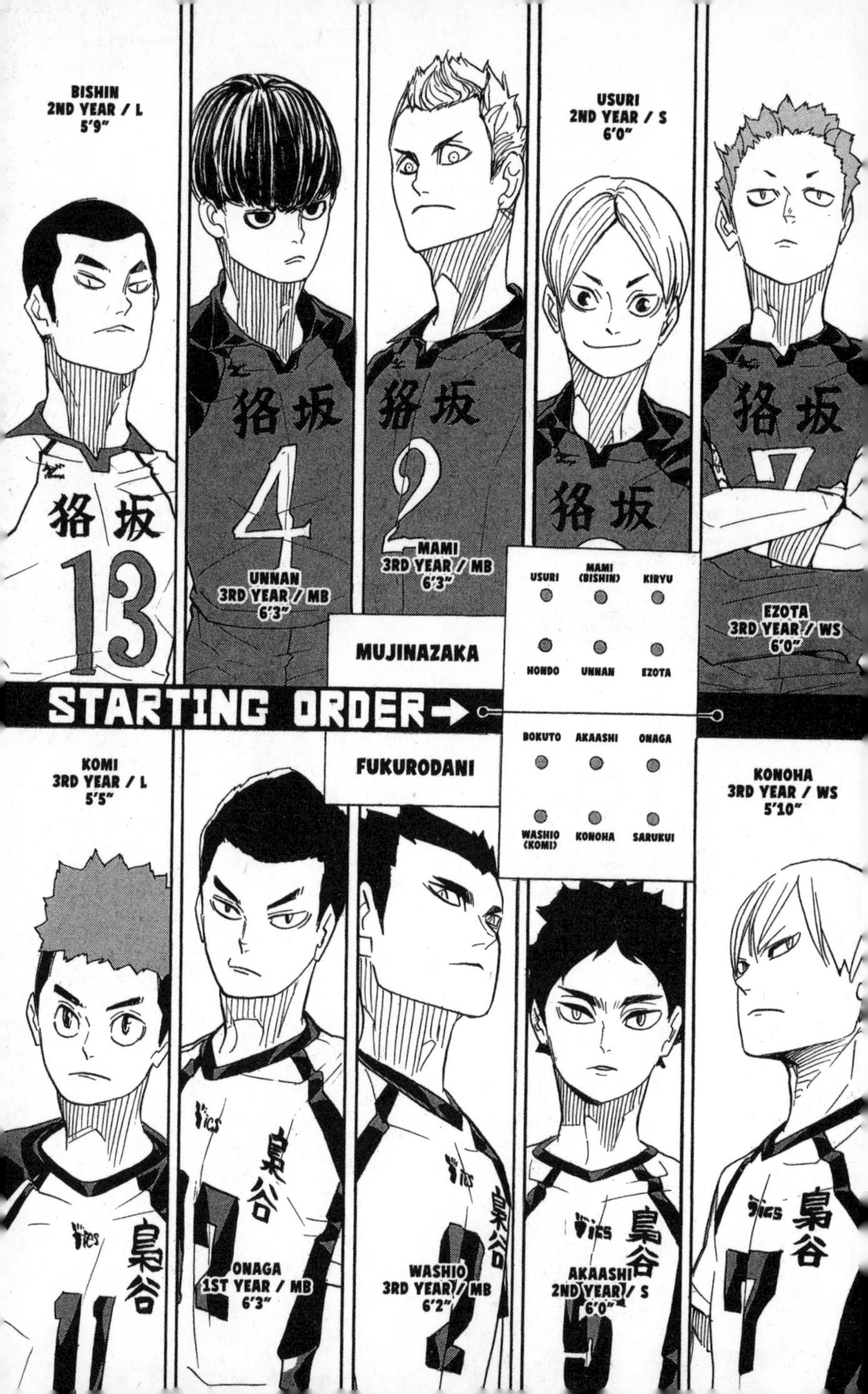
EZOTA
3RD YEAR / WS
6'0"
USURI
2ND YEAR / S
6'0"
MAMI
3RD YEAR / MB
6'3"
UNNAN
3RD YEAR / MB
6'3"
BISHIN
2ND YEAR / L
5'9"
STARTING ORDER→
MUJINAZAKA
USURI
MAMI
(BISHIN)
KIRYU
HONDO
UNNAN
EZOTA
FUKURODANI
BOKUTO
AKAASHI
ONAGA
WASHIO
(KOMI)
KONOHA
SARUKUI
KONOHA
3RD YEAR / WS
5'10"
AKAASHI
2ND YEAR / S
6'0"
WASHIO
3RD YEAR / MB
6'2"
ONAGA
1ST YEAR / MB
6'3"
KOMI
3RD YEAR / L
5'5"

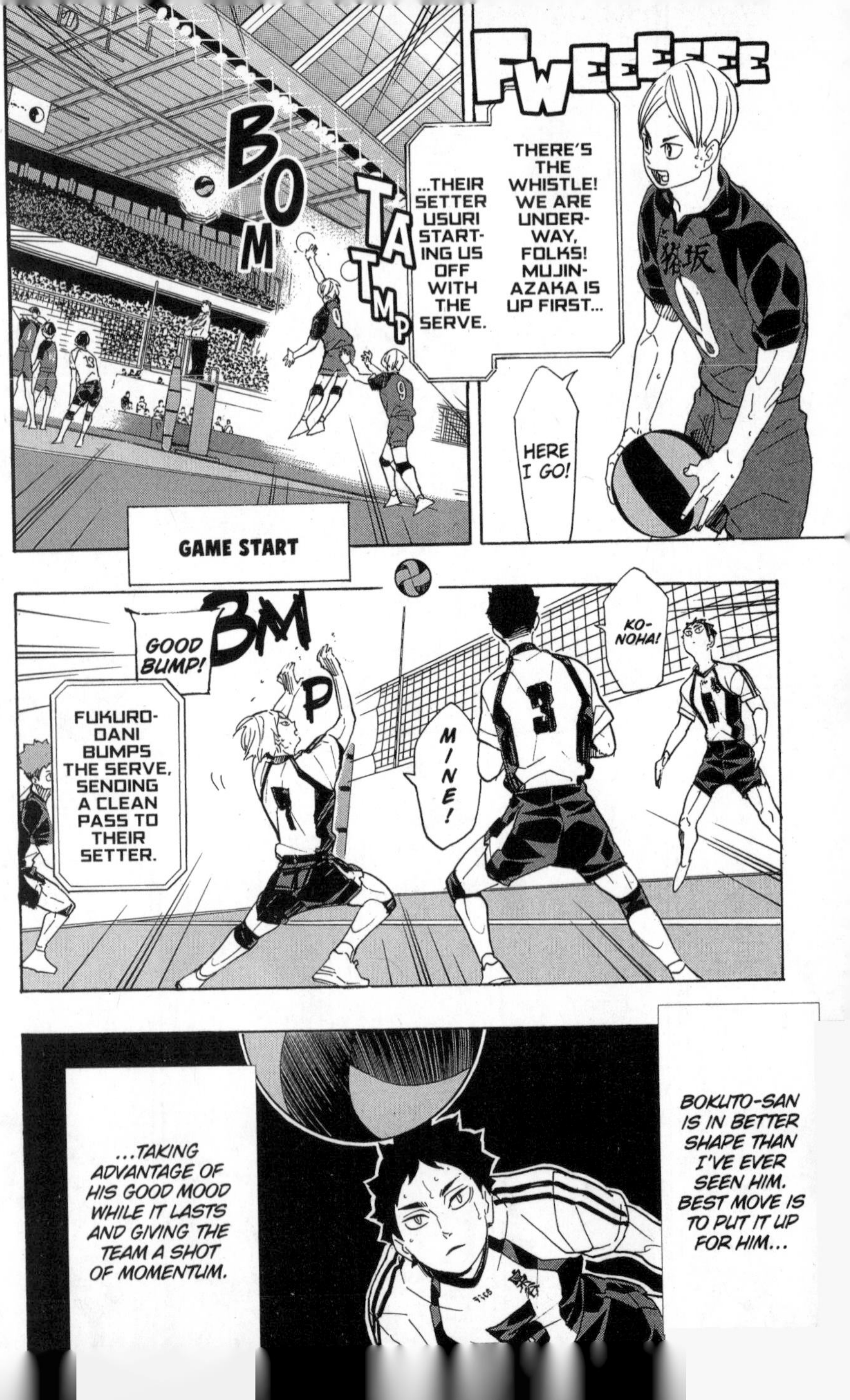
FWEEEEEE
THERE'S THE WHISTLE! WE ARE UNDERWAY, FOLKS! MUJINAZAKA IS UP FIRST...
...THEIR SETTER USURI STARTING US OFF WITH THE SERVE.
HERE I GO!
BOM
TA TMP
GAME START
KO-NOHA!
MINE!
BMP
GOOD BUMP!
FUKURODANI BUMPS THE SERVE, SENDING A CLEAN PASS TO THEIR SETTER.
BOKUTO-SAN IS IN BETTER SHAPE THAN I'VE EVER SEEN HIM. BEST MOVE IS TO PUT IT UP FOR HIM...
...TAKING ADVANTAGE OF HIS GOOD MOOD WHILE IT LASTS AND GIVING THE TEAM A SHOT OF MOMENTUM.

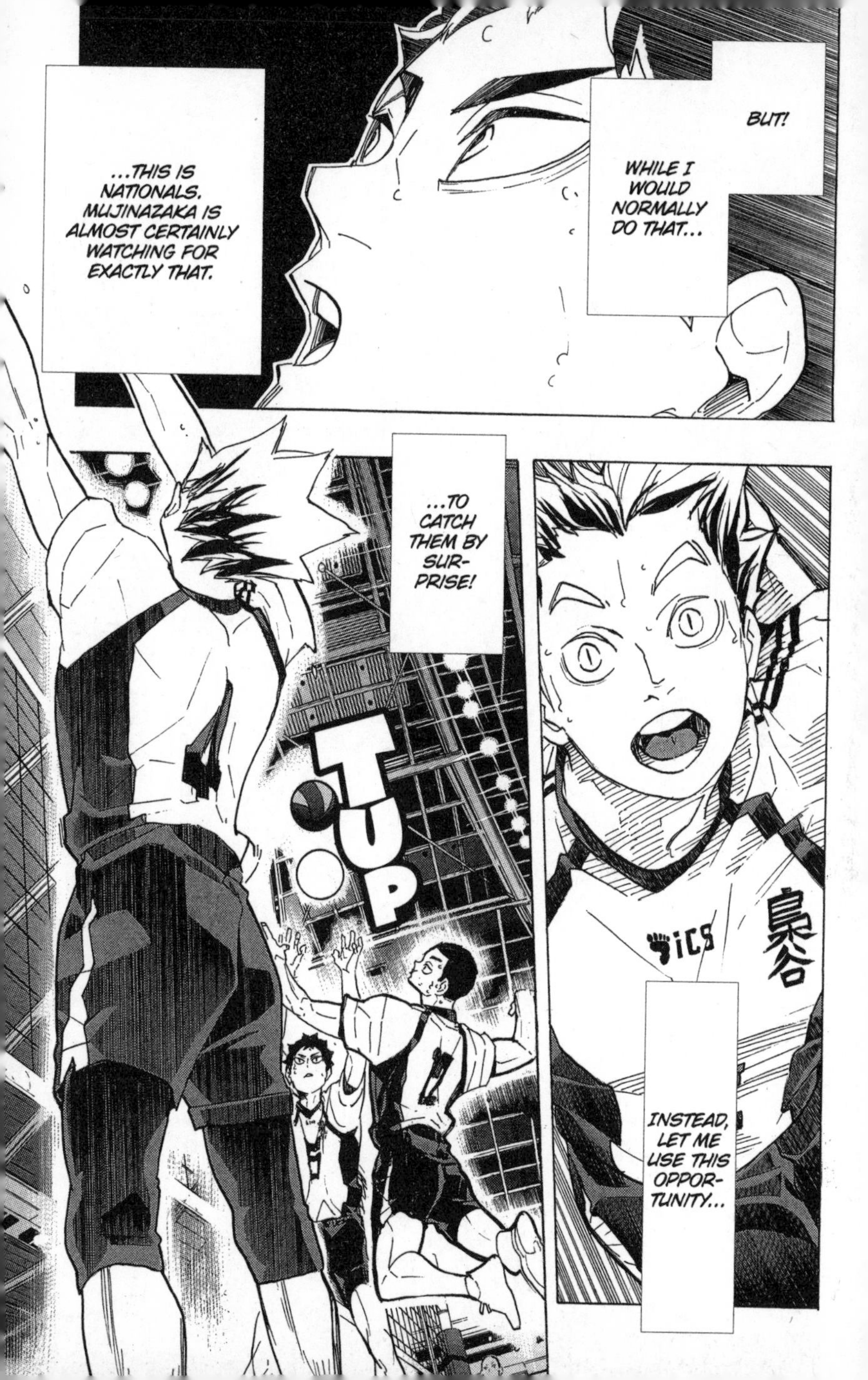
BUT!
WHILE I WOULD NORMALLY DO THAT...
...THIS IS NATIONALS. MUJINAZAKA IS ALMOST CERTAINLY WATCHING FOR EXACTLY THAT.
INSTEAD, LET ME USE THIS OPPORTUNITY...
...TO CATCH THEM BY SURPRISE!
TUP

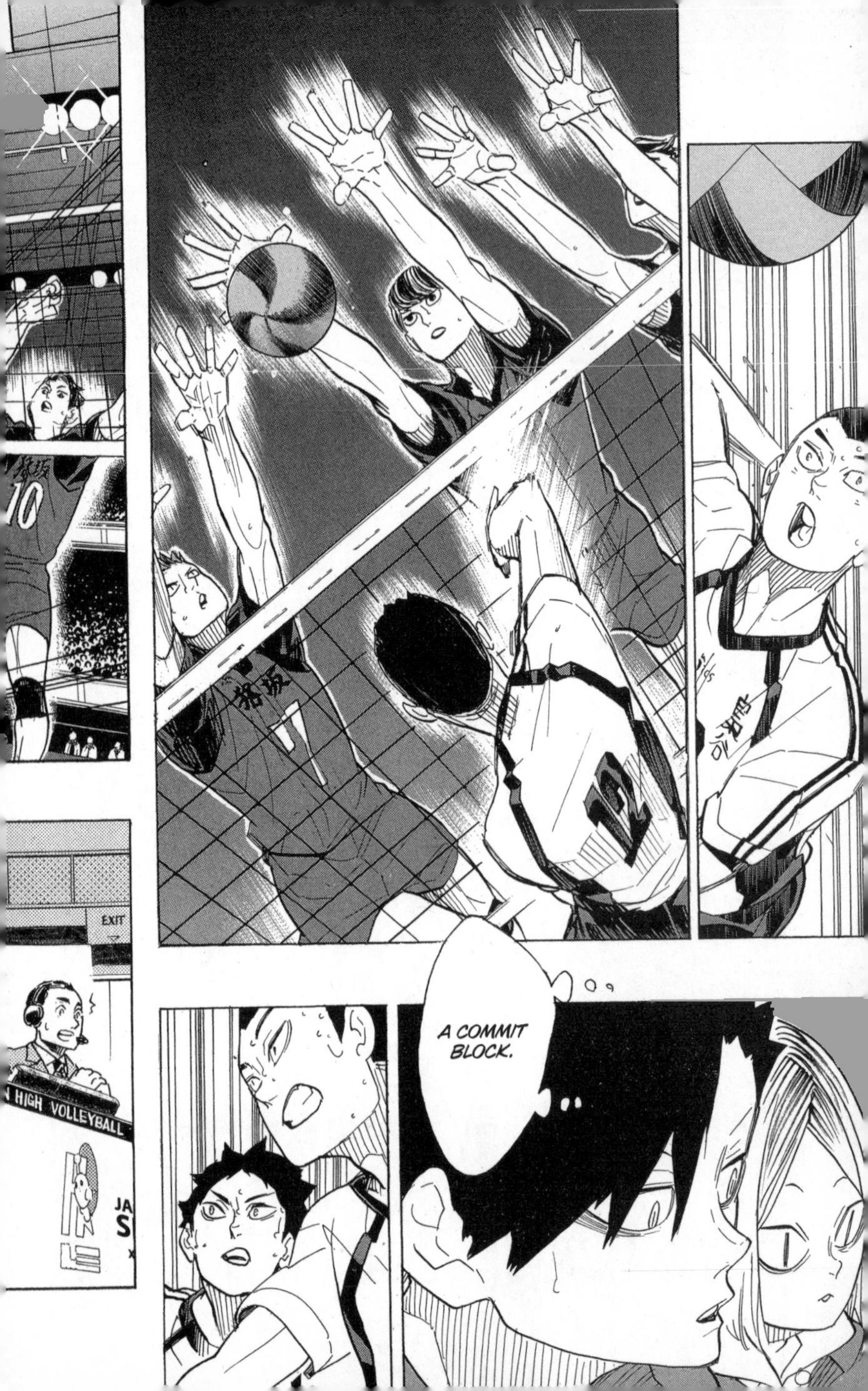
A COMMIT BLOCK.
EXIT
HIGH VOLLEYBALL

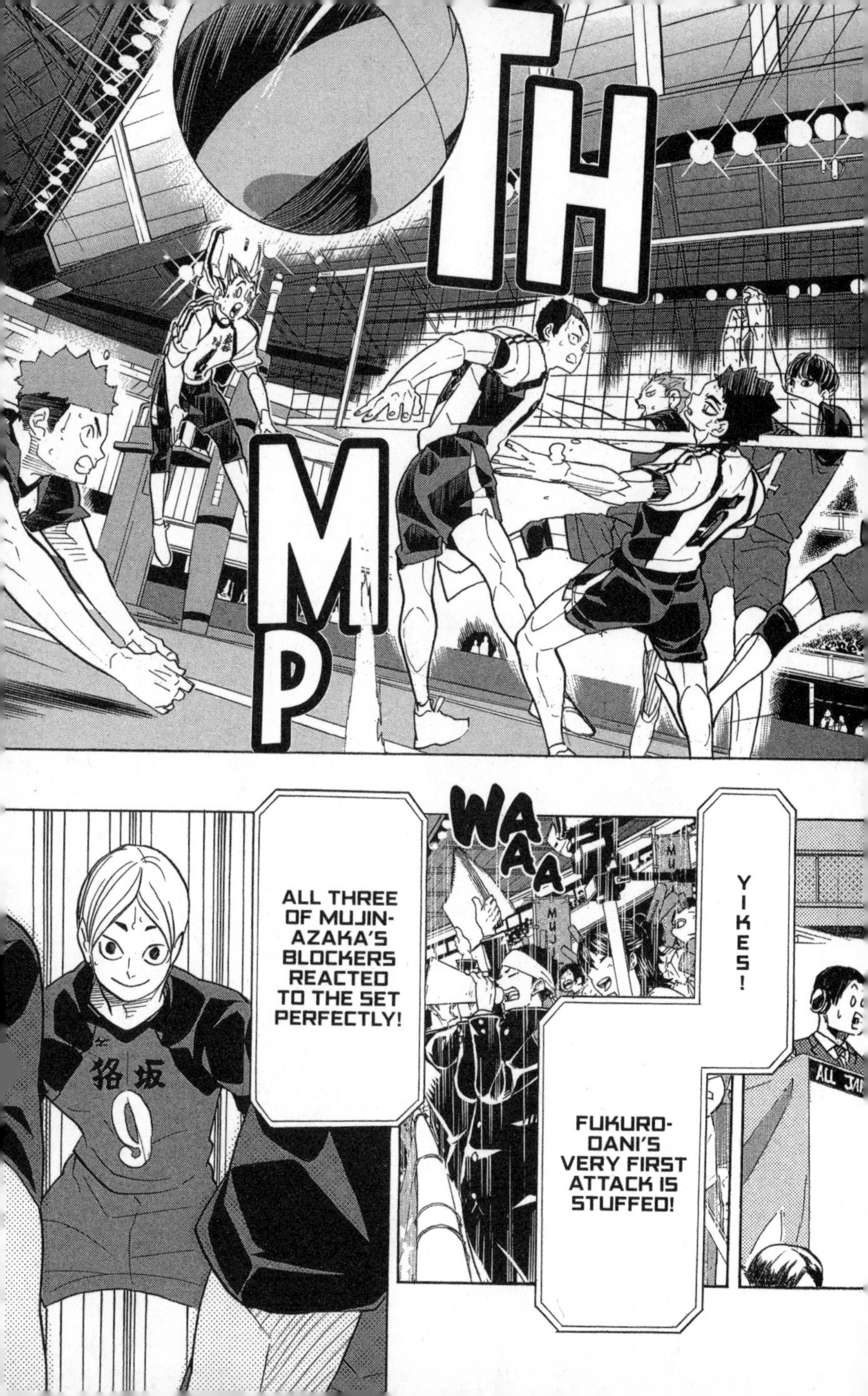
THMP
YIKES!
FUKURO-DANI'S VERY FIRST ATTACK IS STUFFED!
WAAA
ALL THREE OF MUJIN-AZAKA'S BLOCKERS REACTED TO THE SET PERFECTLY!

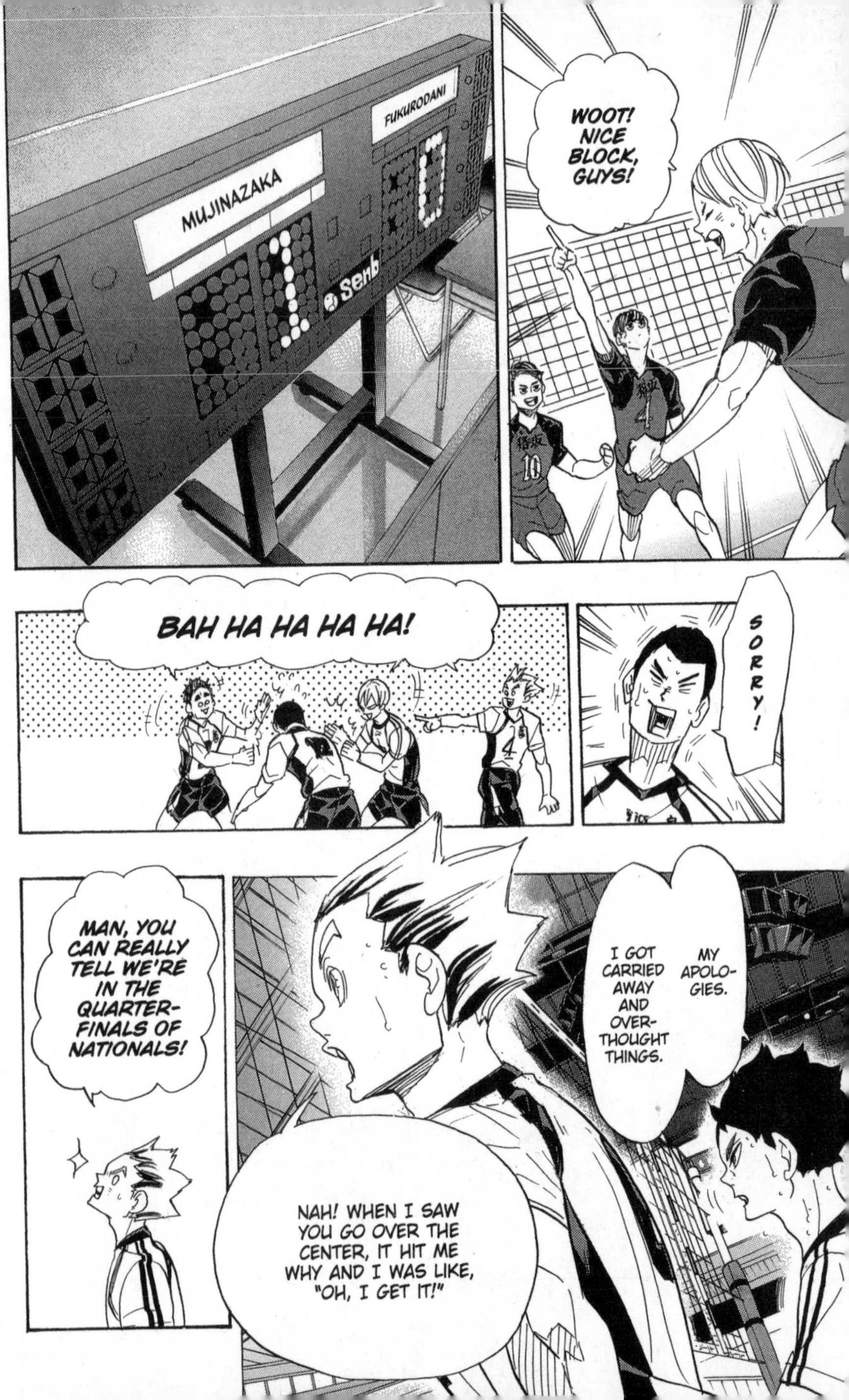
WOOT! NICE BLOCK, GUYS!
FUKURODANI
MUJINAZAKA
SORRY!
BAH HA HA HA HA!
MY APOLOGIES.
I GOT CARRIED AWAY AND OVERTHOUGHT THINGS.
NAH! WHEN I SAW YOU GO OVER THE CENTER, IT HIT ME WHY AND I WAS LIKE, "OH, I GET IT!"
MAN, YOU CAN REALLY TELL WE'RE IN THE QUARTERFINALS OF NATIONALS!

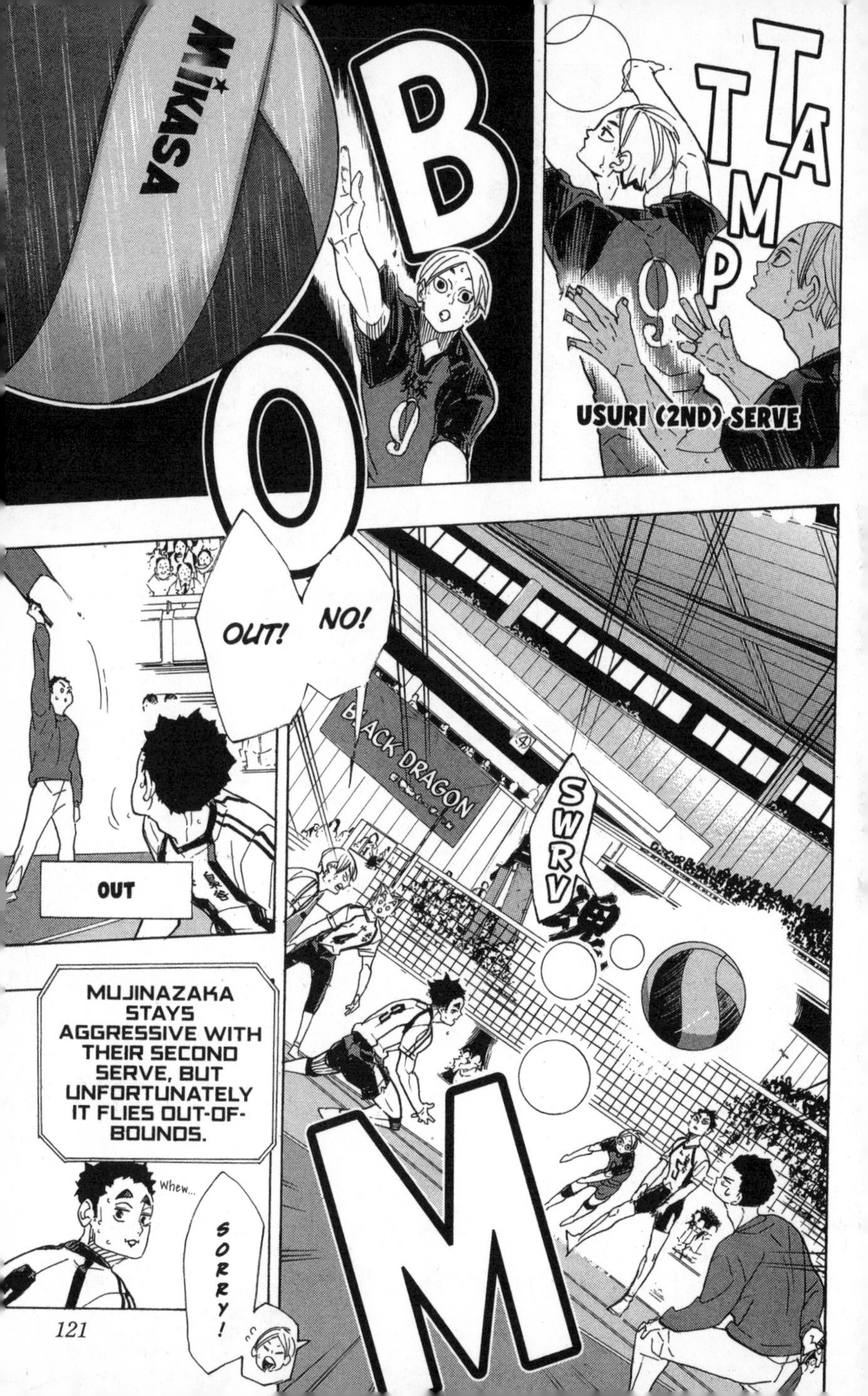
TTAMP
USURI (2ND) SERVE
BOOM
MIKASA
SWRV
OUT!
NO!
OUT
MUJINAZAKA STAYS AGGRESSIVE WITH THEIR SECOND SERVE, BUT UNFORTUNATELY IT FLIES OUT-OF-BOUNDS.
SORRY!
Whew...

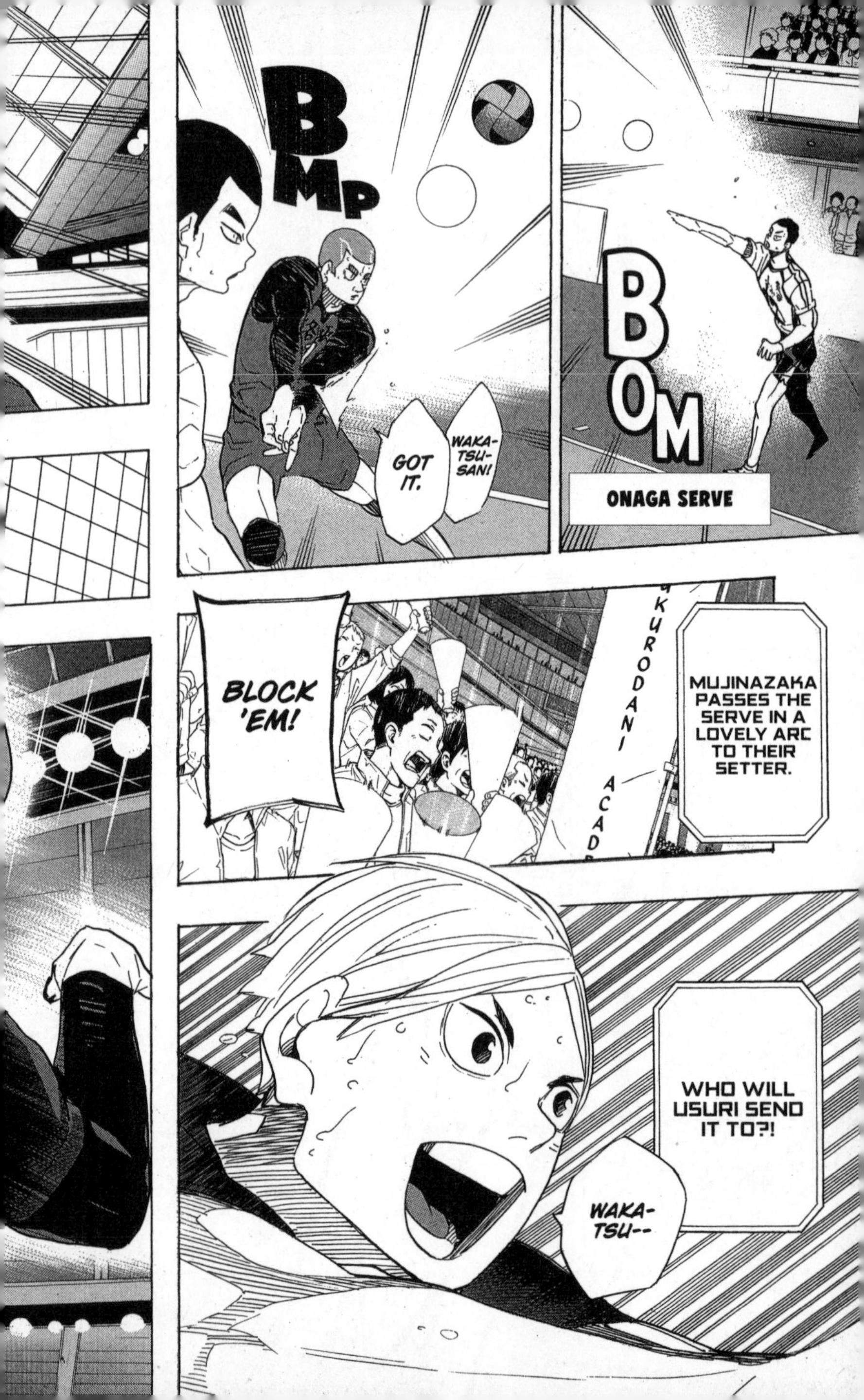
BOM
ONAGA SERVE
BMP
WAKA-TSU-SAN!
GOT IT.
MUJINAZAKA PASSES THE SERVE IN A LOVELY ARC TO THEIR SETTER.
BLOCK 'EM!
WHO WILL USURI SEND IT TO?!
WAKA-TSU--

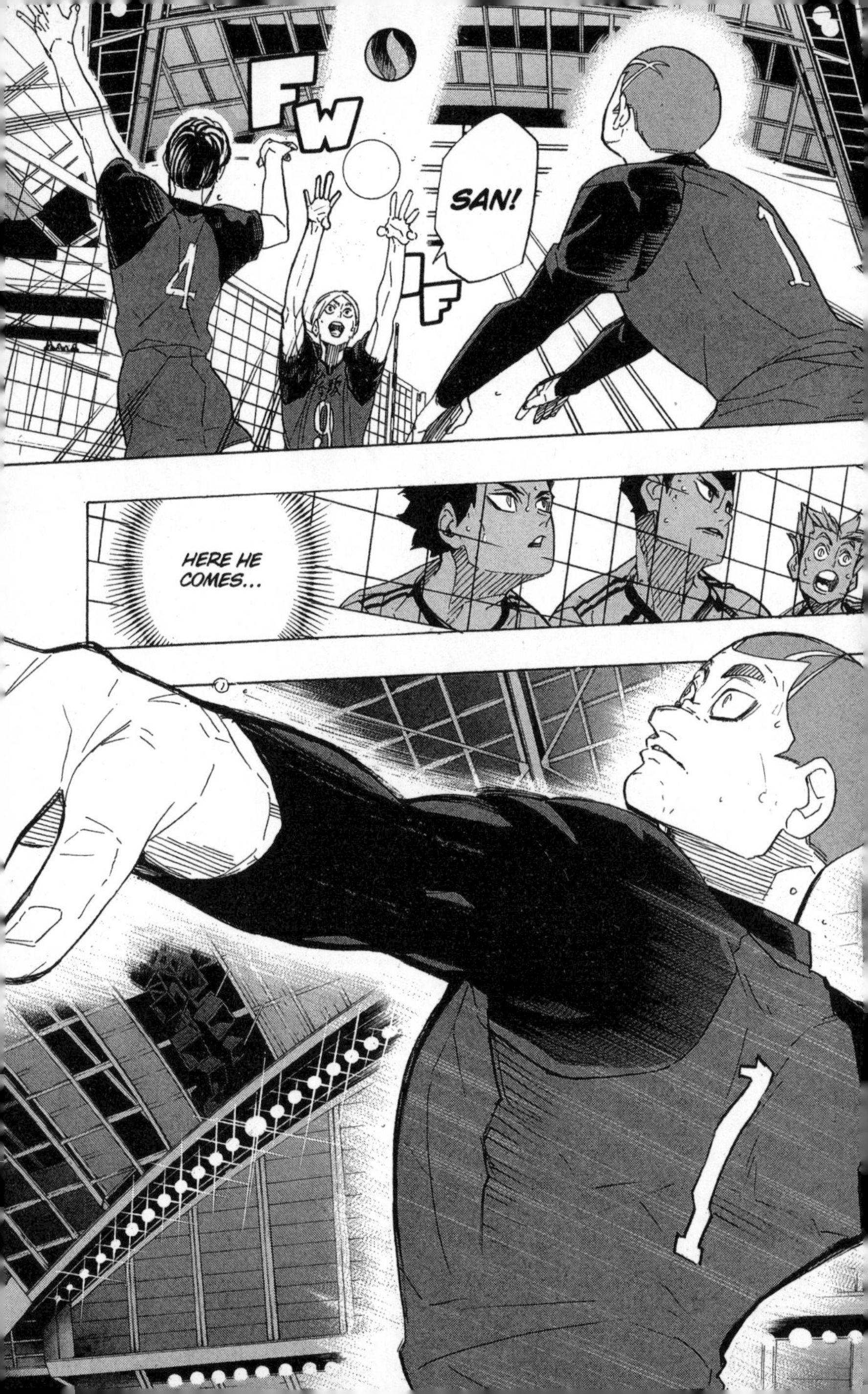
SAN!
FW
HERE HE COMES...

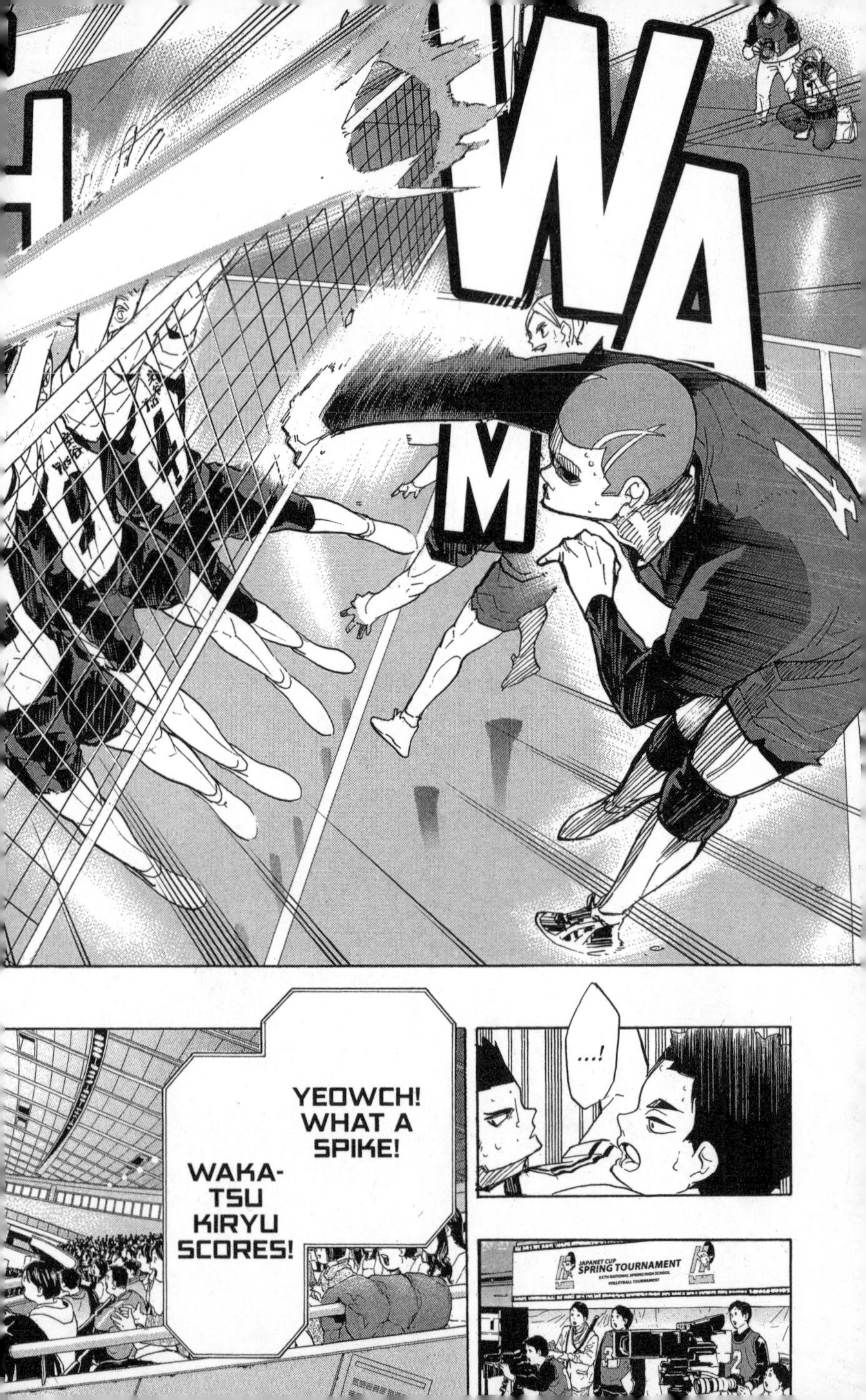
WHAM
...!
JAPANET CUP
SPRING TOURNAMENT
YEOWCH! WHAT A SPIKE!
WAKA-TSU KIRYU SCORES!

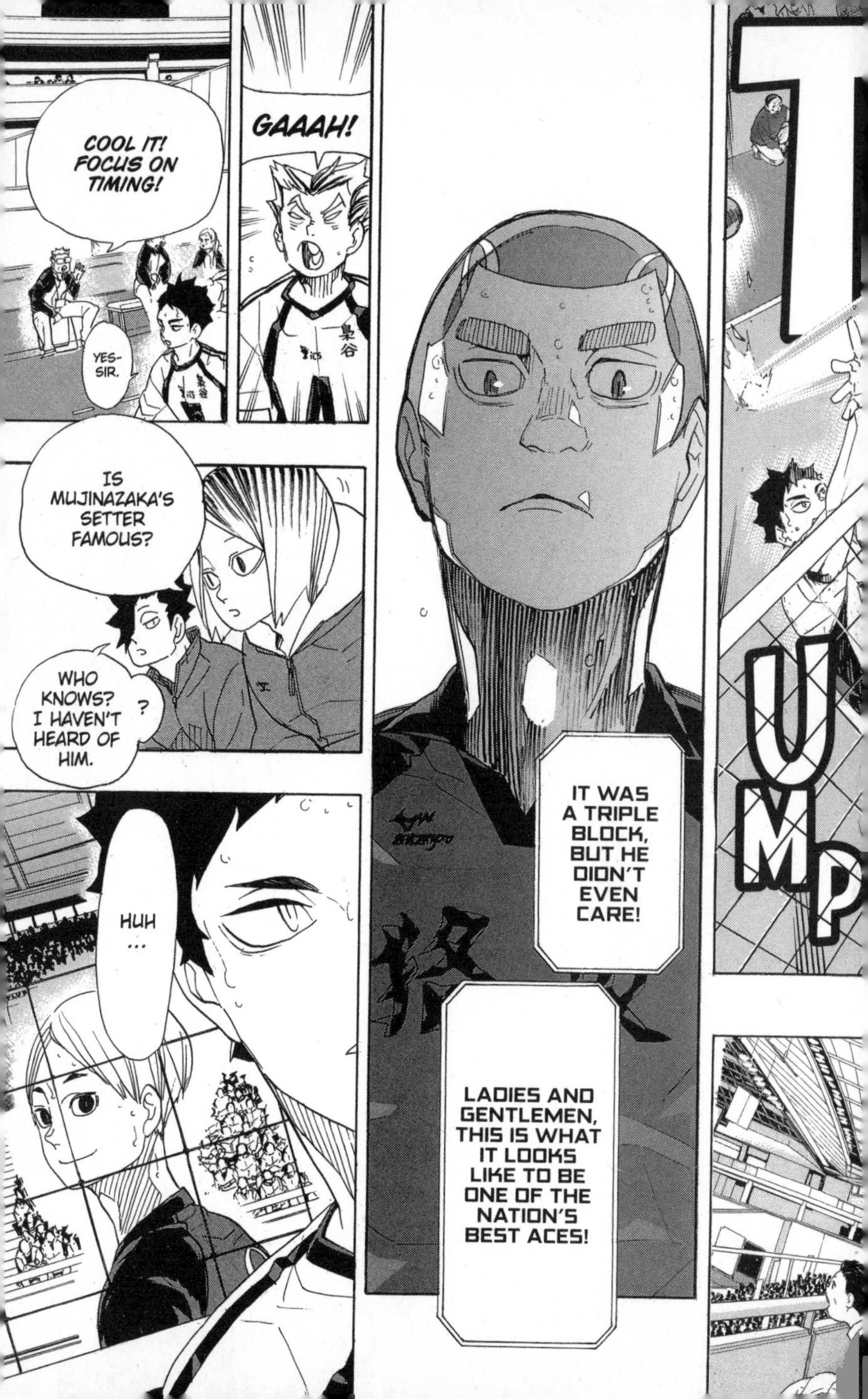
T
UMP
IT WAS A TRIPLE BLOCK, BUT HE DIDN'T EVEN CARE!
LADIES AND GENTLEMEN, THIS IS WHAT IT LOOKS LIKE TO BE ONE OF THE NATION'S BEST ACES!
GAAAH!
COOL IT! FOCUS ON TIMING!
YES-SIR.
IS MUJINAZAKA'S SETTER FAMOUS?
?
WHO KNOWS? I HAVEN'T HEARD OF HIM.
HUH ...

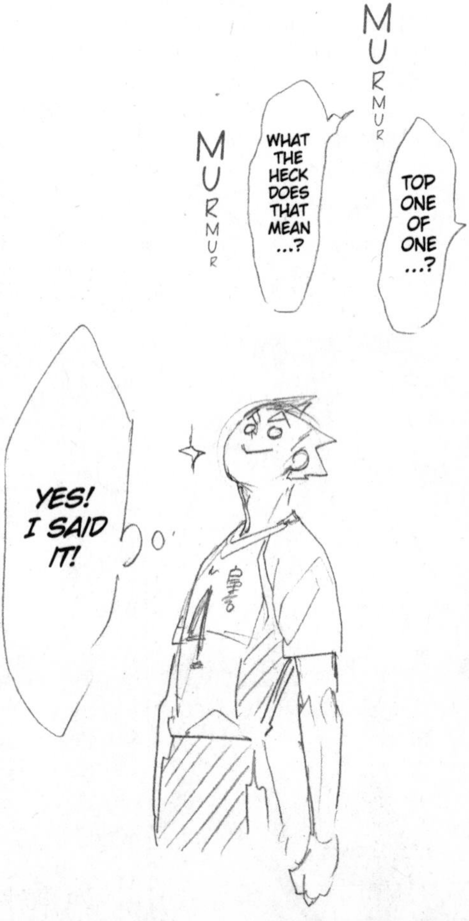
MURMUR
TOP ONE OF ONE ...?
WHAT THE HECK DOES THAT MEAN ...?
MURMUR
YES! I SAID IT!

CHAPTER 329: The Nation's Three Great Aces

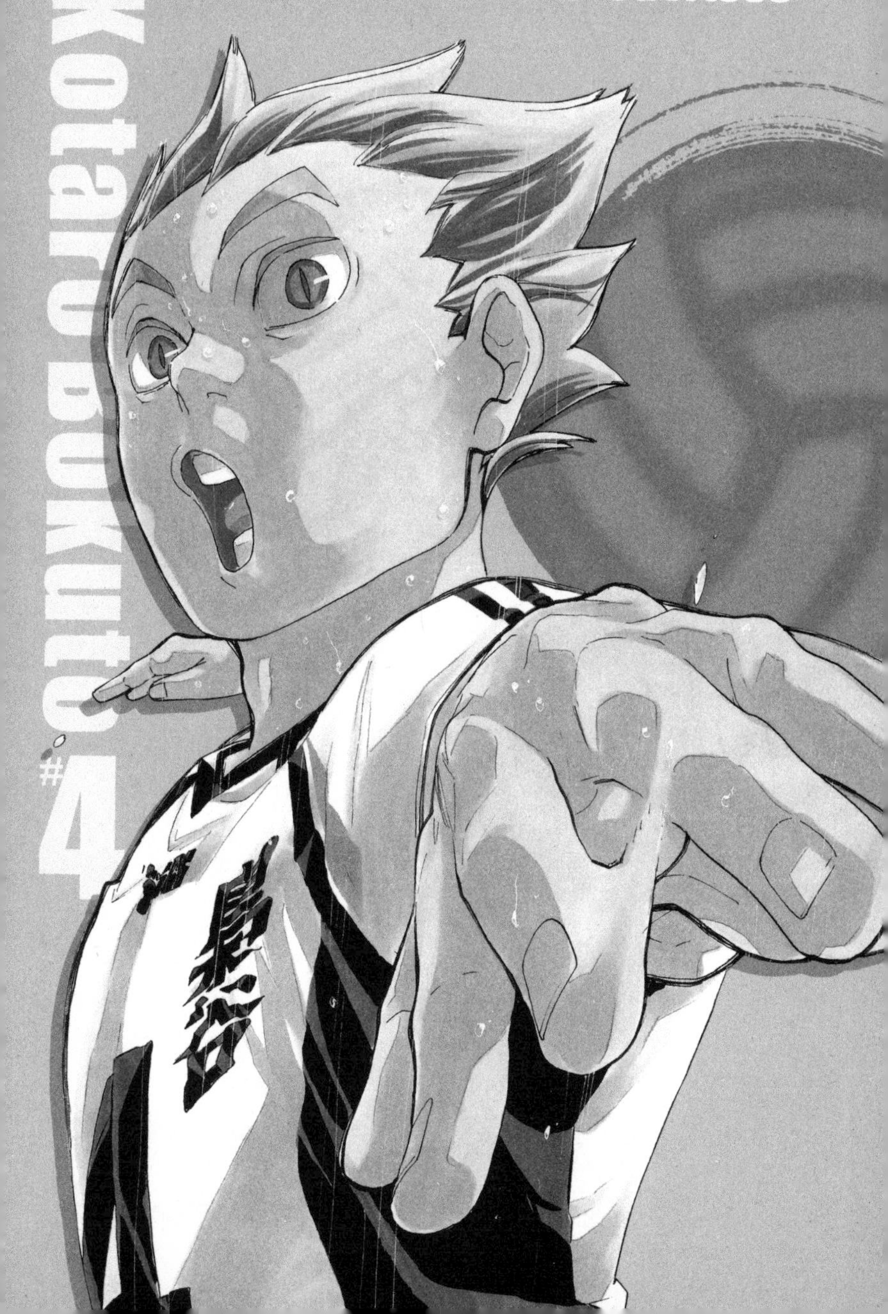
Kotaro Bokuto #4

HAIKYU!!

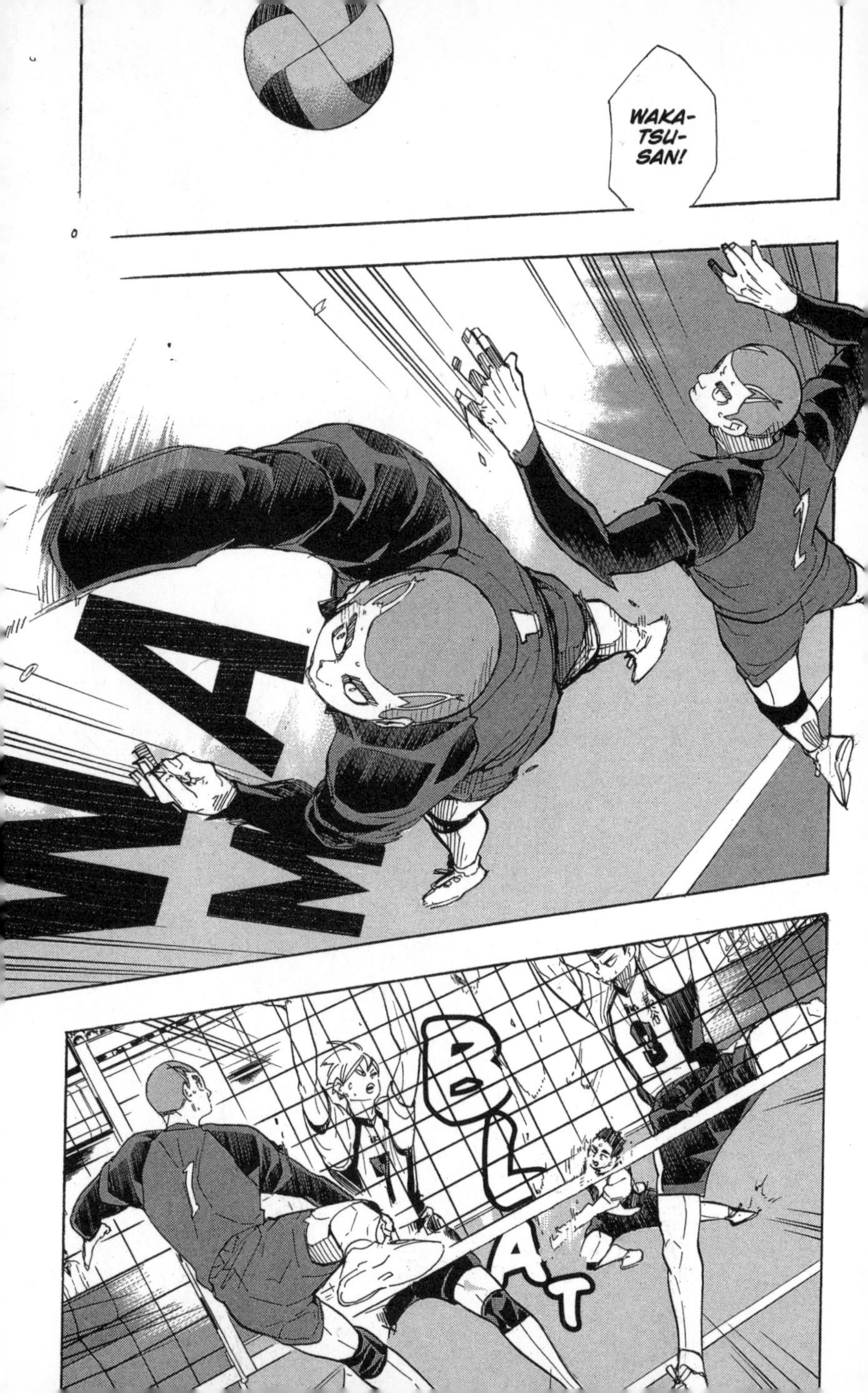
WAKA-TSU-SAN!
WHAM
BAT

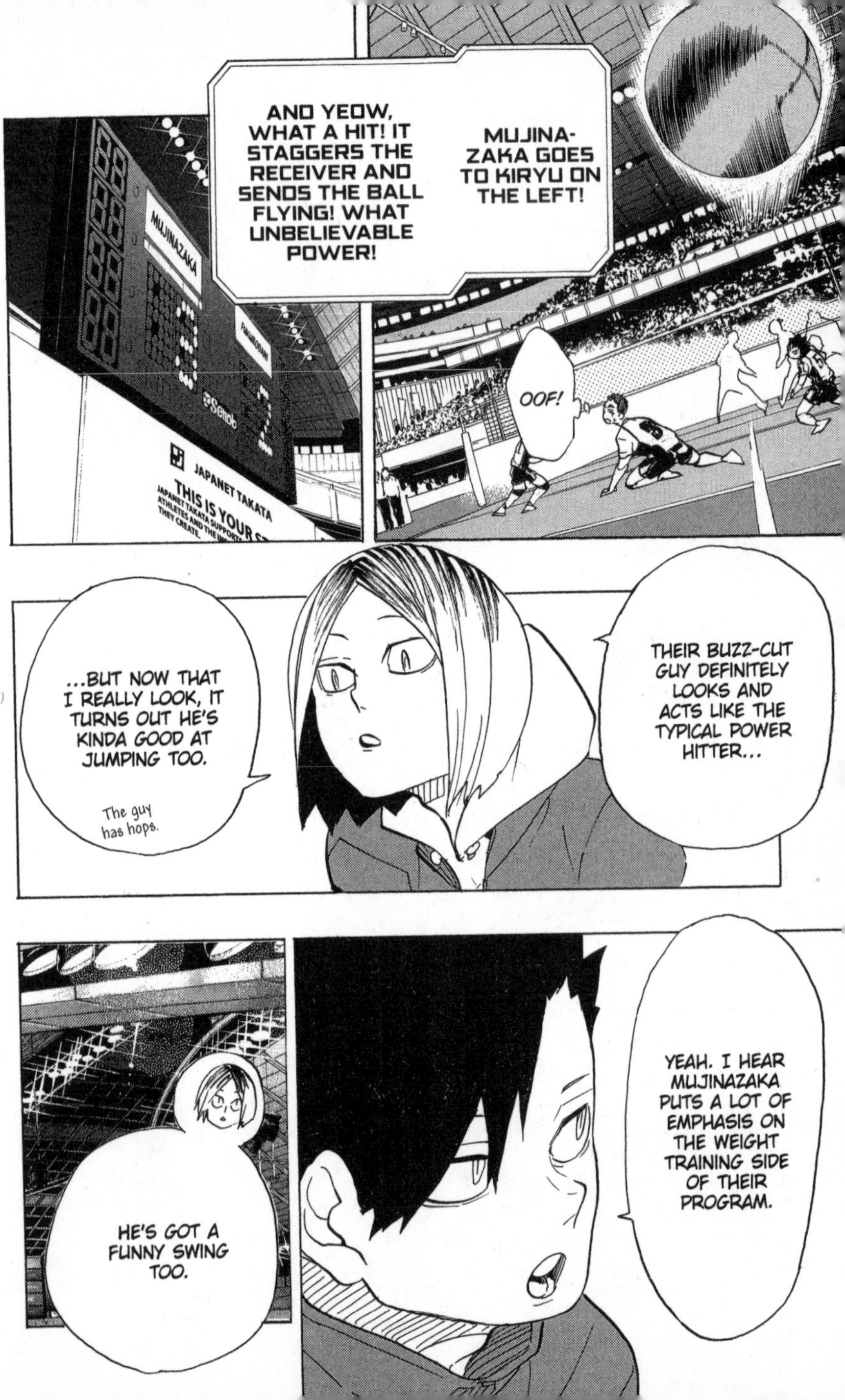
MUJINA-ZAKA GOES TO KIRYU ON THE LEFT!
AND YEOW, WHAT A HIT! IT STAGGERS THE RECEIVER AND SENDS THE BALL FLYING! WHAT UNBELIEVABLE POWER!
OOF!
MUJINAZAKA
JAPANET TAKATA
THEIR BUZZ-CUT GUY DEFINITELY LOOKS AND ACTS LIKE THE TYPICAL POWER HITTER...
...BUT NOW THAT I REALLY LOOK, IT TURNS OUT HE'S KINDA GOOD AT JUMPING TOO.
The guy has hops.
YEAH. I HEAR MUJINAZAKA PUTS A LOT OF EMPHASIS ON THE WEIGHT TRAINING SIDE OF THEIR PROGRAM.
HE'S GOT A FUNNY SWING TOO.

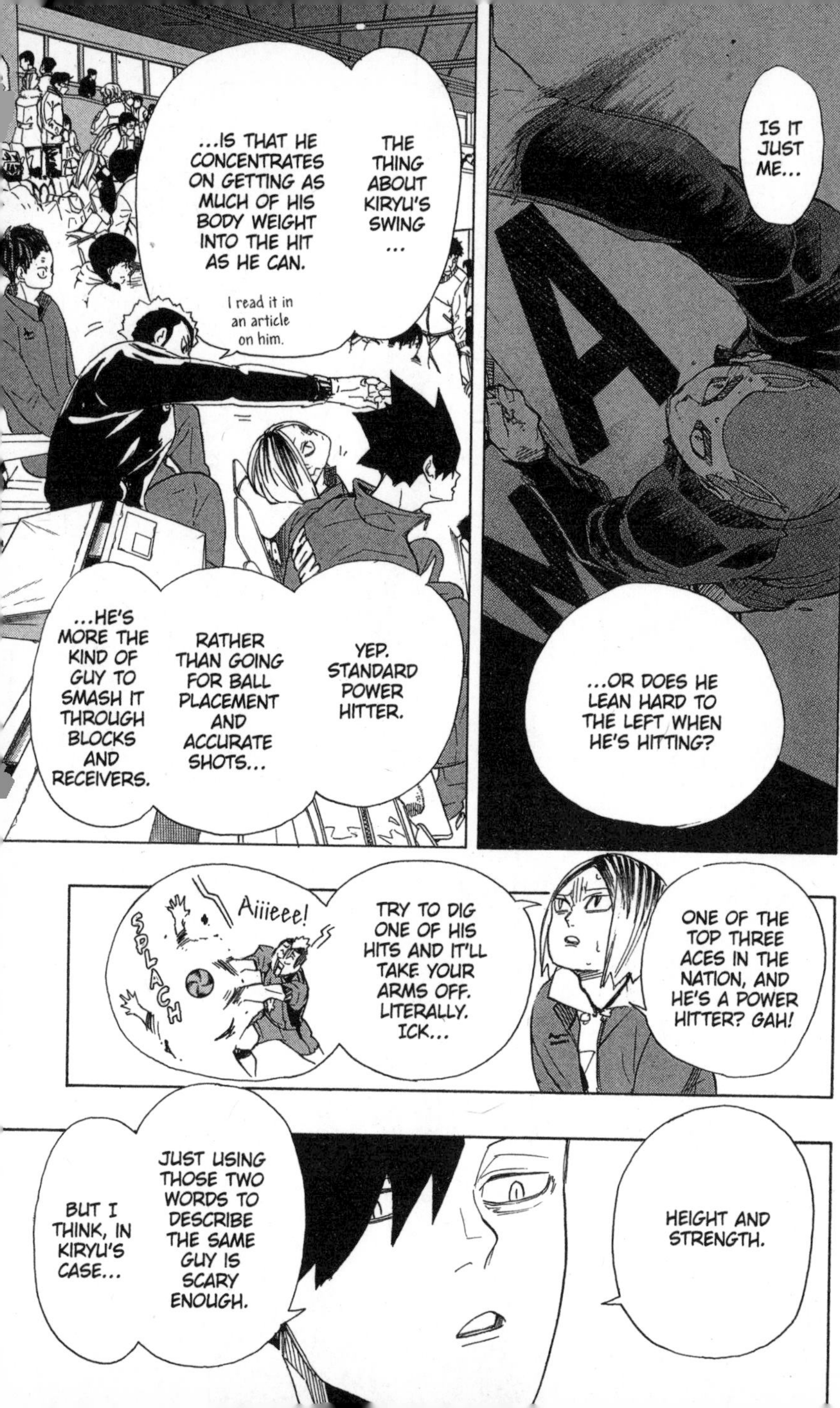
IS IT JUST ME...
...OR DOES HE LEAN HARD TO THE LEFT WHEN HE'S HITTING?
THE THING ABOUT KIRYU'S SWING...
...IS THAT HE CONCENTRATES ON GETTING AS MUCH OF HIS BODY WEIGHT INTO THE HIT AS HE CAN.
I read it in an article on him.
YEP. STANDARD POWER HITTER.
RATHER THAN GOING FOR BALL PLACEMENT AND ACCURATE SHOTS...
...HE'S MORE THE KIND OF GUY TO SMASH IT THROUGH BLOCKS AND RECEIVERS.
ONE OF THE TOP THREE ACES IN THE NATION, AND HE'S A POWER HITTER? GAH!
TRY TO DIG ONE OF HIS HITS AND IT'LL TAKE YOUR ARMS OFF. LITERALLY. ICK...
Aiiieee!
SPLACH
HEIGHT AND STRENGTH.
JUST USING THOSE TWO WORDS TO DESCRIBE THE SAME GUY IS SCARY ENOUGH.
BUT I THINK, IN KIRYU'S CASE...

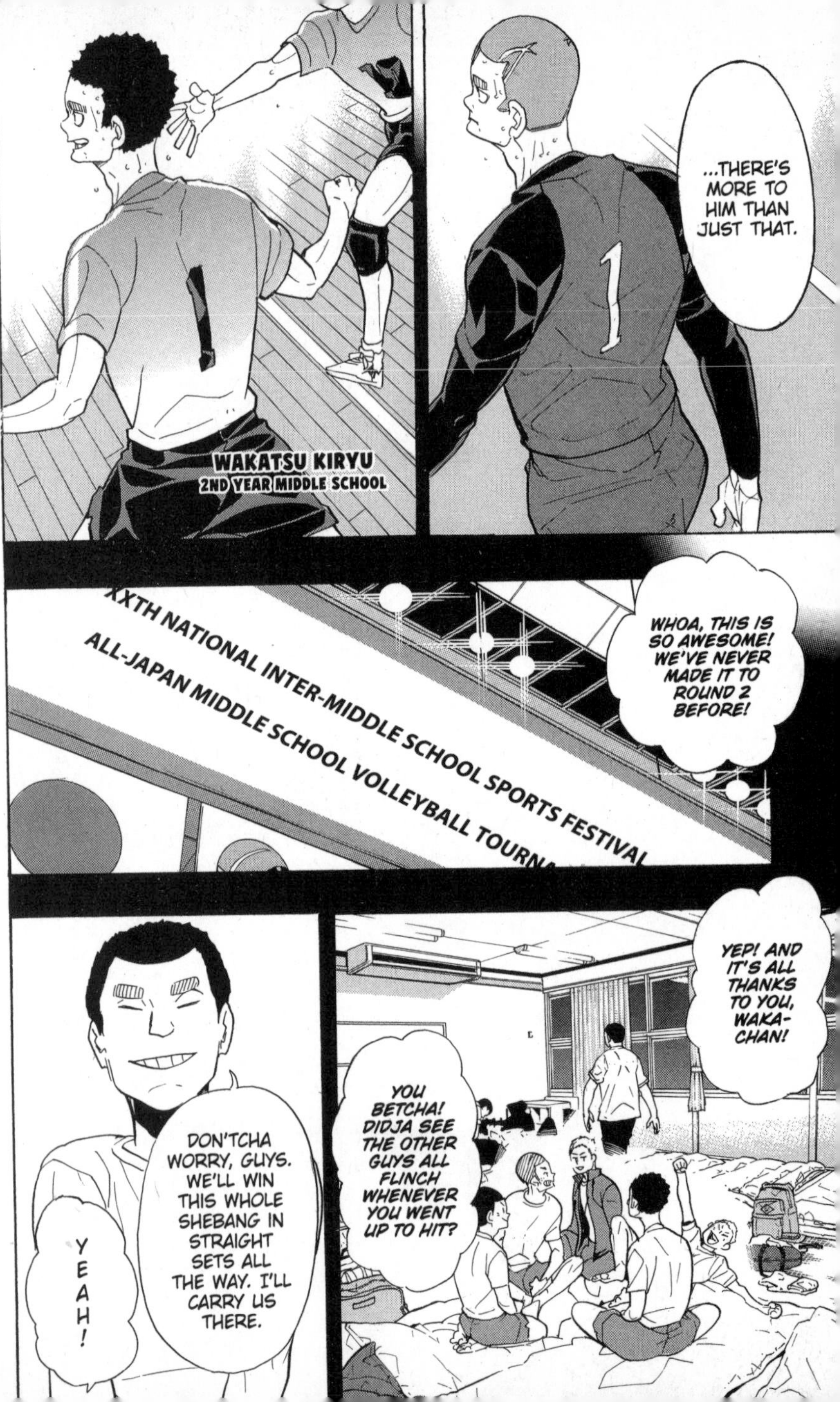
...THERE'S MORE TO HIM THAN JUST THAT.
WAKATSU KIRYU
2ND YEAR MIDDLE SCHOOL
WHOA, THIS IS SO AWESOME! WE'VE NEVER MADE IT TO ROUND 2 BEFORE!
XXTH NATIONAL INTER-MIDDLE SCHOOL SPORTS FESTIVAL
ALL-JAPAN MIDDLE SCHOOL VOLLEYBALL TOURNA
YEP! AND IT'S ALL THANKS TO YOU, WAKA-CHAN!
YOU BETCHA! DIDJA SEE THE OTHER GUYS ALL FLINCH WHENEVER YOU WENT UP TO HIT?
DON'TCHA WORRY, GUYS. WE'LL WIN THIS WHOLE SHEBANG IN STRAIGHT SETS ALL THE WAY. I'LL CARRY US THERE.
YEAH!

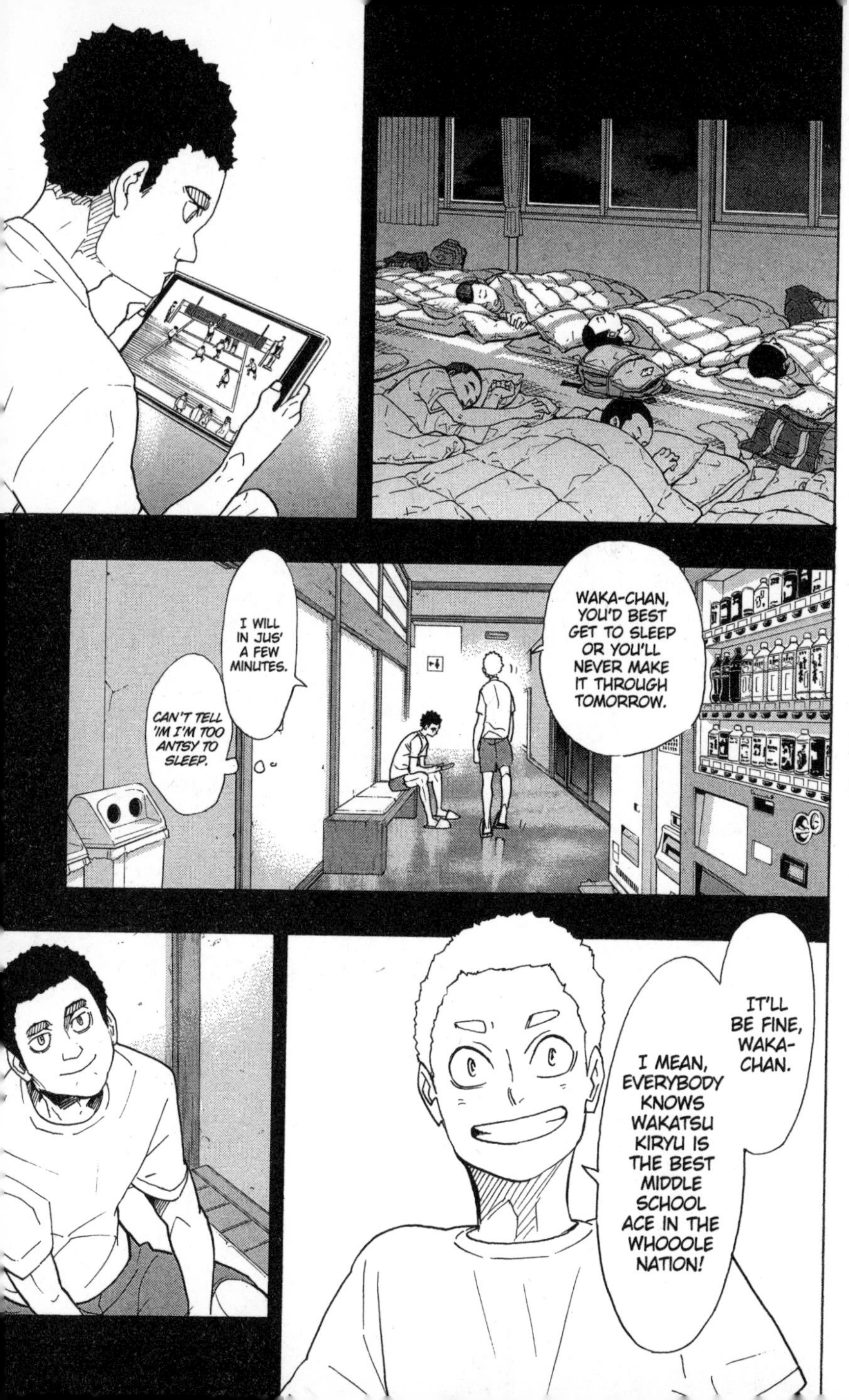
WAKA-CHAN, YOU'D BEST GET TO SLEEP OR YOU'LL NEVER MAKE IT THROUGH TOMORROW.
I WILL IN JUS' A FEW MINUTES.
CAN'T TELL 'IM I'M TOO ANTSY TO SLEEP.
IT'LL BE FINE, WAKA-CHAN.
I MEAN, EVERYBODY KNOWS WAKATSU KIRYU IS THE BEST MIDDLE SCHOOL ACE IN THE WHOOOLE NATION!

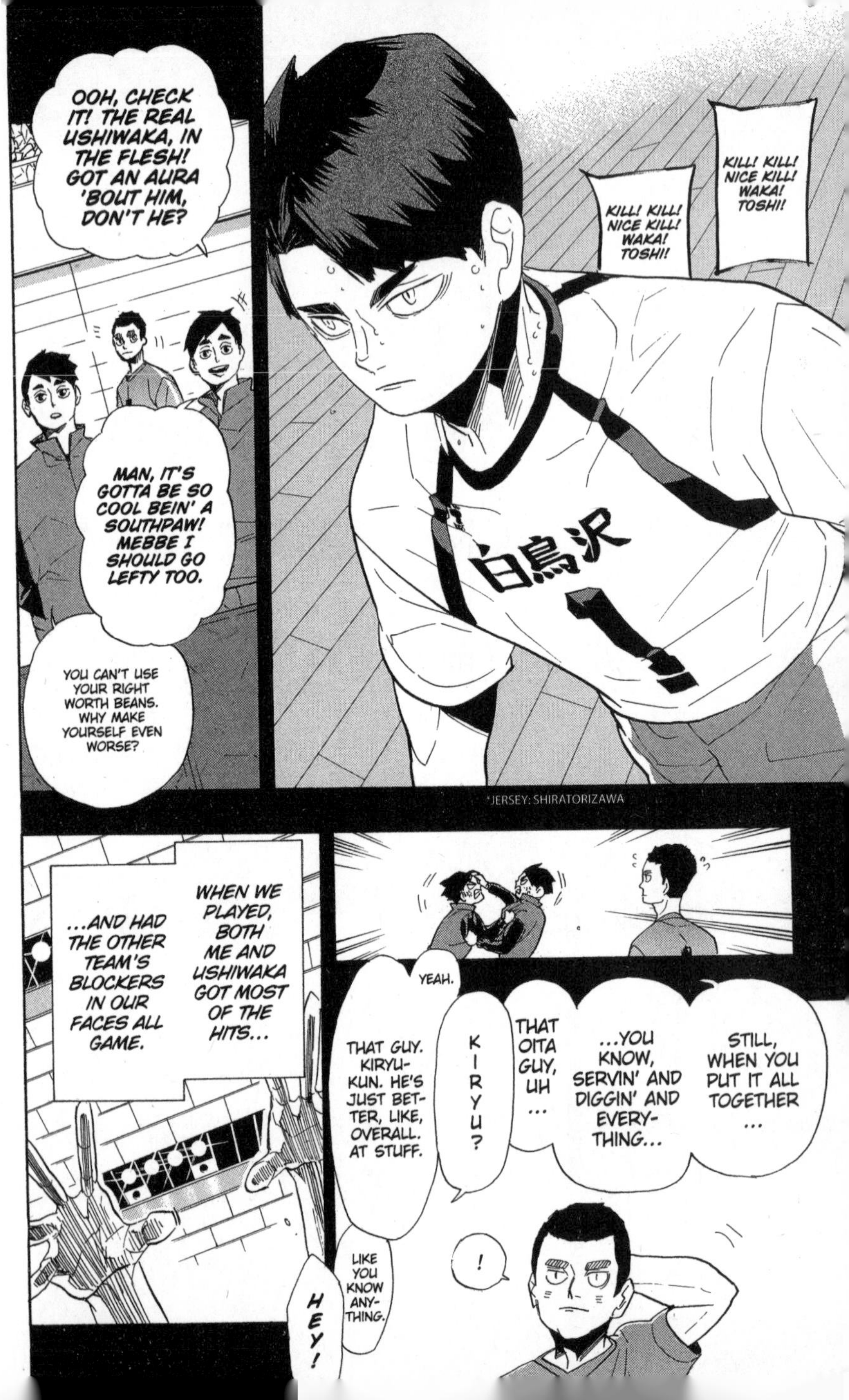
KILL! KILL! NICE KILL! WAKA! TOSHI!
KILL! KILL! NICE KILL! WAKA! TOSHI!
白鳥沢
*JERSEY: SHIRATORIZAWA
OOH, CHECK IT! THE REAL USHIWAKA, IN THE FLESH! GOT AN AURA 'BOUT HIM, DON'T HE?
MAN, IT'S GOTTA BE SO COOL BEIN' A SOUTHPAW! MEBBE I SHOULD GO LEFTY TOO.
YOU CAN'T USE YOUR RIGHT WORTH BEANS. WHY MAKE YOURSELF EVEN WORSE?
STILL, WHEN YOU PUT IT ALL TOGETHER...
...YOU KNOW, SERVIN' AND DIGGIN' AND EVERY-THING...
THAT OITA GUY, UH...
KIRYU?
YEAH.
THAT GUY. KIRYU-KUN. HE'S JUST BET-TER, LIKE, OVERALL. AT STUFF.
!
LIKE YOU KNOW ANY-THING.
HEY!
WHEN WE PLAYED, BOTH ME AND USHIWAKA GOT MOST OF THE HITS...
...AND HAD THE OTHER TEAM'S BLOCKERS IN OUR FACES ALL GAME.

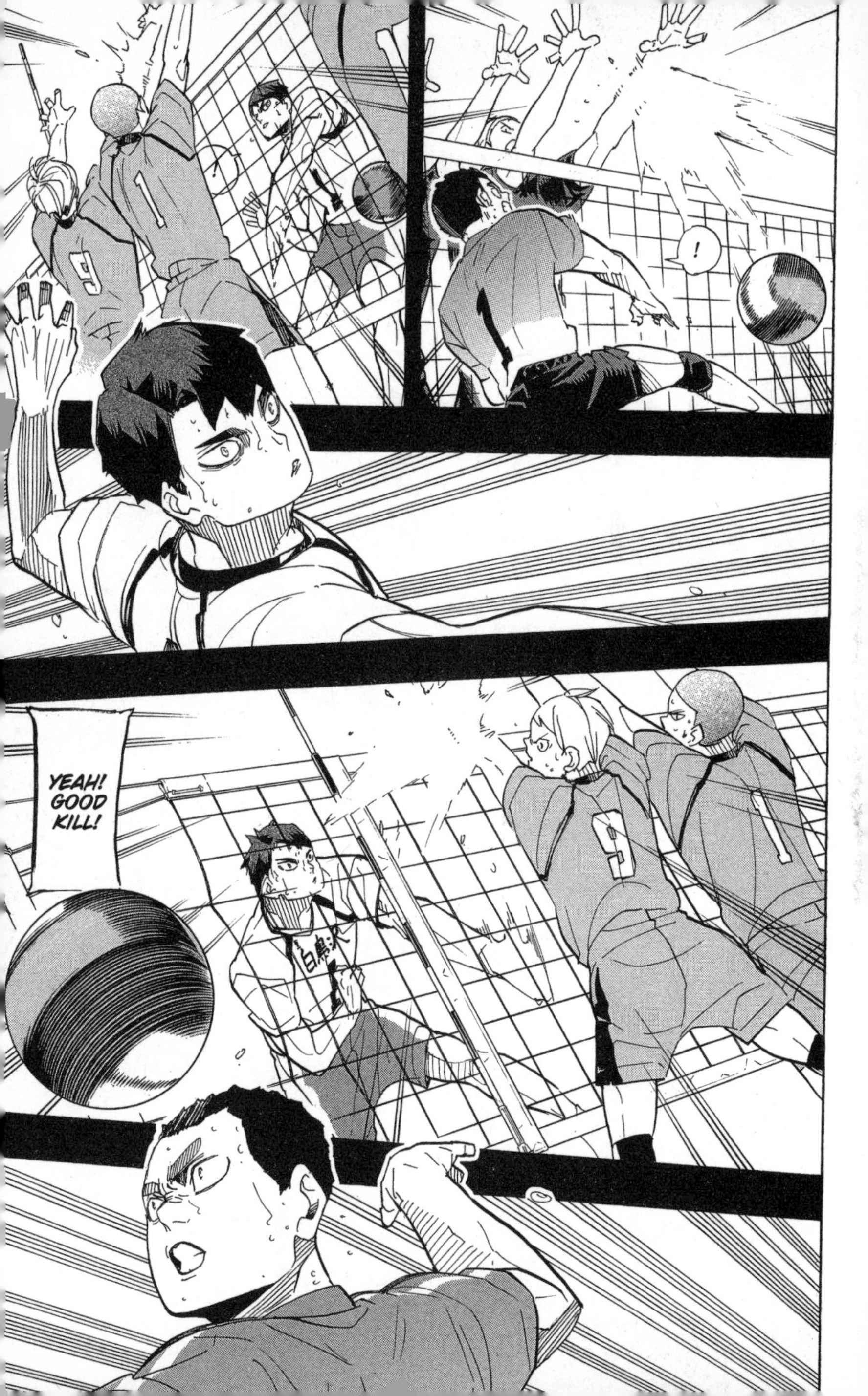
!
!
YEAH! GOOD KILL!

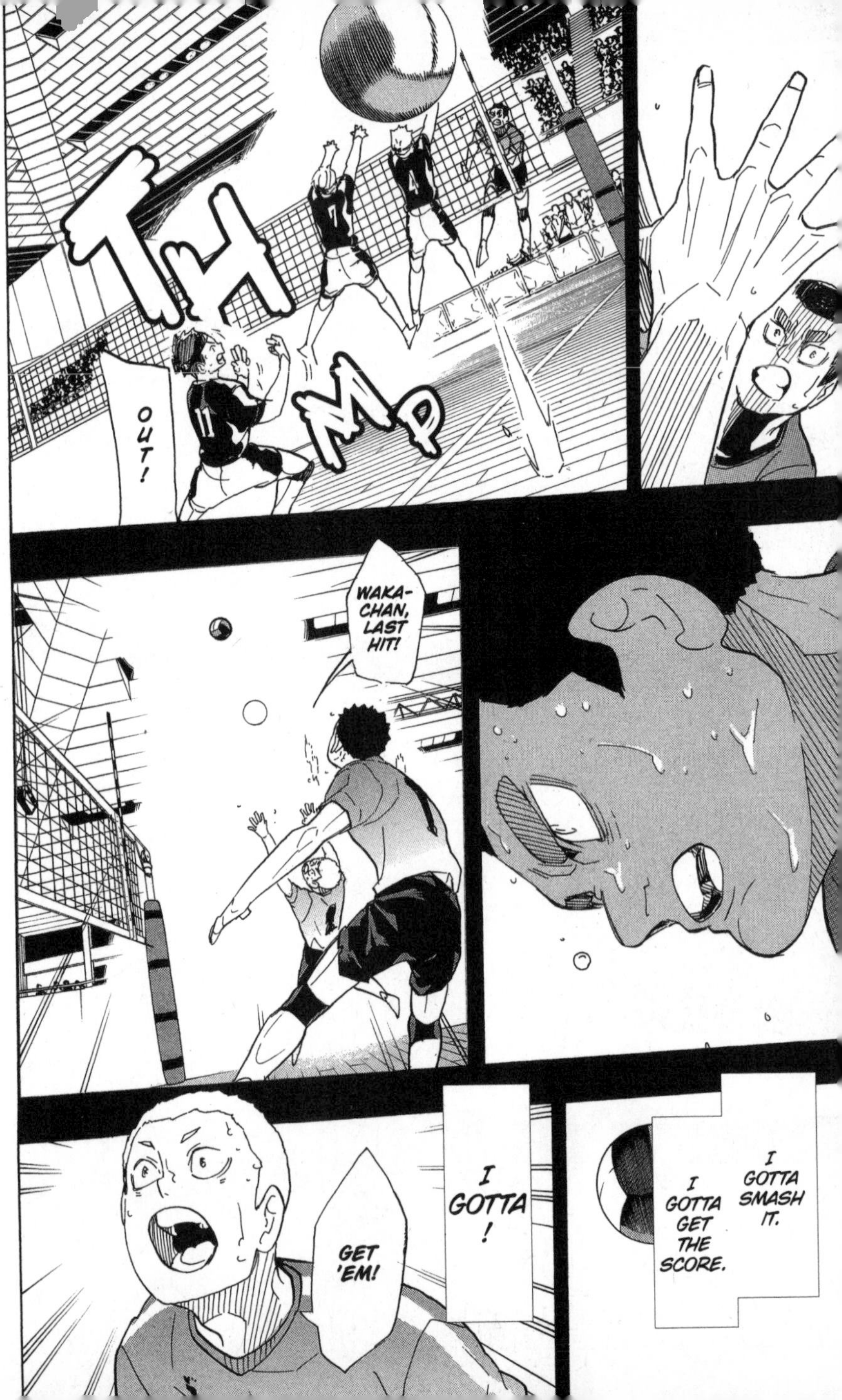
THMP
OUT!
WAKA-CHAN, LAST HIT!
I GOTTA SMASH IT.
I GOTTA GET THE SCORE.
I GOTTA!
GET 'EM!

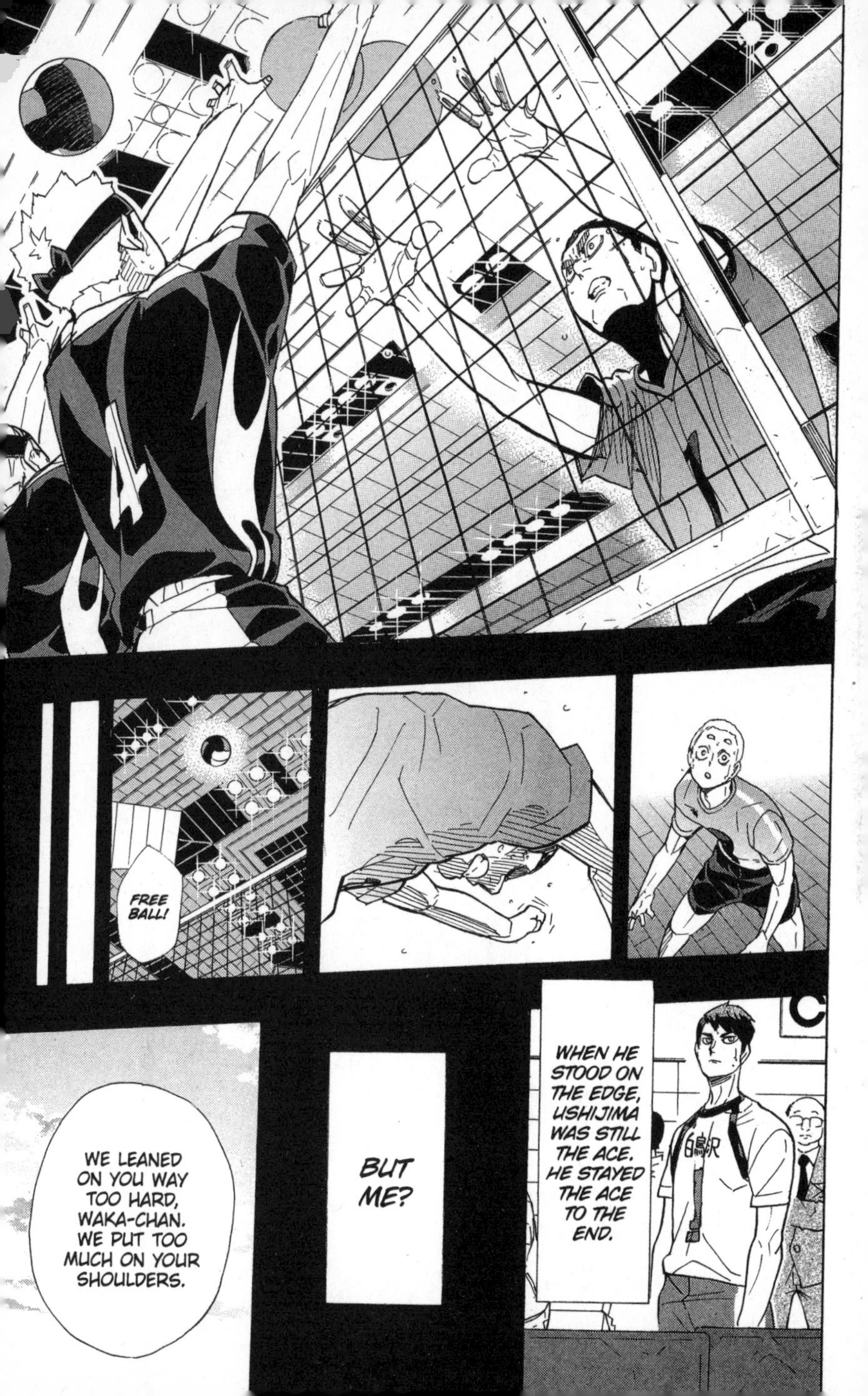
FREE BALL!
WHEN HE STOOD ON THE EDGE, USHIJIMA WAS STILL THE ACE. HE STAYED THE ACE TO THE END.
BUT ME?
WE LEANED ON YOU WAY TOO HARD, WAKA-CHAN. WE PUT TOO MUCH ON YOUR SHOULDERS.

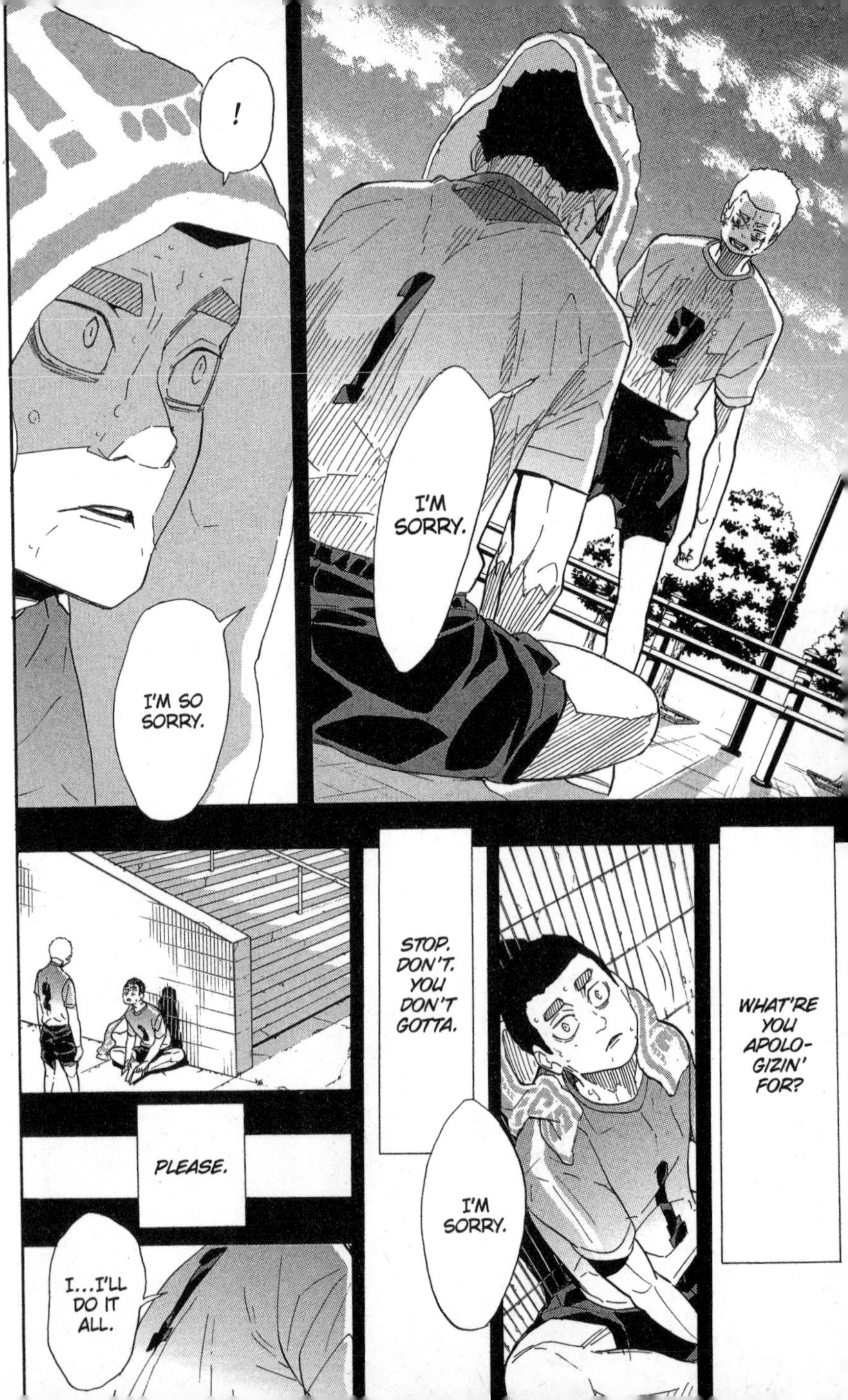
I'M SORRY.
!
I'M SO SORRY.
WHAT'RE YOU APOLOGIZIN' FOR?
I'M SORRY.
STOP. DON'T. YOU DON'T GOTTA.
PLEASE.
I...I'LL DO IT ALL.

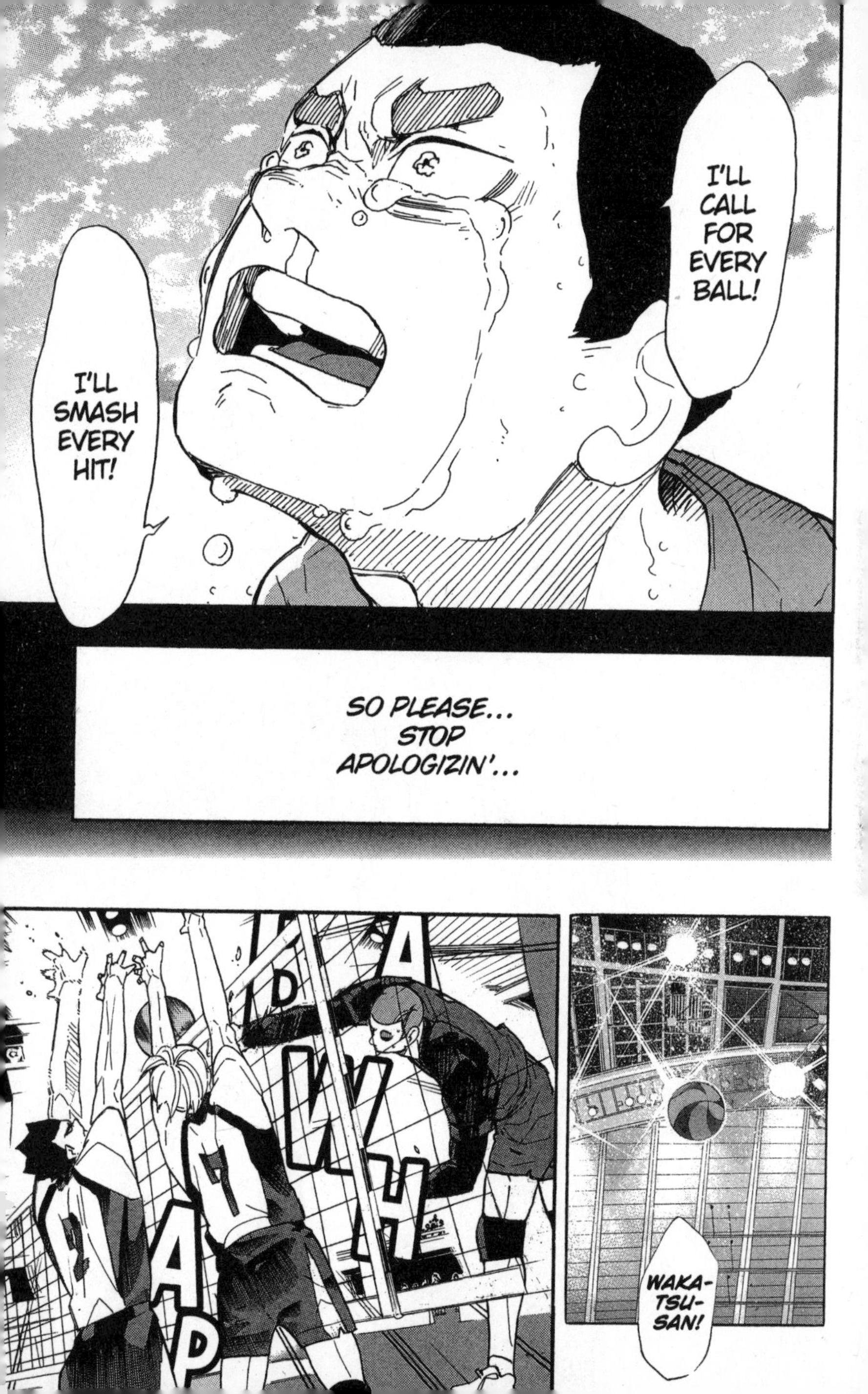
I'LL CALL FOR EVERY BALL!
I'LL SMASH EVERY HIT!
SO PLEASE... STOP APOLOGIZIN'...
WAKA-TSU-SAN!

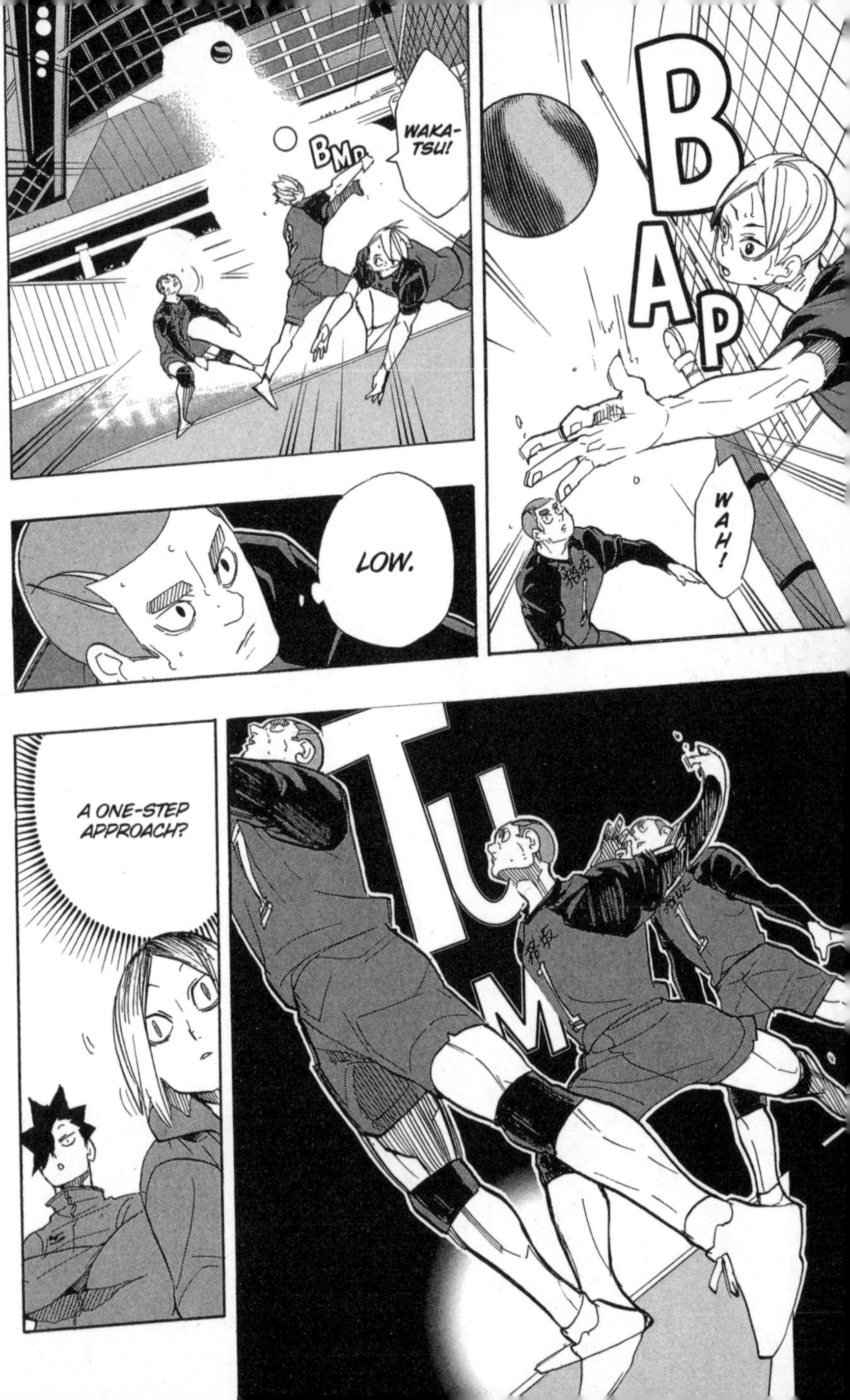
BAP
WAH!
WAKA-TSU!
BMP
LOW.
TUMP
A ONE-STEP APPROACH?

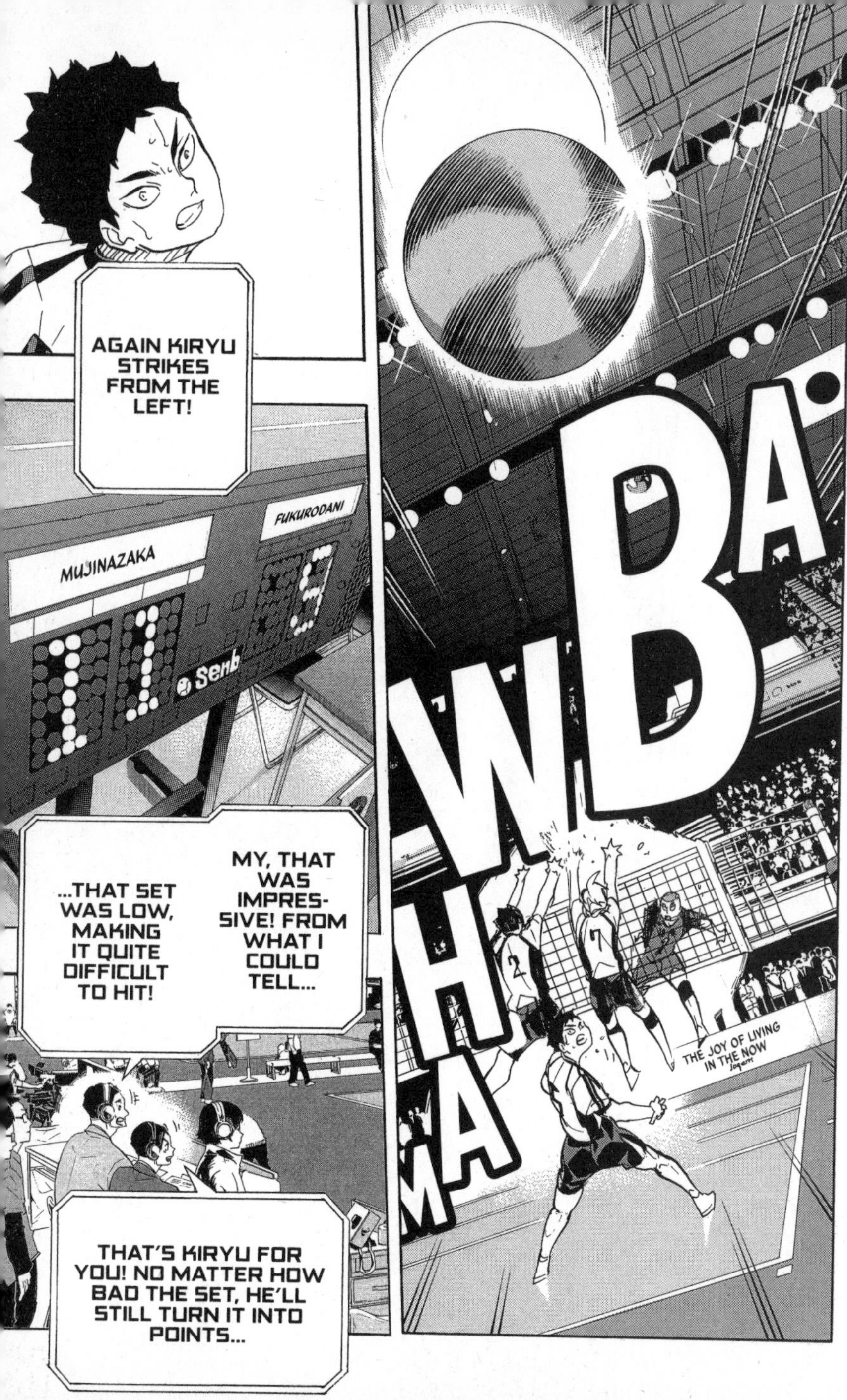
THE JOY OF LIVING IN THE NOW
AGAIN KIRYU STRIKES FROM THE LEFT!
FUKURODANI
MUJINAZAKA
MY, THAT WAS IMPRES-SIVE! FROM WHAT I COULD TELL...
...THAT SET WAS LOW, MAKING IT QUITE DIFFICULT TO HIT!
THAT'S KIRYU FOR YOU! NO MATTER HOW BAD THE SET, HE'LL STILL TURN IT INTO POINTS...

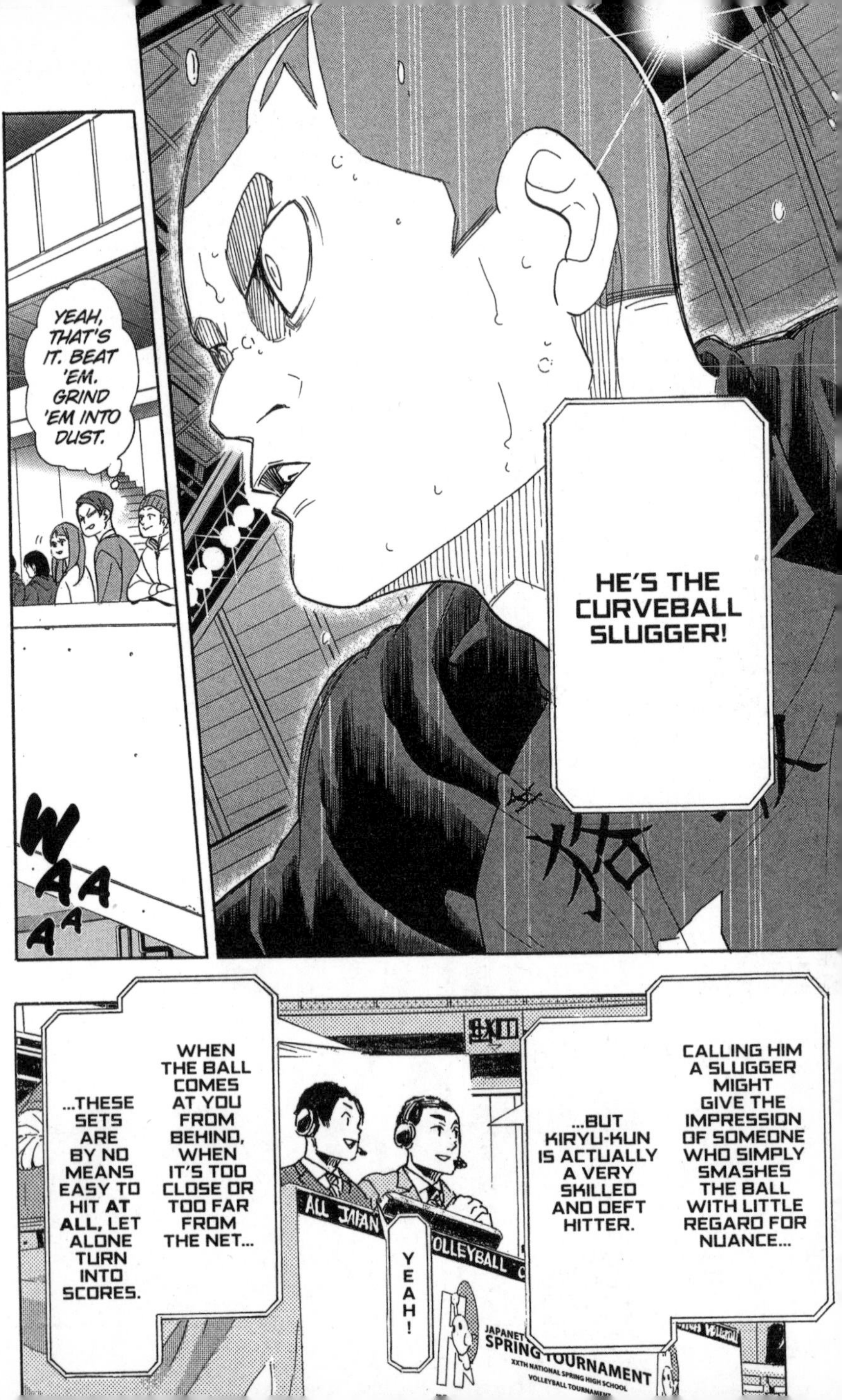
HE'S THE CURVEBALL SLUGGER!
YEAH, THAT'S IT. BEAT 'EM. GRIND 'EM INTO DUST.
WAAAA
CALLING HIM A SLUGGER MIGHT GIVE THE IMPRESSION OF SOMEONE WHO SIMPLY SMASHES THE BALL WITH LITTLE REGARD FOR NUANCE...
...BUT KIRYU-KUN IS ACTUALLY A VERY SKILLED AND DEFT HITTER.
YEAH!
WHEN THE BALL COMES AT YOU FROM BEHIND, WHEN IT'S TOO CLOSE OR TOO FAR FROM THE NET...
...THESE SETS ARE BY NO MEANS EASY TO HIT **AT ALL**, LET ALONE TURN INTO SCORES.
ALL JAPAN VOLLEYBALL
JAPANET
SPRING TOURNAMENT
XXTH NATIONAL SPRING HIGH SCHOOL
VOLLEYBALL TOURNAMENT

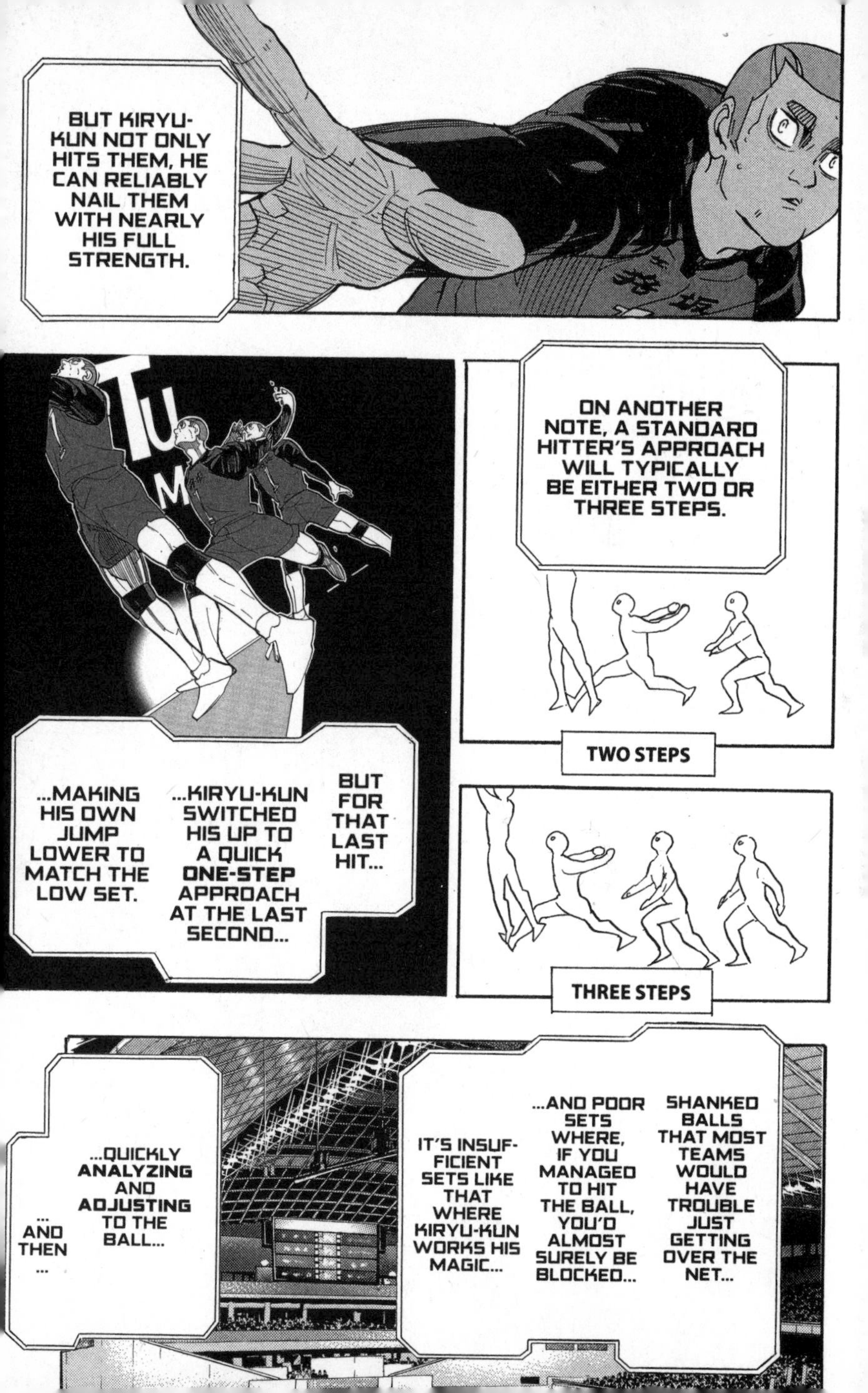
BUT KIRYU-KUN NOT ONLY HITS THEM, HE CAN RELIABLY NAIL THEM WITH NEARLY HIS FULL STRENGTH.
ON ANOTHER NOTE, A STANDARD HITTER'S APPROACH WILL TYPICALLY BE EITHER TWO OR THREE STEPS.
TWO STEPS
THREE STEPS
TUM
BUT FOR THAT LAST HIT...
...KIRYU-KUN SWITCHED HIS UP TO A QUICK ONE-STEP APPROACH AT THE LAST SECOND...
...MAKING HIS OWN JUMP LOWER TO MATCH THE LOW SET.
SHANKED BALLS THAT MOST TEAMS WOULD HAVE TROUBLE JUST GETTING OVER THE NET...
...AND POOR SETS WHERE, IF YOU MANAGED TO HIT THE BALL, YOU'D ALMOST SURELY BE BLOCKED...
IT'S INSUFFICIENT SETS LIKE THAT WHERE KIRYU-KUN WORKS HIS MAGIC...
...QUICKLY ANALYZING AND ADJUSTING TO THE BALL...
... AND THEN ...

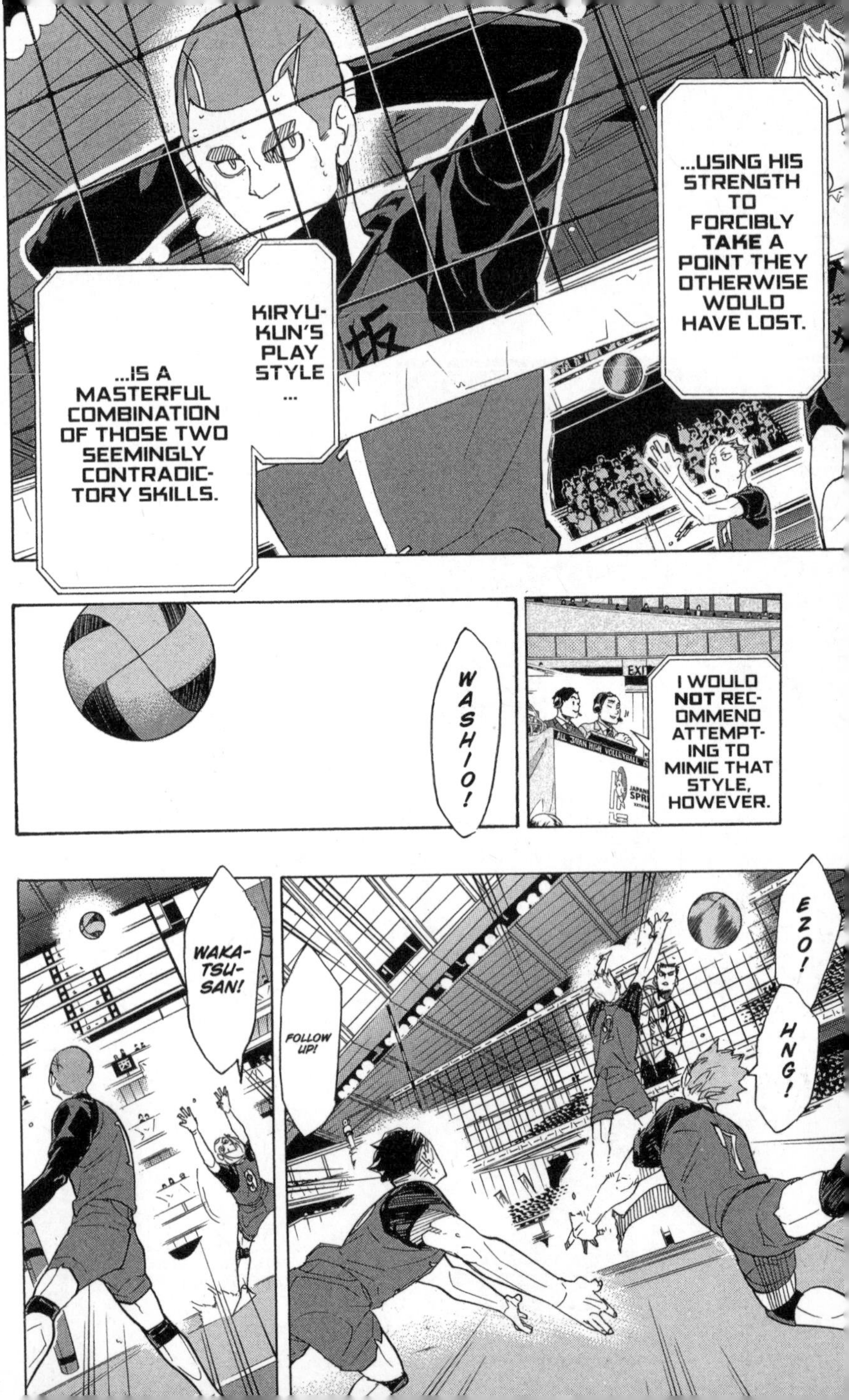
...USING HIS STRENGTH TO FORCIBLY **TAKE** A POINT THEY OTHERWISE WOULD HAVE LOST.
KIRYU-KUN'S PLAY STYLE ...
...IS A MASTERFUL COMBINATION OF THOSE TWO SEEMINGLY CONTRADICTORY SKILLS.
I WOULD **NOT** RECOMMEND ATTEMPTING TO MIMIC THAT STYLE, HOWEVER.
WASHIO!
EZO!
HNG!
FOLLOW UP!
WAKATSU-SAN!

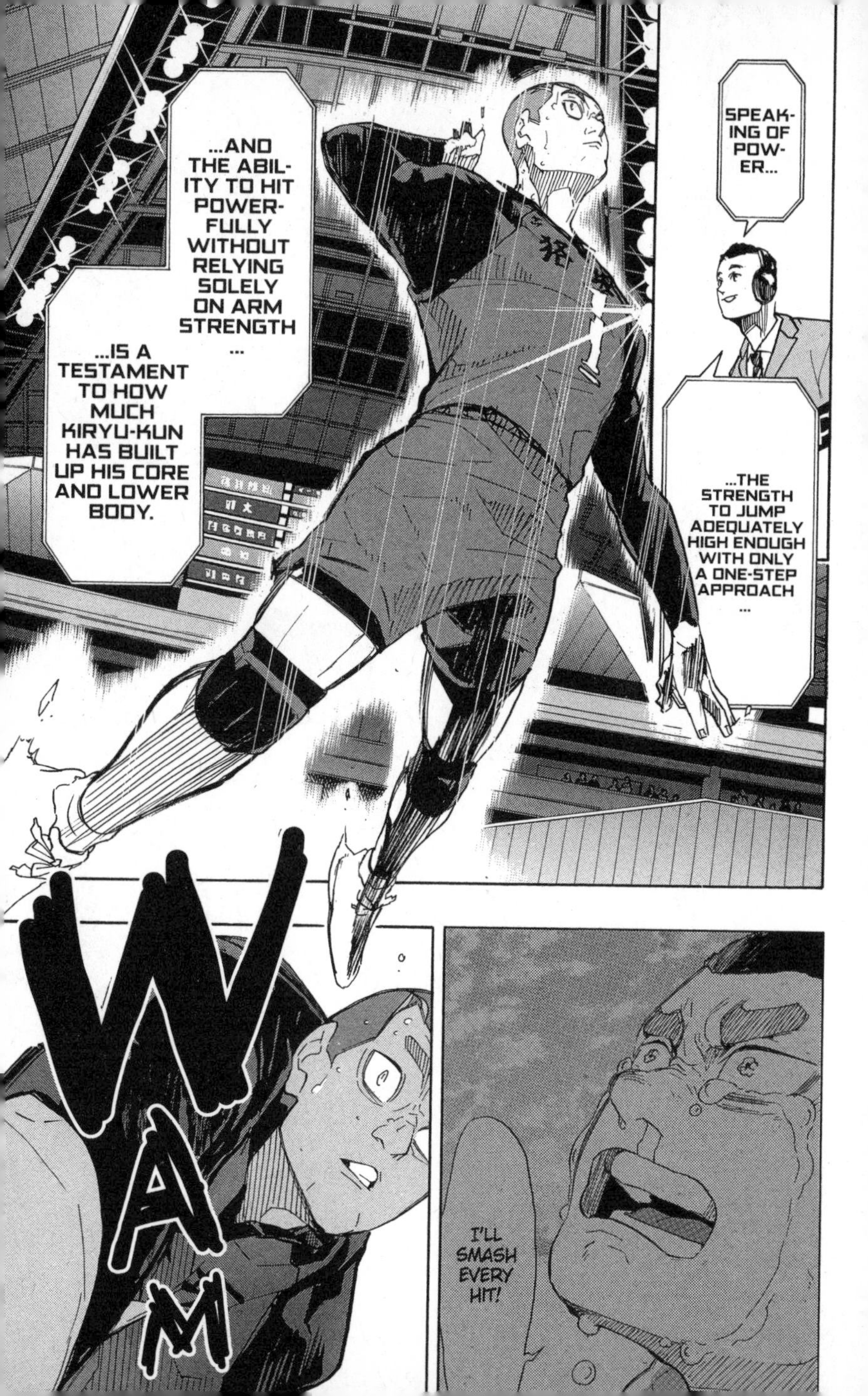
SPEAKING OF POWER...
...THE STRENGTH TO JUMP ADEQUATELY HIGH ENOUGH WITH ONLY A ONE-STEP APPROACH ...
...AND THE ABILITY TO HIT POWERFULLY WITHOUT RELYING SOLELY ON ARM STRENGTH ...
...IS A TESTAMENT TO HOW MUCH KIRYU-KUN HAS BUILT UP HIS CORE AND LOWER BODY.
I'LL SMASH EVERY HIT!
WAM

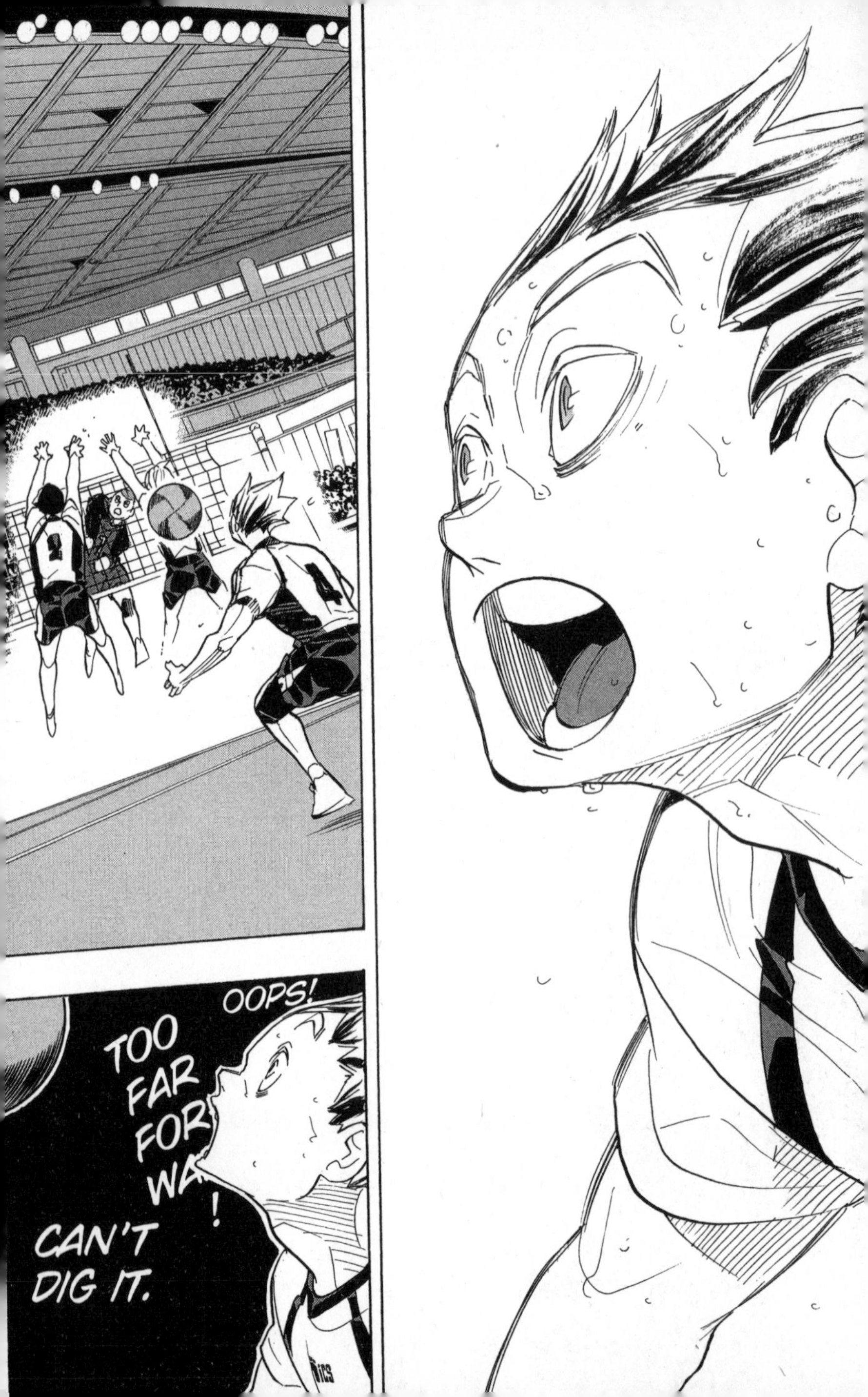
OOPS!
TOO FAR FOR WA- !
CAN'T DIG IT.

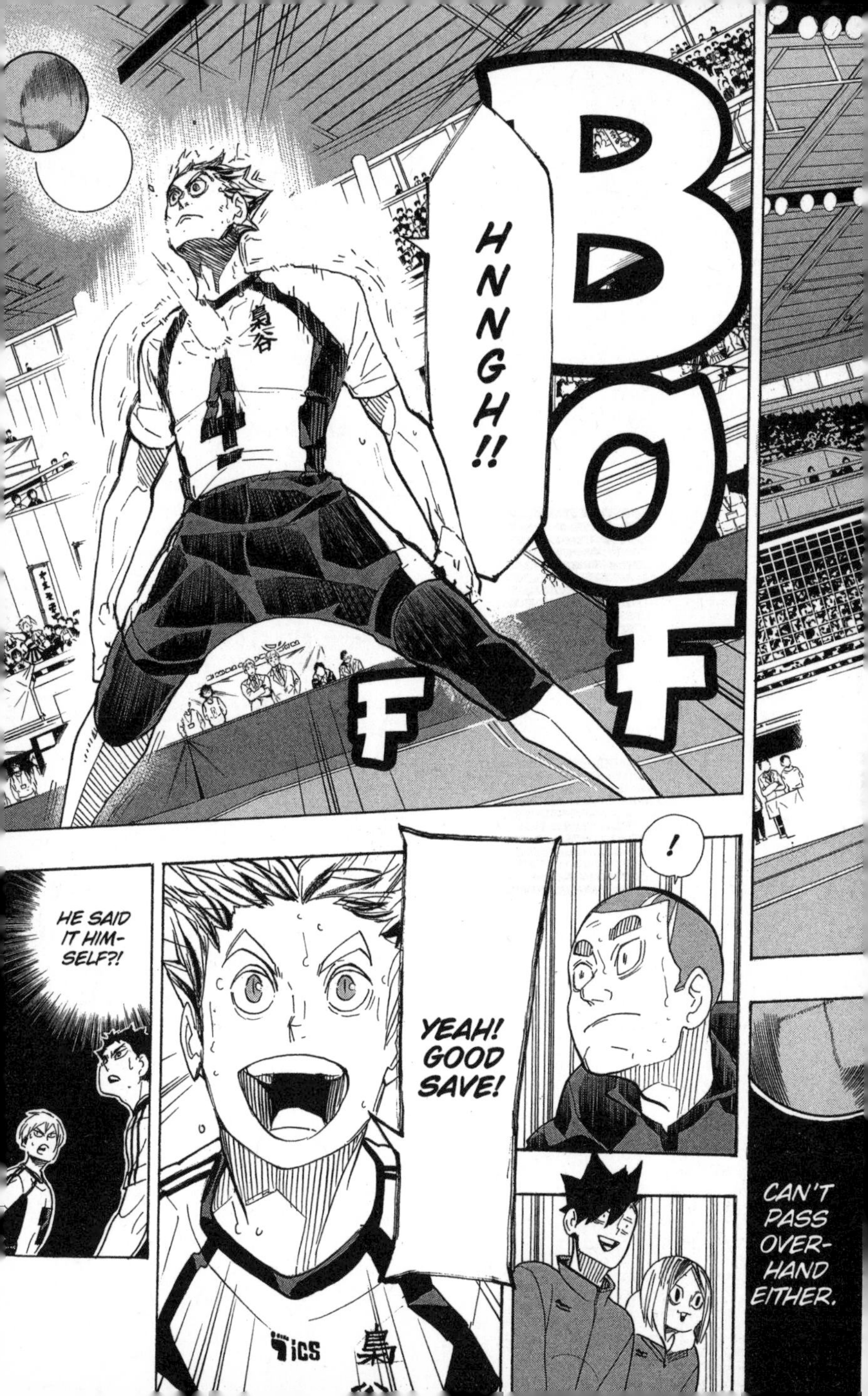
HNNNGH!!
BOFF
CAN'T PASS OVER-HAND EITHER.
!
YEAH! GOOD SAVE!
HE SAID IT HIM-SELF?!

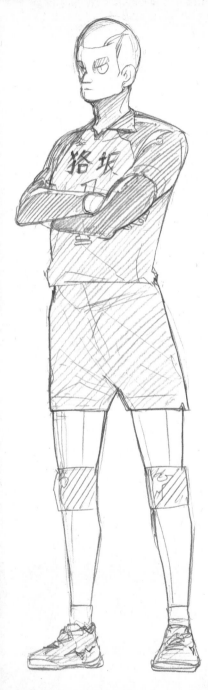

WAKATSU KIRYU

MUJINAZAKA HIGH SCHOOL, CLASS 3-1

VOLLEYBALL CLUB CAPTAIN

POSITION: WING SPIKER

HEIGHT: 6'2"

WEIGHT: 189 LBS. (AS OF JANUARY, 3RD YEAR OF HIGH SCHOOL)

BIRTHDAY: APRIL 8

FAVORITE FOOD: RAW OYSTERS

CURRENT WORRY:

• HIS SERVE DEFENSE

• HOW TO GUIDE HIS JUNIORS AND PROVIDE A GOOD EXAMPLE FOR THEM

• HIS LITTLE SISTER BLEACHED HER HAIR

• THE SPARROW THAT COMES TO HIS HOUSE EVERY YEAR THAT HASN'T COME YET

ETC., ETC....

ABILITY PARAMETERS (5-POINT SCALE)

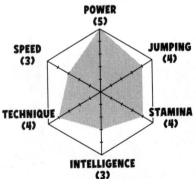

POWER (5)
JUMPING (4)
SPEED (3)
STAMINA (4)
TECHNIQUE (4)
INTELLIGENCE (3)

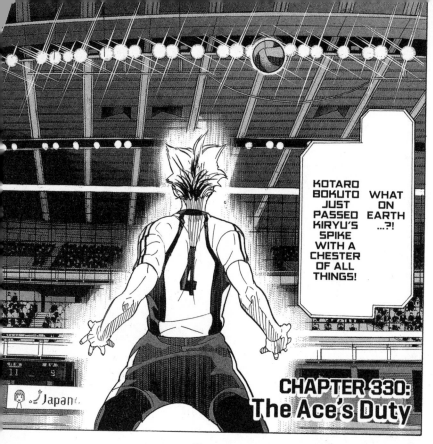

KOTARO BOKUTO JUST PASSED KIRYU'S SPIKE WITH A CHESTER OF ALL THINGS!

WHAT ON EARTH ...?!

CHAPTER 330:
The Ace's Duty

COPY-CAT.

UH, GOOD PASS?

MY GOOD-NESS, WHAT A CREATIVE SPIRIT! [LOL]

WOW!

HA HA HA!

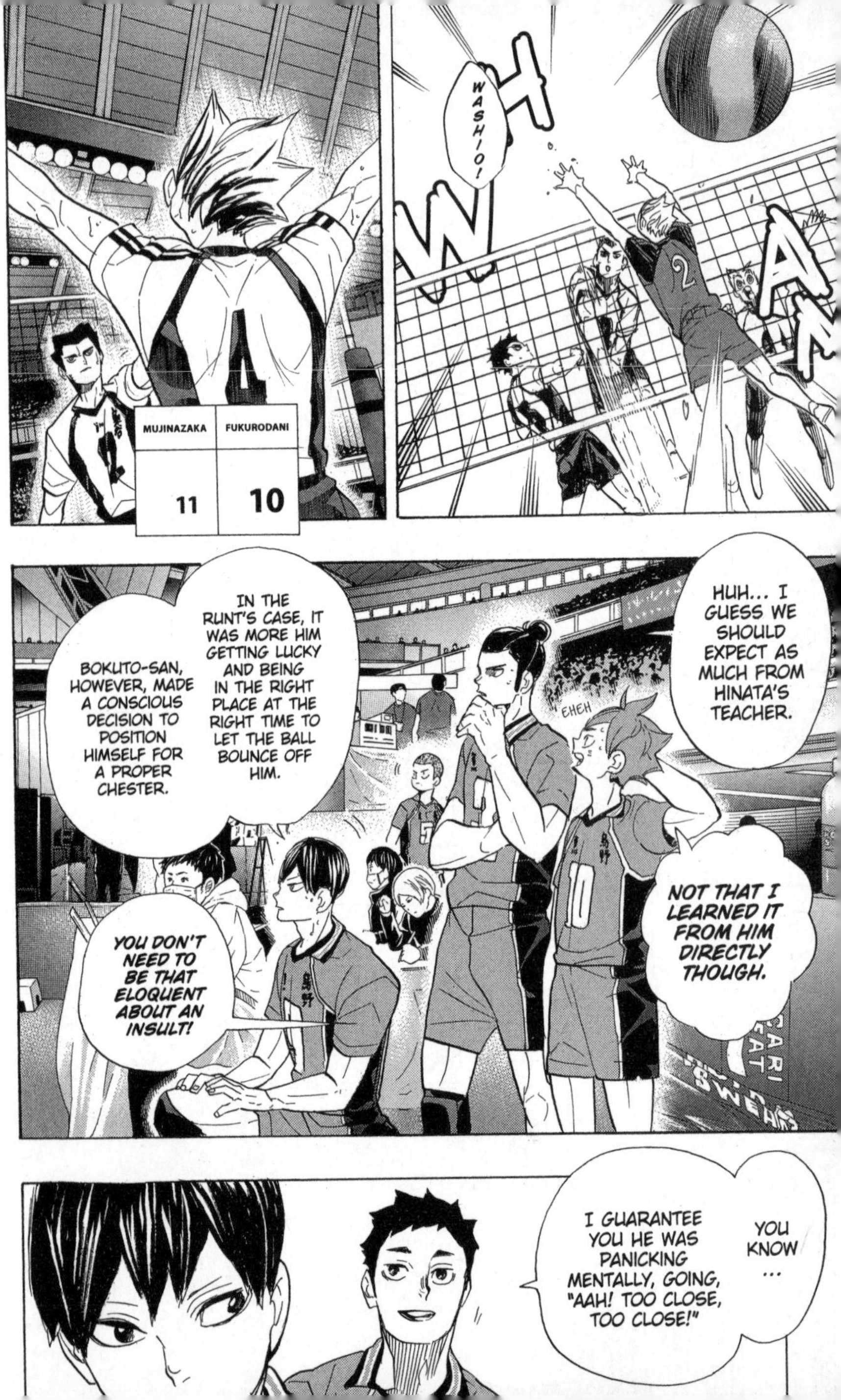
WASHIO!
MUJINAZAKA
FUKURODANI
11
10
HUH... I GUESS WE SHOULD EXPECT AS MUCH FROM HINATA'S TEACHER.
EHEH
NOT THAT I LEARNED IT FROM HIM DIRECTLY THOUGH.
IN THE RUNT'S CASE, IT WAS MORE HIM GETTING LUCKY AND BEING IN THE RIGHT PLACE AT THE RIGHT TIME TO LET THE BALL BOUNCE OFF HIM.
BOKUTO-SAN, HOWEVER, MADE A CONSCIOUS DECISION TO POSITION HIMSELF FOR A PROPER CHESTER.
YOU DON'T NEED TO BE THAT ELOQUENT ABOUT AN INSULT!
YOU KNOW...
I GUARANTEE YOU HE WAS PANICKING MENTALLY, GOING, "AAH! TOO CLOSE, TOO CLOSE!"

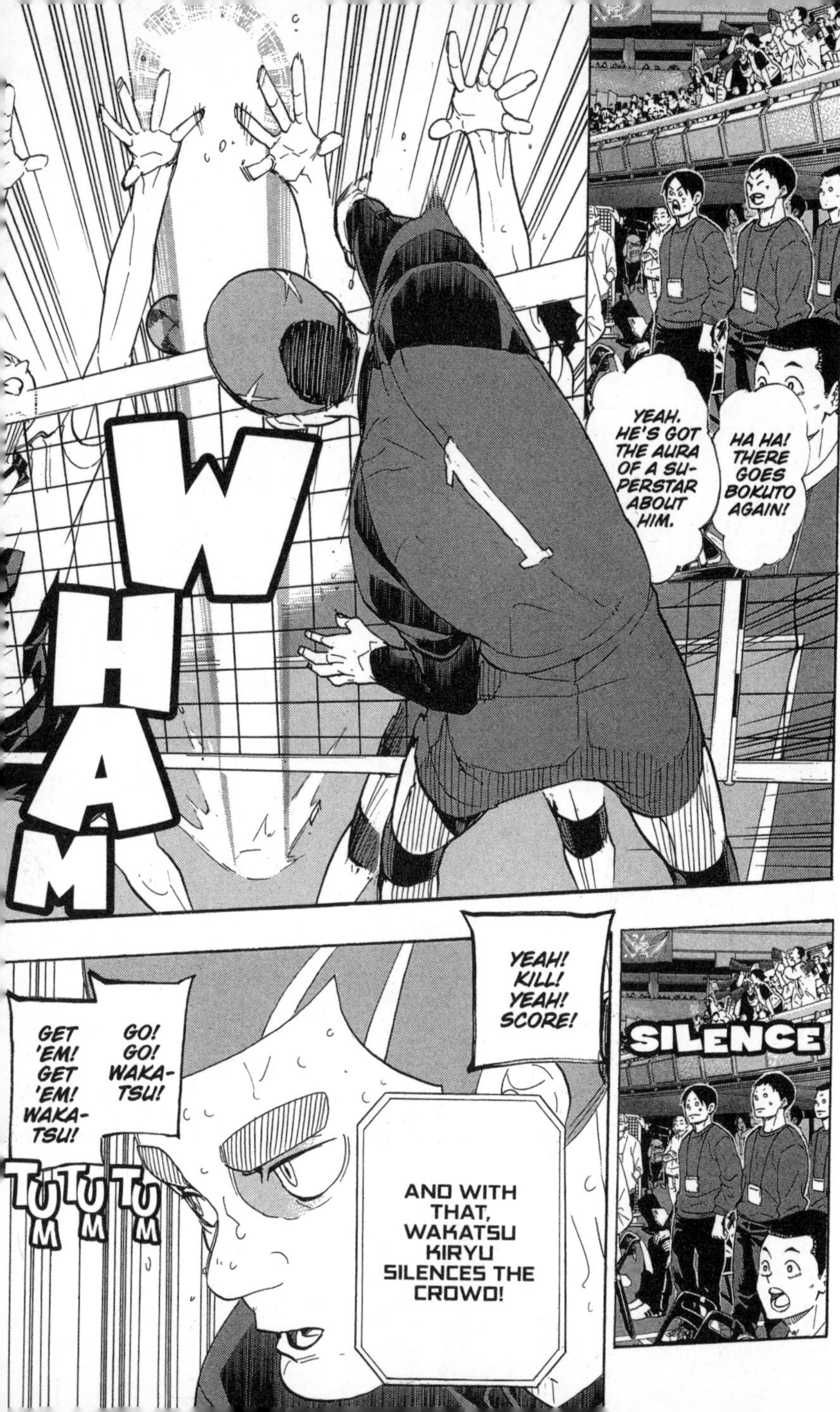
HA HA! THERE GOES BOKUTO AGAIN!
YEAH. HE'S GOT THE AURA OF A SU-PERSTAR ABOUT HIM.
WHAM
SILENCE
YEAH! KILL! YEAH! SCORE!
GO! GO! WAKA-TSU!
GET 'EM! GET 'EM! WAKA-TSU!
TUTUM TUTUM TUTUM
AND WITH THAT, WAKATSU KIRYU SILENCES THE CROWD!

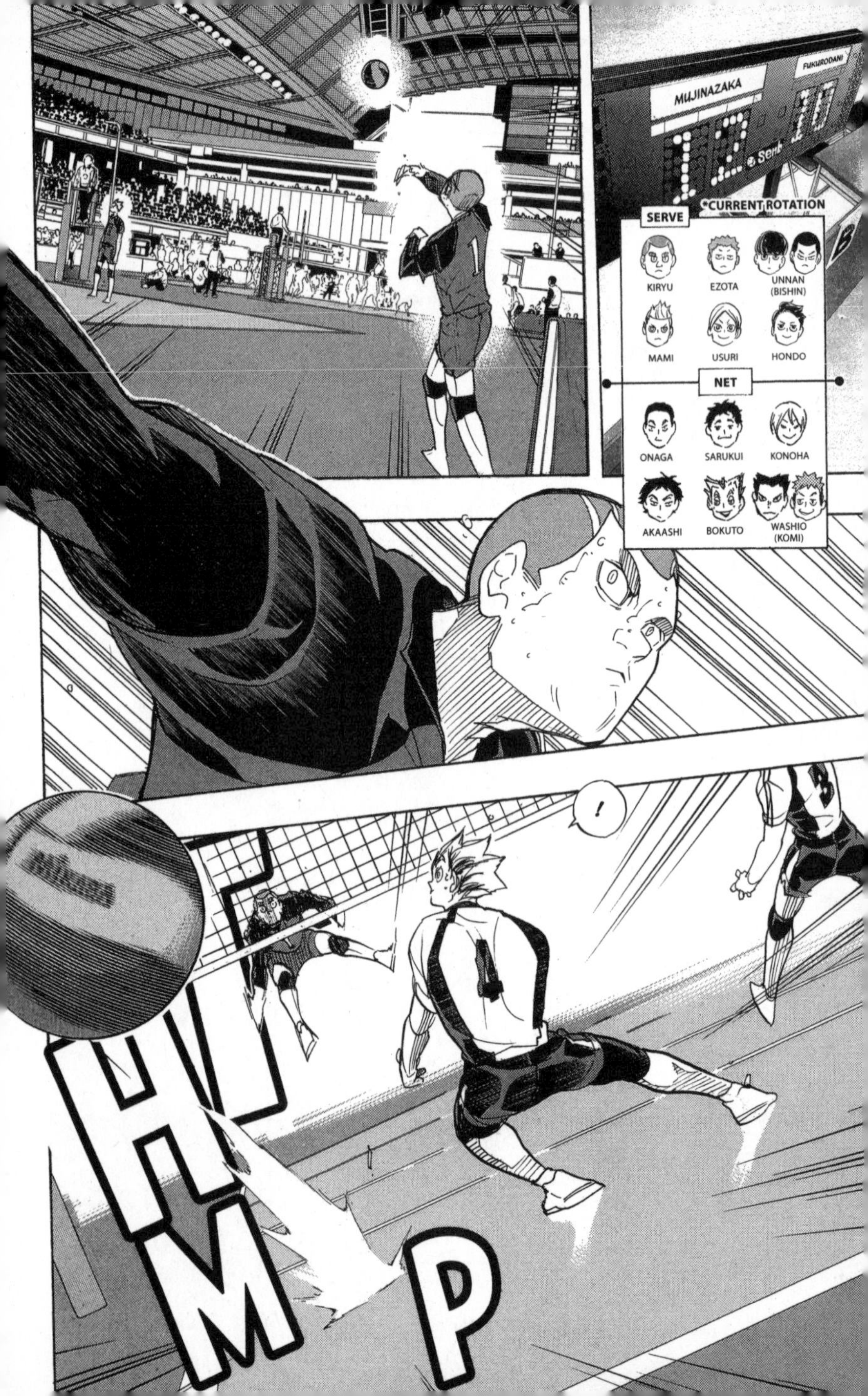
FUKURODANI
MUJINAZAKA
*CURRENT ROTATION
SERVE
KIRYU
EZOTA
UNNAN (BISHIN)
MAMI
USURI
HONDO
NET
ONAGA
SARUKUI
KONOHA
AKAASHI
BOKUTO
WASHIO (KOMI)
!

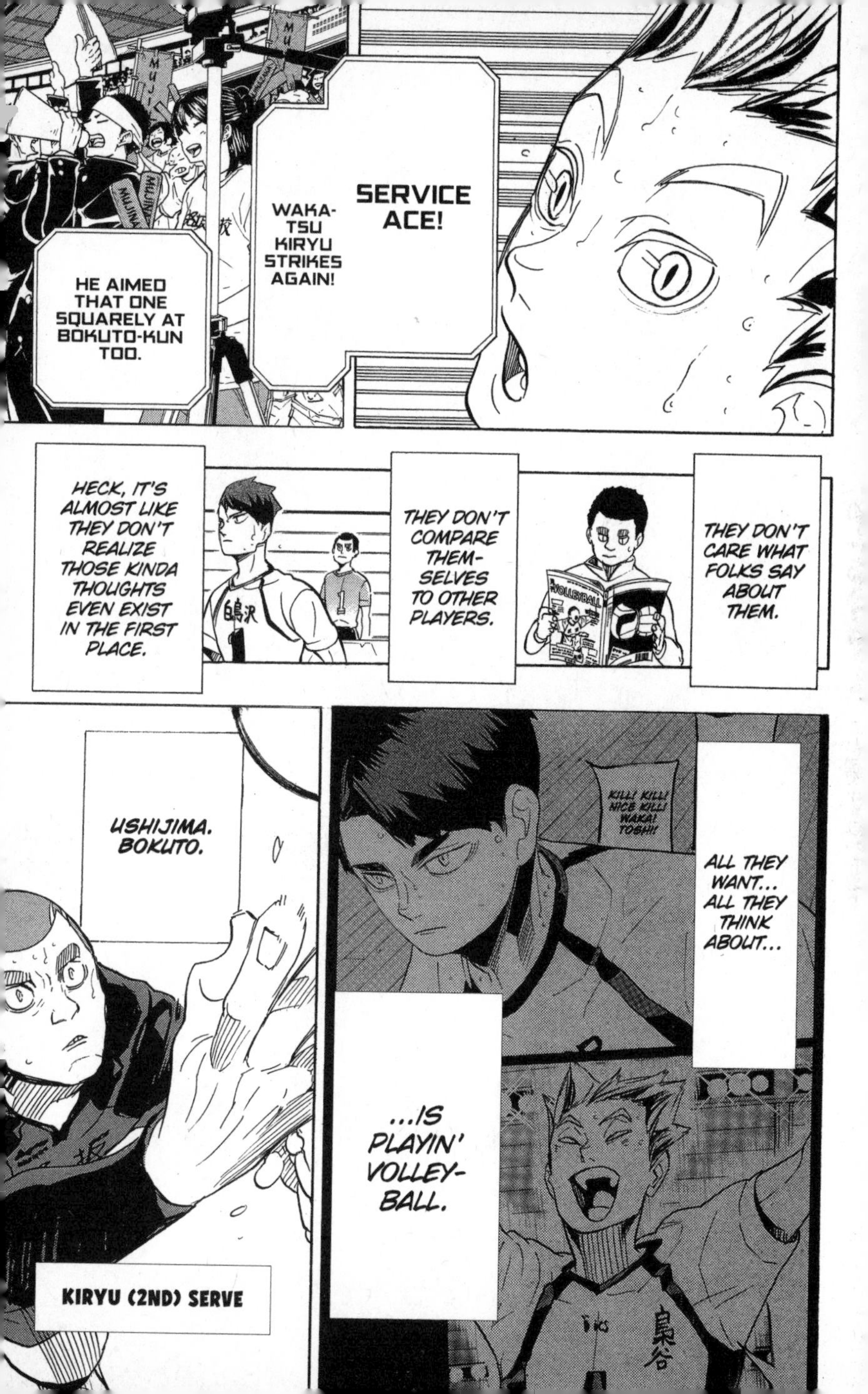

SERVICE ACE!
WAKA-TSU KIRYU STRIKES AGAIN!
HE AIMED THAT ONE SQUARELY AT BOKUTO-KUN TOO.
THEY DON'T CARE WHAT FOLKS SAY ABOUT THEM.
THEY DON'T COMPARE THEM-SELVES TO OTHER PLAYERS.
HECK, IT'S ALMOST LIKE THEY DON'T REALIZE THOSE KINDA THOUGHTS EVEN EXIST IN THE FIRST PLACE.
KILLI KILLI NICE KILLI WAKA! TOSHI!
ALL THEY WANT... ALL THEY THINK ABOUT...
...IS PLAYIN' VOLLEY-BALL.
USHIJIMA. BOKUTO.
KIRYU (2ND) SERVE

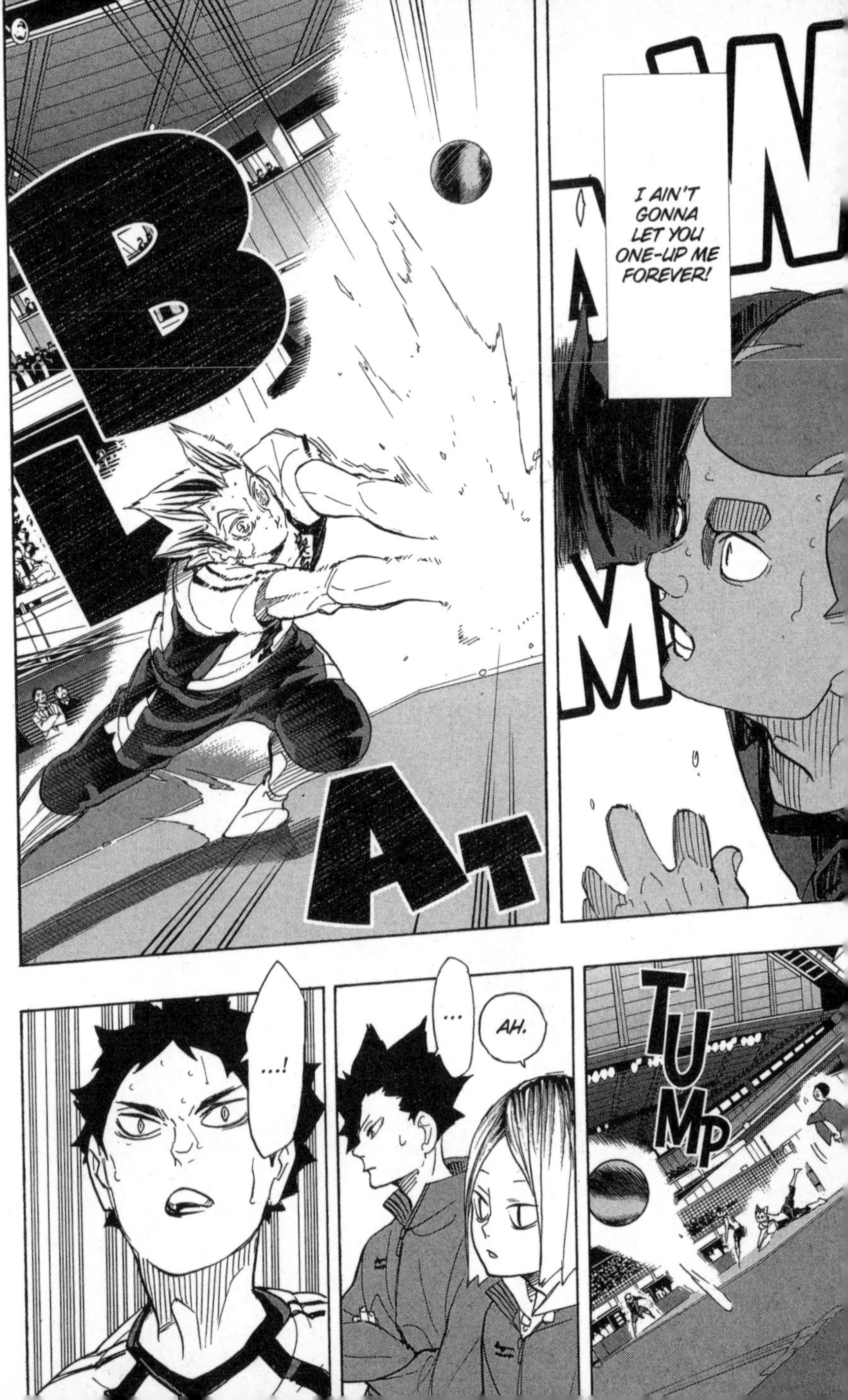

I AIN'T GONNA LET YOU ONE-UP ME FOREVER!
TUMP
...
AH.
...!

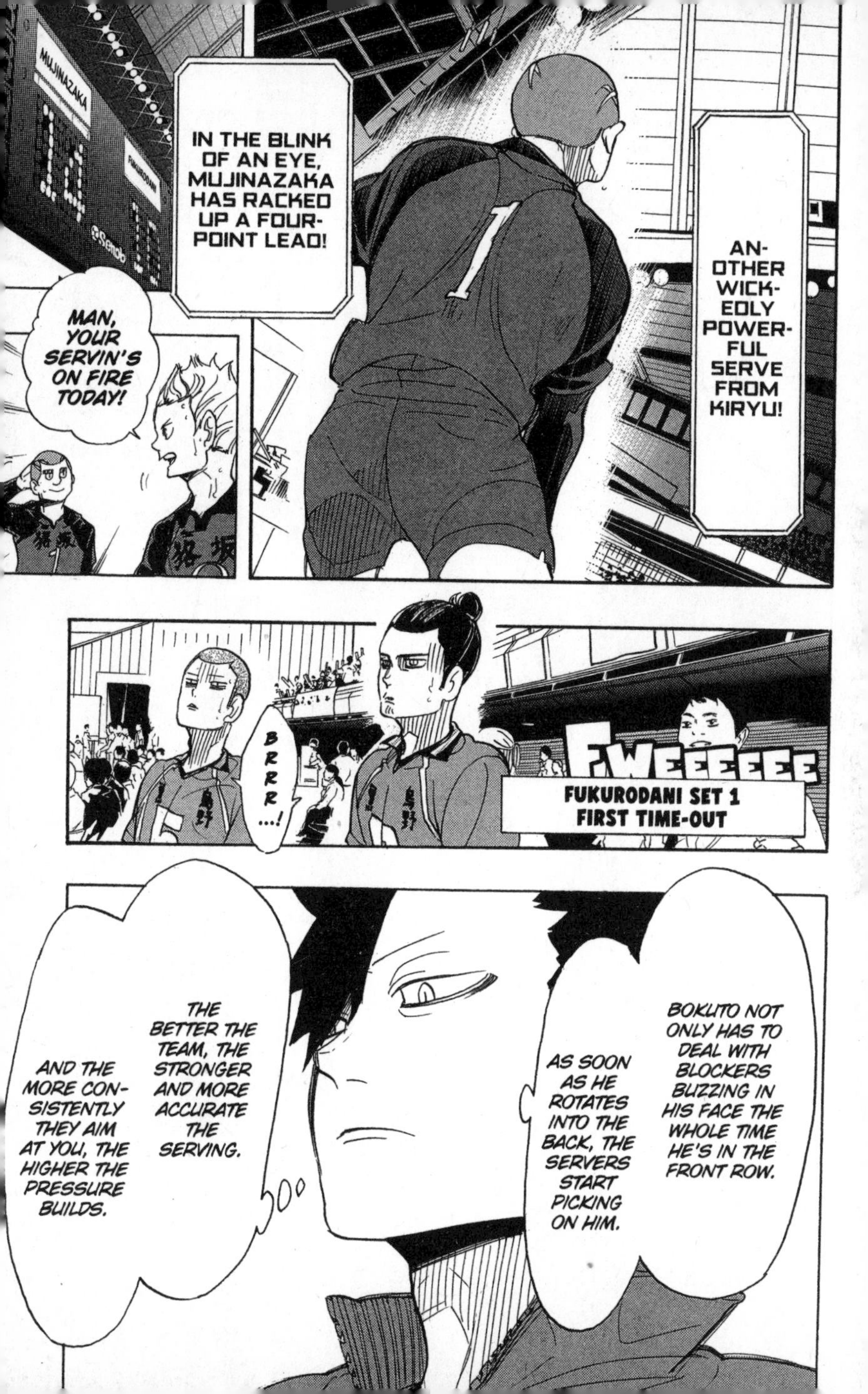
ANOTHER WICKEDLY POWERFUL SERVE FROM KIRYU!
IN THE BLINK OF AN EYE, MUJINAZAKA HAS RACKED UP A FOUR-POINT LEAD!
MUJINAZAKA
FUKURODANI
MAN, YOUR SERVIN'S ON FIRE TODAY!
FWEEEEEE
FUKURODANI SET 1 FIRST TIME-OUT
BRRR...!
BOKUTO NOT ONLY HAS TO DEAL WITH BLOCKERS BUZZING IN HIS FACE THE WHOLE TIME HE'S IN THE FRONT ROW.
AS SOON AS HE ROTATES INTO THE BACK, THE SERVERS START PICKING ON HIM.
THE BETTER THE TEAM, THE STRONGER AND MORE ACCURATE THE SERVING.
AND THE MORE CONSISTENTLY THEY AIM AT YOU, THE HIGHER THE PRESSURE BUILDS.

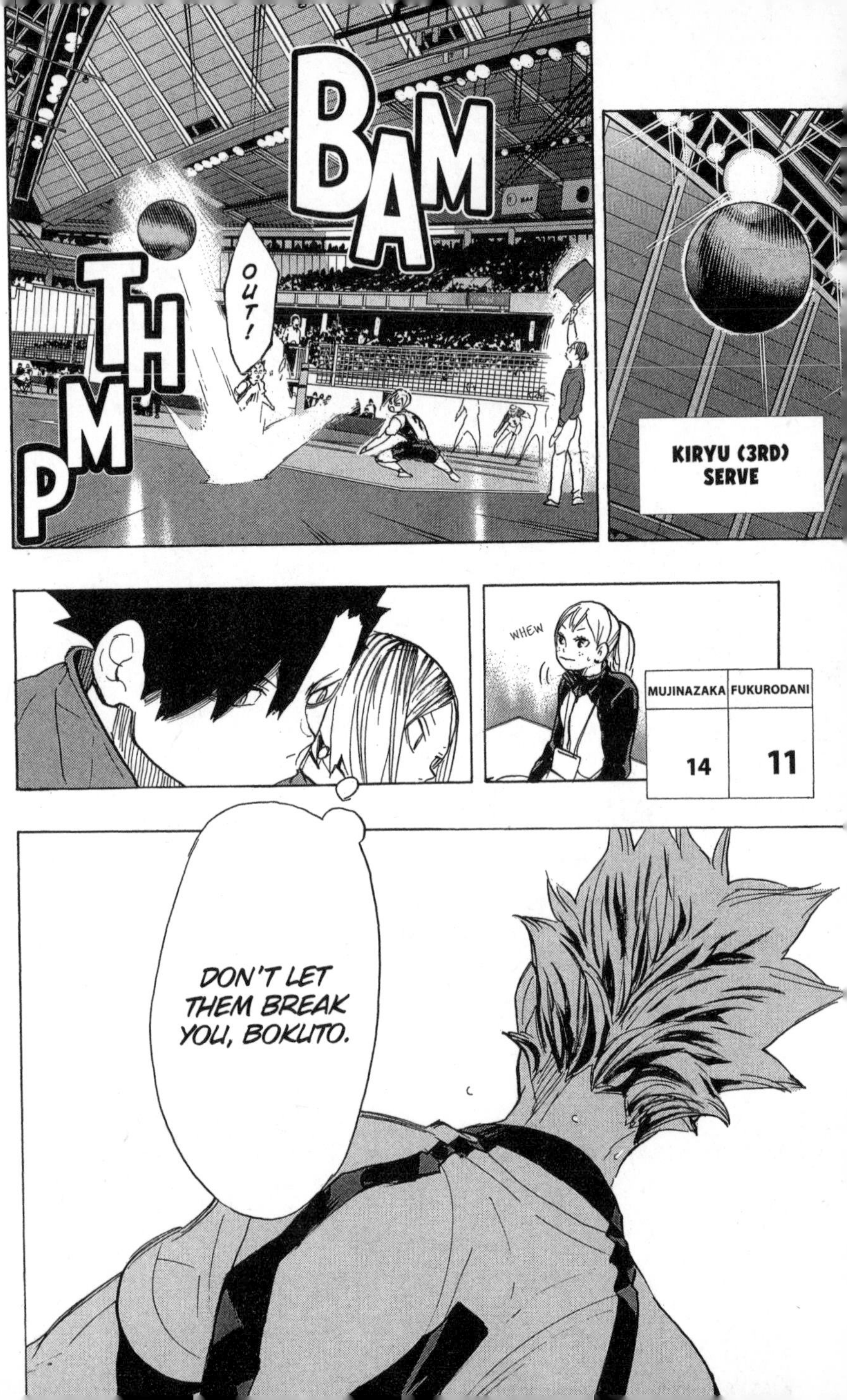
KIRYU (3RD) SERVE
BAM
OUT!
THMP
WHEW
MUJINAZAKA 14
FUKURODANI 11
DON'T LET THEM BREAK YOU, BOKUTO.

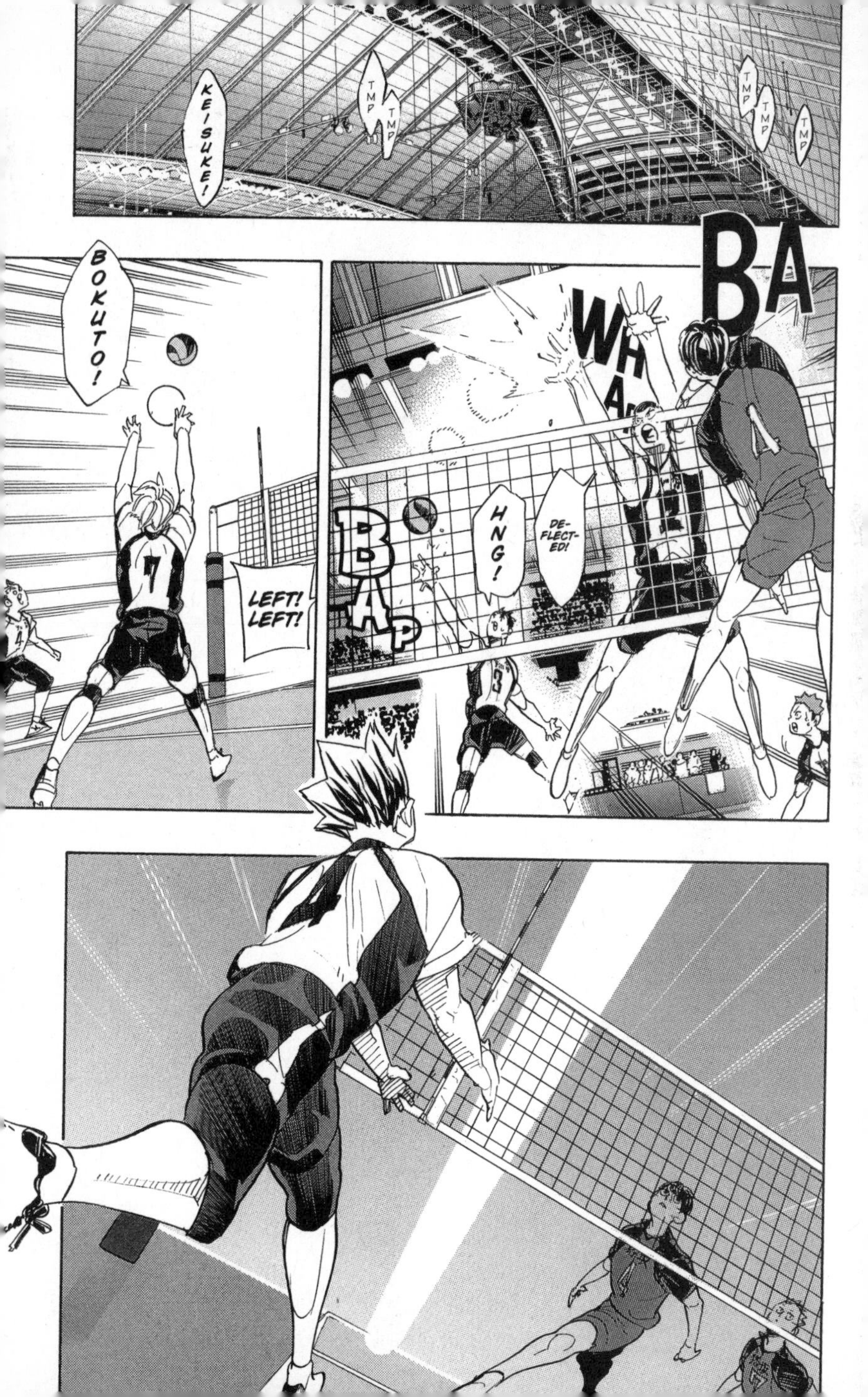
TMP
TMP
TMP
TMP
TMP
KEISUKE!
BA
WHA
DE-FLECT-ED!
HNG!
BAP
BOKUTO!
LEFT! LEFT!

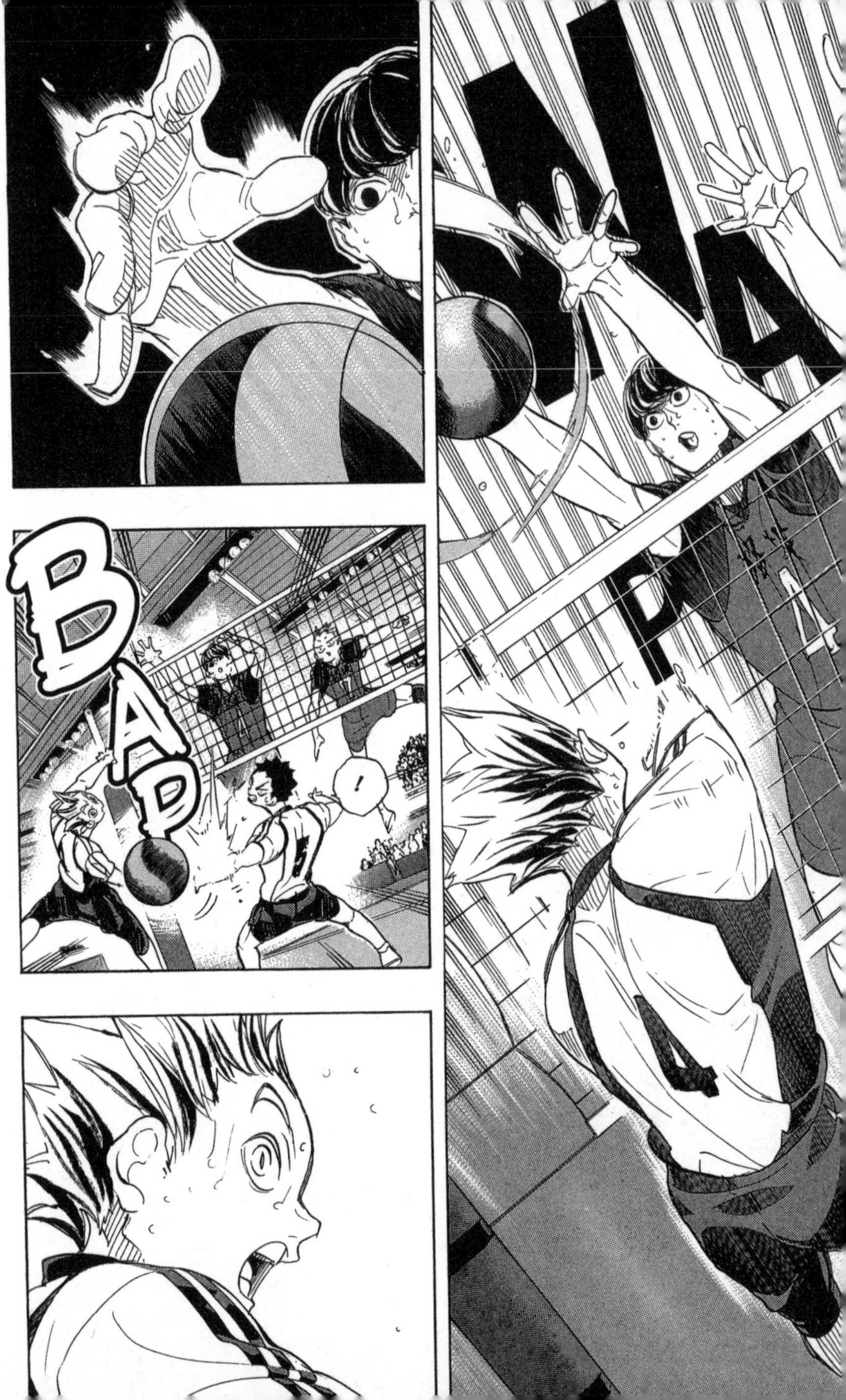
BAP
!

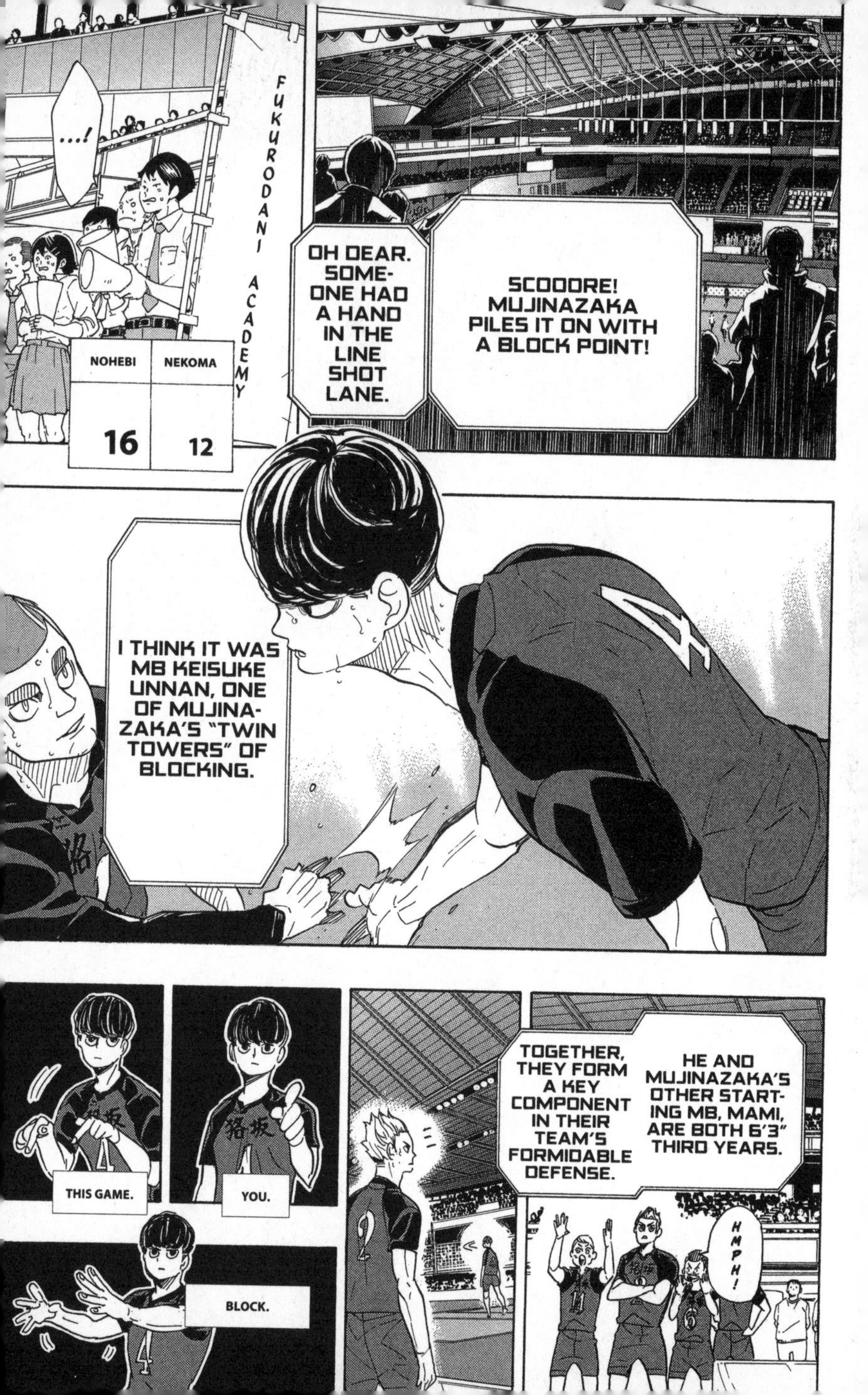

SCOOORE! MUJINAZAKA PILES IT ON WITH A BLOCK POINT!
OH DEAR. SOME-ONE HAD A HAND IN THE LINE SHOT LANE.
...!
FUKURODANI ACADEMY
NOHEBI NEKOMA
16 12
I THINK IT WAS MB KEISUKE UNNAN, ONE OF MUJINA-ZAKA'S "TWIN TOWERS" OF BLOCKING.
HE AND MUJINAZAKA'S OTHER START-ING MB, MAMI, ARE BOTH 6'3" THIRD YEARS.
TOGETHER, THEY FORM A KEY COMPONENT IN THEIR TEAM'S FORMIDABLE DEFENSE.
HMPH!
YOU.
THIS GAME.
BLOCK.

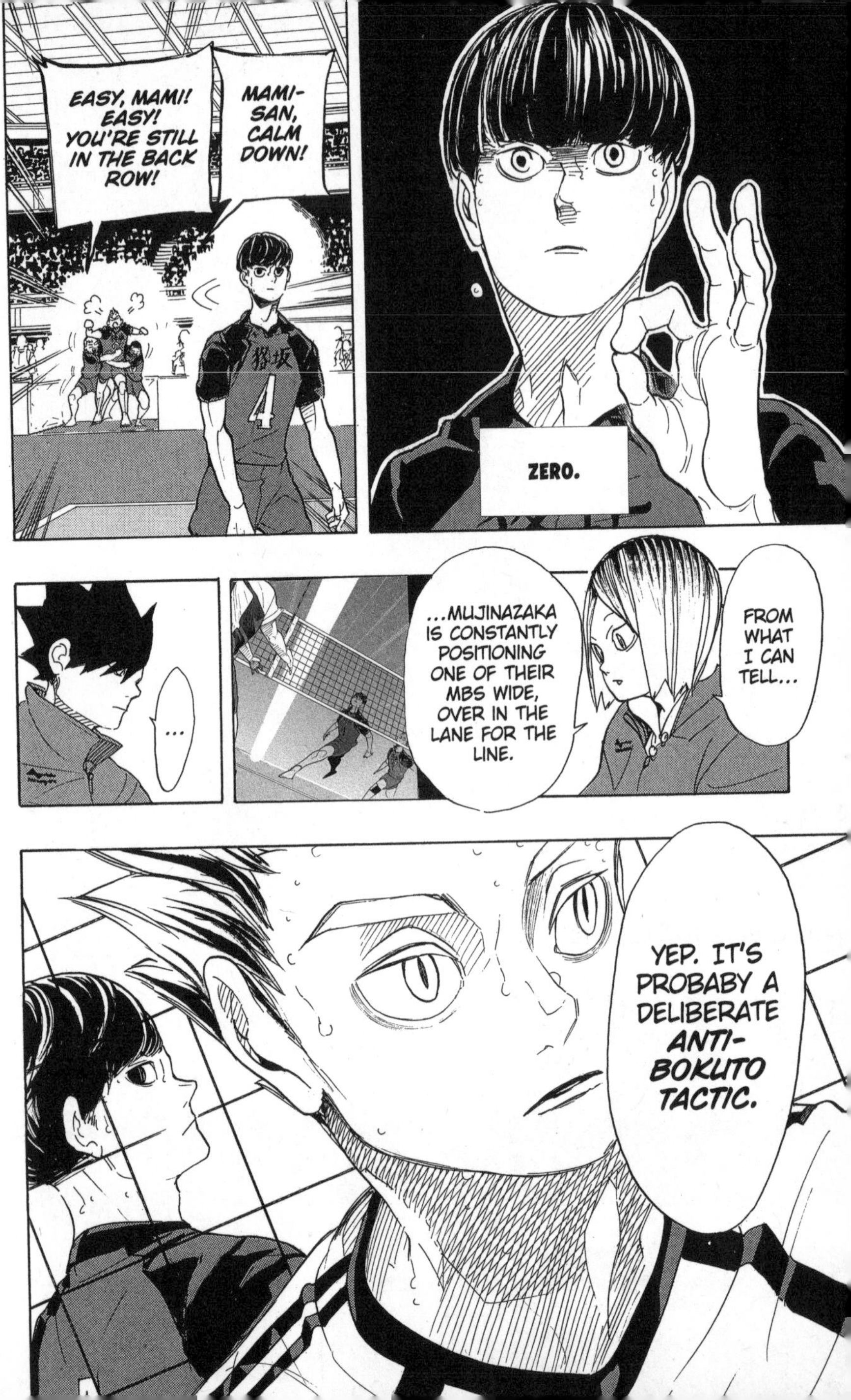
ZERO.
MAMI-SAN, CALM DOWN!
EASY, MAMI! EASY! YOU'RE STILL IN THE BACK ROW!
FROM WHAT I CAN TELL...
...MUJINAZAKA IS CONSTANTLY POSITIONING ONE OF THEIR MBS WIDE, OVER IN THE LANE FOR THE LINE.
...
YEP. IT'S PROBABY A DELIBERATE ANTI-BOKUTO TACTIC.

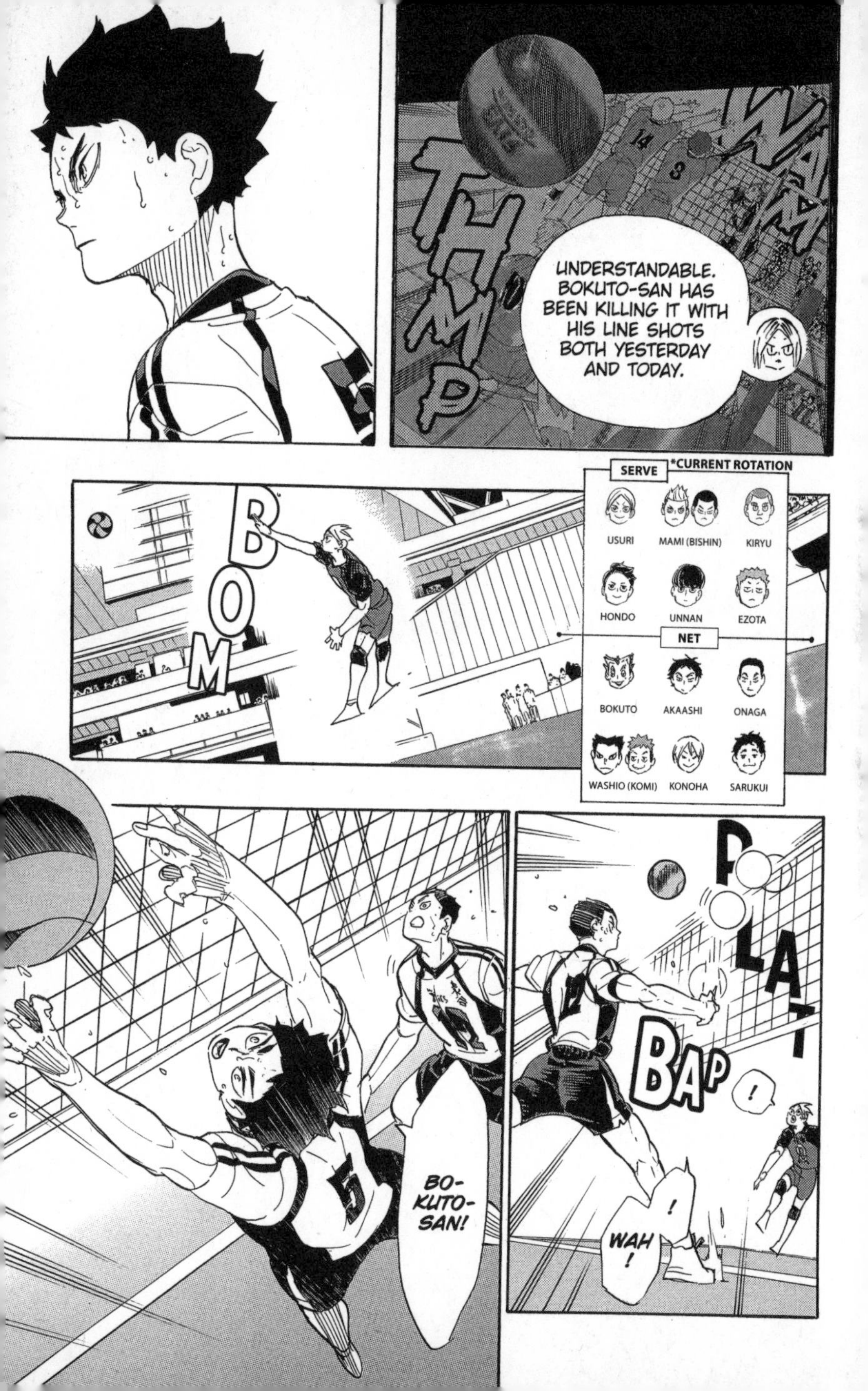
WAM
THUMP
UNDERSTANDABLE. BOKUTO-SAN HAS BEEN KILLING IT WITH HIS LINE SHOTS BOTH YESTERDAY AND TODAY.
*CURRENT ROTATION
SERVE
USURI
MAMI (BISHIN)
KIRYU
HONDO
UNNAN
EZOTA
NET
BOKUTO
AKAASHI
ONAGA
WASHIO (KOMI)
KONOHA
SARUKUI
BOOM
POP
PLAT
BAP
!
!
WAH!
BO-KUTO-SAN!

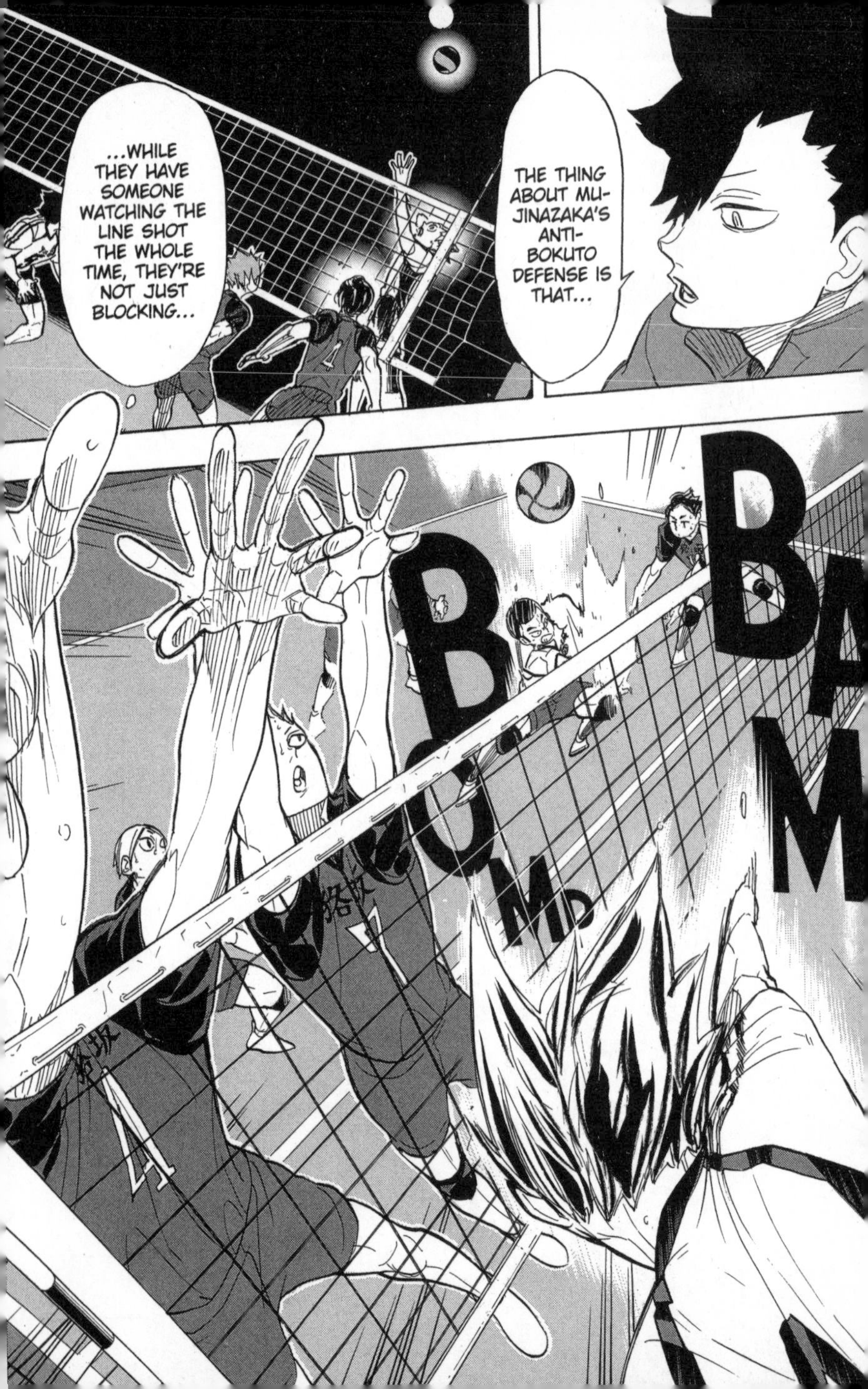
THE THING ABOUT MUJINAZAKA'S ANTI-BOKUTO DEFENSE IS THAT...
...WHILE THEY HAVE SOMEONE WATCHING THE LINE SHOT THE WHOLE TIME, THEY'RE NOT JUST BLOCKING...
BAM
BOOM

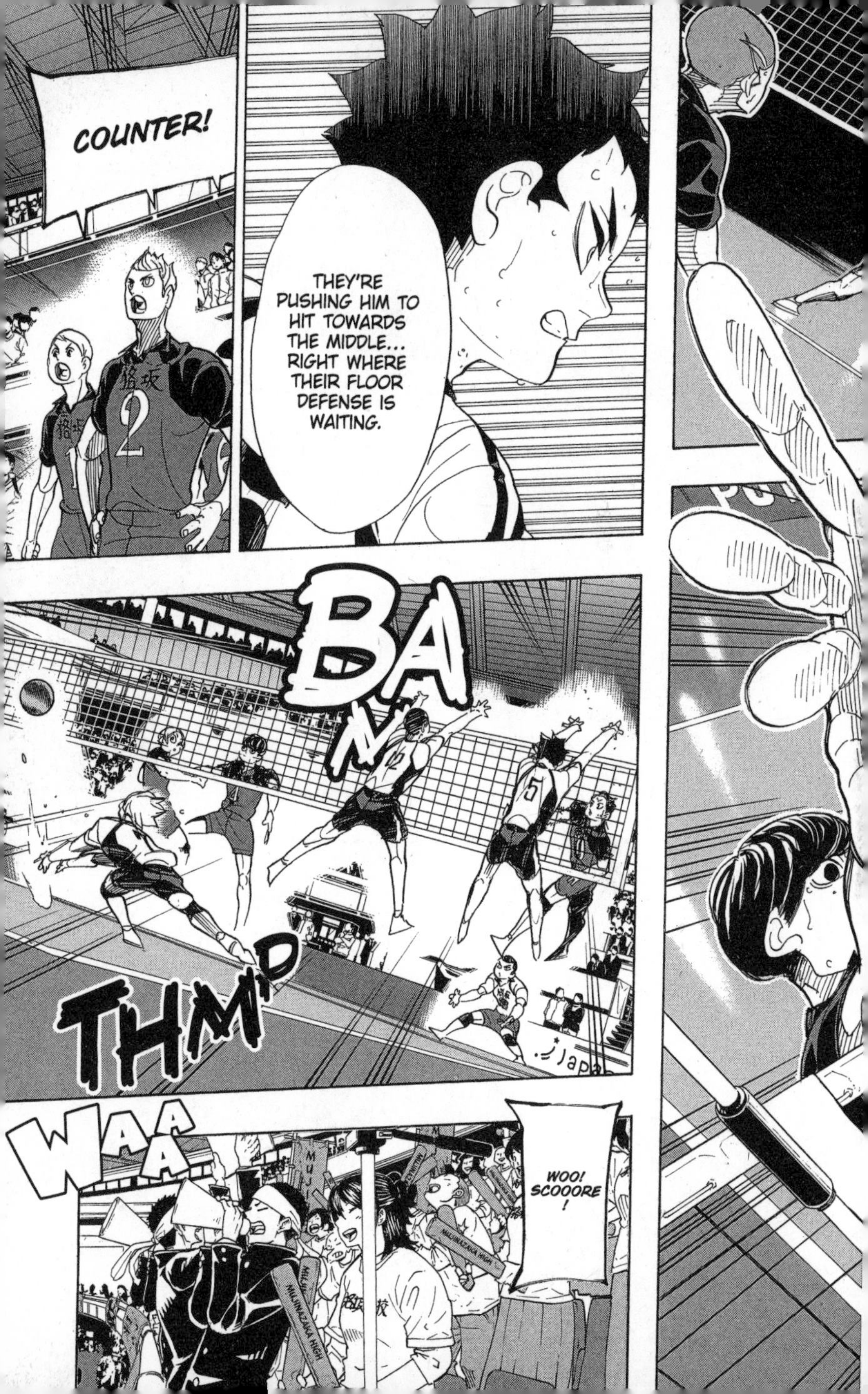
THEY'RE PUSHING HIM TO HIT TOWARDS THE MIDDLE... RIGHT WHERE THEIR FLOOR DEFENSE IS WAITING.
COUNTER!
BAM
THMP
WOO! SCOOORE!
WAAA...

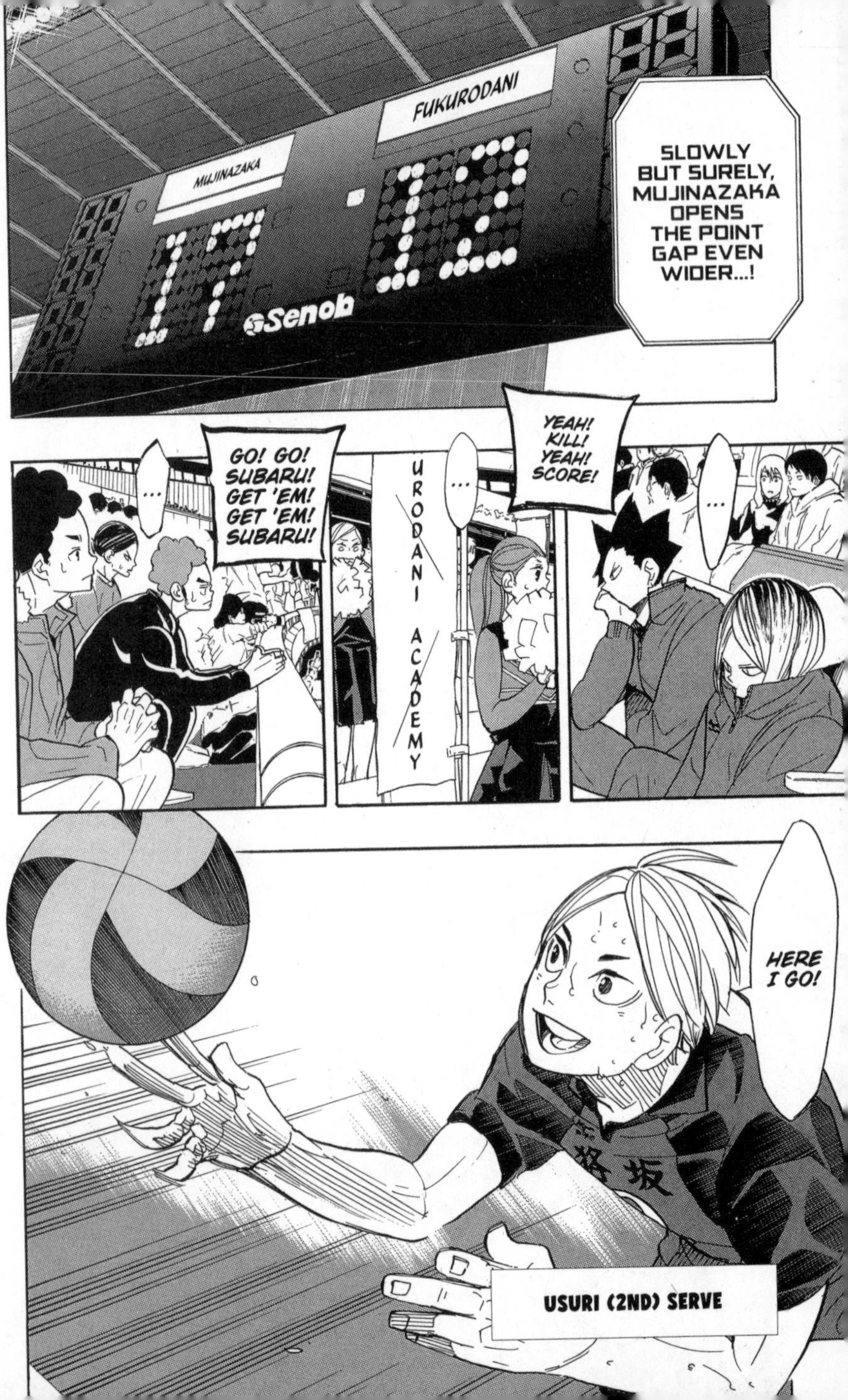
FUKURODANI
MUJINAZAKA
Senob
SLOWLY BUT SURELY, MUJINAZAKA OPENS THE POINT GAP EVEN WIDER...!
...
YEAH! KILL! YEAH! SCORE!
...
URODANI ACADEMY
GO! GO! SUBARU! GET 'EM! GET 'EM! SUBARU!
...
HERE I GO!
USURI (2ND) SERVE

BAFF

SARU!

NASTY!

GOOD BUMP!

HE MADE THAT LOOK EASY, BUT IT TOOK SKILL TO MAKE THAT BUMP.

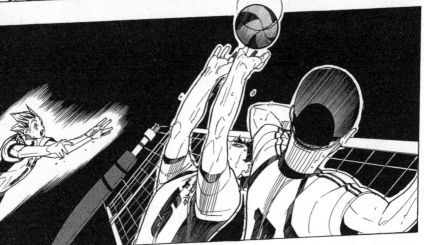

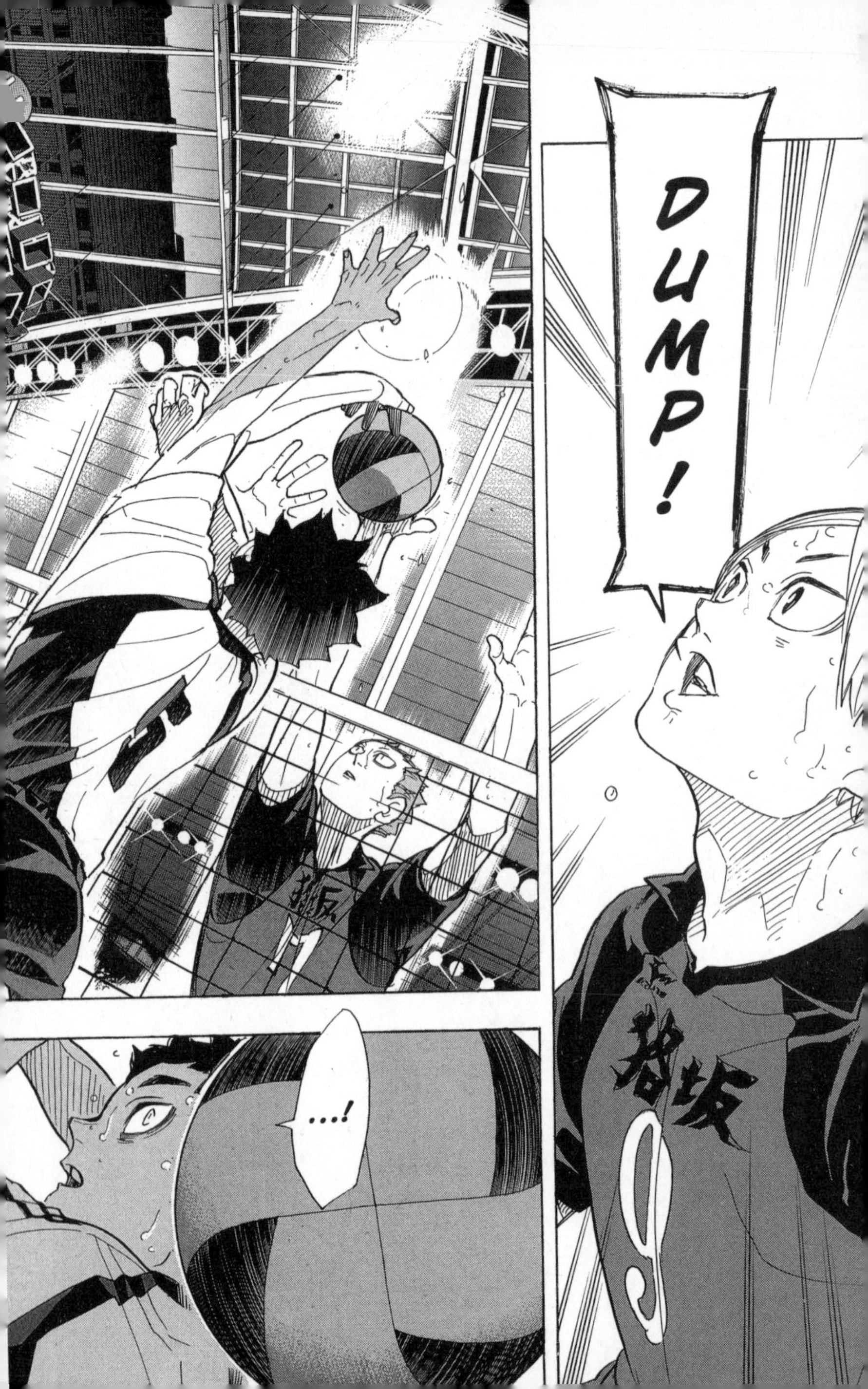
DUMP!
...!

TU
MP
BDM
BDM
BDM
Aha!
I knew it!
狢坂
MUJINAZAKA
FUKURODANI
12
12

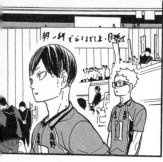

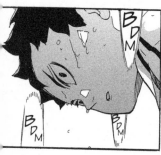

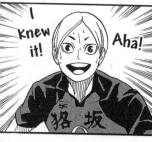

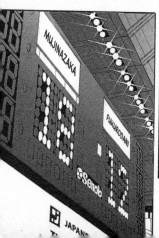

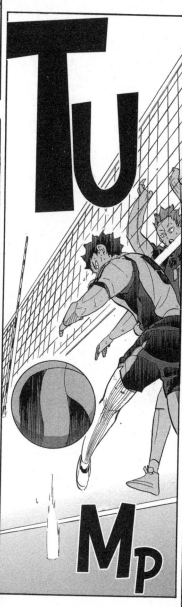

HELLO FROM BEYOND THE (PAGE) EDGE!! GUESS WHICH PANEL THIS IS!!

FROM CH. 330

<MONSTER HAND-CLINGER CROW>

A SUBSPECIES OF THE MONSTER HINA CROW. ONCE IT CLINGS TO YOUR HAND, IT WON'T LET GO UNTIL YOU SCORE (VIA SPIKE OR SERVE).

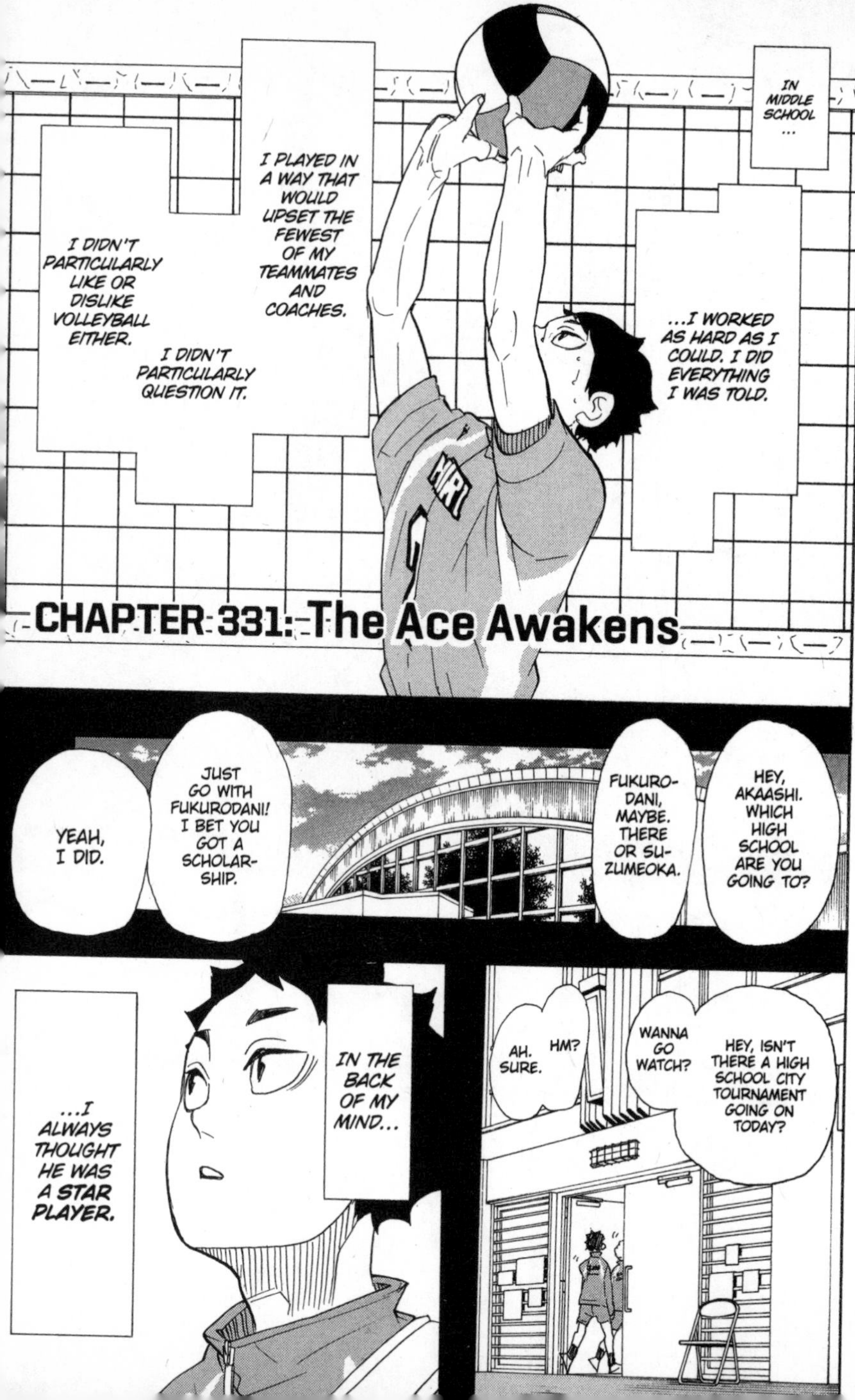
IN MIDDLE SCHOOL...
...I WORKED AS HARD AS I COULD. I DID EVERYTHING I WAS TOLD.
I PLAYED IN A WAY THAT WOULD UPSET THE FEWEST OF MY TEAMMATES AND COACHES.
I DIDN'T PARTICULARLY QUESTION IT.
I DIDN'T PARTICULARLY LIKE OR DISLIKE VOLLEYBALL EITHER.
CHAPTER 331: The Ace Awakens
HEY, AKAASHI. WHICH HIGH SCHOOL ARE YOU GOING TO?
FUKURODANI, MAYBE. THERE OR SUZUMEOKA.
JUST GO WITH FUKURODANI! I BET YOU GOT A SCHOLARSHIP.
YEAH, I DID.
HEY, ISN'T THERE A HIGH SCHOOL CITY TOURNAMENT GOING ON TODAY?
WANNA GO WATCH?
HM?
AH. SURE.
IN THE BACK OF MY MIND...
...I ALWAYS THOUGHT HE WAS A STAR PLAYER.

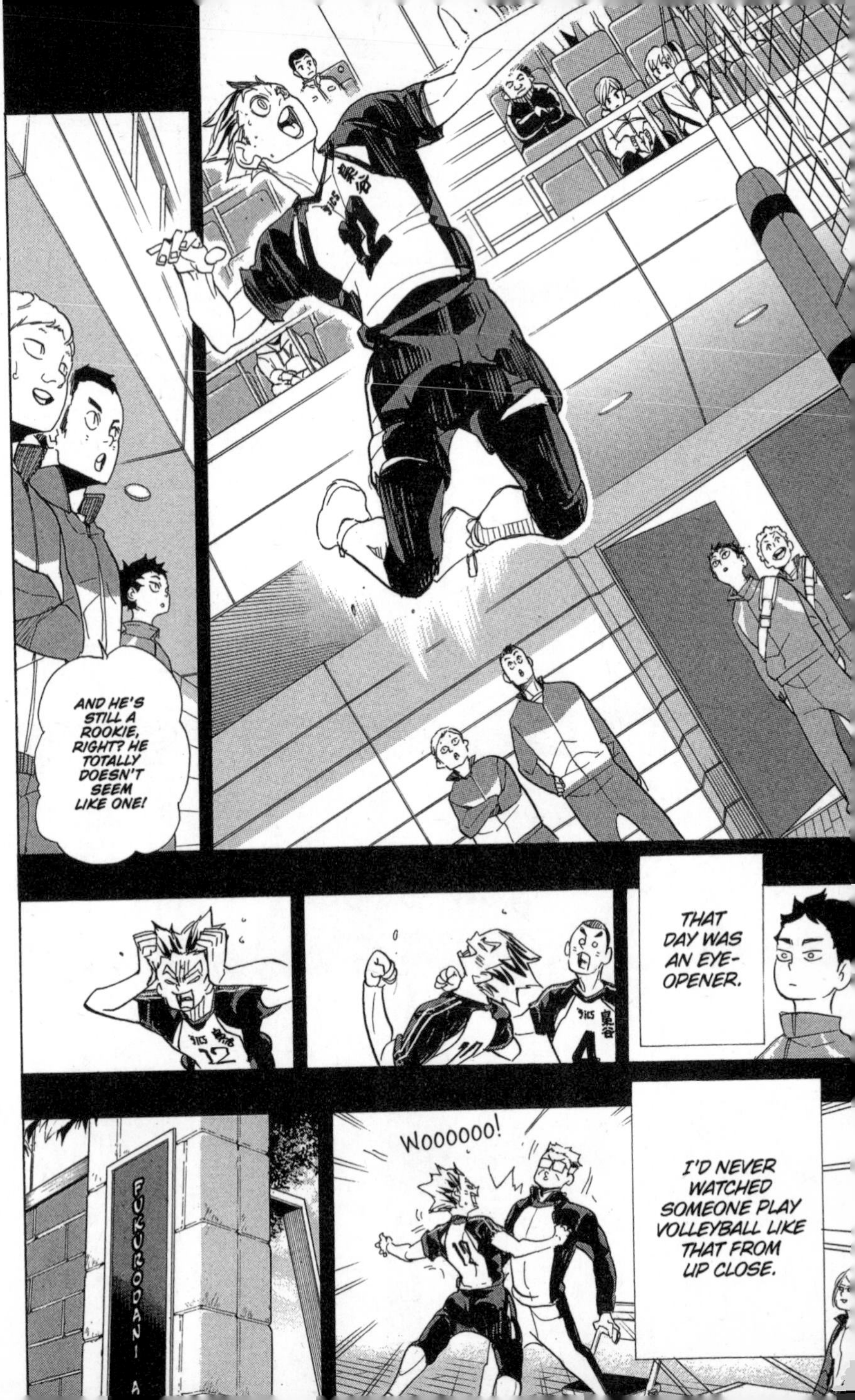
AND HE'S STILL A ROOKIE, RIGHT? HE TOTALLY DOESN'T SEEM LIKE ONE!
THAT DAY WAS AN EYE-OPENER.
I'D NEVER WATCHED SOMEONE PLAY VOLLEYBALL LIKE THAT FROM UP CLOSE.
Woooooo!

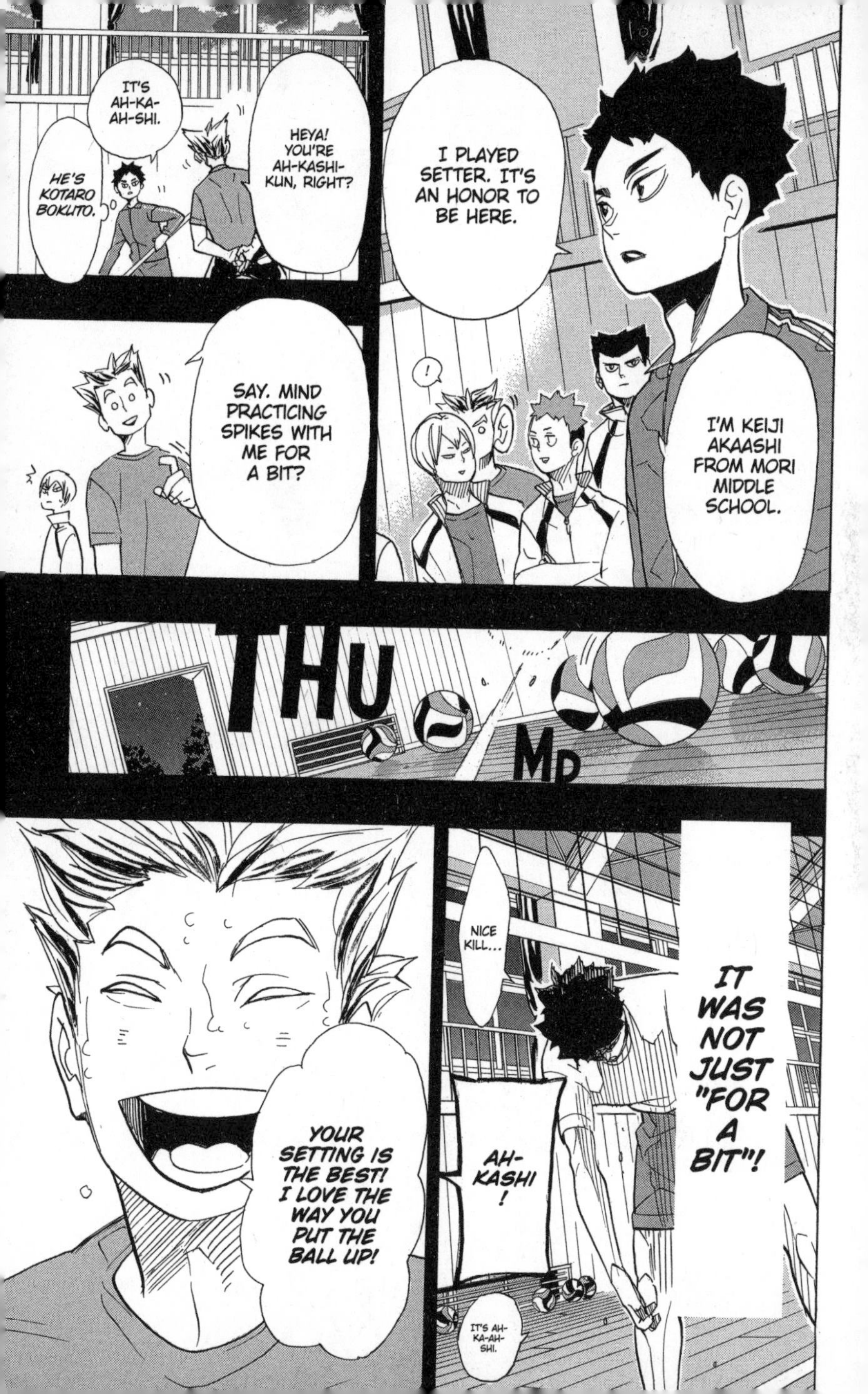

I'M KEIJI AKAASHI FROM MORI MIDDLE SCHOOL.
I PLAYED SETTER. IT'S AN HONOR TO BE HERE.
!
HEYA! YOU'RE AH-KASHI-KUN, RIGHT?
IT'S AH-KA-AH-SHI.
HE'S KOTARO BOKUTO.
SAY. MIND PRACTICING SPIKES WITH ME FOR A BIT?
THUMP
IT WAS NOT JUST "FOR A BIT"!
NICE KILL...
AH-KASHI!
IT'S AH-KA-AH-SHI.
YOUR SETTING IS THE BEST! I LOVE THE WAY YOU PUT THE BALL UP!

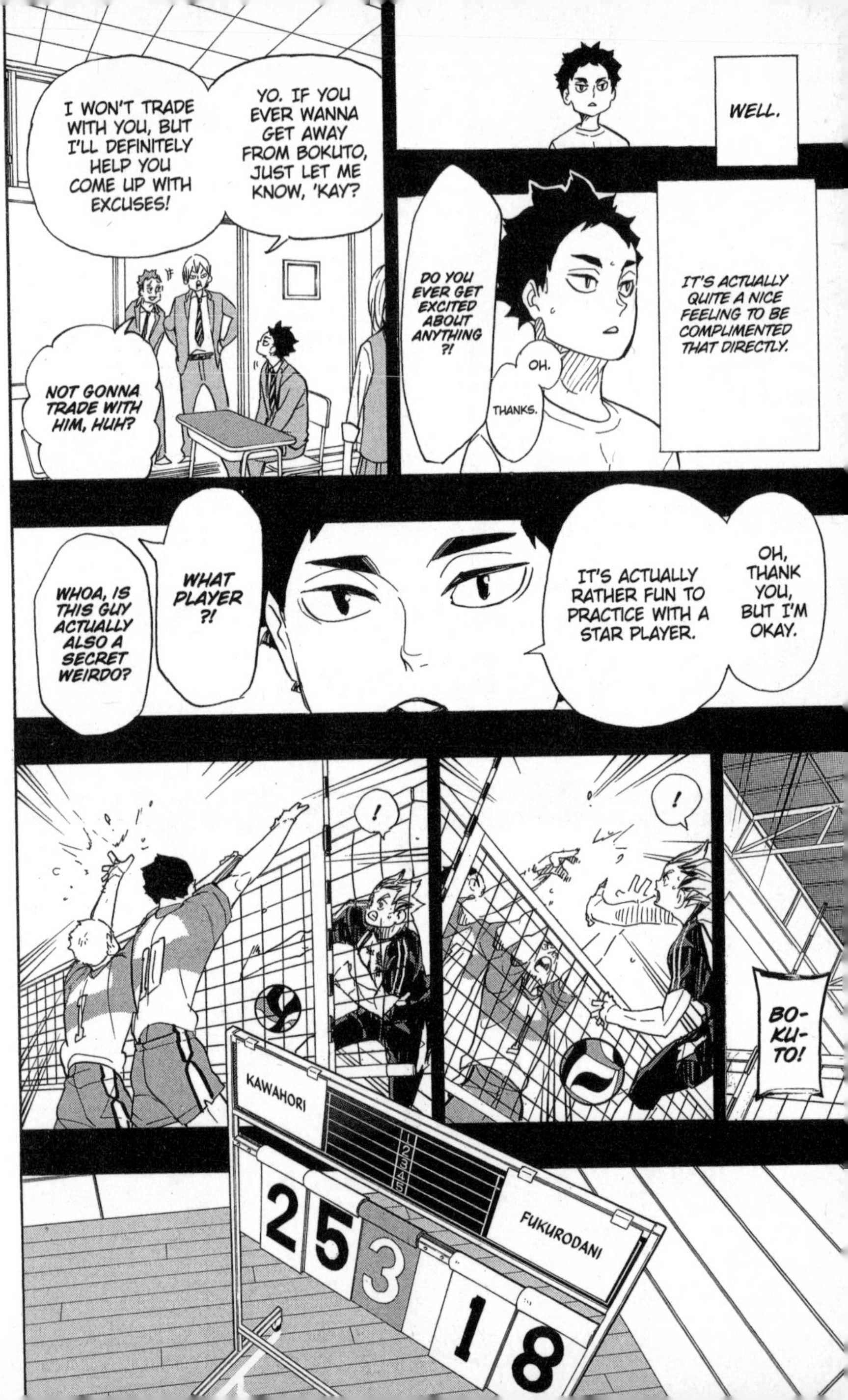
WELL.
IT'S ACTUALLY QUITE A NICE FEELING TO BE COMPLIMENTED THAT DIRECTLY.
OH.
THANKS.
DO YOU EVER GET EXCITED ABOUT ANYTHING ?!
YO. IF YOU EVER WANNA GET AWAY FROM BOKUTO, JUST LET ME KNOW, 'KAY?
I WON'T TRADE WITH YOU, BUT I'LL DEFINITELY HELP YOU COME UP WITH EXCUSES!
NOT GONNA TRADE WITH HIM, HUH?
OH, THANK YOU, BUT I'M OKAY.
IT'S ACTUALLY RATHER FUN TO PRACTICE WITH A STAR PLAYER.
WHAT PLAYER ?!
WHOA, IS THIS GUY ACTUALLY ALSO A SECRET WEIRDO?
BO-KUTO!
!
!
KAWAHORI
FUKURODANI
12345
25
3
18

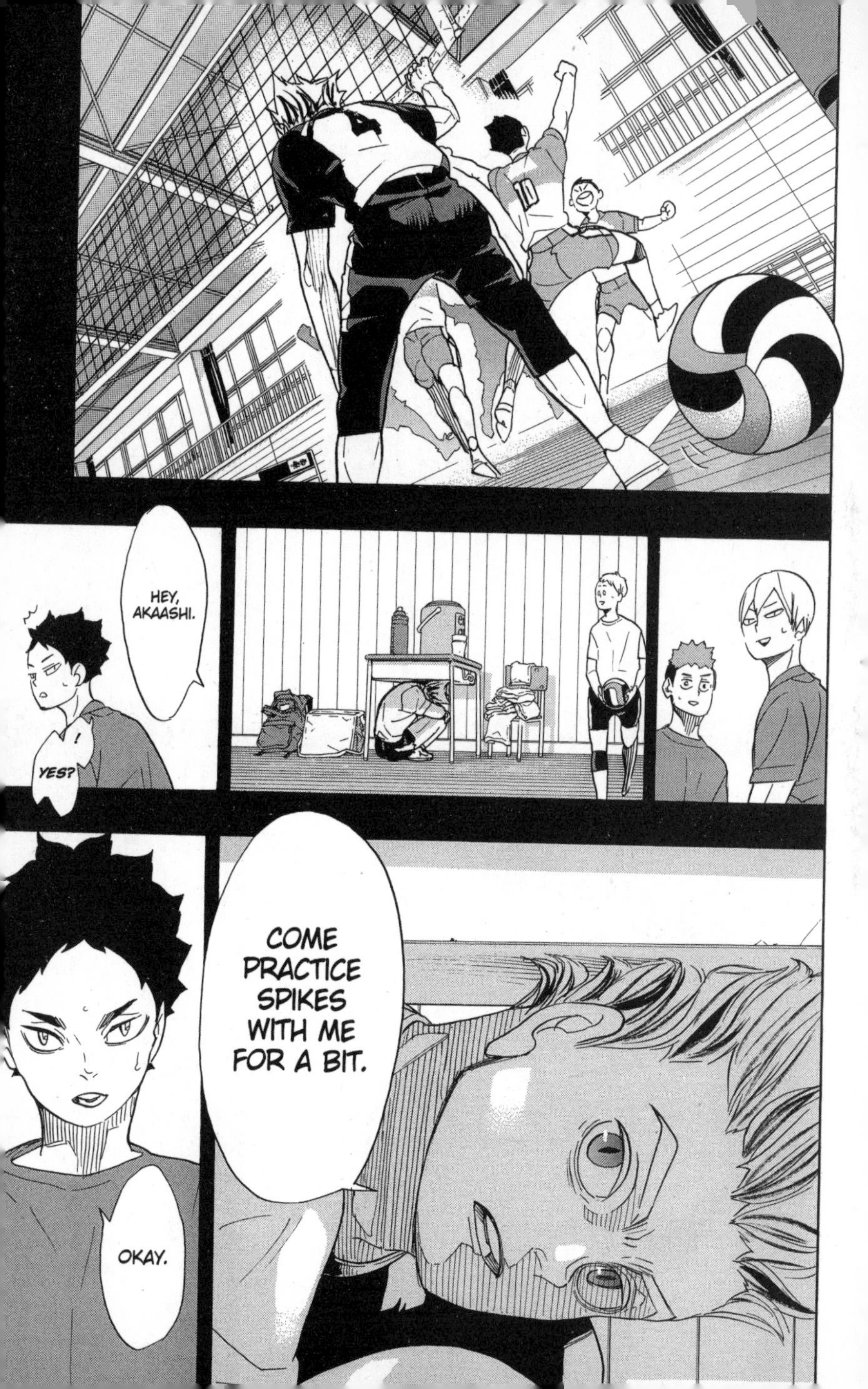
HEY, AKAASHI.
YES?
COME PRACTICE SPIKES WITH ME FOR A BIT.
OKAY.

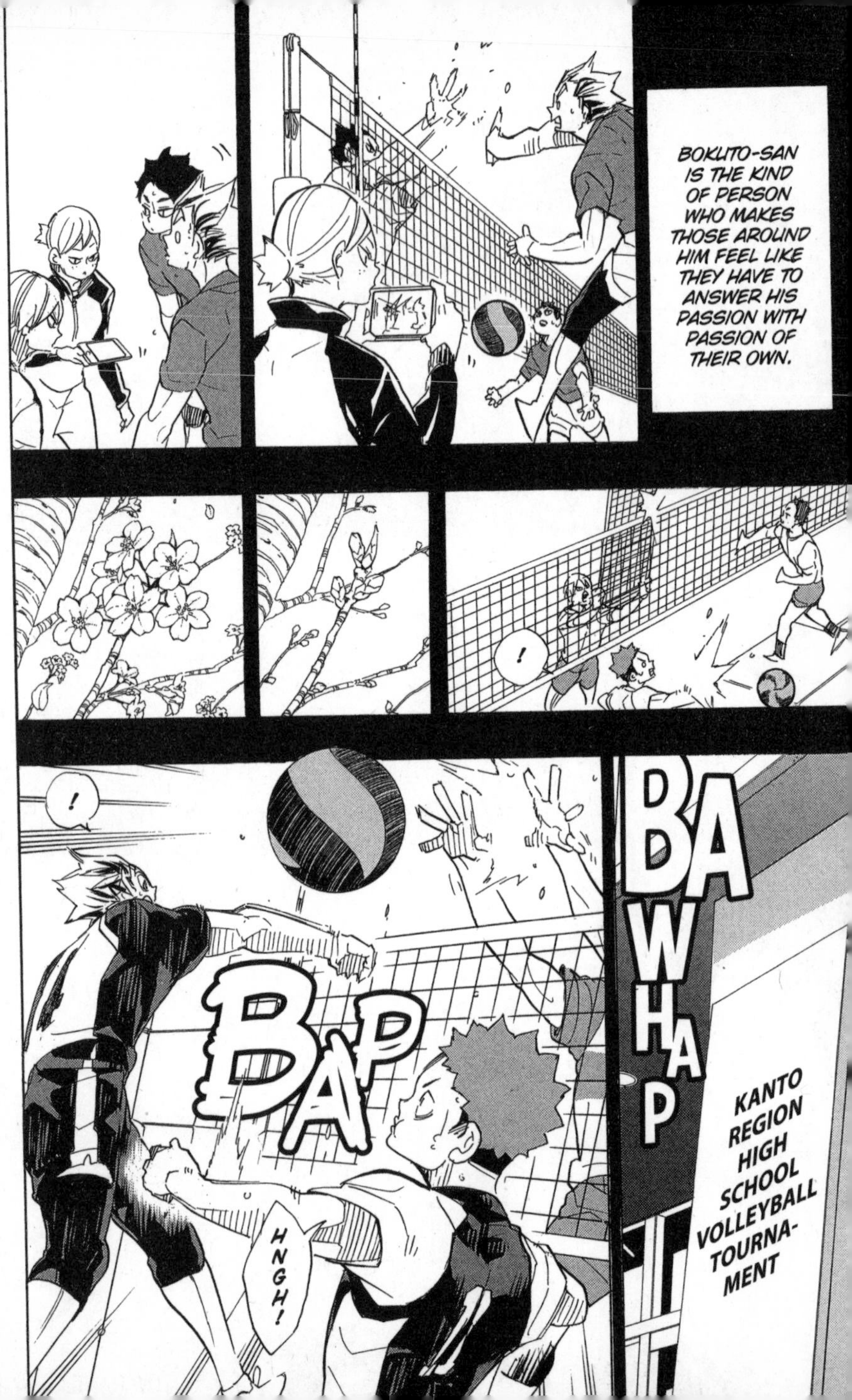
BOKUTO-SAN IS THE KIND OF PERSON WHO MAKES THOSE AROUND HIM FEEL LIKE THEY HAVE TO ANSWER HIS PASSION WITH PASSION OF THEIR OWN.
!
BAWHAP
!
BAPA
KANTO REGION HIGH SCHOOL VOLLEYBALL TOURNA-MENT
HNGH!

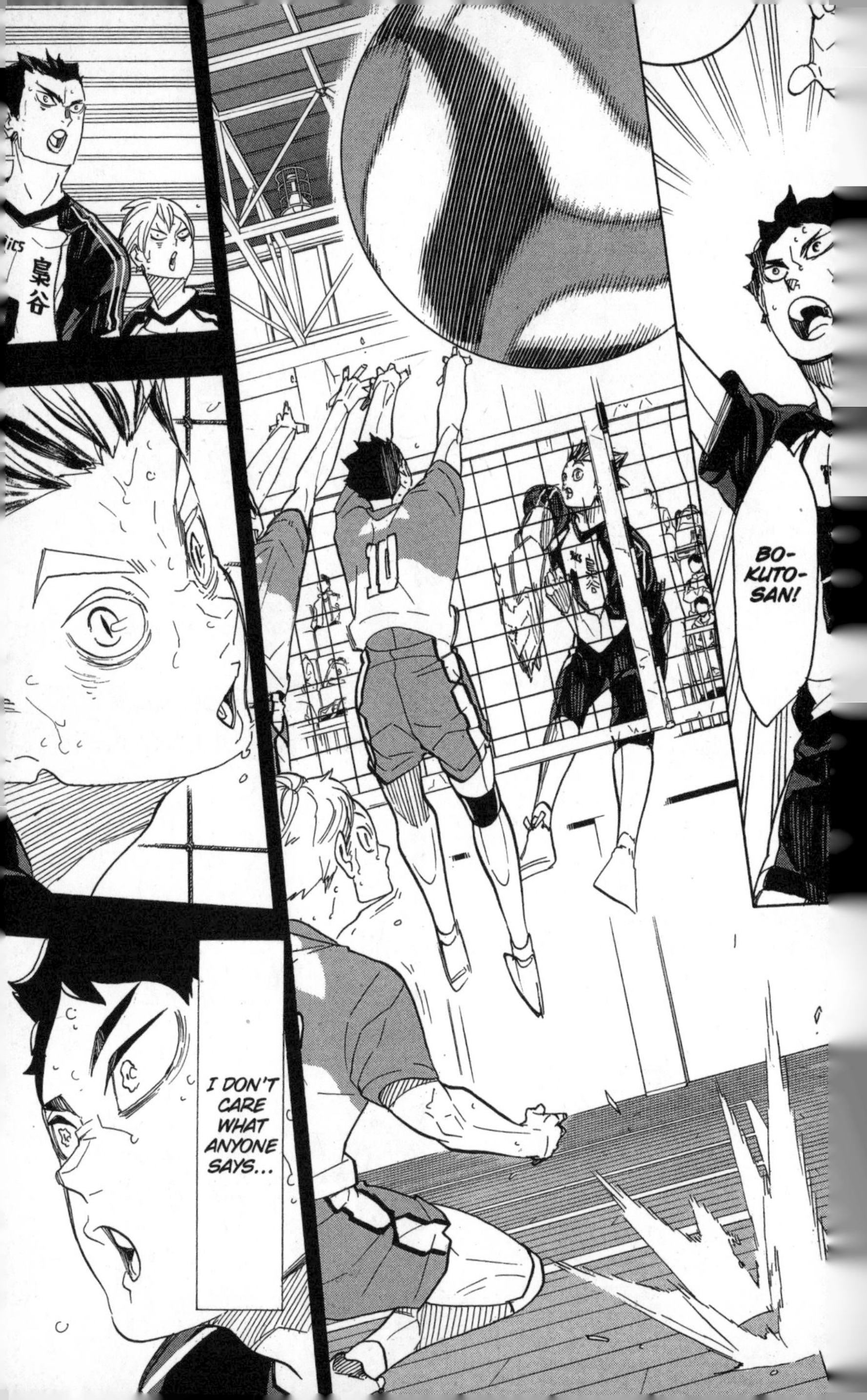
BO-KUTO-SAN!
I DON'T CARE WHAT ANYONE SAYS...

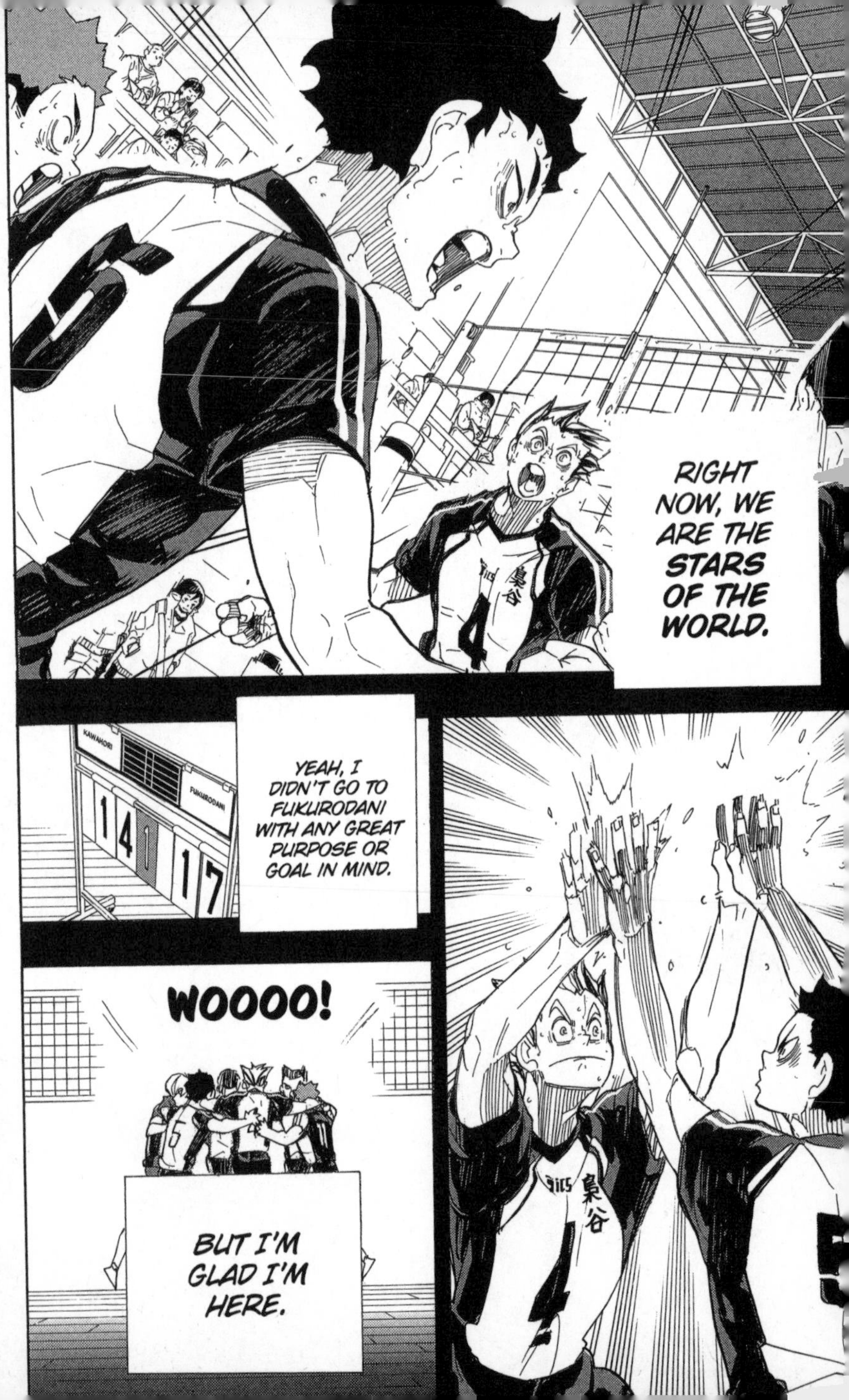
RIGHT NOW, WE ARE THE STARS OF THE WORLD.
YEAH, I DIDN'T GO TO FUKURODANI WITH ANY GREAT PURPOSE OR GOAL IN MIND.
KAWAHORI
FUKURODANI
14
17
WOOOO!
BUT I'M GLAD I'M HERE.

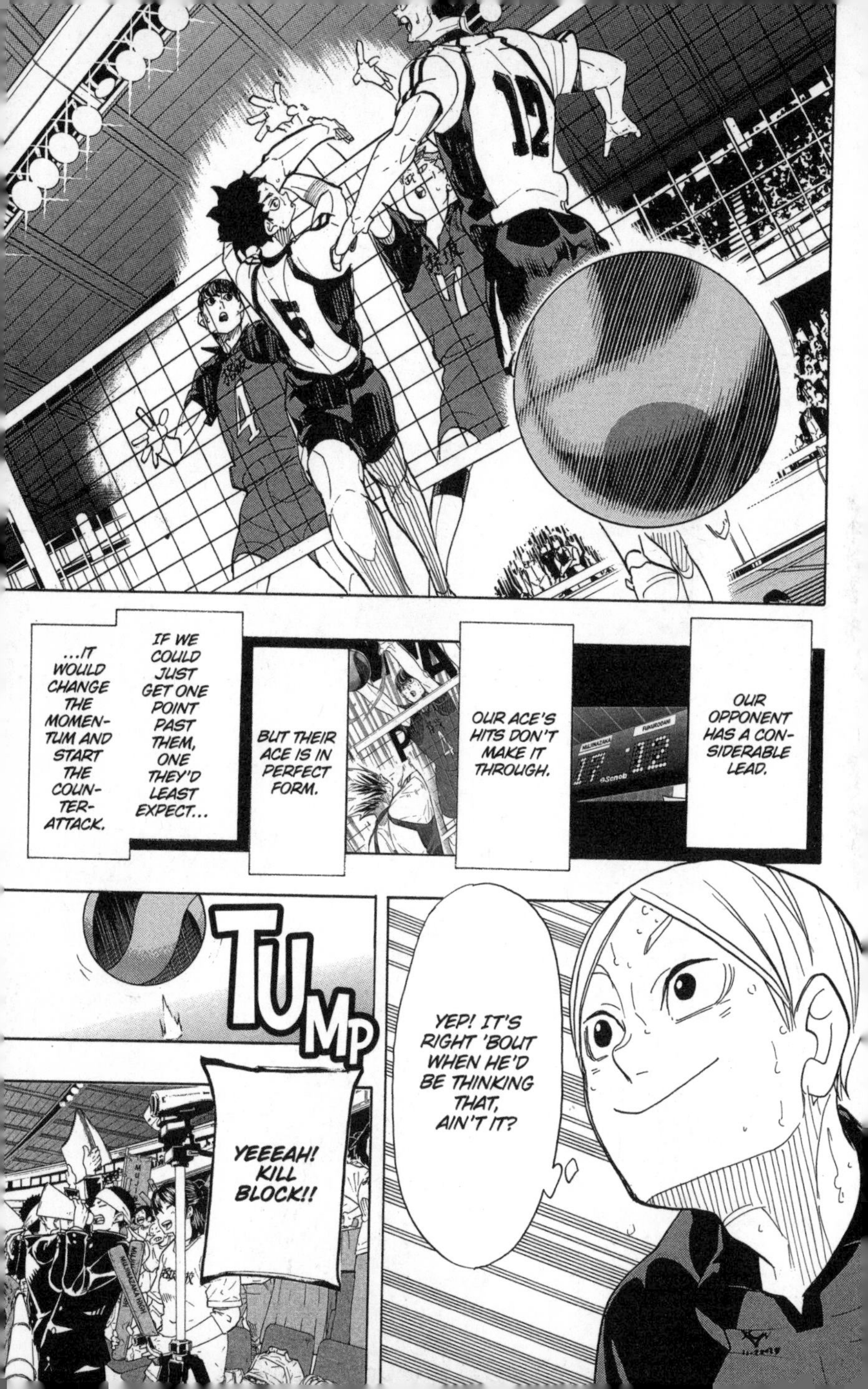
OUR OPPONENT HAS A CONSIDERABLE LEAD.
OUR ACE'S HITS DON'T MAKE IT THROUGH.
BUT THEIR ACE IS IN PERFECT FORM.
IF WE COULD JUST GET ONE POINT PAST THEM, ONE THEY'D LEAST EXPECT...
...IT WOULD CHANGE THE MOMENTUM AND START THE COUNTER-ATTACK.
YEP! IT'S RIGHT 'BOUT WHEN HE'D BE THINKING THAT, AIN'T IT?
TUMP
YEEEAH! KILL BLOCK!!

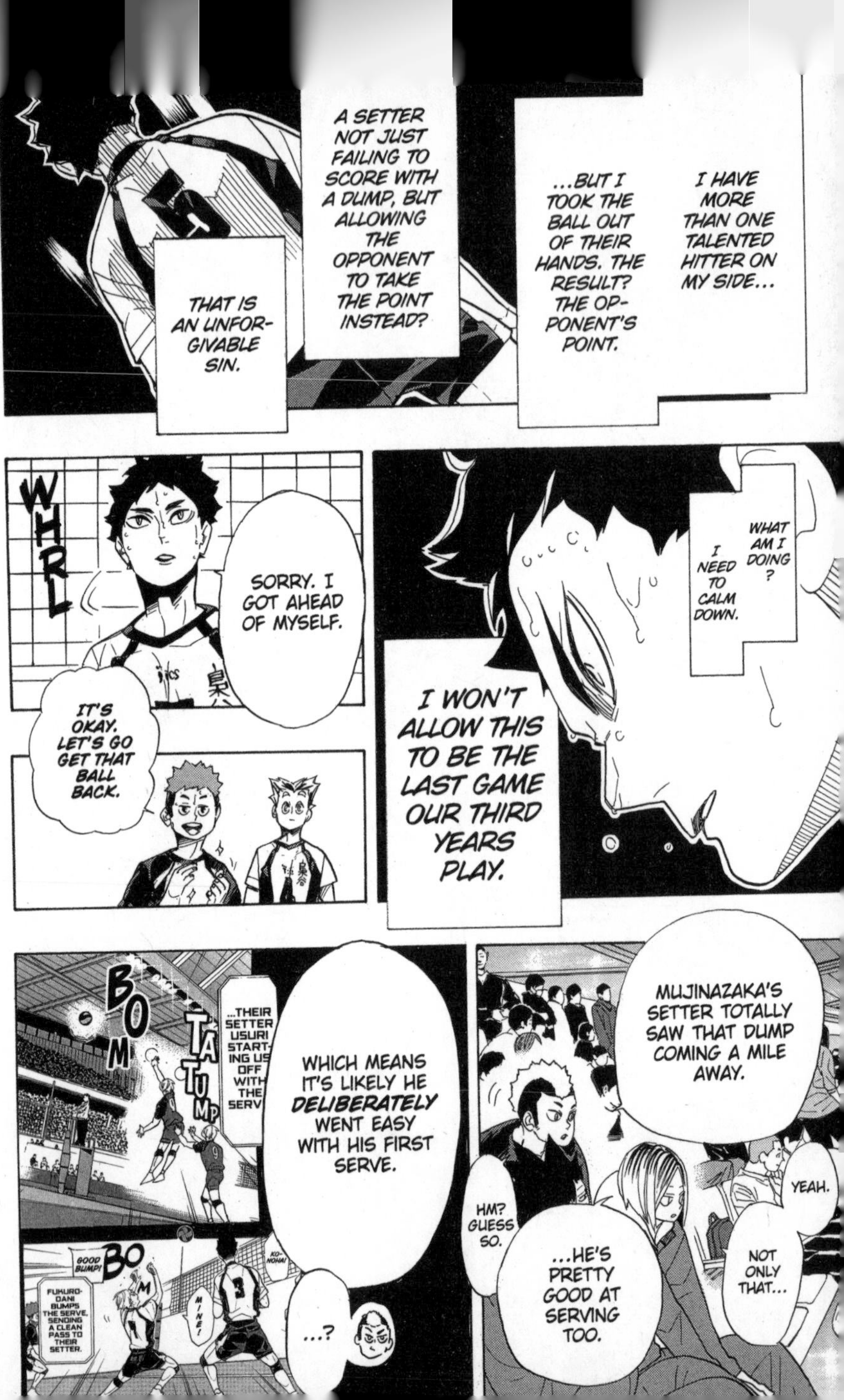
I HAVE MORE THAN ONE TALENTED HITTER ON MY SIDE...
...BUT I TOOK THE BALL OUT OF THEIR HANDS. THE RESULT? THE OPPONENT'S POINT.
A SETTER NOT JUST FAILING TO SCORE WITH A DUMP, BUT ALLOWING THE OPPONENT TO TAKE THE POINT INSTEAD?
THAT IS AN UNFORGIVABLE SIN.
WHAT AM I DOING?
I NEED TO CALM DOWN.
I WON'T ALLOW THIS TO BE THE LAST GAME OUR THIRD YEARS PLAY.
WHRL
SORRY. I GOT AHEAD OF MYSELF.
IT'S OKAY. LET'S GO GET THAT BALL BACK.
MUJINAZAKA'S SETTER TOTALLY SAW THAT DUMP COMING A MILE AWAY.
YEAH.
HM? GUESS SO.
NOT ONLY THAT...
...HE'S PRETTY GOOD AT SERVING TOO.
WHICH MEANS IT'S LIKELY HE DELIBERATELY WENT EASY WITH HIS FIRST SERVE.
...?
...THEIR SETTER USURI STARTING US OFF WITH THE SERV
BOM
TA TUMP
KONOHA!
BOM
GOOD BUMP!
MINE!
FUKURODANI BUMPS THE SERVE, SENDING A CLEAN PASS TO THEIR SETTER.

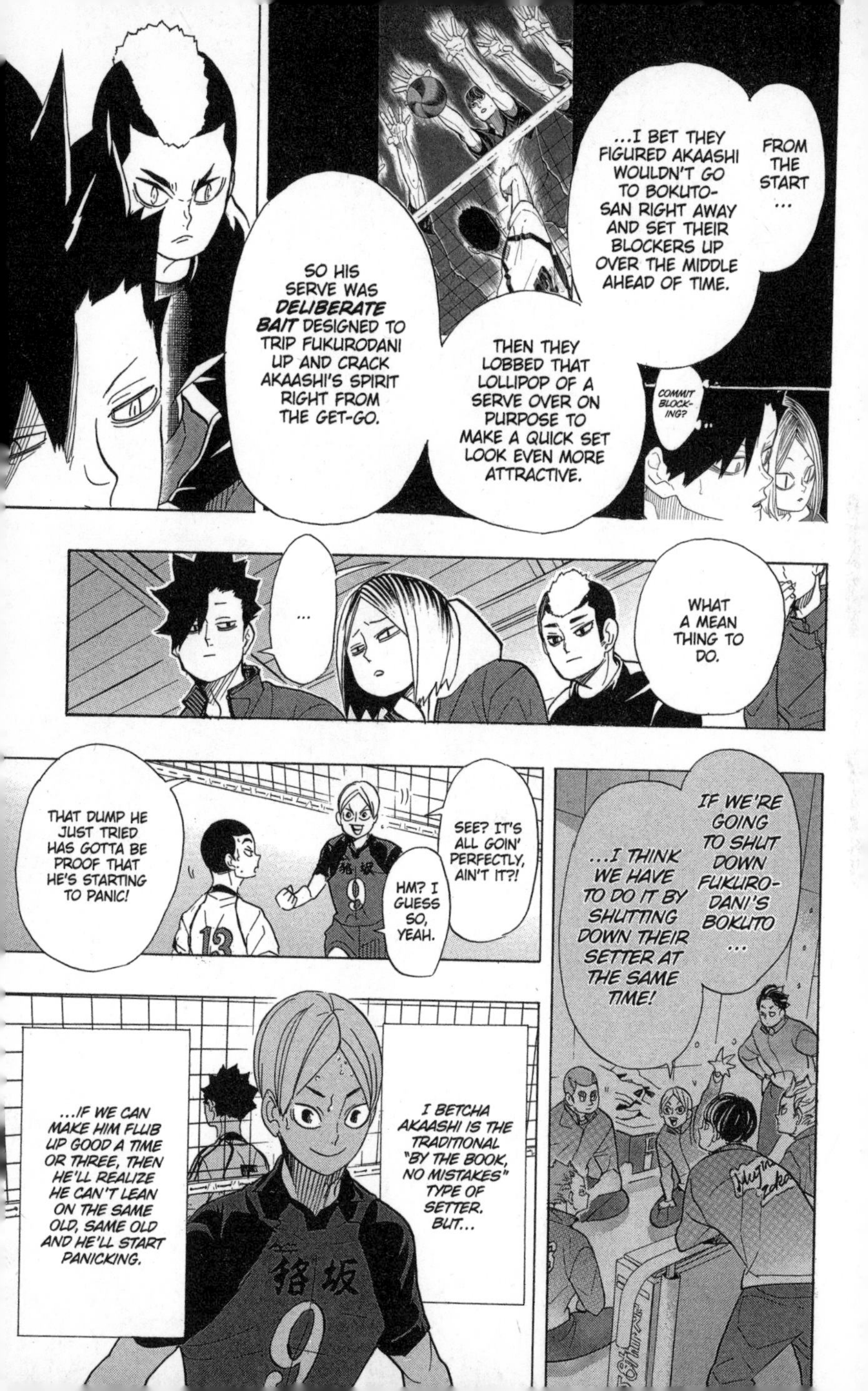
FROM THE START...
...I BET THEY FIGURED AKAASHI WOULDN'T GO TO BOKUTO-SAN RIGHT AWAY AND SET THEIR BLOCKERS UP OVER THE MIDDLE AHEAD OF TIME.
THEN THEY LOBBED THAT LOLLIPOP OF A SERVE OVER ON PURPOSE TO MAKE A QUICK SET LOOK EVEN MORE ATTRACTIVE.
COMMIT BLOCKING?
SO HIS SERVE WAS DELIBERATE BAIT DESIGNED TO TRIP FUKURODANI UP AND CRACK AKAASHI'S SPIRIT RIGHT FROM THE GET-GO.
WHAT A MEAN THING TO DO.
...
IF WE'RE GOING TO SHUT DOWN FUKURODANI'S BOKUTO...
...I THINK WE HAVE TO DO IT BY SHUTTING DOWN THEIR SETTER AT THE SAME TIME!
SEE? IT'S ALL GOIN' PERFECTLY, AIN'T IT?!
HM? I GUESS SO, YEAH.
THAT DUMP HE JUST TRIED HAS GOTTA BE PROOF THAT HE'S STARTING TO PANIC!
I BETCHA AKAASHI IS THE TRADITIONAL "BY THE BOOK, NO MISTAKES" TYPE OF SETTER. BUT...
...IF WE CAN MAKE HIM FLUB UP GOOD A TIME OR THREE, THEN HE'LL REALIZE HE CAN'T LEAN ON THE SAME OLD, SAME OLD AND HE'LL START PANICKING.

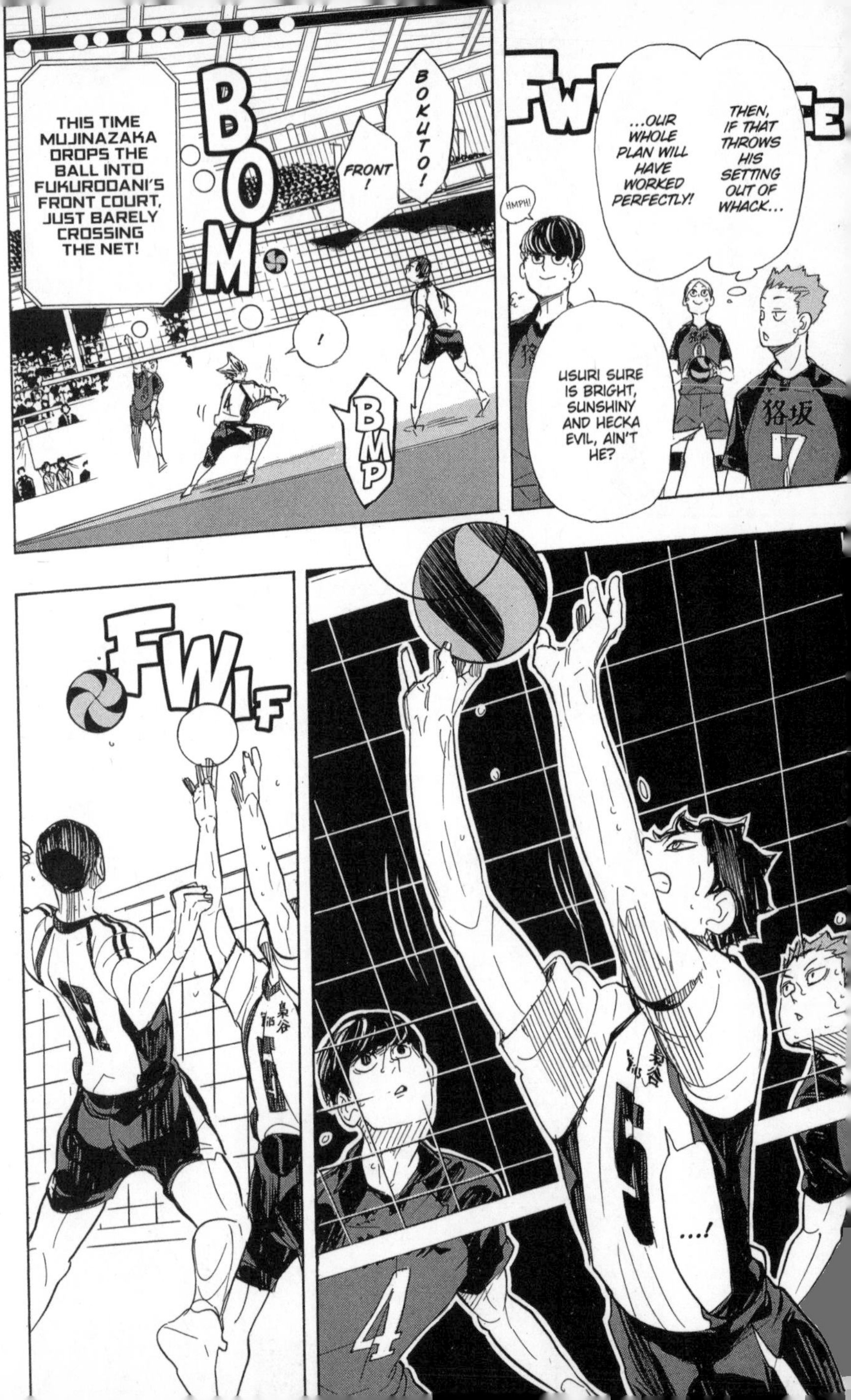
THEN, IF THAT THROWS HIS SETTING OUT OF WHACK...
...OUR WHOLE PLAN WILL HAVE WORKED PERFECTLY!
HMPH!
USURI SURE IS BRIGHT, SUNSHINY AND HECKA EVIL, AIN'T HE?
BOKUTO!
FRONT!
BOOM
THIS TIME MUJINAZAKA DROPS THE BALL INTO FUKURODANI'S FRONT COURT, JUST BARELY CROSSING THE NET!
!
BMP
...!
FWIF

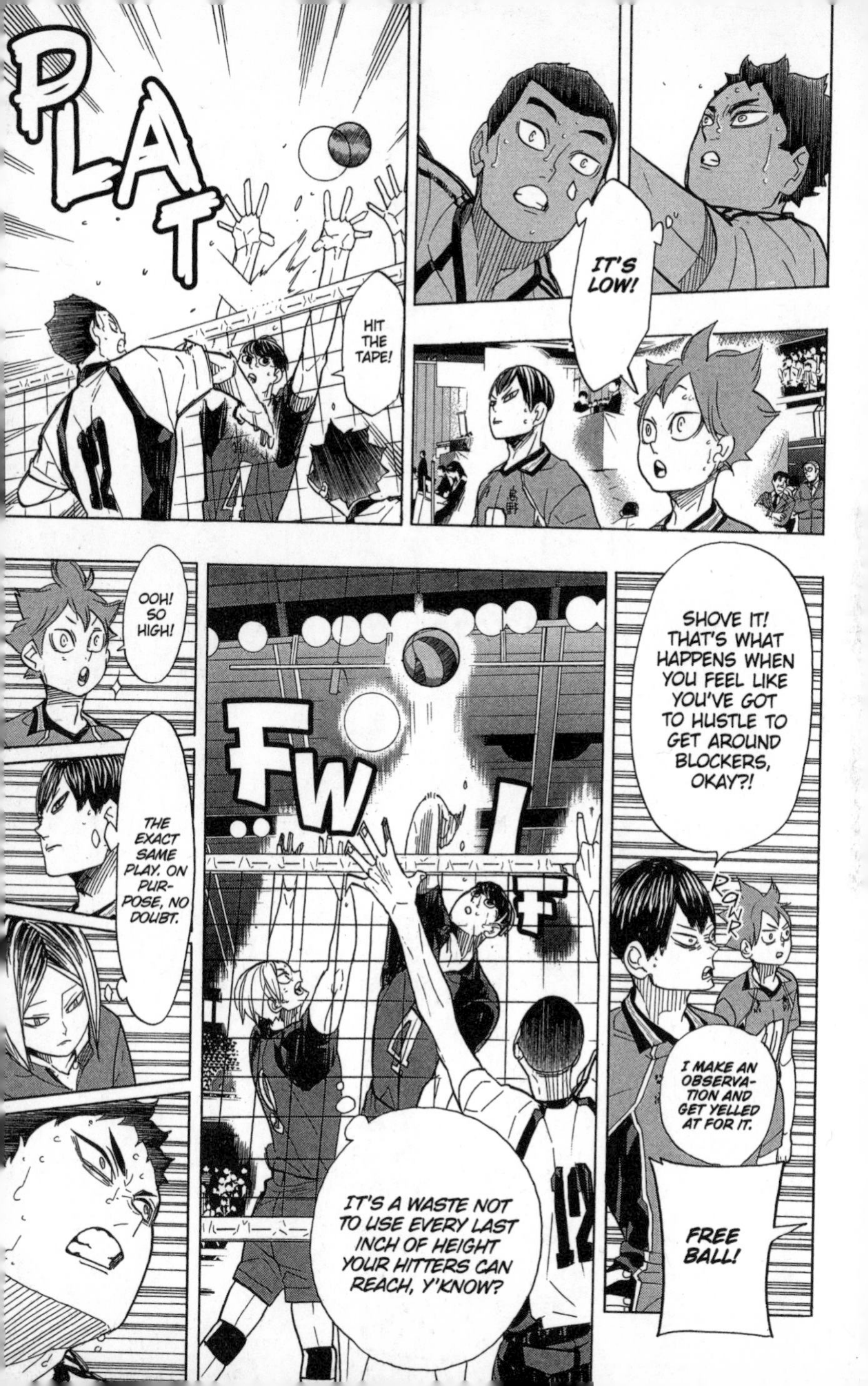
IT'S LOW!
PLAT
HIT THE TAPE!
SHOVE IT! THAT'S WHAT HAPPENS WHEN YOU FEEL LIKE YOU'VE GOT TO HUSTLE TO GET AROUND BLOCKERS, OKAY?!
RAWR
I MAKE AN OBSERVATION AND GET YELLED AT FOR IT.
FREE BALL!
FW
IT'S A WASTE NOT TO USE EVERY LAST INCH OF HEIGHT YOUR HITTERS CAN REACH, Y'KNOW?
OOH! SO HIGH!
THE EXACT SAME PLAY. ON PURPOSE, NO DOUBT.

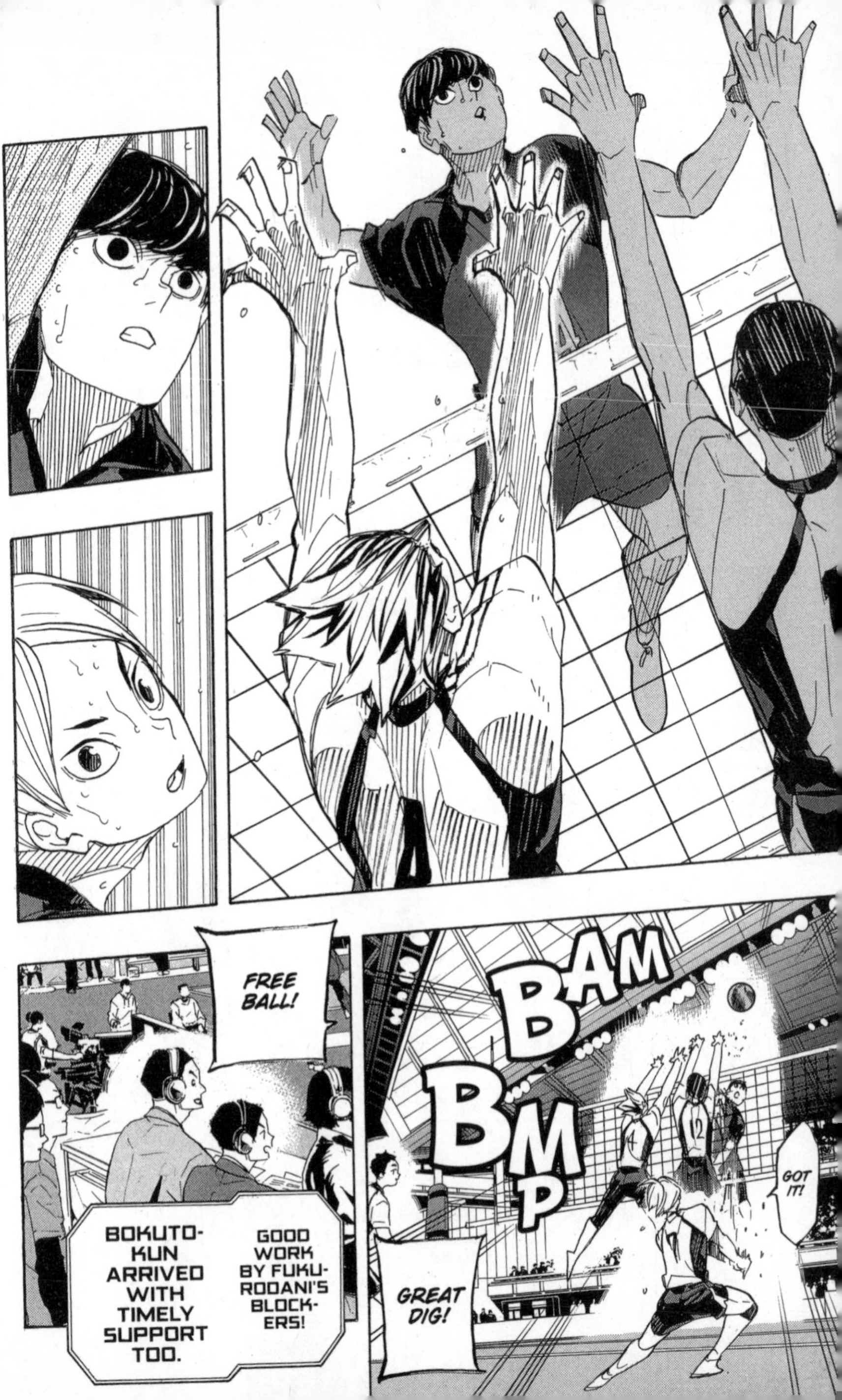
BAM
BMP
GOT IT!
GREAT DIG!
FREE BALL!
GOOD WORK BY FUKURODANI'S BLOCKERS!
BOKUTO-KUN ARRIVED WITH TIMELY SUPPORT TOO.

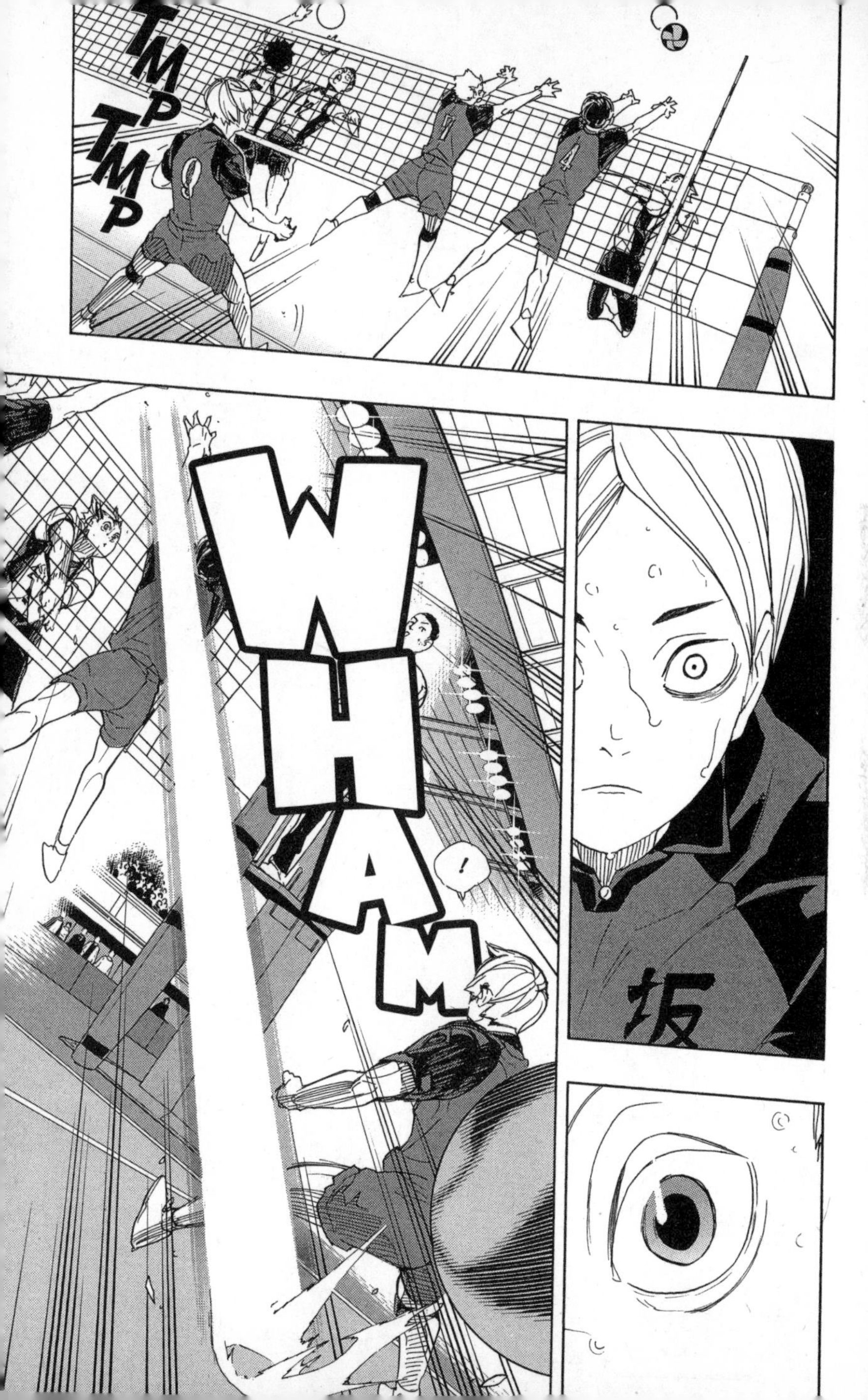
TMP TMP TMP
坂
WHAM
!

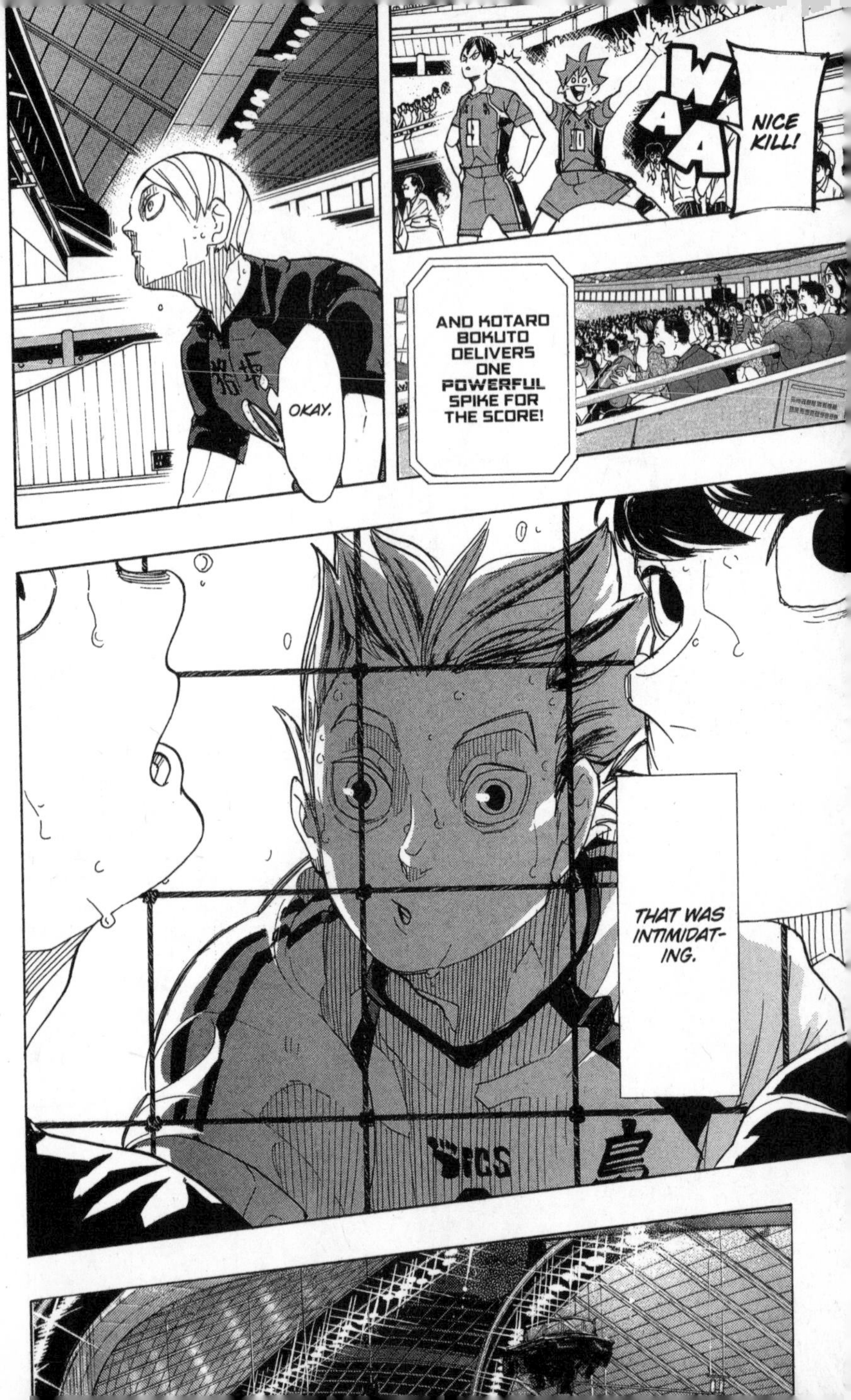
NICE KILL!
WAAA
AND KOTARO BOKUTO DELIVERS ONE POWERFUL SPIKE FOR THE SCORE!
OKAY.
THAT WAS INTIMIDAT-ING.

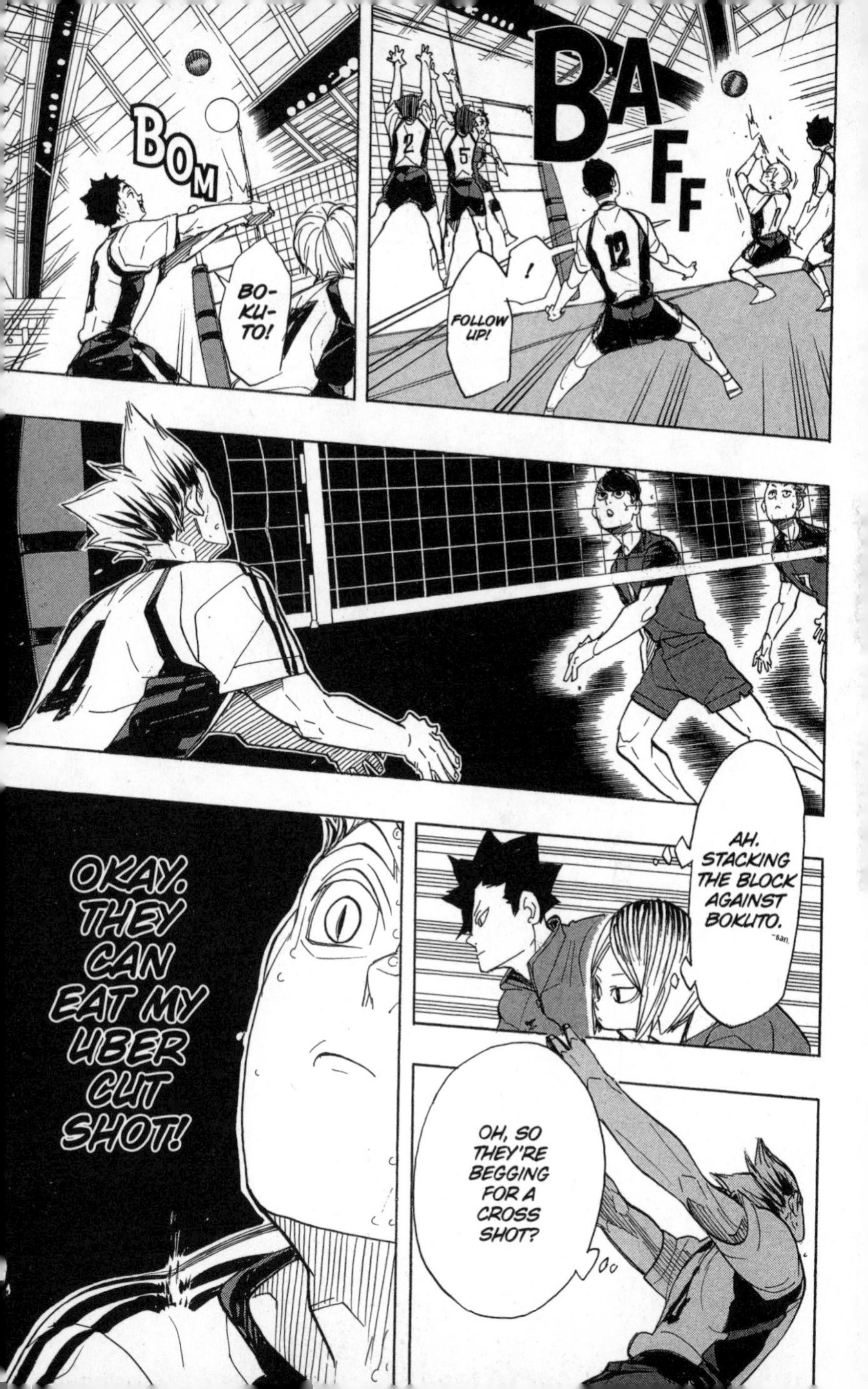
BAFF
!
FOLLOW UP!
BOM
BO-KU-TO!
AH. STACKING THE BLOCK AGAINST BOKUTO.
-san
OH, SO THEY'RE BEGGING FOR A CROSS SHOT?
OKAY. THEY CAN EAT MY UBER CUT SHOT!

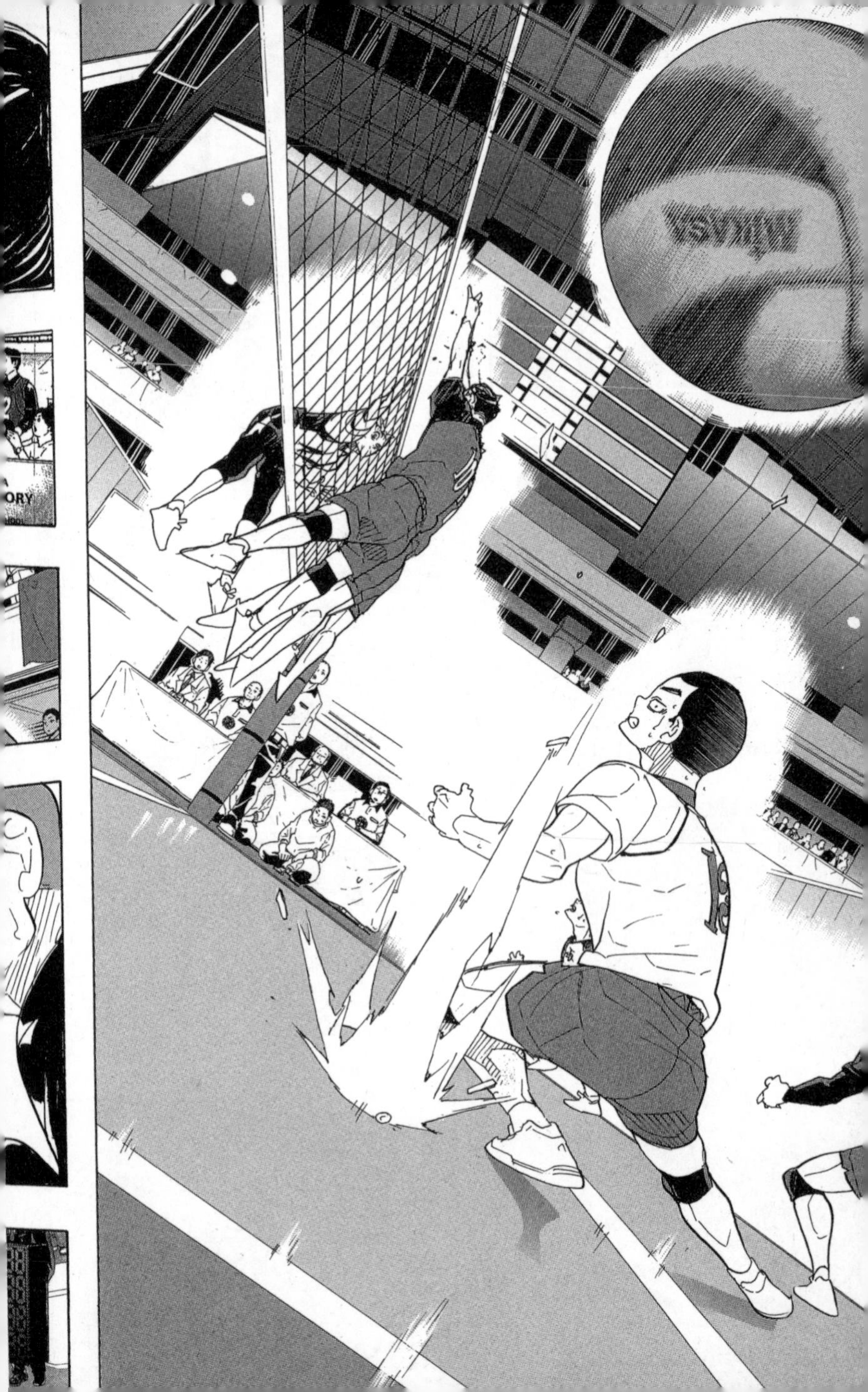

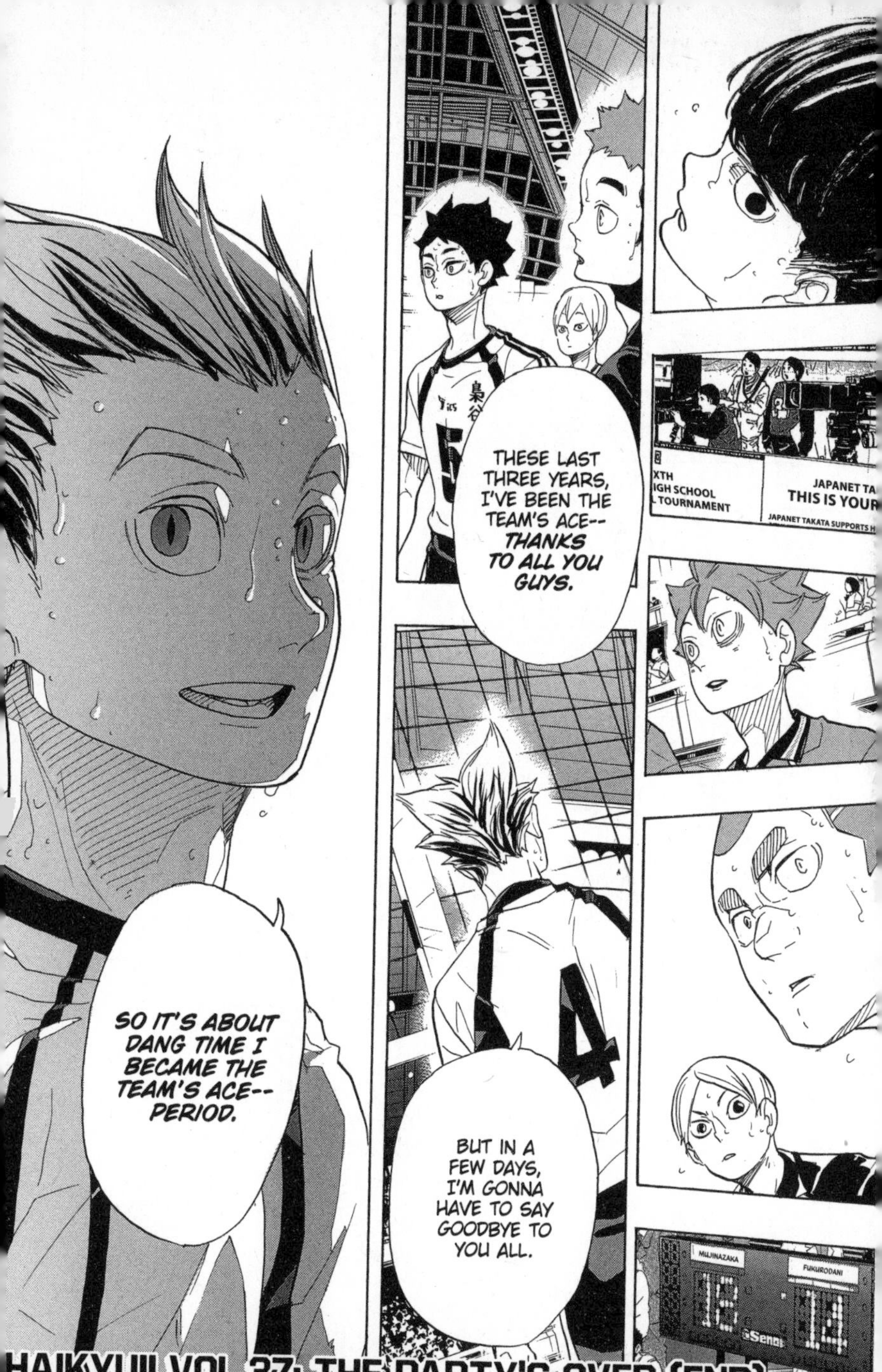
XTH
IGH SCHOOL
L TOURNAMENT
JAPANET TA
THIS IS YOUR
JAPANET TAKATA SUPPORTS H
MUJINAZAKA
FUKURODANI
THESE LAST THREE YEARS, I'VE BEEN THE TEAM'S ACE-- *THANKS TO ALL YOU GUYS.*
BUT IN A FEW DAYS, I'M GONNA HAVE TO SAY GOODBYE TO YOU ALL.
SO IT'S ABOUT DANG TIME I BECAME THE TEAM'S ACE-- PERIOD.

HAIKYU!! VOL 37: THE PARTY'S OVER (END)

BONUS STORY (COUPLES)

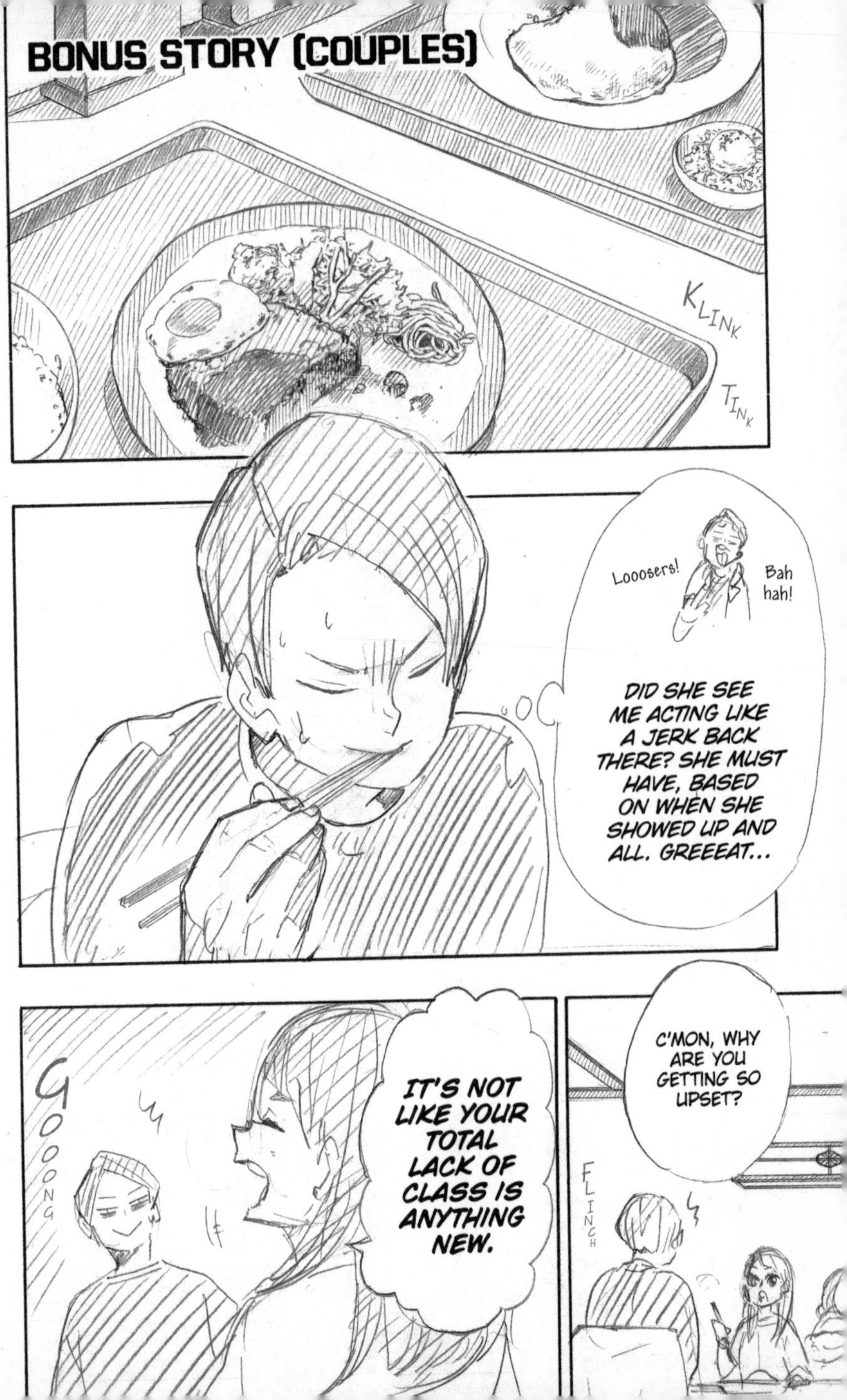
KLINK
TINK
Looosers!
Bah hah!
DID SHE SEE ME ACTING LIKE A JERK BACK THERE? SHE MUST HAVE, BASED ON WHEN SHE SHOWED UP AND ALL. GREEEAT...
C'MON, WHY ARE YOU GETTING SO UPSET?
FLINCH
GOOOONG
IT'S NOT LIKE YOUR TOTAL LACK OF CLASS IS ANYTHING NEW.

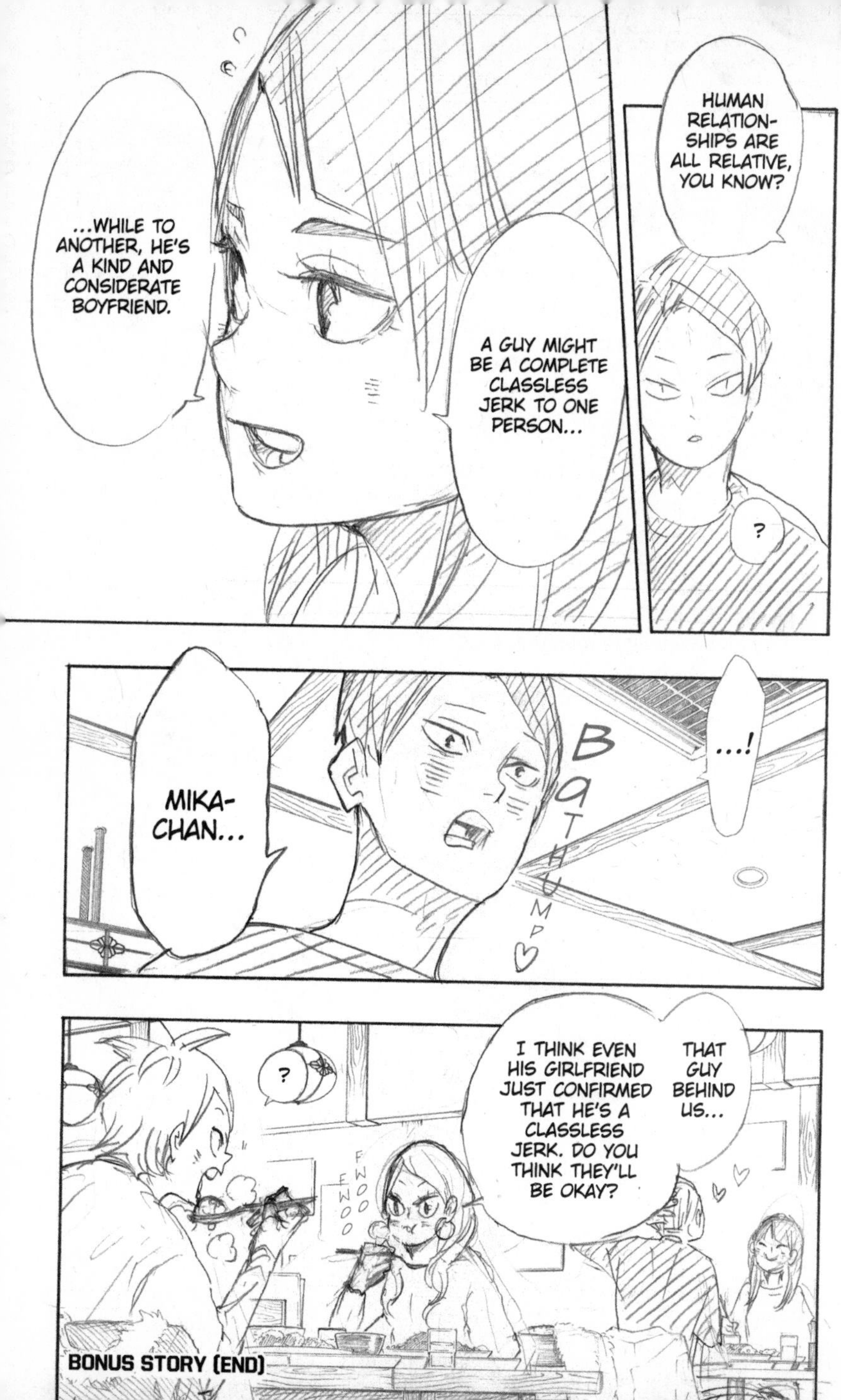
HUMAN RELATION-SHIPS ARE ALL RELATIVE, YOU KNOW?
?
A GUY MIGHT BE A COMPLETE CLASSLESS JERK TO ONE PERSON...
...WHILE TO ANOTHER, HE'S A KIND AND CONSIDERATE BOYFRIEND.
...!
BATHUMP
MIKA-CHAN...
THAT GUY BEHIND US...
I THINK EVEN HIS GIRLFRIEND JUST CONFIRMED THAT HE'S A CLASSLESS JERK. DO YOU THINK THEY'LL BE OKAY?
FWOO
FWOO
?
BONUS STORY (END)

EDITOR'S NOTES

The English edition of Haikyu!! maintains the honorifics used in the original Japanese version. For those of you who are new to these terms, here's a brief explanation to help with your reading experience!

When saying someone's name in Japanese, a suffix is often attached to indicate how familiar the speaker is with the person. Some are more polite and respectful, while others are endearing.

1 ***-kun*** is often used for young men or boys, usually someone you are familiar with.

2 ***-chan*** is used for young children and can be used as a term of endearment.

3 ***-san*** is used for someone you respect or are not close to, or to be polite.

4 ***Senpai*** is used for someone who is older than you or in a higher position or grade in school.

5 ***Kohai*** is used for someone who is younger than you or in a lower position or grade in school.

6 ***Sensei*** means teacher.

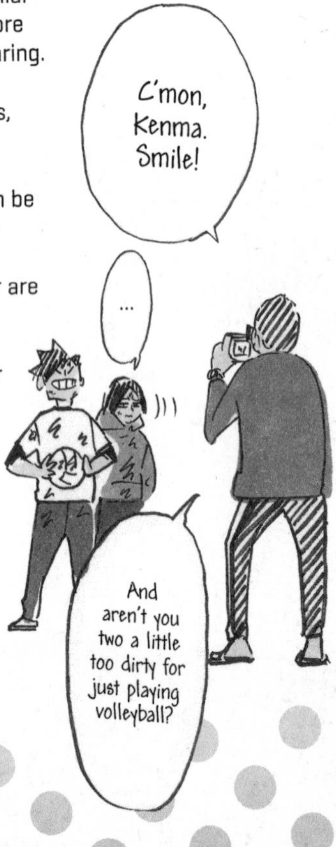
C'mon, Kenma. Smile!
...
And aren't you two a little too dirty for just playing volleyball?